EXETER ESSAYS IN GEOGRAPHY

£4·20

Photo by Henry Wykes

Arthur Haurés
16 Dec. 1970.

EXETER ESSAYS
IN
GEOGRAPHY

in honour of ARTHUR DAVIES

Edited by

K. J. GREGORY

and

W. L. D. RAVENHILL

Department of Geography, University of Exeter

UNIVERSITY OF EXETER

1971

Set in Monotype Bembo 270, 11 on 12 point
Printed in Great Britain by James Townsend and Sons Limited

Contents

CONTENTS

List of Illustrations

FIGURES

PLATES

The Contributors

W. J. ARMSTRONG, BA MAgrSci
Assistant Lecturer in Geography, University of Exeter 1969–

A. M. Y. BLACKSELL, MA DPhil
Lecturer in Geography, University of Exeter 1970–
Assistant Lecturer 1967–1970

J. R. BLUNDEN, BA PhD
Senior Lecturer in Geography, The Open University
BA(*Exon*) 1958, PhD(*Exon*) 1965

D. J. BONNEY, BA
Royal Commission on Historical Monuments of England
BA(*Exon*) 1955, Research student 1963

D. S. BRYANT, BA
Senior Lecturer in Geography, North-Western Polytechnic
BA(*Exon*) 1963, Research student 1963–1965

K. J. GREGORY, BSc PhD
Lecturer in Geography, University of Exeter 1964–
Assistant Lecturer 1962–1964

MARY GRIFFITHS, BA PhD
Lecturer in Geography, University of Exeter 1968–1969
Assistant Lecturer 1965–1968
BA(*Exon*) 1964, PhD (*Exon*) 1969

J. B. HARLEY, BA PhD
Lecturer in Geography, University of Exeter 1970–

E. M. JOHNS, MA
Senior Lecturer in Geography, University of Exeter 1966–
Lecturer in Geography 1948–1966

C. KIDSON, BA PhD
> Professor and Head of Geography Department, University College of Wales, Aberystwyth
> Lecturer in Geography, University of Exeter 1947–1954

B. S. MORGAN, BA PhD
> Lecturer in Geography, King's College, University of London
> BA(*Exon*) 1964, PhD(*Exon*) 1970

P. T. NEWBY, BA
> Lecturer in Geography, Hendon College of Technology
> BA(*Exon*) 1966, Research student 1966–1968

ETHEL S. PATTERSON, MA PhD
> Lecturer in Geography, University of Exeter 1931–1935, 1941–1966
> Montefiore Reader in Geography 1934–1936

W. L. D. RAVENHILL, MA PhD
> Professor of Geography, University of Exeter 1969–
> Senior Lecturer 1962–1969
> Lecturer 1948–1962

P. TOYNE, BA
> Lecturer in Geography, University of Exeter 1968–
> Assistant Lecturer 1965–1968

D. WALLING, BA PhD
> Assistant Lecturer in Geography, University of Exeter 1968–
> BA(*Exon*) 1966, PhD(*Exon*) 1971

R. S. WATERS, MA
> Professor and Head of Geography Department, University of Sheffield
> Lecturer in Geography, University of Exeter 1954–1962

Preface

When the Geographical Association held their Spring Conference at Exeter in April 1954, among the papers presented to the members was one entitled 'The Personality of the South West'—it was written and read by Arthur Davies. This subject was an abrupt departure from his then current interests and though he soon afterwards returned to his former research 'loves' he had, by his example, aroused among his colleagues an enthusiasm for and an interest in the pursuit of the study of the Geography of the South-West peninsula. Although, over the years, he stayed loyal to his early research themes and was only occasionally again tempted by the scenic beauties and attractive problems of the West Country, he was always at hand to encourage and to provide facilities for others to seek their research fortunes within the province surveilled by the University College of the South West and later by the University of Exeter. It seems appropriate, therefore, at the close of Arthur Davies' long tenure of the chair of Geography at Exeter to honour him with a volume of essays on a subject which he did so much to foster. Just as the variety of the topics in the 'Exeter Essays' is integrated by the common theme of South-West England, so the contributors are linked with Professor Davies by a common bond of association as colleagues or as students, or as both.

During twenty-three years in Exeter Professor Davies has seen, and has encouraged, expansion and intensification of geographical investigation. Within the subject his interests have been wide-ranging and the essays collected in this volume are an indication of the breadth of study which he has encouraged, a reflection of the development of geographical research in Exeter, and a review of some aspects of the character and evolution of the South West. The contributors include two who were members of staff at the time of Professor Davies' appointment, eight who are members of staff in 1971, and five who are former research students. Their essays, utilising a variety of geographical techniques, indicate some of the character of that part of England described by Professor Davies as one 'of which men may well be proud.' The long and varied coastline of the South West includes a wealth of geomorphological information and the use of this in relation to the chronology of the Quaternary is reviewed in the first essay. Head deposits, first described in Britain in west Cornwall, are widely distributed over the peninsula and they provide the subject for the second contribution. A variety of contrasting morphogenetic systems are imprinted upon the physical landscape, not least upon the valley network as shown by the third study, and the magnitude of the variation of contemporary streamflow against the background of the detail of the physical landscape is investigated in Essay 4. The mapping of this part of England forms the subject of two essays: the contribution of John Norden to the early mapping of Cornwall is documented in the sixth essay, while the seventh traces the relationships between the Ordnance Survey and the pioneer geological mapping of Sir H. T. De la Beche. The record of settlement in the region is long and continuous, and Essay 5 utilises the information contained in the present landscape for a study of eastern Dartmoor. Subsequently, the 1851 census provides material for the eighth study which concerns the nineteenth century population of a part of south Devon. Two dominant characteristics of the South West are the development of mining in the nineteenth century, and the growth of the holiday industry up to the present day: the early growth of the latter in a part of what is now Torbay forms a revealing subject for Essay 13, while the revival and future potential of Cornish tin is a topic of contemporary interest (11). The fact that the holiday industry is essentially seasonal has led to attempts to attract light industry to the region, and the industrialists' perception of the opportunities available are described in the twelfth essay. The seasonal volume of the holiday industry creates problems which are apparent not least in the Dartmoor National Park (9). Whereas Dartmoor has been the subject of numerous and diverse researches, the peripheral Culm Measures have not received equal attention and so it is appropriate that one essay (10) should discuss the problems of land classification on the difficult soils of this part of Devon. The city of Exeter provides subjects for the last three contributors: the morphological variety within Exeter's urban area is investigated (15); a study is made (14) of the medical geography of one of the contained urban zones, and finally, the analysis of retailing (16) demonstrates the way in which Exeter serves a considerable area of Devon. These sixteen essays illustrate some aspects of the past and present of the South West, both relevant to the appreciation of this *Region with a Future*.

We wish to thank the essayists who gave freely of their time and research labours to create this volume and who by their diligence and punctuality made the task of editing a joy and the intended date of publication a reality. It is also a deeply-felt pleasure to record our appreciation of the cartographic work performed by Miss Pat Gregory and Mr Andrew Teed under the direction of Mr Rodney Fry, who relieved us completely of any anxiety for the production and compilation of the maps and diagrams. To Miss Marion Bethel, Miss Gillian Stiling, Mrs Barbara Whinham and Miss Jenny Williams we are indebted for their patience, fortitude and skill in turning the essays into typescript copy for the printers. Miss Susanna Guy of Exeter University Library kindly assisted with the preparation of the bibliography of works published by Arthur Davies, and to a very old friend of his, Miss Mollie Dexter, we are especially grateful for her reading of all the essays in typescript and in proof, and for her kindly guidance with the many pitfalls of our language. We express our sincere thanks to the University of Exeter for willingly undertaking to publish the volume, particularly to Mr R. A. Erskine and to Dr Joyce Youings and her colleagues on the Publications Committee, and finally to the printers James Townsend and Sons Limited for the care and interest which they have devoted to the work.

KENNETH GREGORY
WILLIAM RAVENHILL

13th March 1971

Professor Arthur Davies: A Memoir

ETHEL SIMKINS PATTERSON

Arthur Davies was appointed to the Reardon Smith Chair of Geography in the University College of the South West in March 1948. The department of geography at that time was small, but it was well established, and had a high standing in the West Country whence came most of its students. But it was circumscribed in its studies by the demands of the external syllabus of the University of London whose degree examinations it took, and by the inadequacy of accommodation, equipment and staffing owing to the financial stringency of the times.

Professor Davies retires from the Chair in 1971, leaving a large and ever-expanding department of the University of Exeter, granting its own degrees based on a thorough coverage of modern geographical studies, and having a high national reputation. It is housed in fine and well-equipped modern buildings which are a far cry from its beginnings in an old army hut in Gandy Street. It has about 260 students drawn from all over the country, and the staff, which in 1947 numbered four, is now thirteen, including two professors, each with a specialised field of study. It has also a tutorial system which guarantees close contacts between students and staff.

The success of this development in the space of twenty years was due in no small measure to the man who planned and directed it, and who, in his person, had a rare combination of qualities, intellectual, practical and human, which fitted him so uniquely for the job he undertook. He was an academic of brilliant mind and exact scholarship, with a clear vision of the future development and application of his subject. He was fortunate in that his mentor at the University College of Wales, Aberystwyth, was one of the great founding fathers of British geography, the late H. J. Fleure. Under him he took a brilliant degree in geography, physics and mathematics, which gave him the scientific training so necessary to a geographer. But he also studied and took a first class degree in anthropology, giving him an interest in the human side of his subject which was evidenced later in his major field of research—the exploration and discovery of the Americas. By close and expert study of old maps and manuscripts he reconstructed and interpreted the results of many of the voyages of the fifteenth and sixteenth centuries, and his publications on Henry the Navigator, Columbus, Amerigo Vespucci and the Cabots earned him international recognition—in Genoa in 1951, where he was awarded the Columbus medal, and in Portugal in 1960, where he delivered two lectures at the Lisbon Congress in honour of Prince Henry the Navigator. His dual interest in the scientific and human factors in his studies made him give full weight not only to the scientific interest of the voyages, but also to the lives and characters of the men who made them. One feels, as one reads his work, that he was not only writing about these journeys, but also adventuring along with the men who made them. Because of his balanced training and interest he never lost sight of the concept of geography as a whole, in spite of modern trends which split it more and more into special-ised branches. It was this knowledge of the 'wholeness' of his subject which made him so well fitted to plan, and to bring into operation, a syllabus which, though wide in its range of specialities, nevertheless preserved the unity of geography.

He believed firmly that a geographer should never lose contact with the ground which was his starting point—hence his insistence on regular field work for which the South West was a superb laboratory He took many field excursions and study courses to Europe for the LePlay Society: to Poland in 1931; to Yugoslavia in 1932; to Czechoslovakia in 1937; to Auvergne in 1951; and in 1966, at the request of the British Council, he visited Rumania. From these many visits there developed his main regional interest—the geography of Europe, and especially of Eastern Europe, recorded in many articles. He hopes to write a major work on this region.

His concept of geography was passed on to generations of students at Manchester, Leeds and Exeter by his superb gifts as a teacher. He was not only a natural teacher but also a highly trained and experienced one. This is not surprising, for both his parents were head teachers in his native Merthyr Tydfil. His lectures were lucidly and graphically presented, with that verve which told of the Celtic strain in him, and his subtle knowledge of his audiences was based on experience of many types outside a university—in Adult Education, Learned Societies, the Army, and many others less academic, for he was much in demand at social gatherings. He knew well the value of a light touch in heavy matters, as the gales of laughter which sometimes came from his lecture room showed.

His University experience included much administration. At Leeds he served as Sub-Dean of the Faculties of Arts, Law and Commerce, and also as admissions officer for General and Honours students. He was an active member of many faculty committees on which his clear head, sound common sense, and forthright expression of views made him a valuable member.

He had wide experience as an examiner, acting externally for the Universities of London, Belfast, Leeds, Bristol, Reading, Durham and Southampton. In 1961 he became Dean of the Faculty of Social Studies at Exeter, and Chairman of the Southern Universities Joint Panel of Geography, and in 1969 he was appointed Deputy Vice-Chancellor of the University, a post he has filled with distinction.

One phase of his career, enjoyed keenly by his vigorous and practical spirit, was his six years' service in the Army; these took him to a field that greatly expanded his experience of men and matters. He had been a member of the O.T.C. at Aberystwyth and a champion shot, and, on the outbreak of war, he volunteered and was commissioned after training. He rose to the rank of Major, R.A. With his battery he crossed to Normandy on D-Day and went through the campaign to the Elbe. He was twice mentioned in despatches, and recommended for the M.C. At the end of hostilities he became commandant of the town and port of Wedel, and of a Polish camp of three thousand Displaced Persons. Also, because of his knowledge of military law, he was appointed one of the three judges of the

High Military Tribunal in Hamburg, the supreme court of the British Zone of Germany. Some of his impressions of the invasion and of post-war Europe are recorded in articles in the American Geographic Review, and in publications of the Royal Institute of International Affairs.

His years in the army enriched his innate capacity for dealing with human beings with sympathy, understanding and firmness. He loved people, and had a warm outgoing personality which instantly impressed all who came into contact with him—a personality eager to understand and to help to the limit of its capacity. No one went to him for help or encouragement in vain.

To his colleagues he was an admirable 'chief'. All were part of a team, and no plans were made or decisions taken without full discussion in a staff meeting. Yet he never forgot that he was the captain of the team, and that the ultimate decisions and responsibilities were on his shoulders. His colleagues appreciated also his innate modesty, which admitted that in their own fields they needed no advice or interference from him. It was a good team, and made for a happy department for staff and students alike.

In the long run, however, he will be remembered by his colleagues and students alike not only as a fine geographer and an inspiring teacher, but also as a sincere and warm-hearted friend. With one accord they wish him and his wife well in their retirement, hoping that it will be fruitful in the studies which, because of his many duties so faithfully performed, have yet to be written.

List of Publications by Arthur Davies

1926   'A critical analysis of the census returns of Merthyr Tydfil' *Geography* 11 (1926), 473–9

1929   'Man's nasal index in relation to climate' *Man* (1929), 8–14

1932   'A resurvey of the morphology of the nose in relation to climate' *Journ. Royal Anthrop. Inst.* (1932), 337–59

1933   *Slovene Studies* ed. A. Davies and L. Dudley Stamp (LePlay Society 1933), 1–70
       'A study in city morphology and historical geography' *Geography* 18 (1933), 25–27

1934   *Polish Studies* ed. A. Davies (LePlay Society 1934), 1–66

1935   *Mills Catalogue of Ancient Maps* (University of Manchester 1935)

1938   'John Cabot and the Viking tradition' *Leeds Phil. Lit. Soc. Proc.* 4 (1938), 362–71
       'The morphology of Prague' *Leeds Phil. Lit. Soc. Proc.* 5 (1938), 202–8

1939   'The evolution of the ship in relation to its geographical background' (with H. Robinson) *Geography* 24 (1939), 95–109

1946   'War damage in western Europe' *World Today* (1946), 144–61
       'War damage in Germany' *World Today* (1946), 197–206
       'Geographical factors in the invasion and Battle of Normandy' *Geog. Rev.* 36 (1946), 613–31

1948   'Logarithmic analysis and population studies' *Geography* 33 (1948), 53–60

1949   'An interrupted zenithal world map' *Scottish Geog. Mag.* 65 (1949), 1–6
       The discovery of America An Inaugural Lecture (University College of the South-West 1949)

1950   'Climatic regions and climatic numbers' *Scottish Geog. Mag.* 66 (1950), 4–13
       'Columbus and King John' *Brasilia* 5 (Coimbra Univ. 1950), 669–77

1951   'Origins of Columbian cosmography' *V Centenario della Nascita di Cristoforo Colombo, Convegno Internazionale di Studi Colombiani* (Genoa 1951), 59–67

1952   'The "First" voyage of Amerigo Vespucci' *Geog. Journ.* 118 (1952), 331–7

1953   'The loss of the Santa Maria' *Amer. Hist. Rev.* 58 (1952/3), 854–65

1954   'The miraculous discovery of South America by Christopher Columbus' *Geog. Rev.* 44 (1954), 573–82
       'The personality of the South West' *Geography* 39 (1954), 242–9
       'O problema Vespuciano' *Revista de Historia* (São Paulo, Brazil 1954), 195–9
       'The Egerton MS 2903 map of 1510 and the Padron Real of Spain' *Imago Mundi* 11 (1954), 47–52

1955   'A note on the views of Prof. Nowell regarding the third voyage of Columbus' *Geog. Rev.* 45 (1955), 254
       'The last voyage of John Cabot' *Nature* 176 (1955), 996–9

1956 'The first discovery and exploration of the Amazon' *Trans. Inst. Brit. Geographers* 22 (1956), 87–96
'The "English" coasts on the map of Juan de la Cosa' *Imago Mundi* 13 (1956), 26–9
'Man of mystery' *Isca* 14 (1956), 68–74

1960 Six biographies of the 15th and 16th century explorers and cosmographers for Encyclopaedia Britannica, 1960
'João Fernandes and the Cabot voyages' *Resumo dos Communicaçoes, Congresso Internacional de Historia dos Descobrimentos* (Lisbon 1960), 95–9
'The 1501–02 voyage of Amerigo Vespucci' *Resumo dos Communicaçoes, Congresso Internacional de Historia dos Descobrimentos* (Lisbon 1960), 99–103

1961 'A navegacao de Fernâo de Magalhaes' *Revista de Historia* 45 (São Paulo, Brazil 1961), 173–89

1962 'Select bibliography: Exploration and Discovery' *Handbook for History Teachers* (University of London, Inst. Educ. 1962), 675–8
'Portugaliae Monumenta Cartographica' (Review article) *Scottish Geog. Mag.* 78 (1962), 178–80

1964 'Prince Henry the Navigator' (Prize essay Camoens Award 1960) *Trans. Inst. Brit. Geographers* 35 (1964), 119–28
'The South West Peninsula of England' in *Field Studies in the British Isles* (Royal Society of London 1964) 14–22
Review article on Bernard G. Hoffman: 'Cabot to Cartier, Sources for an ethnography of north-eastern North America 1497–1550' *Bull. Brit. Assoc. American Studies* New Series 8 (Univ. Manch. 1964), 67–9

1965 'Biography of João Fernandez' *Dictionary of Canadian Biography* (Univ. Toronto Press, 1965), 675–9

1966 'The Vinland Map and the Tartar Relation' *Geography* 51 (1966), 259–65

1967 'Columbus divides the world' *Geog. Journ.* 133 (1967), 337–44

1969 'Introduction to the South-West Region' in *Exeter and its Region* ed. F. Barlow (Exeter 1969), 3–4

I

The Quaternary History of the Coasts of South-West England, with special reference to the Bristol Channel Coast[*]

C. KIDSON

Evidence of recent changes of sea level, in the form of raised shore platforms bearing ancient beach deposits and of 'submerged' forests, are so numerous around the coasts of the south-western counties that they have been under discussion for more than two centuries. In 1839 de la Beche[1] was able to review a wide range of papers on the subject as far back as Borlase[2] in 1758. Prestwich's[3] classic paper in 1892 discussed every major site known today, with the sole exception of that at Trebetherick Point in Cornwall, first described in detail by Arkell[4] in 1943. However, despite this long record of scientific enquiry no generally agreed chronology of the events of the Quaternary has emerged. Radiometric dating techniques do not, as yet, cover the Middle and Lower Pleistocene, and organic material yielding pollen of demonstrable interglacial age has not yet been found in the area. There is much faunal evidence, particularly relating to the Upper Pleistocene, but large areas of doubt remain. We are forced still to rely largely on the same deductive methods as Ussher[5] used (almost one hundred years ago) in arriving at his time scale of events. Everard et al[49] have reviewed some of the problems still to be solved. The present paper seeks to review again the considerable volume of work carried out in recent years and to summarise the state of knowledge in 1970. In the absence of an agreed chronology, this can perhaps best be done by considering in turn each of the seven major elements which make up the coastal sequence in the South West. They range from the buried rock channels of all the major rivers, graded to base levels some hundreds of feet below Ordnance Datum, to the erosion surfaces of proved early Pleistocene age at heights close to +213 metres (+700 feet) O.D. They are:

  i the deep rock channels of the rivers which can be traced not only within the present estuaries but also across the floors of the surrounding seas;

[*]For the purposes of this paper, the Bristol Channel coast is defined as stretching from Hartland Point, Devon, to Weston-super-Mare, Somerset.

ii   the 'submerged forests' frequently exposed in the intertidal zone at low tide;

iii   the shore platforms close to present sea level (from about —6 to +20 metres (—20 to +65 feet) O.D.);

iv   the giant erratics together with the contemporaneous (?) boulder clay;

v   the raised beach deposits of sand and shingle, containing marine faunas, which rest on the shore platforms;

vi   the Head and Till(s) (?) overlying the raised beach deposits;

vii   the higher level erosion surfaces.

i   The Buried Channels

All the rivers of the South West have deeply entrenched, often narrow rock channels grading to base levels much below present sea level. Many of them were discovered in the boom years of railway building in the middle of the last century. Codrington[6] discussed some of those in South-West England in a well-known paper written in 1898. Much has been learned in recent years of the form of these channels .Anderson[7] has traced the buried channel of the Severn to depths of —51 metres (—168 feet) off Porthcawl and has shown how the rock channels of the South Wales rivers grade to this proto-Severn. McFarlane[8] carried out a series of geophysical traverses which showed that the buried channels of the Taw-Torridge in north Devon (Fig. 1.1) and of the Erme in south Devon attain depths of —26 to 27 metres (—85 to 88 feet) close to their mouths and appear to be graded to a sea level of —46 metres (—150 feet) O.D. Clarke,[9] on the basis of 43 gravity cores collected from the seabed, has traced the buried channel of the River Exe to depths in excess of— 46 metres (—150 feet) in the neighbourhood of Hope's Nose.

These buried channels were clearly eroded during periods of lowered sea level at the maxima of Pleistocene glacial periods. Stride[10] has drawn attention to 'near-shore' benches at —107 metres (—360 feet) and —128 metres (—420 feet) to the west of the Isles of Scilly, which, he suggests, were cut when a Pleistocene sea level stood considerably below that of the present. Not surprisingly the upper sections of the channels close to the present coastline are filled with Flandrian sediments. Clarke[9], for example, was able to show that the sediments in the Exe channel between —43 metres (—140 feet) and —17 metres (—55 feet) were laid down in pollen zones IV to VIc. Anderson[7] has, however, shown that not only do some of the buried channels contain boulder clays of more than one glaciation, but also that the form of some of them can be described as 'valley in valley'. The implication is that down-cutting during a Weichselian low sea level was only the last such erosional episode. It is reasonable to infer that during each glacial phase of the Pleistocene the development of the buried channels was carried one stage further. Renewed erosion in each glacial period removed some of the sediments deposited in the earlier interglacials. The buried channels cannot be assigned to any single period of the Quaternary. Their development took place throughout the Pleistocene. Their down-cutting was completed in the Weichselian. They were infilled for the last time in the Flandrian.

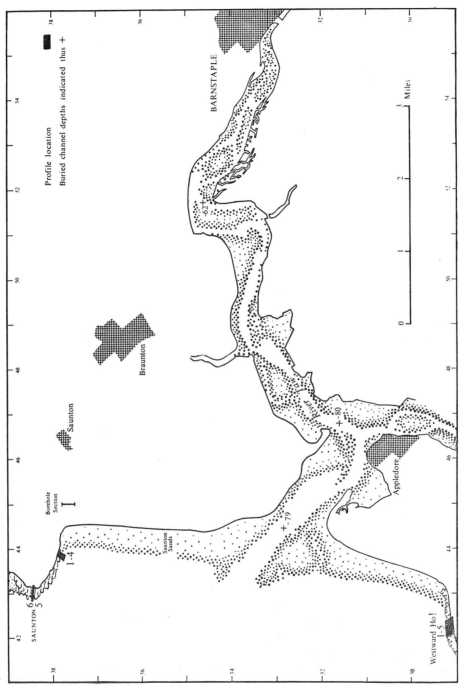

Fig. 1.1 The Taw–Torridge estuary and Barnstaple Bay. The heights below O.D. of the buried rock channel of the Taw are given in feet. The locations of the profiles at Saunton (Fig. 1.2) and Westward Ho (Fig. 1.3) and of the borehole (Fig. 1.4) are shown.

ii   The 'Submerged Forests'

De la Beche[1] recorded in 1839 that ' "submerged forests" are so common that it is difficult not to find traces of them . . . at the mouths of all the numerous valleys (of Cornwall, Devon and west Somerset) which open upon the sea . . .'. He recorded particularly, amongst others, those in Tor Bay, near Looe, near Falmouth, at Perranporth, in Mount's Bay, in the Hayle and Camel estuaries, in Barnstaple Bay, at Porlock and at Stolford, near the mouth of the river Parrett. He agreed with Horner,[11] who first recorded the Stolford 'submarine' forest (Plate 1) in detail, that they were inundated by a relative rise in sea level but he wrongly deduced that this had occurred since Roman times. The work of Godwin, [12, 13] amongst others, has shown that the coastal peats and the 'forests' exposed in the intertidal area are but the highest members of a series of intercalating peats and marine sediments which mark the progress of the post-glacial or Flandrian recovery of the sea from its extreme Weichselian low level. Godwin and his colleagues calculated this to be more than 109 metres (360 feet) below O.D. Few of the coastal peats of the South West have been studied in detail. Clarke's[9] work off south-east Devon shows that, since the end of Pollen Zone IV (circa 7700 B.C.), the later stages of the transgression have brought sea level from —43 metres (—140 feet) to that of the present. Kidson et al[14] have shown that peats in the coastal parts of the Somerset Levels record a rise of 26 metres (85 feet) since Pollen Zone VIc (circa 6000 B.C.). This latter work does not confirm the suggestion by Godwin et al[13] that sea level rise was largely completed by about 3500 B.C.; it indicates rather that it continued at a reducing rate. Jelsergma[15] has shown that a world-wide alternation of peats and marine sediments has led some workers to argue that the Flandrian Transgression was spasmodic, with minor advances and retreats superimposed on the general upward movement of the sea. Others have argued that only climatic fluctuations are involved and that, when due account is taken of the compaction of sediments, isostatic rebound and tectonic warping, the curve of sea level rise is a smooth one, beginning rapidly in the late glacial and slowing considerably from about 5,000 years ago and continuing at a diminishing rate to the present day. The work by Kidson et al,[14] referred to above, supports the latter view.

iii   The shore platforms close to the present sea level

Shore platforms occur very widely around the coasts of the South West. Wright[16] has shown, for example, that between Start Point and the Helford river, they are present along more than 60 per cent of the coast. They occur at different heights in relation to the present sea. Where raised beach deposits are absent, it is possible to argue with Cotton[17] that even those well above sea level are the product of contemporary erosion. However, many shore platforms in the South West carry raised beach and glacial or periglacial deposits (Plates 2, 3) which testify to their pre-glacial, interglacial or interstadial age. Just as the rock channels of the rivers were cut during low glacial sea levels, so the shore platforms were developed during high sea levels in the interglacials. In many Quaternary sections in the South-West peninsula, the shore platform is the basal member.

There is no agreement about either the height(s) or the age(s) of the shore platforms.

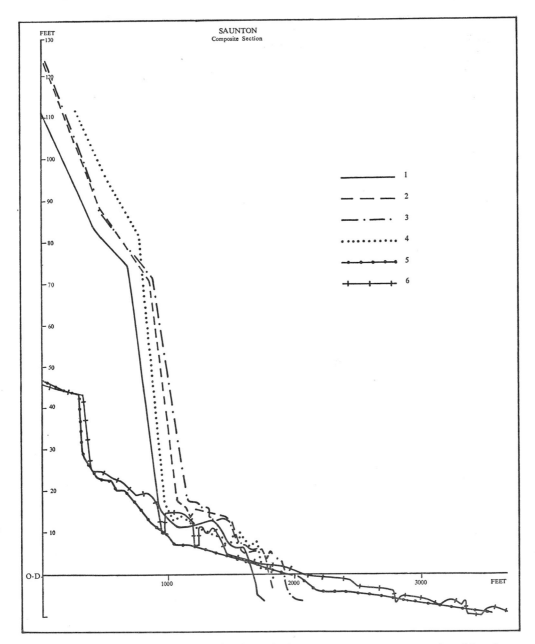

Fig. 1.2 Superimposed profiles across the shore platforms at Saunton, Devon, produced by photogrammetry supplemented by ground survey. Significant heights are given in the text.

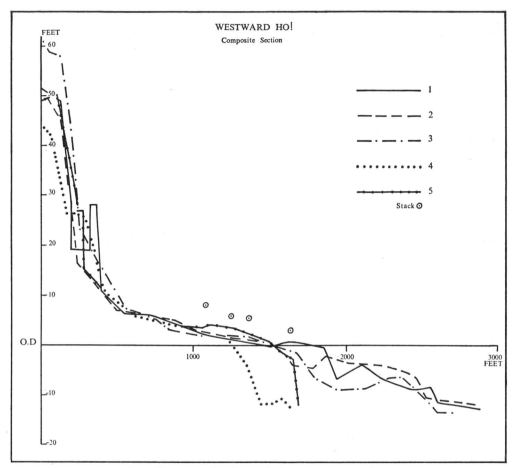

Fig. 1.3 Superimposed profiles across the shore platforms at Westward Ho, Devon, produced by photogrammetry supplemented by ground survey. Significant heights are given in the text.

Some workers, for example Zeuner,[18] distinguished a number of distinct levels, but Stephens and Synge[19] argued that, in Barnstaple Bay, 'it is by no means certain that three distinct platforms are present . . .'. Wright,[16] discussing the shores of the English Channel west of the Teign, concluded that, after allowing for differences in height resulting from variations in exposure and after eliminating the effects of varying geological structure and lithology, 'these multiple levels reflect changes in sea level'. Figures 1.2 (Saunton) and 1.3 (Westward Ho) show superimposed shore profiles in Barnstaple Bay. Their locations are shown in Figure 1.1. Here distinct and separate platforms are to be seen with upper limits at —1.5 metres (—5 feet), +5 to 5.5 metres (+16 to 18 feet) and +8 to 8.5 metres (+26 to 28 feet). At Saunton (Plate 2) the most marked feature is the 5-metre platform. At Westward Ho this has been largely destroyed in the production of the —1.5 metre platform and of the contemporary feature, but remnants still remain. The dominant platform here is, however, the +8 metre surface (Plates 4 and 5). In the South West as a whole the platform heights which occur most frequently fall into four groups. Referred to Ordnance Datum the cliff notches at the upper limit of the platform lie at:

(a) —6 metres (—20 feet) to 0 metres,
(b) +3.7 metres (+12 feet) to +5.5 metres (+18 feet),
(c) +6 metres (+20 feet) and +9.5 metres (+31 feet),
(d) +20 metres (+65 feet).

A good deal of confusion arises from references in the literature to the so-called '25-foot' platform, a term applied with little discrimination to surfaces from sea level to well above 10.7 metres (35 feet). This arises from a failure to recognise, or to concede the existence of more than one feature. Table 1 summarises recent views on platform heights, views which, unlike some expressed earlier, are based on surveyed heights referred to a stated datum. Most authors now recognise the multiplicity of platforms but some still retain doubts. Everard et al[49] recorded detailed surveys of a large number of platforms and identified a greater number of distinct features, but these fall within the groupings given above.

Table 1 also summarises the wide range of views on the age of these features. Many follow Zeuner,[18] who distinguished three sea levels at +18 metres (+60 feet), +7.5 metres (+25 feet) and +3.6 metres (+12 feet) and dated them as Main Monastirian (=Eemian), Late Monastirian (=Late Eemian) and Epi-Monastirian (=the Gottweig Interstadial of the Weichselian). Much confusion arises in published dates since some authors refer to platforms at both of Zeuner's lower levels as the '25-foot' shore platform, whilst others equate the age of the platform with that of the raised beach deposits which lie upon them. The major divergence of opinion appears to be between those who, like Zeuner,[18] place the cutting of the platforms in the last interglacial (Eemian) and those who, like Mitchell,[23] argue for a much earlier Pleistocene age.

ApSimon and Donovan[20] were able to ascribe the Howe Rock platform at Weston-super-Mare, Somerset, to the Paudorf Interstadial and to equate it with the Worcester Terrace of the Severn, because its landward end passes below the Lower Breccia of Brean Down. The other shore platforms in the South West are clearly also older than the raised beach deposits which they carry but the age of the deposits tells us nothing of the maximum age which the platform could have. In an attempt to obtain greater precision the present author secured a sample of fossil *Balanus balanoides* (?) from the surface of the +5-metre (+16 feet) platform at Saunton in Barnstaple Bay; these were obtained from *beneath* the Eemian (?) raised beach deposits (Plate 2) and gave a C14 age (N.P.L. 115) of >40,800 B.P. Shell dates are now generally regarded as untrustworthy and all that an infinite date such as this reveals is that the specimen is not younger than 40,800 years. No greater precision was, therefore, achieved. However, the width of this single element, the 5-metre platform (Fig. 1.4) (in Barnstaple Bay cut across resistant Devonian rocks) in the sequence of shore platforms seems a strong argument against its cutting in an interglacial as short as the Eemian. Even this single feature would seem to require a very long period of time for its

TABLE I

Shore Platforms in South-West England. Some recent views on heights and ages.
(ages have been converted, where necessary, from the author's terminology to modern European terms)

AUTHOR	−6m (−20 ft.) to 0m.	+3.7m (+12 feet) to +5·5m. (+18 feet).	+6m. (+20 feet) to +9.5m. (+31 feet)	+20m. (+65 ft.)
1 *Arkell*[4] Trebetherick Cornwall		←+15 to +20 ft.* (10 feet above HWM) Hoxnian and Eemian →		
2 *Dewey*[21],[22] a. Mousehole Cornwall b. Saunton, Devon		+15 feet		+65 ft.
3 *Zeuner*[18] a. Hope's Nose to Hall Sands, Devon Croyde, Saunton Devon b. Hope's Nose to Plymouth Hoe, Devon c. Mousehole, Cornwall; Portland, Dorset		3.6 metres Epi-Monastirian (=Gottweig Interstadial)	7.5 metres Late Monastirian (=Late Eemian)	60 ft. Main Monastirian (=Eemian)
4 *Mitchell*[23] Irish Sea, North France, E & SE England		←5–25 ft. (18 ft. mean) Cromerian →		
5 *Orme*[24] South Devon		14 ft. Weichselian Interstadial	24 ft. Late Eemian *Orme*[31]**	65 ft. Eemian
6 *ApSimon and Donovan*[20] Brean Down, Somerset	−20 ft. —O.D. (Howe Rock) Paudorf Interstadial			

Source	Lowest	Low raised beach	Higher raised beach	Highest
7 Donovan[25] Bristol Channel		←+3m Swallow Cliff Epi-Monastirian		
8 Bird[26] Dodman, Cornwall		12–15 ft. Interglacial		
9 Clarke[27] Camel Estuary, Cornwall		15 ft. (6 ft. above HWM) (Poorly marked and discontinuous) Interglacial (last) stillstand	25 ft. (15 ft. above HWM) (well marked) Late Monastirian	65 ft. Main Monastirian
10 Stephens and Synge[19] Stephens[30] Barnstaple Bay	↑	Early Pleistocene 0–50 ft. Only possibly more than one platform ——→ possibly Cromerian		
11 Wright[16] Teignmouth to the Lizard ***		12 feet No reliable date	26 feet No reliable date	
12 Mitchell and Orme[28] Scillies		6–18 ft. Composite, possibly Hoxnian/Eemian		
13 James[29] South Cornwall		16 ft. (less well defined) Epi-Monastirian	25 ft. (well marked) Late Monastirian	
14 Kidson[14] This paper Barnstaple Bay	−5 feet	16–18 feet Saunton Composite from Cromerian to	28 feet (Westward Ho) Composite from Cromerian to Flandrian —→	

* Arkell.[4] This surface carries the raised beach which Arkell described as the '10-foot', 'Pre-glacial' or 'Patella' beach.

** Orme[31] suggested an Eemian retrimming of Hoxnian or even older coastal zone.

*** See also Everard et al[149].

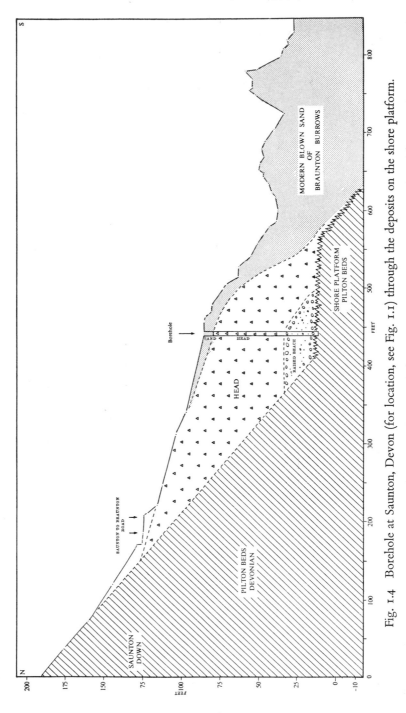

Fig. 1.4 Borehole at Saunton, Devon (for location, see Fig. 1.1) through the deposits on the shore platform.

development. It may well have been rejuvenated several times throughout the Quaternary. When all the surfaces between the intertidal Howe Rock platform at Weston-super-Mare[20] and the '60-foot' feature at Mousehole and Portland[18] are considered, a composite age stretching from the early Pleistocene, possibly the Cromerian, to the youngest of the Weichselian interstadials seems the logical conclusion. Just as the modern sea is retrimming the older shore platforms, so the interglacial seas throughout the Pleistocene are likely to have modified pre-existing features. In these circumstances a number of steps over quite a wide height range seem more likely than a single feature. One of the most convincing arguments for the blocking out of the shore platforms at least as early as the Hoxnian interglacial lies in the presence on them of the giant erratics.

iv   The giant erratics together with the contemporaneous (?) boulder clay

A characteristic feature, and a significant unit in the Pleistocene stratigraphical record of coastal development in the South West, is the train of 'giant erratics' which have been recorded all round the coast of the peninsula. Prestwich[3] described a boulder of trap rock at Cawsand Bay, Plymouth; Ussher[48] discussed the erratics at Prawle Point and Flett and Hill[32] drew attention to the now famous 50-ton Porthleven erratic. The 'giant erratics' of north Devon have been known for a very long time and are particularly well documented. Williams[33] described the Saunton erratic as long ago as 1837, and papers by Pengelly,[34] Hall,[35] and Dewey[36] have examined a whole series of similar rocks located between Croyde Bay and Fremington. Dewey established from a petrological study that the pink granite boulder from Saunton and the dark grey-green granophyre from Combrew Farm, near Fremington, probably originated from the coast of north-west Scotland. Recent papers by Taylor[37, 38] and Arber[39] lead the present author to agree with Zeuner's[18] correlation of the 'giant erratics' of the coast with those included within the Fremington Clay. Doubts about the glacial origin of the Fremington Clay, first discussed in detail by Maw[40], must now be regarded as untenable[23, 39]. If the Fremington Clay is, as it now appears, a true boulder clay, the agency responsible for transporting the boulders was an ice sheet, not icebergs. The erratics on the English Channel coast can scarcely be accounted for other than by ice rafting, however, and here the discussion in Stephens and Synge[19] on the height of glacial sea levels is relevant. The Fremington Clay is probably Saale in age[18, 23] laid down by an ice sheet extending as far as the Scillies[28] and impinging on the coasts of Devon and Cornwall. If the coastal erratics belong to the same glacial period as the Fremington Clay, as they appear to do, their precise position in the Pleistocene coastal stratigraphy is critical. Plate 3 clearly shows the Saunton granite boulder 'cemented' to the '5-metre' shore platform *beneath* the raised beach deposits. This means that the platform cannot be younger than Hoxnian and the raised beach deposits are probably not older than Eemian. This seems to be the true stratigraphic position of all the *giant* erratics. It does, however, raise one major difficulty. Maw[40] believed that the Fremington Clay lay *above* the raised beach. Mitchell[23] supported this view and Stephens[30] claimed to have traced the raised beach gravels along stream sections from beneath the clay to the cliffs at Fremington Quay and Penhill. However, recent (as yet unpublished) detailed work by Wood,[41] involving drilling and geophysical examination, has shown conclusively that the clays and beach gravels, as distinct from outwash material, occur *side by side* at Fremington and neither is superposed upon the other. The true relationship of the giant erratics together with the Fremington Clay can thus be as indicated in the Saunton coastal section (Plate 3). Zeuner's argument[18] that the Fremington Clay must be older than the raised beach seems, therefore, to have been well founded.

v   The raised beach deposits

Throughout the South West, ancient beaches are to be seen, in cliff sections, resting on the upper landward parts of the shore platforms (Plate 2). Sometimes a giant erratic is found just in front of the eroding seaward edge of the beach deposits, or, as at Saunton (Plate 3), is cemented by them on to the surface of the underlying platform. Frequently the deposits incorporate other smaller erratic stones. The marine character of the deposits was recognised very early and Prestwich[3] was able to compare studies, carried out by his contemporaries, of the Mollusca of the raised beaches at Portland, Torquay, Barnstaple and Bridgwater. These old beach materials are as variable in character as those of the present-day beaches above which they rest. In places they are almost exclusively composed of pebbles and cobbles as, for example, at Westward Ho (Plate 4). Elsewhere, as at Saunton, they are mainly current-bedded sands cemented, into a form of sandrock with pebble bands, by calcium carbonate or iron oxides. In many places the sands of the raised beaches pass upwards into false-bedded blown sands yielding a terrestrial fauna. These dune sands extend to much greater heights than the beach deposits with which they are frequently confused.

The raised beach deposits ought to make it easier to unravel the events of the Quaternary. Instead, they make the problem more complex. Prestwich[3] and his contemporaries seem to have had little doubt that a simple tri-partite stratigraphical relationship existed, consisting of shore platform, raised beach and overlying 'head' or 'rubble drift'. Had they used modern European Quaternary terminology they might have ascribed the beach to the Eemian interglacial and the head to the Weichselian, whilst recognising that the beach incorporated erratic material from an earlier glaciation. Doubts now exist not only about the age of the raised beach sediments but also about correlations between beaches in different parts of the peninsula. These difficulties arise because nowhere do two undoubted raised beach deposits occur in the same coastal section with a clearly defined stratigraphical relationship. They are complicated by the belief that more than one till and/or head, representing more than one glaciation, is present in South-West England as in Ireland[19, 23, 30] and that these are to be found above raised beach deposits, for example, those at Saunton in north Devon, which have been dated[18] as Late Monastirian (Late Eemian). This has led these workers to ascribe a Hoxnian age to the Saunton beach and to other deposits correlated with it. The picture is still further complicated by the mistaken belief (see Section iv above) that the Fremington Clay, now recognised as a true till, overlies the raised beach in Barnstaple Bay. Mitchell[23] resurrected this latter belief from the early work of Maw.[40]

Arkell's[4] work at Trebetherick Point, Cornwall, had earlier emphasised the difficulties of dating and correlation in the South West. He ascribed the raised beach there at 4.6 to 6 metres (15 to 20 feet)—the so-called 'pre-glacial', 'patella' or '25-foot' beach—to the Boyn Hill or Middle Acheulian Interglacial (Hoxnian). He originally equated this beach with that at Saunton, referred to above, but subsequently changed his views (Arkell[50]) to place the Saunton beach in the last interglacial (Eemian). Whilst he did not positively identify a higher raised beach at Trebetherick, he regarded the Boulder Gravel as either a beach or as having been derived by solifluction processes from higher (Tertiary?) surfaces and moved by the river Camel into an estuarine position during the Wolvercote or Mioquian Interglacial (Eemian). He considered it to be of the same age and related to the same sea level (18 metres =60 feet) as the Portland and Torbay beaches.

Zeuner[18] placed the 18-metre beach which he described at Portland, Torbay and Mousehole, Cornwall, in the Main Monastirian (Early Eemian). He also recognised a 7.5 metre (25 feet) beach which he dated as Late Monastirian (Late Eemian) and a 3.6 metre (11 to 12 feet) feature which he referred to the Epi-Monastirian (Gottweig Interstadial of the Weichselian). He argued that "there is no evidence of ice transgression of the 25-foot beach anywhere in Devon."

Mitchell and Orme[28] recognised two beaches in the Isles of Scilly. They placed the Chad Girt beach in the Hoxnian and they equated the higher Porth Seal beach with Zeuner's 7.5 metre (25-foot) beach and with the Eemian beach at Selsey.[42] Whilst all these workers recognise strand lines at different levels there is clearly no consensus of opinion either on correlation or on age. In the absence of absolute dating techniques which can be applied to the middle Pleistocene, there is a temptation to assign each beach deposit and each till or head to a separate interglacial or glacial period. However, nowhere in the South West is there a clear cut section showing two distinct beaches separated by an undoubted till, which would confirm that a beach had survived a glacial period in which it had been overridden by ice. Even Stephens and Synge[19], who claimed to identify tills or heads from two glaciations above the raised beach deposits at Saunton and Croyde, asserted that 'there is one and only one raised beach to be seen around Barnstaple Bay.' The most extensive interglacial deposits in the South West itself are the Burtle Beds of Somerset (Figs. 1.5 and 1.6). Bulleid and Jackson[43, 44] recorded the presence in the Burtle Sands of three valves of *Corbicula fluminalis* and of antlers of *Cervus browni* and from this fossil evidence inferred that the deposits are not younger than the terrace gravels of Crayford in the Thames Valley, where flint implements date the deposits as Mousterian. This implies a *youngest* age of Eemian. They did, however, also compare the Burtle Beds with gravels at Clacton-on-Sea, and on this basis, a Hoxnian age is *possible*. ApSimon and Donovan[47] correlated the marine Pleistocene deposits of the Vale of Gordano, Somerset, which reach 13.7 metres (45 feet) above O.D. and the Kenn gravels, with the Burtle Beds and suggested a Main Monastirian (early Eemian) age. There is, however, nothing in the faunal evidence[45] which precludes a Hoxnian age.

The Burtle Sands are found in a borehole at Highbridge, Somerset, beneath head deposits. Their stratigraphical position is, therefore, similar to that of the raised beach sands on the 5-metre shore platform at Saunton in Devon, which Zeuner[18] regarded as Late Monastirian (late Eemian); which Stephens[30] dates as Hoxnian; and about which Arkell[4, 50] had changing

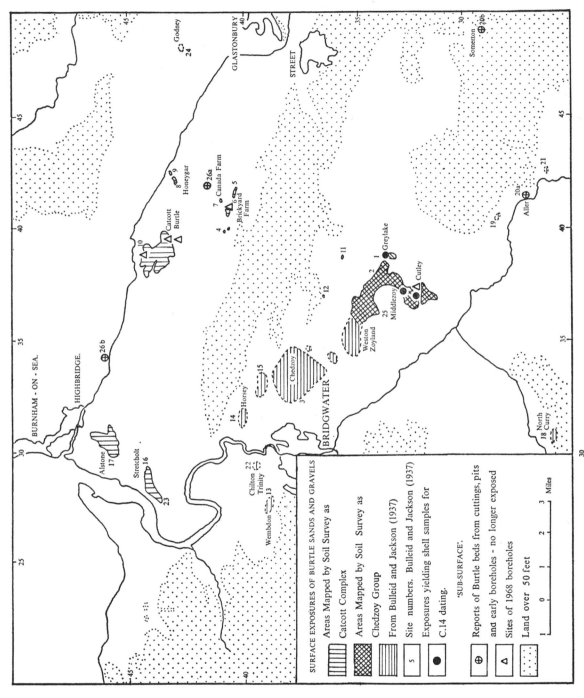

Fig. 1.5   Surface exposures of the sands and gravels of the Burtle Beds of Somerset. An Eemian age is suggested.

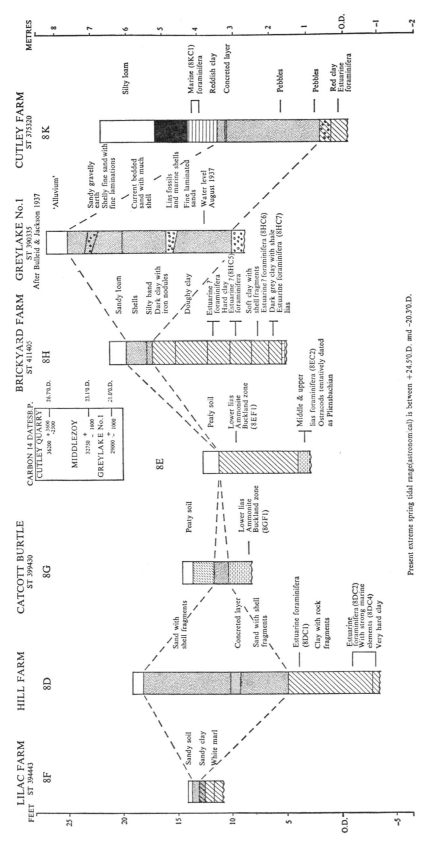

Fig. 1.6 Boreholes through the Burtle Beds. These show that the Burtle Beds rest on an eroded Lias/Trias base and consist of two elements, (i) a clay beginning as estuarine and grading to marine, and (ii) a sand and gravel member containing a marine fauna suggesting a sandbank rather than a beach environment. The C 14 dates are discussed in the text.

c

views. Curiously a C 14 date from marine shells obtained from the base of the sandrock at Saunton (I-2981) of 33,200±2,800-1,800 B.P. falls within the same time range as shells from the Burtle Sands.[45] Whilst this might suggest that the Burtle Sands are comparable in age with the Saunton beach (a view held until recently by the present author) the known unreliability of shell-dates, together with the obvious lack of credibility of a sea level at this late date reaching to heights suggested by the Burtle Beds, makes these dates of no value in correlation, despite the views of Emery in the U.S.A.[46] In addition, the sand bank, as distinct from beach character of the Burtle Beds,[45] shows that they must be related to a sea level much higher than that at which the Saunton beach was formed. Whilst there is no conclusive evidence to indicate the interglacial period from which the Burtle Beds date or their exact relationship to the Saunton deposit, the balance of probability is that both are Eemian. An early Eemian age is suggested for the Burtle Beds and a late Eemian date for the Saunton deposits which may be correlated with the raised beach at Selsey in Sussex. Here West and Sparks,[42] in the most thorough study of interglacial deposits yet carried out in southern England, clearly demonstrated the Eemian age of fossiliferous deposits below the raised beach shingle.

There seems to be little convincing evidence of a beach of Hoxnian age anywhere in the South West. It would indeed be surprising if such a beach had survived the Saale glaciation which overrode the shore platforms on which the major raised beach deposits are found. The balance of probability is for the survival of beaches from the Eemian interglacial, which as far as South-West England is concerned was succeeded by a glacial period in which periglacial, rather than glacial processes operated. Zeuner's[18] suggested oscillations of sea level in the Eemian interglacial seem to be in accordance with the observed stratigraphical relationships in the South West.

vi   The head(s) and till(s) (?) overlying the raised beach deposits

For the greater part of the Pleistocene the South-West Peninsula lay outside the limits of ice penetration. Certainly during the last glaciation (Weichsel) it experienced periglacial rather than glacial conditions. There is now a good deal of evidence[23, 28] that, during the penultimate glaciation (Saale), ice penetrated as far as the Isles of Scilly and pressed in upon the west coasts of Devon and Cornwall. The Fremington Clay is now recognised as a true till and the balance of opinion is that it is Saale in age. Elsewhere, although deposits have been suggested or claimed as tills, for example, by Arkell,[4] Stephens,[30] and Mitchell and Orme,[28] sufficient doubt remains in each location for judgment to be reserved. Periglacial or 'head' deposits are widespread around the coast and an upper and a lower head are frequently identified. No deposits are more difficult to date or to correlate and height is of no significance. Frequently fabric analysis is of little help in separating two heads since the influence of the coastal slope predominates. Even when more than one head can be shown to be present, it is a matter for conjecture whether they represent two glacial periods or two stages within a single glaciation. The only tool available is stratigraphy. In the South West there is argument and doubt about the true stratigraphical relationship of the one undoubted till, the

Fremington Clay. Nowhere is there a single site where two undoubted raised beach deposits can be seen *together,* separated by a till or head. Indeed, in the South West, only for the Isles of Scilly[28] has a claim been made that two raised beaches separated by a cold phase have been identified.

The difficulties not only of identifying but also of correlating heads and tills can be demonstrated from the Barnstaple Bay area. Stephens[30] has argued that there is only one raised beach here. This includes the sandrock deposit at Saunton which Zeuner[18] regarded as part of the 7.5 metre (25 foot) Main Monastirian (Eemian) beach. Stephens,[30] however, considered the Barnstaple Bay/Croyde Bay raised beach to be Hoxnian in age largely because he believed that the equivalent at Fremington extends below the Fremington Clay of Saalian age. This means that the deposits above the raised beach are all that remains to span the whole of the Upper Pleistocene. In the variable thickness of head above the raised beach at Saunton and Croyde, Stephens discerned a lower or main head and what he calls a weathered till which he dates as Saale and an upper cryoturbated head which he regards as Weichselian. No marine deposits separate the two heads but a 'weathering sand layer' between them is dated as Eemian. The present author cannot accept this interpretation of the periglacial deposits overlying the north Devon raised beach. In his view only one glacial period is represented by the whole of the head deposit. Figure 1.4 shows a borehole (located on Fig. 1.1) away from the coastal exposure, where slope washes, vegetation and turf-slipping contribute to a very confused section. In the borehole only a single blocky head is present. All the variations in the head on the coast can be accounted for in terms of differences in the lithology of the country rock; by the presence of blown sand of the same age as the raised beach; and by the present-day colluvial processes to say nothing of climatic variations within a glacial period, which produce stadial and interstadial oscillations. Where the local rocks are highly shattered, as they are at Croyde, head-like colluvial deposits can be seen to be developing under present processes on the coastal slope and the view of the present author is that the Weichsel and Flandrian are long enough to account for the whole of the head and alleged till deposits.

In interpreting the deposits overlying the raised beach, insufficient account appears to be taken of the role of the Saale (?) till and its coastal equivalent—the erratic boulders. The raised beach clearly developed in a coastal zone covered with glacial debris: indeed, glacial material is incorporated in the raised beach in many places. It would be surprising if some of the pre-raised beach glacial deposits had not been left *above* the raised beach level and the subsequent fate of this material in the succeeding glacial period may well account for till-like lenses in the overlying head. It must have been subjected to the same solifluction processes as the country rock.

There are thus two possible interpretations of the Barnstaple Bay/Croyde Bay stratigraphy, depending on, firstly, where in the sequence the Fremington Clay is placed—below the raised beach or above it;[23] secondly, whether the raised beach is dated as Hoxnian,[23, 30] at the very end of the preceding Elster glaciation,[4] or whether it is regarded as Eemian;[18, 50] thirdly, whether there is a single head (this paper) with minor lithological variations or whether there are two heads/tills separated by a distinct warm phase.[30]

These two interpretations are:

	Stephens, Mitchell, Arkell	*This paper (Zeuner)*
Weichsel	Upper cryoturbated Head	Single Head
Eem	Weathering Horizon/ sand layer	Raised Beaches
Saale	Till/Lower Head (=Fremington Clay)	Giant Erratics= Fremington Clay
Hoxne	Raised Beach	Shore Platform (multiple age)
Elster	Giant Erratics	
Early Pleistocene	Shore Platform	

Similar reasoning can be applied to other major sites in the South West. Arkell[4] adopted a sequence and dating comparable to Stephens, though Arkell later modified his views.[50] He identified a Younger Head and a Main Head at Trebetherick Point separated by the Trebetherick Boulder Gravel. This he regarded as either marine or fluvially emplaced solifluctes material related to a sea level higher than the present. Both he and Mitchell[28] regarded the upper part of the Boulder Gravel, described as a 'pebbly clay bed', as possibly a till. Once again the present author finds this interpretation unsatisfactory. If the 'patella' beach is Eemian, as Zeuner[18] believed it to be, then the overlying deposits must be thought of as Weichsel in age. As at Saunton, with which beach Arkell correlated that at Trebetherick, this is a possible interpretation—indeed, in the view of the present author, a probable one.

Mitchell and Orme[28] present a wealth of new evidence from the Isles of Scilly, which can be interpreted as corroborating the view of Stephens and Arkell given above. The Chad Girt beach is said to underlie glacial deposits which are equated with the Fremington Clay. This tends to support Mitchell's[23] own interpretation of the stratigraphic position of the Fremington Clay. If the Chad Girt and Porth Seal beaches are indeed distinct and separate and belong to two different interglacial periods, and if, as Mitchell and Orme argue, the Porth Seal beach can be correlated with the Eemian beach at Selsey, Sussex, the Scilly evidence would resolve doubts about which of the two stratigraphical interpretations given above to accept. However, this evidence is complex and open to other interpretations. The same arguments about the overlying glacial and periglacial deposits can be advanced here as elsewhere in the South West.

vii   The higher level erosion surfaces

The glacio-eustatic oscillations of sea level in the Quaternary were superimposed on a sea level falling throughout the period from a height of the order of 180 to 210 metres (600 to 690 feet). Zeuner[18] suggested that this early Pleistocene (Calabrian) sea level had fallen to 80 to 85 metres (264 to 280 feet) by the late Sicilian (Cromerian); to 56 metres (184 feet) by the end of the Milazzian (early Hoxnian); to 32 metres (105 feet) by the Tyrrhenian (later Hoxnian); and to 7.5 metres (25 feet) in the late Monastirian (late Eemian). Each interglacial sea level was, therefore, lower than that in the preceding interglacial. Low sea levels in the early glacial periods may have been *higher* than present sea level. General summaries of views on this non-glacially induced fall in sea level between the beginning of the Pleistocene and the present are given by Holmes,[51] Fairbridge,[52] and Guilcher.[53] High-level erosion surfaces have been recognised throughout the South West at a wide variety of levels and have been attributed to marine erosion not only in the Quaternary but also in earlier geological periods. Wooldridge[54] has summarised some views on this subject. There is now agreement among many geomorphologists[55] that a surface of marine origin, related to a sea level of 210 metres (690 feet) exists throughout the South West and is part of a feature extending throughout southern England. In the South East this has been dated by faunal evidence as Early Pleistocene (possibly Calabrian) in age.[56] Some sceptics[57] remain, however. Many workers have described erosion surfaces below the Calabrian and recently the tendency has been to regard these as of Pleistocene, rather than of Tertiary age.[55] Clarke[27] has studied the cliff profiles of the Padstow area and discerned notches at between 50 and 55 metres (163 and 180 feet) which he suggested are Milazzian in age. Similarly he described notches at between 24 and 38 metres (80 and 125 feet) which he referred to still stands in the Great Interglacial (Tyrrhenian=Hoxnian) and at 20 metres (65 feet) which he regarded as the Main Monastirian (Early Eemian) of Zeuner. Earlier Orme[31] had described fossil sea cliffs which he attributed to a Hoxnian sea.

It is not surprising that there is little agreement on the origin or age of those 'cliff notches' and high level erosion surfaces which do not carry dateable sediments. Even if a marine origin is conceded, dating is impossible when they are cut in much older rocks. Even when they are developed on glacial or periglacial deposits their dating can scarcely be regarded as reliable when the age of the deposits themselves is doubtful. Thus Arber[58] records erosion surfaces at 30 metres (100 feet) and 15 metres (50 feet) cut across the main head in the Barnstaple area and relates them to Eemian high sea levels. The arguments about the age of the head in north Devon in Section vi above suggest, however, that even the age of these erosion features which may belong to the Upper Pleistocene cannot be accepted without question. Orme[55] described planation surfaces at a wide range of heights in the South Hams and concluded "whilst it may be possible to equate some of the lower strandlines with similar Mediterranean sea levels, their precise placing in the Pleistocene sequence of north-west Europe remains problematical." This conclusion remains a valid one. Correlation and dating of erosion surfaces based on heights alone is clearly unsatisfactory.

Not all the higher surfaces are devoid of marine sediments. Unfortunately such deposits are few and their age and relationship to the surface sequence remains problematical. Reid[59] related the St Erth beds of Cornwall to the 130 metres (430 feet) platform and dated them as Pliocene. Mitchell[60], however, re-examined the St Erth beds, with which he had earlier[23] correlated the Hele gravels near Barnstaple and similar gravels in the Isles of Scilly. He related them to a sea level at 56 metres (185 feet), assigned them to the Cromerian and suggested that they may have been disturbed by Lowestoft (Elster) ice. Subsequently, he modified his views[61] and referred them to the Antian (pre-Cromerian). Wood[41] has suggested that the Hele gravels are fluvio-glacial and thus unrelated to the sea in which the

St Erth deposits were laid down. Clearly the last word has not been written on the significance of the high level erosion surfaces, and of the deposits which rest on them, for the chronology of the Middle and Upper Pleistocene.

CONCLUSION

There is clear evidence throughout the South West of oscillations of sea level from the early Pleistocene to the present day. The range in height represented by erosion features attributed to Pleistocene seas is +210 metres (+690 feet) to perhaps —128 metres (—420 feet). The buried rock channels of the rivers of the peninsula appear to grade to sea levels much below that of the present sea. Whilst these channels are probably composite in age they were probably downcut to their lowest level in the Weichselian. Flandrian sediments infill the rock channels and are to be found together with the peat beds of the 'submerged' forests in nearshore and intertidal areas. These show that the last 46 metres (150 feet) of the postglacial rise of sea level had been accomplished since the end of Pollen Zone IV (7700 B.C.).

Ice of Saale age probably reached as far south as the Isles of Scilly. The Fremington Clay is now recognised as a true till dating from this glaciation but there is still no agreement on its stratigraphical relationship either to the raised beaches in Barnstaple Bay or to the 'giant erratics'.

There is no general agreement on the ages or on correlations between the raised beaches of the South West. Many workers date the beaches below 20 metres (65 feet) as Eemian in age but others seek to refer some of them to the Hoxnian Interglacial. This latter view has been severely criticised by Guilcher[53] as being at variance with the bulk of evidence from Western Europe.

There is still a considerable divergence of view on the number of 'head' deposits above the so-called '25-foot' (7.5 metre) raised beach and argument as to whether, in the Barnstaple Bay area, a till (the Fremington Clay and its equivalent) is found above it or below it. Bowen[62] has suggested that the raised beaches are Eemian in age and their overlying periglacial slope deposits are Weichselian. This seems to the present author to be more in accordance with the evidence than the alternative sequence, worked out in north Devon, of a Hoxnian beach overlain by till of Saale age and by Weichselian head.

There remain varying opinions of the age of the shore platforms but a composite origin involving periodic retrimming throughout the Quaternary now has wide support.

Further work will be necessary before the place in the Pleistocene succession of the higher erosion surfaces, and the deposits which lie upon them, can be determined.

All these problems can only be finally solved by the emergence of reliable absolute dating techniques which can reach back into the Middle and Upper Pleistocene. The Th^{230}/U^{234} method is the most promising and may well resolve at least some of the outstanding problems. Guilcher[53] has suggested that shells from the raised beaches of Devon and Cornwall be dated by this method and one can but support his proposal. If reliable dates can be obtained in this way the most acute stratigraphical disagreements will disappear.

REFERENCES

1 De la Beche, H. T. *Report on the geology of Cornwall, Devon and West Somerset* (London 1839), 395–434

2 Borlase, W. *Natural History of Cornwall* (1758)

3 Prestwich, J. 'The raised beaches and "Head" or rubbledrift of the South of England: their relation to the valley drifts and to the glacial period: and on a late post-glacial submergence' *Q. Jl. Geol. Soc. Lond.* 48 (1892), 263–342

4 Arkell, W. J. 'The Pleistocene rocks at Trebetherick Point, North Cornwall: their interpretation and correlation' *Proc. Geol. Ass.* 54 (1943), 141–70

5 Ussher, W. A. E. 'The chronological value of the Pleistocene deposits of Devon' *Q. Jl. Geol. Soc. London* 34 (1878), 449–58

6 Codrington, T. 'On some submerged rock valleys in South Wales, Devon and Cornwall' *Q. Jl. Geol. Soc. Lond.* 54 (1898), 251–78

7 Anderson, J. G. C. 'The concealed rock surface and overlying deposits of the Severn valley and estuary from Upton to Neath' *Proc. South Wales Inst. Engrs.* 83 (1968), 27–47

8 McFarlane, P. B. 'Survey of two drowned river valleys in Devon' *Geol. Mag.* 92 (1955), 419–29

9 Clarke, R. H. 'Quaternary sediments off south-east Devon' *Q. Jl. Geol. Soc. Lond.* 125 (1970) (for 1969), 277–318

10 Stride, A. H. 'Low Quaternary sea levels' *Proc. Ussher Soc.* 1 (1962), 6–7

11 Horner, L. 'Sketch of the geology of the South-Western part of Somersetshire' *Geol. Trans.* 3 (1815), 338–84

12 Godwin, H. *History of the British Flora* (Cambridge University Press 1956)

13 Godwin, H., Suggate, R. P. and Willis, E. H. 'Radiocarbon dating of the eustatic rise in ocean level' *Nature* 181 (1958) 1518–9

14 Kidson, C., Heyworth, A., and Manton, M. M. Evolution of Bridgwater Bay. In preparation.

15 Jelsergma, S. 'Sea level changes during the last 10,000 years' R. Met. Soc. Proc. Intern Symposium (1969) *World Climate from 8000 to B.C.* 54–71

16 Wright, L. W. 'Some characteristics of the shore platforms of the English Channel Coast and the northern part of the North Island, New Zealand' *Z. für Geomorphologie* N.F. II (1967), 36–46

17 Cotton, C. A. 'Level of Plantation of Marine Beaches' *Z. für Geomorphologie* 7 (1963), 97–111

18 Zeuner, F. E. *The Pleistocene Period* (London 1959) (2nd edn.)

19 Stephens, N. and Synge, F. M. 'Pleistocene Shorelines' in *Essays in Geomorphology* ed. G. Dury (London 1966), 1–52

20 ApSimon, A. M. and Donovan, D. T. 'The stratigraphy and archaeology of the Late-glacial and Post-glacial deposits at Brean Down, Somerset' *Proc. Univ. of Bristol Spelaeological Soc.* 9 (2) (1960/1), 67–136

21 Dewey, H. *British Regional Geology, South-West England* (HMSO 1948), 64

22 Dewey, H. 'The raised beach of North Devon: its relation to others and to Palaeolithic man' *Geol. Mag.* 10 (1913), 154–63

23 Mitchell, G. F. 'The Pleistocene History of the Irish Sea' *Adv. Sci.* 17 (1960), 313–25

24 Orme, A. R. 'The raised beaches and strand lines of South Devon' *Field Studies* 1 (2) (1960), 1–22

25 Donovan, D. T. 'Sea levels of the last glaciation' *Bull. Geol. Soc. Am.* 73 (1962), 1297–8

26 Bird, E. C. F. 'Coastal landforms of the Dodman district' *Proc. Ussher Soc.* 1 (1963), 56–7

27 Clarke, B. B. 'The superficial deposits of the Camel estuary and suggested stages in its Pleistocene history' *Trans. Roy. Geol. Soc. Cornwall* 19 (1961/2), 257–79

28 Mitchell, G. F. and Orme, A. R. 'The Pleistocene deposits of the Isles of Scilly' *Q. Jl. Geol. Soc. Lond.* 123 (1967), 59–92

29 James, H. C. L. 'Aspects of the raised beaches of South Cornwall' *Proc. Ussher Soc.* 2 (1968) 55–6

30 Stephens, N. 'Some Pleistocene Deposits in North Devon' *Biuletyn Peryglacjalny* 15 (1966), 103–14

31 Orme, A. R. 'Abandoned and composite sea cliffs in Britain and Ireland' *Ir. Geogr.* 4 (1962), 279–91

32 Flett, J. S. and Hill, J. B. 'Geology of Lizard and Meneage' *Mem. Geol. Surv.* (1912)

33 Williams, D. 'Raised Beaches of Saunton Down End and Baggy Point' *Proc. Geol. Soc.* 2 (1837), 535

34 Pengelly, W. 'The Granite Boulder on the shore of Barnstaple Bay, North Devon' *Trans. Devon Ass.* 6 (1873), 211

35 Hall, T. M. 'Notes on Granite Boulders near Barnstaple' *Trans. Devon Ass.* 11 (1879), 429–34

36 Dewey, H. 'Notes on some igneous rocks from North Devon' *Proc. Geol. Soc.* 21 (1910), 429–34

37 Taylor, C. W. 'Erratics of the Saunton and Fremington areas' *Trans. Devon Ass.* 88 (1956), 52–64

38 Taylor, C. W. 'The Saunton Pink Granite Erratic' *Trans. Devon Ass.* 90 (1958), 179–86

39 Arber, M. A. 'Erratic Boulders within the Fremington Clay of North Devon' *Geol. Mag.* 101 (1964), 282–3

40 Maw, G. 'On a supposed deposit of Boulder Clay in North Devon' *Q. Jl. Geol. Soc. Lond.* 20 (1864), 445–51

41 Wood, T. R. Personal communication based on unpublished work for a PhD on 'Some aspects of the Quaternary deposits of South-West England' (1970)

42 West, R. G. and Sparks, B. W. 'Coastal interglacial deposits of the English Channel' *Phil. Trans. R. Soc. B.* 243 (1960/1), 95–133

43 Bulleid, A. and Jackson, J. W. 'The Burtle Sand Beds of Somerset' *Proc. Somerset Arch. and Nat. Hist. Soc.* 83 (1937), 171–95

44 Bulleid, A. and Jackson, J. W. 'Further notes on the Burtle Sand Beds of Somerset' *Proc. Somerset Arch. and Nat. Hist. Soc.* 83 (1941), 111–4

45 Kidson, C. 'The Burtle Beds of Somerset' *Proc. Ussher Soc.* 2 (1970), 189–91

46 Emery, K. O. and Milliman, J. D. 'Sea levels during the past 35,000 years' *Science* 162 (1968), 1121–23

47 ApSimon, A. M. and Donovan, D. T. 'Marine Pleistocene deposits of the Vale of Gordano, Somerset' *Proc. Spelaeological Soc. Univ. of Bristol* 7 (3) (1956), 130–6

48 Ussher, W. A. E. in *The Geology of the Country around Kingsbridge and Salcombe.* Mem. Geol. Surv. 1904

49 Everard, C. E., Lawrence, R. H., Witherick, M. E. and Wright, L. W. 'Raised beaches and marine geomorphology' in K. F. G. Hosking and G. J. Shrimpton *"Present views of some aspects of the Geology of Cornwall and Devon."* Royal Geol. Soc. Cornwall (Penzance 1964), 283–310

50 Arkell, W. J. 'Three Oxfordshire Palaeoliths and their significance for Pleistocene correlation' *Proc. Prehist. Soc. New Ser.* 11 (1945), 20–32

51 Holmes, A. *Principles of Physical Geology* (London 1965) (2nd edn.), 711–15

52 Fairbridge, R. W. 'Quaternary Period,' 912–31 in *The Encyclopaedia of Geomorphology* (Reinhold, New York 1968)

53 Guilcher, A. 'Pleistocene and Holocene sea level changes' *Earth-Science Reviews* 5 (2) (1969), 69–97

54 Wooldridge, S. W. 'The Physique of the South West' *Geography* 39 (1954), 231–42

55 Brunsden, D., Kidson, C., Orme, A. R. and Waters, R. S. 'Denudation Chronology of parts of South-Western England' *Field Studies* 2 (1) (1964), 115–32

56 Kidson, C. 'The Role of the sea in the evolution of the British landscape' Chapter I in *Geography at Aberystwyth* (Univ. of Wales Press 1968)

57 Simpson, S. 'On the supposed 690-foot marine platform in Devon' *Proc. Ussher Soc.* 1 (3) (1964), 89–91

58 Arber, M. 'Pleistocene sea levels in North Devon' *Proc. Geol. Assoc.* 71 (1960), 169–76

59 Reid, C. in C. Reid and J. S. Flett *The Geology of the Land's End District.* Mem. Geol. Surv. (1909)

60 Mitchell, G. F. 'The St Erth Beds—an alternative explanation' *Proc. Geol. Assoc.* 76 (1965), 345–66

61 Mitchell, G. F. and Watt, O. 'The History of the Ericaceae in Ireland during the Quaternary' in West, G. R. and Walker *Studies in the Vegetational History of the British Isles* (Cambridge University Press 1970)

62 Bowen, D. Q. 'A new interpretation of the Pleistocene succession in the Bristol Channel area' *Proc. Ussher Soc.* 2 (2) (1969), 86

2

The Significance of Quaternary Events for the Landform of South-West England

R. S. WATERS

In essence the Palaeozoic massif of South-West England may be described as a region of narrow steep-sided valleys and broad 'flat-topped' interfluves. This distinctive association of forms is common to all parts of the peninsula irrespective of their general elevations. It is as characteristic of the high summit plains of Dartmoor and Exmoor as of the intervening lower tract of central Devon and as typical of the locally dominant Cornish uplands as it is of the less elevated plateaulands from which they rise.

But in almost every view it is the interfluves which appear to dominate the scene and to run together as a continuous upper surface of gentle gradients and small relief, whereas the intervening incised valleys are lost to sight below their sharply convex rims. And it is the interfluve surfaces of low relief which for the past 150 years have impressed topographers and attracted the attention of geologists and geomorphologists.[1] They have been recognized over the greater part of the peninsula, mapped at many different elevations between the summit of Dartmoor and the top of the coastal cliffs and interpreted as remnants of planation surfaces or stripped planes of unconformity.[2]

Although it is generally agreed that the surfaces were fashioned in descending order, there is no agreement on the number that are present nor on the manner of their fashioning. Nevertheless few workers would dissent from the view that little evidence exists in the landscape of the operation of any process other than those of sub-aerial weathering and erosion and that "only locally . . . does it appear that any shoreline earlier than that at 130 metres (430 feet) can be recognized as having transgressed notably within the present coastline."[3] Indeed a more recent interpretation would limit marine planation entirely to those narrow coastal areas which now stand at or below 130 metres (430 feet).[4] In short the geomorphological history of the peninsula has been conceived almost wholly in terms of alternate episodes of base-levelling or stripping and rejuvenation.

According to the necessarily rough chronology of denudation which has been suggested, the higher more extensive 'flats' are regarded as fragments of Tertiary surfaces, the oldest of which are believed to have been tilted or warped during the Miocene orogeny, and the lower cliff-top platforms are interpreted as Pleistocene strand-flats. In other words the recurrent phases of planation and valley cutting are presumed to have begun with the regression of the Upper Cretaceous Sea and to have continued ever since.

In this 'classical' interpretation of the denudation chronology the only Quaternary events that are accorded morphogenetic significance are the fluctuations in sea-level, and their effects are recognized only in the relatively narrow coastal zone and along the lower reaches of the streams. But despite their importance, sea level variations are but one of the many events which have affected the landform of South-West England during the last three million years. The comparative neglect, save at coastal sites, of the local morphological and sedimentary evidence of those other events may be attributed to the understandable preoccupation of research workers with the more readily observed and delineated elements in the landform—namely, the interfluve surfaces.

QUATERNARY MORPHOGENESIS, THE DETERMINANTS OF CHANGE

According to current geological usage the Quaternary period comprises the two epochs, Pleistocene and Holocene (or Recent). West,[5] following Flint,[6] suggests that the distinguishing of the Holocene epoch is unnecessary, but the geomorphologist can surely justify the retention of the term Holocene for the last 10,000 years during which Man has emerged as a significant geomorphological process.

This most recent, shortest and apparently most abnormal of geological periods is strikingly differentiated from the preceding 60 million years of Tertiary time by the rate and intensity of its climatic fluctuations and by the far-reaching hydrological and biotic changes generated by those fluctuations of climate. The morphological consequences of these short-term climatic changes of great intensity have been identified in most of the world's landscapes and form the basis of Thornbury's conclusion that most of the earth's topography is no older than Pleistocene.[7]

Geomorphological development was affected in two ways by Quaternary changes of climate. First, changes in temperature caused worldwide variations in the sea level, which fell with the development of land-borne ice-sheets during the cold phases and rose again as the ice melted during warm phases. This purely glacio-eustatic fall in sea level had begun already in the Tertiary when the gradual lowering of the temperature led to the growth of ice-sheets over Antarctica and Greenland. By the end of the Pliocene the pre-glacial sea level had fallen from 72 metres above to near present sea level.[8] The maximum fluctuation in response to continental glaciations during the Pleistocene is considered to have been from 4 to 12 metres (13 to 40 feet) above to at least 200 metres (656 feet) below present sea level.[9] Clearly the morphological consequences of these movements of base-level are restricted mainly to coastal areas. Secondly, the rates of operation and in some cases the nature of geomorphological processes altered with changes in the bioclimatic and hydrological conditions in such a way that the alternation of glacial and interglacial phases was marked in many of the world's landscapes by an alternation of morphogenetic systems. But because of the rapidity of the alternation it is considered that landforms can rarely have developed in equilibrium with either system. By contrast the late Tertiary landform, developed as it was over a long period of relatively slowly changing bioclimatic conditions, may be an equilibrium form in areas of crustal stability.

The emergence of Man as a geomorphological process during the Holocene must also be recognized as an event of high significance for the landforms of many areas. Man is adept at creating or modifying landforms, both directly and indirectly. His direct influence, as Professor E. H. Brown has noted, may be either purposeful, as in the case of a railway cutting, or incidental to his other activities, as witness for example the hollow ways or sunken lanes.[10] But his most effective morphogenetic activities, like the effects of climate, may not be direct but realized via a long series of linked consequential changes. For instance he may, during the course of his agricultural, industrial or recreational activities, bring about changes in the nature and density of the vegetation cover and in the related density, nature, depth and mass of roots in the soil; all of these in turn effect changes in the run off/infiltration ratio and hence in the weathering/removal ratio and, through the latter, in the geometry of the land surface. In other words, with the addition of even primitive man, the morphogenetic system is modified and its expression in the landscape begins to change.

THE RESULTS IN SOUTH-WEST ENGLAND

(1) *Movements of base-level*

As indicated above, so long as geomorphologists were chiefly concerned with the genesis of the most obvious and most extensive elements in the landform, the significance of Quaternary events was underestimated. So long as all of those elements were interpreted as remnants of base-levelled surfaces, the primary aim was to seek a mechanism to account for successive negative movements of base-level during the Late Tertiary, and for alternating negative and positive movements throughout the Pleistocene. Thus the Quaternary events that were considered were the glacio-eustatic fluctuations of sea level, which were believed to account for the lower base-levels of erosion ranging from at least 130 metres (426 feet) above to more than 45 metres (148 feet) below present sea level. Recent findings have demonstrated, however, that although the amplitude of the ice-controlled fluctuations was sufficient to accommodate the range of height of the morphological elements regarded hitherto as Pleistocene in age, 90 per cent of the variation was below present sea level. Even if, as is unlikely, conditions during an early warm phase approached those of the Late Tertiary and all the ice disappeared from Antarctica as well as from the northern hemisphere, the resultant high sea level would still have been far too low to trim the '400-foot platform'. Thus if that most impressive of all platforms on the peninsula be an Early Pleistocene feature —and it must be admitted that its age has never been established, notwithstanding the recent careful re-examination of the supposedly related St Erth beds[11]—either it has been uplifted or the capacity of the ocean basins has increased since its formation. But the necessary introduction of crustal movement of one kind or another into the argument at once renders suspect all chronologies based on 'height above sea level,' and invalidates all attempts to associate particular coastal platforms with specific high sea levels. Consequently further consideration of the nature and effects of glacial eustasy can add little to the generally accepted views on the age and origin of the cliff-top platforms and the other rejuvenation forms that characterise the lower portions of the valleys. Moreover, these views will lack precision until dateable deposits are found in unequivocal association with presumed Pleistocene elements.

(2)   *Alternating morphogenetic systems*

Even if it be accepted that the major subdued elements in the landform are 'ancient', i.e. Tertiary, it is impossible not to regard the minor forms as 'modern'. As Sir Charles Cotton reminded us in 1958, 'The day is long past when it was the fashion to ascribe detailed landscape forms, i.e., any other than the broadest and most generalised features of the relief, to pre-Pleistocene morphogenesis'.[12] All the finer details of surface configuration are assumed 'without further argument' to be the result of processes of land sculpture that have operated during the Quaternary. Fortunately, in the landform of the South-West there are clear indications of the influence of two radically different morphogenetic systems, termed by Cotton the rain-and-rivers and the cryergic systems. The rain-and-rivers system, formerly the so-called 'normal' system, was dominant during the mild phases; the cryergic or cryo-nival (periglacial) system dominated during the cold phases. Of the warm and cold phases themselves there is, of course, ample independent evidence, principally in the form of mammalian remains found in the limestone caves of Devon, of which two, Kent's Cavern and Tornewton, are of particular stratigraphic importance.[13] It is nevertheless the virtually ubiquitous and unequivocal documentation of the two contrasted geomorphic systems, in the superficial geology and in the landform, that merits more detailed attention.

Indications of cryergic activity are legion.[14] Unmistakable evidence of the frost weathering of coherent rock (gelifraction) and frost action on incoherent material (cryo-turbation or geliturbation) is provided by regoliths and rock outcrops throughout the peninsula, irrespective of either altitude or distance from the present coastline. Frost-split cobbles and pebbles are as typical of head deposits on the raised beach platform as of the thoroughly churned mélange of Tertiary gravels and clay-with-flints and chert at 225 metres (738 feet) O.D. on the Haldon Hills; and the metadolerite of Cox Tor (430 metres [1410 feet] O.D.) is shattered no more nor less than the grit tors (100 metres [328 feet] O.D.) overlooking the Valley of Rocks west of Lynton or the schist arête (20 metres [65 feet] O.D.) above Start Point. Indeed the debris mantle everywhere contains products of gelifraction in greater or lesser abundance. The coarser fraction in every pit and cliff section consists of relatively fresh, angular rock and mineral fragments, and the surface clitters on the granite uplands contain both frost-detached blocks and frost-broken boulders. The manifestations of geliturbation are distributed no less widely. Wherever the surface of the regolith is sensibly flat, such indications of frost disturbance as vertically disposed pebbles and rock fragments persist to a depth of approximately one metre (3.3 feet) and clear examples of sorting are also common to about half that depth. Thus pit sections on Haldon show superficial pockets of loess-like silty material separated by flakes and cobbles of flint and chert in the top of the Tertiary gravels, and the presumed Early Pleistocene deposits of sand, rounded quartz and flint pebbles and gabbro cobbles at Crousa Common on the Lizard platform are similarly sorted. Other indications of the effects of geliturbation are well seen on the granite uplands. One of the most instructive is provided by sections in a gravel pit at 414 metres (1358 feet) O.D. on Dartmoor, which show a series of involutions consisting of downward hanging lobes or pods of head separated by upward projecting swirls of growan (rotted granite) above a layer of undisturbed but equally incoherent growan.[15] This is the clearest example yet noted in South-West England of the effects of the seasonal thawing and re-freezing from the top downwards of a superficial layer of incoherent material underlain by still frozen ground. It is considered to be indicative of an earlier phase of more intense cryergic activity than that which gave rise to the other examples of regoliths disturbed and sorted to a maximum depth of one metre (3.3 feet).

If the distribution of the examples of frost weathering, disturbance and sorting is very wide, that of the evidence for the periglacial variety of solifluxion i.e. congelifluxion, is ubiquitous. Indeed, at very few sites has the entire regolith weathered from the immediately subjacent bedrock; most, and in some cases all, of it is *head*. Head has been identified and mapped by officers of the Geological Survey ever since the publication in 1839 of De La Beche's report on the geology of the West Country, in which he applied the quarryman's term to a superficial deposit of the kind first described by Borlase in 1758 at Porth Nanven near St Just. It is defined as weathered material moved downslope by solifluxion and associated processes during the Pleistocene cold phases. Unfortunately its ubiquity cannot be indicated in the drift sheets of the 1-inch-to-the-mile geological map. At best only the thicker spreads are shown; from some sheets it is omitted entirely.[16] Two solifluxion layers have been identified at many widely separated inland sites. On Dartmoor they are represented by an upper head of large stones and boulders of sound granite (of which the well-known clitters form a major part) and a lower or main head of much smaller weathered granite and crystal fragments set in a fine matrix of sandy or gritty loam. From observations of their field relations it is apparent that the two heads which differ so strikingly in physical constitution represent two cold phases; indeed in several sections they are separated by an erosional unconformity.[17] Two heads of comparable constitution, separated by a layer of peat, have been recorded from Bodmin Moor and attributed to the Middle and Late Weichselian.[18]

Confirmation of the former existence of periglacial, tundra-like bioclimatic conditions is provided by Late Pleistocene deposits of wind-borne, loess-like material on the Lizard platform,[19] by fossil floras with arctic or alpine characters in the Bovey Basin and on Bodmin Moor[20] and by ice-vein and ice-wedge pseudomorphs in many cliff sections of head. In fact, all the evidence supports the view that the landscapes of South-West England were affected by a frost-dominated complex of geomorphic processes on at least two occasions during the latter part of the Pleistocene.[21] It is surely inconceivable that the results of the operation of those processes should not be clearly expressed in the landform of a region which has been affected by the subsequent rain-and-rivers system for a mere 10,000 years.

(3) *Modifications to the landform*

It would appear, from the ubiquity and constitution of the solifluxion deposits, that the most significant modifications to the pre-existing landform were the direct result of a wholesale stripping and re-distribution of its regolith. The lower, or main, head, which is associated with the earlier, more intense of the Weichselian cold phases, is nowhere a simple product of the frost weathering of bedrock, though it may contain rock flakes and mineral chips. For example, on Dartmoor it consists of a dull yellow- to strong-brown sandy or gritty loam containing coherent but easily broken granite stones up to 15 centimetres (6 inches) long. Whatever may be the proportion of fine matrix to stones—and it is rarely lower than two to one—the bimodal distribution of particle sizes is a distinctive characteristic. Its matrix appears to be a thorough mixture of the secondary products of chemical weathering with silt-, sand- and fine grit-sized particles of less weatherable minerals, predominantly quartz. It is of uniform colour and consistency throughout and betrays no evidence of having been weathered since it was deposited, though its uppermost portions may exhibit some degree of horizon differentiation through post-depositional soil development. In every respect, therefore, it appears to represent a pre-existing regolith that has been redistributed by solifluxion and/or wash. Indeed at many sites on Dartmoor it has overrun and preserved the vestiges of a pre-periglacial weathering profile; at others it is separated from basal, *in situ,* weathered material (growan) by a layer of downwashed regolith or bedded growan. This consists of a number of thin, moderately sorted, alternating bands of silty clay and fine to coarse sand or fine gravel. Frequently the coarser bands pass laterally into lenses of head. Therefore it is reasonable to infer that the bedded slope deposits are the first indications of the re-distribution of waste to which the main head bears witness.

In some areas the mass downslope transfer of largely pre-existing material obliterated minor elements in the landform (as witness the head-filled gullies in the Upper Greensand scarp of the Haldon Hills)[22] and reduced the amplitude of its local relief almost everywhere. Relatively thick accumulations of soliflual debris remain on the raised-beach platform in sheltered coastal locations, occupy the floors of first- and second-order basins and form the so-called rubble-drift terraces along third-order streams on the granite outcrops. Their absence from the valley floors of higher-order streams may be accepted as evidence of the continued, albeit seasonal, operation of fluvial processes during the cold phases. Confirmation of the efficacy of those processes of linear erosion is provided by the now-buried valleys off the mouths of the major rivers. The cliffed head deposits around the coast suggest that the soliflual transfers of waste also continued well beyond the present shoreline towards a greatly lowered sea level. But large as it is, the amount of head remaining on the land surface can give no real clue to the total volume of material removed from the region. The layer of head mantling the interfluve slopes is indicative only of the thickness of the seasonally-thawed material that was subject to downslope transfer. It represents the moving sheet of debris that was stopped in its tracks, as it were, at the end of the cold phase. That the total ablation was very great can only be inferred by the thickness of the coastal accumulations, which so obviously owe their preservation to their position on the raised, wave-cut platform. They are clearly the last surviving remnants of the landward portions of seaward-sloping aprons of soliflual debris which were alternately extended beyond the present shoreline during two cold phases and cut back by wave action during the intervening and subsequent warm phases. Confirmation, not only of the magnitude of the ablation during the Main Weichselian but also of its morphological consequences, is provided by evidence from higher elevations inland.

On the granite uplands the large-scale, downslope transfer of pre-existing regoliths, represented by the lower (main) head, was responsible for lowering the broad interfluve surfaces and laying bare the tors. The history of the progressive emergence of the tors—after they had been differentiated by selective, sub-surface weathering[23]—and their subsequent modification has been reconstructed from a study of the debris layers in numerous pits. 'During the earlier cold phase successive horizons of the pre-existing weathering profile were removed from the upper parts of slopes and deposited in reverse order lower down as the main head. The succeeding intercryergic phase seems to have been too short, or perhaps bioclimatically unfavourable, for a new weathering profile to develop on the stripped portions of the slopes, though the main head commonly shows evidence of truncation. The latter cold phase was characterized by the downslope transfer of boulders and blocks of sound bedrock, detached from the newly exposed tors, and their deposition as the upper head.'[24] Thus as a result of the substitution of the cryergic morphogenetic system—in which the rate of removal of waste greatly exceeded its rate of production by weathering—for the pre-existing rain-and-rivers system (under which weathering rates exceeded those of removal) all the granite uplands were considerably lowered. By how much this was so, is given by the heights of the tors, for the vertical extent of a tor is an indication of the minimum amount by which the surrounding surface has been lowered. Beyond the immediate environs of the tors with their encircling masses of clitter, some of which display rudimentary patterns of nets and stripes, the slow downslope movement of the lower head merely preserved or enhanced the smoothness of interfluve slopes on all the granite outcrops. The thickness of the pre-existing weathering mantle available for cryergic redistribution precluded the exposure of bedrock and the creation of the benched hillslopes which are another distinctive legacy of the cryergic system to the landform of the South West.

On the indurated arenaceous rocks of Exmoor and on the metamorphosed sediments and intrusives which surround the granite outcrops,[25] the mantle of head is rarely as deep or as continuous as it is on the granite. Yet these well-bedded and well-jointed rocks are highly susceptible to frost weathering; clearly, removal of their small-calibre products was relatively rapid. Consequently their slopes were greatly modified. Initially irregular hillsides with gradients of between 8 and 10 degrees were converted by selective gelifraction and solifluxion into flights of steps with broad treads and steep risers. They are particularly well developed on Cox Tor, where it is clear from their attitude that they are structurally controlled and—from their current modification by spring sapping—that they are relict forms, possibly representing the cumulative effects of several periglacial phases. As on the granite uplands so in certain other parts of the Palaeozoic country, selective surface degradation, operating over entire interfluvial areas, created a 'structural relief' by giving topographic expression to subtle geological differences. Elsewhere on the peninsula the effects of the cryergic metamorphosis are less explicit in the landform, though the ubiquitous head would appear to indicate that the broadly rounded interfluves bounded by convexo-concave slopes on the shales of central Devon and on the slates and shales south of Dartmoor and Bodmin Moor are an expression of the latest alternation of cryergic and rain-and-rivers systems.

Indeed is it possible any longer to deny the efficacy of Quaternary morphogeny in South-West England? Virtually all of the morphological features which immediately come to mind when we attempt to visualize typical Dartmoor scenery owe their origins or their dominant characteristics to the operation of cryergic processes. None of the details of the relief of any of the granite areas is older than the periglacial phase to which the lower (main) head testifies. But the preceding warm phase of selective bedrock decomposition, together with the production of deeply weathered regoliths, was a necessary prerequisite to the extensive periglacial metamorphosis, after which virtually no trace of the pre-existing landform remained. It follows that on the granite uplands it is futile to attempt to define any high-level planation surface within narrow altitudinal limits. The broad, 'flat'-topped interfluves of Dartmoor and Bodmin Moor can no longer be interpreted as the terminal surfaces of pre-Pleistocene planations; they are, rather, surfaces at the base of the zone of weathering, stripped of their mantles of waste; their negligible gradients are indicative only of the minimal slopes across which the soliflual transfers were effected. Indeed, if a similar wholesale stripping of regoliths occurred during each of the preceding cold phases, the uplands may well have been lowered by some 40 to 60 metres (131 to 197 feet) during the Quaternary. Unfortunately it is not possible even to hazard a guess at the magnitude of the denudation of the Palaeozoic areas, where preperiglacial weathering was less, but frost weathering more, important than it was on the granites.

REFERENCES

1 Shorter, A. H., Ravenhill, W. L. D. and Gregory, K. J. *Southwest England* (London 1969), 23–52
   Balchin, W. G. V. 'The denudation chronology of South-West England' in *Present Views of Some Aspects of the Geology of Cornwall and Devon* ed. K. F. G. Hosking and G. J. Shrimpton (Penzance 1964), 267–81
2 Gregory, K. J. 'Geomorphology' in *Exeter and its Region* ed. Frank Barlow (Exeter 1969), 27–42
   Simpson, S. 'Geology' in *Exeter and its Region* ed. Frank Barlow (Exeter 1969), 5–26
3 Linton, D. L. 'Tertiary Landscape evolution' in *The British Isles: a Systematic Geography* ed. J. W. Watson and J. B. Sissons (London 1964), 110–30
4 Simpson, S. op. cit.
5 West, R. G. *Pleistocene Geology and Biology* (London 1968)
6 Flint, R. F. *Glacial and Pleistocene Geology* (New York 1957)
7 Thornbury, W. D. *Principles of Geomorphology* (New York 1954)
8 Mercer, J. H. 'The discontinuous glacio-eustatic fall in Tertiary sea-level' *Palaeogeogr. Palaeoclimat. Palaeoecol.* 5 (1968), 77–86
9 Jongsma, D. 'Eustatic sea-level changes in the Arafura Sea' *Nature* 228 (1970), 150–1

10 Brown, E. H. 'Man shapes the Earth' *Geogr. Journ.* 136 (1970), 74–85
11 Mitchell, G. F. 'The St Erth beds—an alternative explanation' *Proc. Geol. Ass. Lond.* 74 (1965), 345–66
12 Cotton, C. A. 'Alternating Pleistocene morphogenetic systems' *Geol. Mag.* 95 (1958), 125–36
13 Sutcliffe, A. J. 'Pleistocene faunas of Devon' in *Exeter and its Region* ed. Frank Barlow (Exeter 1969), 66–70 and references cited therein
14 Waters, R. S. 'The geomorphological significance of Pleistocene frost action in south-west England' in *Essays in Geography for Austin Miller* ed. J. B. Whittow and P. D. Wood (Reading 1965), 39–57
15 Waters, R. S. 'The Pleistocene legacy to the geomorphology of Dartmoor' in *Dartmoor Essays* ed. I. G. Simmons (Torquay 1964), 73–96
16 For example, sheet 324, Okehampton
17 Waters, R. S. 1964 op. cit.
18 Conolly, A. P., Godwin, H. and Megaw, E. M. 'Studies in the post-glacial history of British vegetation: XI. Late glacial deposits in Cornwall' *Phil. Trans. Roy. Soc.* B 234 (1950), 397–469
19 Coombe, D. E. and Frost, L. C. 'The nature and origin of the soils over the Cornish serpentine' *J. Ecol.* 44 (1956), 605–15
20 Heer, O. 'On the fossil flora of Bovey Tracey' *Phil. Trans. Roy. Soc.* 152 (1862), 1039–86
   Conolly, A. P. et al. op. cit.
21 Although no evidence of earlier cold phases has yet been obtained from an inland site, more extended Pleistocene sequences have been reported from coastal locations, for example Stephens, N. 'Some Pleistocene deposits in north Devon' *Biuletyn Peryglacjalny* 15 (1966), 103–14
22 Waters, R. S. 'Dartmoor Excursion' *Biuletyn Peryglacjalny* 15 (1966), 123–8
23 Linton, D. L. 'The problem of tors' *Geogr. Journ.* 121 (1955), 478–87
24 Waters, R. S. 1965 op. cit.
25 Guilcher, A. 'Nivation, cryoplanation et solifluction quaternaires dans les collines de Bretagne Occidentale et du Nord du Devonshire' *Rev. Geomorph. Dyn.* 1 (1950), 53–8
   Te Punga, M. T. 'Altiplanation terraces in southern England' *Biuletyn Peryglacjalny* 4 (1956), 331–8
   Waters, R. S. 'Altiplanation terraces and slope development in Vest Spitsbergen and South-West England' *Biuletyn Peryglacjalny* 11 (1962), 89–101

3

Drainage Density Changes in South-West England

K. J. GREGORY

Drainage density was defined by Horton[1] as the length of stream channel per unit area. This fundamental parameter is useful because it provides a simple way of characterising the drainage network. The effects which drainage basin characteristics such as relief and rock type exercise upon processes operating in the drainage basin are often expressed through the nature of the drainage network. In geomorphological research drainage density has therefore been used in two main ways. Firstly, because it is related to other drainage basin characteristics, it can be used as an index of the land form or physical character of an area.[2] Secondly, it is a parameter which can be related to contemporary processes, and numerous equations describing streamflow and sediment yield from drainage basins have included drainage density as a dependent variable.[3] A third use of the parameter, hitherto little explored, may be to compare past and present drainage densities. Underfit valleys described from a wide variety of areas have provided one type of geomorphological evidence for climatic change and they have prompted a suggestion from Dury in 1954[4] that the problem of dry valleys should be re-examined. Schumm[5] has outlined the general ways in which drainage density may vary in response to changing climatic conditions.

Describing the valleys of Dorset and east Devon De la Beche[6] in 1829 wrote 'Could these streams have cut such valleys as they now flow through? If there be any true relation between cause and effect they could not.' Geomorphological research in South-West England has tended to ignore the problem indicated by De la Beche and has concentrated instead upon three main themes. The coast has figured prominently, reflecting the length of the coastline of Devon and Cornwall and the variety contained therein; the denudation chronology has been studied extensively, emphasising the need to document Quaternary sea-level change and to provide a link between highland and lowland Britain; and the periglacial contribution to the landscape has been an important focus of attention in this unglaciated part of the highland zone. Research on these three themes has seen the documentation of portions of the coast in some considerable detail, the identification of the periglacial contribution to the landscape of areas such as Dartmoor,[7] and the isolation of the numerous stages of sea level change.[8] However, at least two notable gaps are evident in the

33

record of geomorphological research. Firstly, certain areas, including south-east Devon to which De la Beche referred, have received less attention than areas such as Dartmoor and Exmoor. Secondly, contemporary geomorphological processes operating in inland areas have received comparatively little study. One explanation for these gaps is that the methods utilised in the study of the denudation chronology and periglacial morphogenesis of Dartmoor, for example, are not readily applied to areas where the slopes are more dissected and the summit areas less extensive. Accordingly Waters[7] has suggested that central Devon and the South Hams are notably lacking in Pleistocene strandflats and are characterised by convexo-concave slopes. In such areas attention can therefore be directed toward the present drainage net and the detailed pattern of the valleys, in the search for traces of morphogenesis equivalent to those recorded on Dartmoor. Inspection of the valley network of the South West shows that it includes dry valleys as well as the type of valley which puzzled De la Beche.

THE PROBLEM

The existence of dry valleys within South-West England has received comparatively little comment. Although areas of limestone outcrop occur (Fig. 3.1A) and characteristically possess large dry valleys, they have been referred to only by Jukes-Brown.[9] The presence of anomalous channels or valleys now dry was noted on the north coast of Devon at the Valley of the Rocks, Hartland Quay and Damehole Point (Fig. 3.1A, Location 1) and these were ascribed to locally rapid cliff recession which truncated an existing valley side and resulted in the production of a dry valley.[10] More recently an additional cause has been suggested to explain the channel-like nature of these now dry valleys (Fig. 3.1A, 1, 2) namely erosion by glacial meltwater. Evidence which includes the till at Fremington has prompted the suggestion[11] that meltwater from ice of the penultimate glaciation abutted on to the north coast of Devon and provided meltwater which was at least partly responsible for producing these features as glacial drainage channels. Funnel-like rounded grooves in west Cornwall and some valleys hanging above the coast between Porthleven and Marazion (Fig. 3.1A, 5) have been interpreted as channels eroded by water derived from melting snow which formerly persisted on the Godolphin-Tregonning Hills.[12] Particular instances of dry valleys have also been noted, such as the Ashburton valley which is dry for a length of some 3 kilometres (1.9 miles) between Ashburton and Bickington (Fig. 3.1A, 3) as a result of river capture.[13] More widely the presence of dry valleys on the Permian breccias south of Exeter has been mentioned;[14] a map showing the distribution of dry valleys within the Exe basin has been presented,[15] and the networks of valleys and streams in five drainage basins in Devon have been analysed.[16]

It is apparent therefore that dry valleys within the South West are not restricted to the limestone outcrops and the coasts of north Devon. Occasionally they have been recorded in sections, as on the flanks of Haldon (Fig. 3.1A, 4) where gullies cut into the Upper Greensand have subsequently been infilled by head deposits.[17] Although there are probably instances of infilled gullies elsewhere in Devon and Cornwall, these are difficult to detect and it is

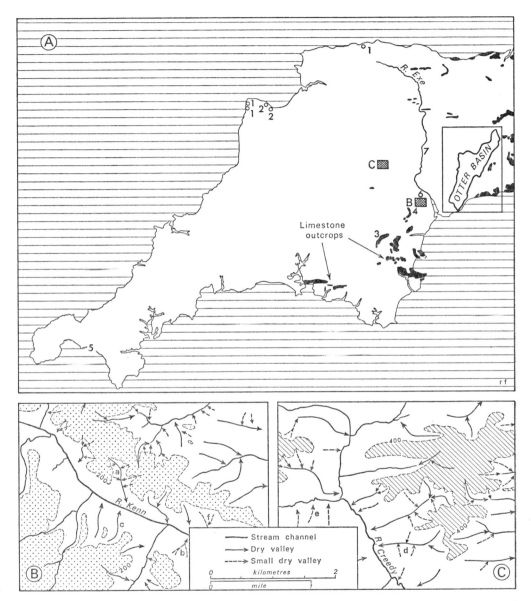

Fig. 3.1 South-West England. Localities referred to in the text are shown in (A) and two examples of networks of streams and valleys based upon field survey are shown in (B) and (C). As drainage density is conventionally quoted in miles per square mile these units are retained in this paper and in Figures 3.2, 3.5 and 3.6.

equally difficult from map evidence alone to determine the extent of the present stream network.[18] For basins in Devon and Cornwall there is, at the 1:25,000 map scale, a substantial number of valleys indicated by contour crenulations but without a stream shown. In Figure 3.2 the relationship between stream length and basin area, obtained from the blue-line data shown on 1:25,000 maps for basins covering some 28.4 per cent of the area of the two counties, is compared with the lengths of valleys, obtained from the blue-line network plus valleys indicated by contour crenulations, also plotted against basin area. This demonstrates (Fig. 3.2) that, whereas the drainage density of the stream network in a sample of basins averages 2.62, that of the valley network averages 4.61: in certain parts of the South West peninsula there is therefore an apparent dry valley density of approximately 2.00 according to the evidence of 1:25,000 maps.

Map scale and map convention explain the magnitude of the difference between these two relationships (Fig. 3.2) to some extent but not completely. Evidence from 1:10,560 maps confirms the existence of dry valleys in some areas and this is borne out by field examination of selected areas, bearing in mind the problem of land drainage, stream diversion and regulation which may give rise to apparently dry valleys. Considering the dynamic nature of any existing drainage network, composed of ephemeral, intermittent and perennial elements, there are still numerous examples within Devon and Cornwall of small valleys which contain no indication of a stream channel at the present time. Two areas are illustrated in Figure 3.1B and C and these show the character of the network of dry valleys on the Permian rocks in relation to the present stream network. Generally there are two scales of dry valley (Fig. 3.1, B and C). The largest are deep, steep-sided features which are very similar morphologically to valleys which contain a stream at the present time (Fig. 3.1B, a). A second group includes smaller features, sometimes mere furrows, with convexo-concave sides and frequently grouped together in twos and threes (Fig. 3.1B, b). The larger dry valleys are usually tributary to the present stream network, although they may hang above the stream to which they are apparently tributary (Fig. 3.1B, c) but the smaller variety, although in some cases found dissecting the sides of large dry valleys or stream-occupied valleys (Fig. 3.1C, d, e) may in certain instances be divorced from the present stream pattern (Fig. 3.1B, f). In some parts of South West England there is, therefore, a difference between the present stream network and the network of valleys, and it is the purpose of this paper to review the explanations available for this difference, and to consider in detail the character of the difference in an area in south-east Devon.

THE AVAILABLE EXPLANATIONS

In Britain the explanations devised to account for the existence of dry valleys have been developed particularly for areas influenced by meltwater erosion, which produced striking and anomalous valleys and channels in the landscape, and also for areas underlain by limestone of Carboniferous, Jurassic and Cretaceous ages. However, although dry valleys are best developed in such areas, their presence has also been noted on outcrops of limestones

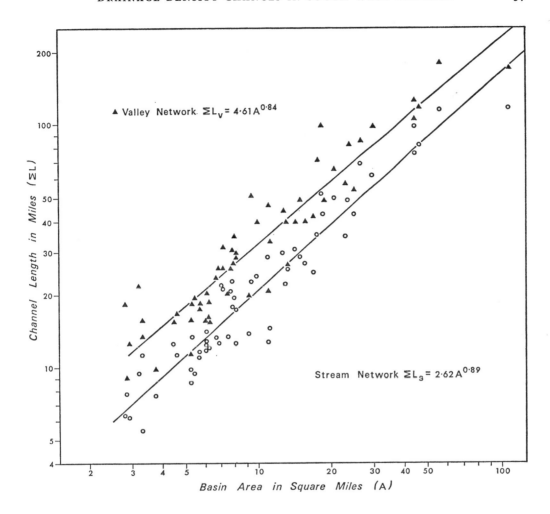

Fig. 3.2   The relationships between stream length and valley length and area for basins in South-West England. The stream channel lengths are based upon the blue line network shown on 1:25,000 maps, the valley lengths are based upon this information plus the additional valleys indicated by contour crenulations. The basins included represent 28.4 per cent of the area of Devon and Cornwall.

of other ages, and similar features occur on sandstones and conglomerates in areas like Cannock Chase and on the Keuper Marl outcrop, where they are confined to valley heads and minor gulleys.[19] As early as 1911 dry valleys on the Bunter Pebble Beds outcrop of Nottinghamshire were noted by the Geological Survey and ascribed to a recent general lowering of the water table in the Bunter rocks.[20] Explanations offered during the last hundred years to account for the presence of dry valleys must be visualised against the background of drainage basin dynamics and they must be set into a framework of geo-morphological time, such as the scales of steady, graded and cyclic time distinguished by Schumm and Lichty.[21]

The dynamics of drainage density

Figure 3.3 attempts to position the various explanations offered for dry valleys against the background of these two themes. The shading should be envisaged as continuing across the diagram and thus as indicating the relationship of a particular mode of origin to the three scales of geomorphological time. The section in the centre of the diagram attempts firstly to portray the drainage basin as the fundamental unit in fluvial geomorphology through which input, in the form of effective precipitation is transformed into output, expressed as streamflow and sediment yield; secondly to represent the drainage network as a dynamic feature composed of ephemeral, intermittent and perennial elements; and thirdly to indicate the several types of flow that may be involved in the passage of water from divide to the outlet of the basin. The drainage net will adjust to the conditions, including input, which obtain at a particular point in time and the network will expand and contract during steady time over a range determined by the climate and by the basin characteristics. For example, the density of the drainage network within one small basin in the Otter drainage basin (SY 054888) ranges from 4.40 at low flows to 6.60 during high discharges. Although the controls of drainage density are not yet precisely determined, it is known that climate exerts an influence.[22] A study comparing the drainage densities of the Unaka Mountains (Carolina, Tennessee) and of Dartmoor concluded that differences in rainfall intensity were responsible for contrasts in drainage density.[23] Rock type also influences drainage density and although the primary contrast is between permeable and impermeable rocks, further variety is occasioned by variations in infiltration rates allowed by the soils supported by various rock types. Brunsden[24] has contrasted drainage density values for small numbers of drainage basins on the Dartmoor granite with those obtaining on adjacent Devonian and Culm Measures rocks. Topographic characteristics of drainage basins can be expressed in a variety of ways[25] and relationships have, for example, been derived between drainage densities and relief measures. Land use can also influence present drainage density values but, because the drainage basin functions as a system, it is difficult to divorce the influence of a single variable from the control exerted by other parameters which influence the system. Thus the drainage network (Fig. 3.3) can be viewed as intermediate between input to, and output from, a drainage basin and the basin characteristics dictate the range over which the present network may expand and contract; this range is within the confines (Fig. 3.3) of occasional catas-trophic events and occurs over storm period, seasonal and annual variation.

Within the steady time scale (Fig. 3.3) any deliberate or accidental modification of the drainage basin characteristics may produce a response in the limits over which the drainage network expands and contracts. Expansion of the drainage network can be achieved deliberately by ditching (Fig. 3.3) for agricultural, forestry, road or urban drainage, and the amount of this has been estimated by one author to average 5 miles per square mile over England and Wales.[26] Such expansion may have contributed to the increased flood hazard, which it has been suggested, has characterized the Exe basin.[27] However, although such changes increase the maximum drainage density they also may be responsible for reducing the lowest values of drainage density within a particular drainage basin. Because a higher

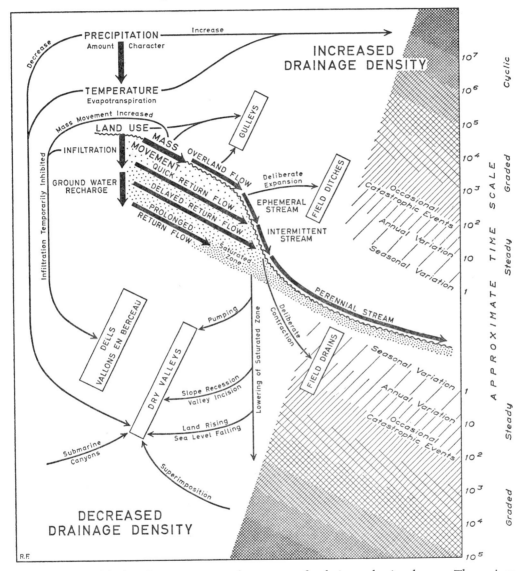

Fig. 3.3 A model of explanations suggested to account for drainage density changes. The various explanations are positioned on the diagram with respect to the geomorphological time scale represented by shading. The types of water flow in the basin, represented in the centre of the diagram, are based upon D. G. Jamieson and C. R. Amerman 'Quick return subsurface flow', *J. Hydrol,* 8 (1969), 122–136.

drainage density allows greater surface runoff to contribute to higher flood peaks, the proportion of infiltration and percolation may be lowered so that base flows may be associated with lower drainage densities. The opposite situation is provided when field drains (Fig. 3.3) afford a means of contraction of the present drainage network.

Explanation for dry valleys

Changes of drainage density on the graded geomorphological time scale (Fig. 3.3) may be viewed as the consequence of changes in climate, which have sometimes been used to explain reductions in drainage density and the presence of dry valleys. Two main groups of explanations for dry valleys are relevant in South-West England. One group envisages that in the past the basin functioned in a way very similar to the present mode of operation but that a gradual evolutionary change prompted a reduction in drainage density; explanations in the second group involve a substantial change in the mode of operation of the drainage basin.

Particularly in areas of Chalk outcrop early suggestions made to explain the presence of dry valleys were in terms of the processes operating at the present time. After the catastrophic school which included the suggestion made by Sedgwick[28] that the dry coombes and valleys of the Chalk appear to have been swept out by a flood of retreating waters during some period of elevation, explanations included those of Taylor who envisaged the dry valleys as the consequence of an enormous increase in rainfall,[29] and of Prestwich[30] who saw the lowering of the plane of saturation in the Chalk, consequent upon deep trenching of the downs, as being responsible for the production of dry valleys. Greenwood in 1877[31] described the dry valleys at the head of present streams as 'rain valleys' and attributed them to rainfall. In his account of the Chalk Downs of north Dorset Jukes-Brown[9] interpreted the coombes and dry valleys, which open into the permanently-watered valleys, as rain gulleys cut by the water flowing off the ridges after heavy rains and snowfalls. He also concluded that, when the rainfall was greater, the water table must have been higher so that springs may have occurred at higher levels; many of the coombes may then have had perennial water-courses fed by springs, and recession of these spring heads may have contributed to the development of the coombes.

From these early foundations have evolved the twentieth century explanations for the presence of dry valleys. Dury[4, 32] concluded that the high rates of runoff demanded by meandering valleys and large meandering channels are adequate to explain the cutting of now-dry valleys in the limestone belts of the Cotswolds and the Chilterns. Support for the hypothesis of wetter climates in the past was provided by Manley,[33] who argued that in the past the occurrence of spring lines at levels higher than those of today could have resulted from the persistence of seasons only slightly wetter than present. The occasional flow of water in dry valleys[34] and the suggestion that, prior to periglacial conditions, the joints of the Chalk may not have been opened sufficiently to permit much percolation,[35] may be relevant to these explanations, which view the dry valley system as an elaboration of the present stream network. More recently several researchers have proposed the lowering of the water table as the reason for the inception of dry valleys. Although a lowering of the water table could have arisen consequent upon reduced precipitation, lowering could also have been achieved in other ways. Fagg[36] suggested recession of the escarpment as the prime cause of lowering of the saturation level in the Chalk and in the Lower Greensand, and this is supported by Small,[37] who views the inception of ramifying systems of dry valleys in the Wiltshire Chalk as being due to a steady decline in elevation of the scarp-foot springs and to the deep incision of the main Chalk valleys. In the Yorkshire Wolds the dry-valley systems have been attributed to a fall in the level of the water table,[38] and an analysis of the Stonehill dry valley, Dorset, showed[39] that it was produced under climatic conditions similar to those of today and not primarily periglacial in character. In some areas a distinction has been drawn between the escarpment dry valleys and the larger dry valleys which dissect the dip slopes. To some extent the processes responsible for fashioning these two types may differ, and in particular spring-sapping under conditions similar to those of today has been advocated as an important element in the development of the dry valleys of the Wiltshire Chalk.[40] The evidence which supports these explanations includes the facts that the extremes of the present climate provide conditions under which dry valleys may function again; the climatic variations of the late Quaternary include ample opportunity, with higher rainfalls and lower temperatures, for greater runoff; higher water tables in the past could have occurred not only under wetter climates but also prior to the most recent phases of local downcutting.

Not all authors have been sufficiently impressed by the nature or amount of this evidence to conclude that the dry valleys originally constituted an extension of the present network under conditions very like those of today. Reid[41] argued in favour of the production of the dry valleys of the South Downs when permafrost rendered infiltration much reduced and gave rise to a much higher drainage density than would occur without permafrost. The high rates of runoff over permafrost occasioned after the Spring thaw could have produced a dense network of valleys similar to those reported from areas of the contemporary Arctic.[42] Such valleys may have been fashioned by water flow over permafrost accompanied by mass movement which is now indicated by the distribution of head deposits. With reference to Europe, Schmitthenner[43] considered that the shallow depressions most frequently referred to as *dellen* resulted from the combined effects of soil movement and of water flowing on the surface. Such shallow, often bowl- or dish-shaped depressions could have developed under periglacial conditions when solifluction complemented water flow and when the relative importance of these two elements varied according to the time of year. Dellen and a variety of related landforms, covering a range of sizes, have been identified in parts of Europe.[44] Dells and derasional valleys have been described in Hungary[45] as transitional in origin between linear and areal destructive features and they have been attributed by Pecsi[46] to the combined action of gelisolifluction, cryoturbation, pluvionation, cryofraction and gravitational movements under periglacial conditions.

Few specific studies have been made of such features in Britain, although the depressions on the Bagshot sands of Hampstead Heath have been interpreted as dells,[47] and dry coombes have been mapped on the Keuper sandstones of the Lapworth valley, Warwickshire.[48] A major scarp dry valley of the North Downs, developed between 10800 and 10300 B.C., has been attributed to niveo-fluvial processes occasioned by the melting of snow accumulated on the crest of the scarp without there necessarily having been any permafrost.[49]

Thus it is thought that under periglacial conditions a variety of dry valley features can be produced, ranging from the large dry valleys such as the dip slope valleys of the English Chalklands to flat-floored dry valleys shorter in length, and to dellen and derasional valleys. This range of phenomena would be formed under periglacial conditions with water flow as one element, supplemented to varying degrees by mass movement especially in the form of solifluction. Some valleys, formerly thought to be exclusively periglacial in origin, have been shown on further analysis to have operated under interglacial as well as periglacial conditions. Klatkowa[50] has shown that the valleys in the Lodz upland are polygenic forms which finally ceased to develop at the end of the Wurm.

Other explanations have been offered to account for the presence of dry valleys in middle latitudes. The presence of dry valleys in areas of limestone has been attributed to superimposition from a less permeable cover rock,[19] and mass movement may sometimes be the major cause.[51] Many of the explanations cited above apply to the graded time scale (Fig. 3.3), but a longer term explanation nearer the cyclic time scale is provided by Winslow's suggestion[52] that the dry valleys of south-east England were initially developed as submarine canyons during the Calabrian transgression, and later modified by solifluction, spring-sapping and other subaerial processes. These various explanations of dry valleys and dellen (Fig. 3.3) provide a background of possible solutions for the reduced drainage densities apparent on various rock types in Devon, and illustrated below for the Otter drainage basin.

SOUTH-EAST DEVON

The drainage basin of the river Otter includes two major rock types (Fig. 3.4). Triassic Pebble Beds, sandstones and marls outcrop in the central and western portions of the basin, and these are overlain in the eastern and northern parts by the Cretaceous Upper Greensand which dips eastwards at a lower angle than the Triassic rocks beneath. The Otter valley is therefore characterised by the dip slope of the Triassic rocks in the west and by a major scarp slope capped by Upper Greensand immediately east of the river Otter. This broad pattern of relief (Fig. 3.5) is diversified in two ways. Remnants of river terraces and valley side benches occur (Fig. 3.5) but are fewer in number and less well-preserved than in the valleys on more resistant rocks to the west.[15] A second reason for diversity is the presence of smaller cuestas (Fig. 3.5), particularly well-developed on the Pebble Beds and on the Upper Sandstone (Fig. 3.4).

Morphometry

Field mapping of stream channels and of dry valleys and depressions throughout the Otter basin[16] revealed numerous instances of dry valleys which at the present time possess no indication of a stream channel. The major ones are indicated in Figure 3.5. The Otter basin

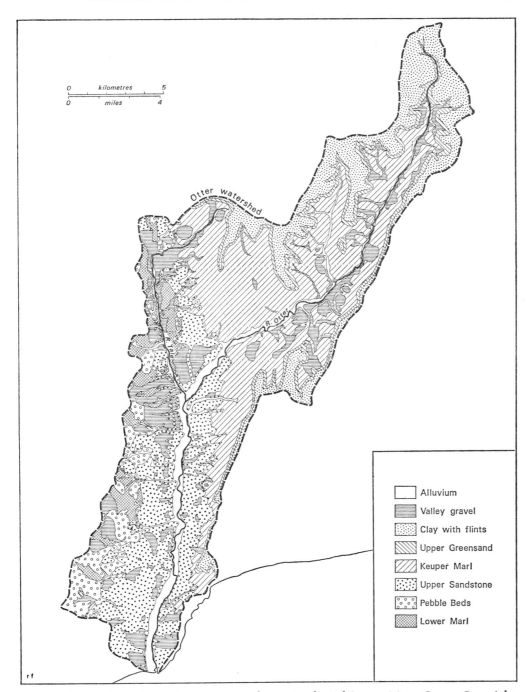

Fig. 3.4 The geology of the Otter Basin. Based upon Geological Survey Maps: Crown Copyright, by permission of the Controller of HM Stationery Office.

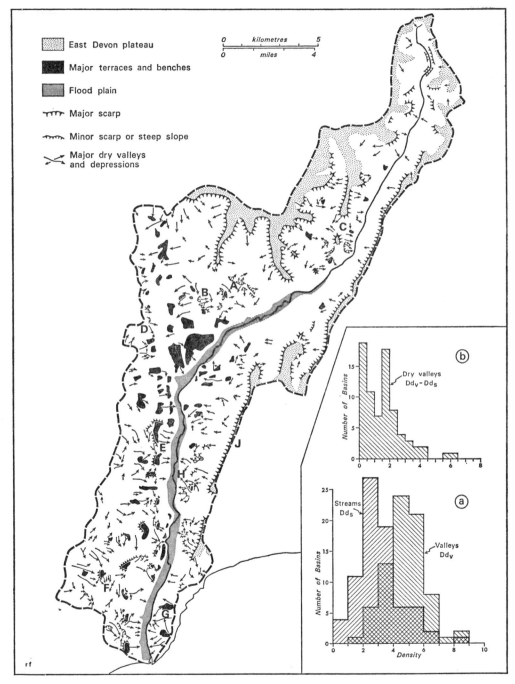

Fig. 3.5   Some geomorphological elements in the Otter Basin. The major dry valleys and remnants of terraces and valley-side benches are based upon field mapping. The terrace fragments occur in three main groups which grade to the present coast at heights of approximately 60m, 40m, 7.5m above present sea level. Localities referred to in the text are denoted A to H, J. The frequency distributions of drainage density according to stream data and valley data for 76 small basins within the Otter watershed are shown in (a), and are significantly different (t-test) at more than 99.9 per cent level. The frequency distribution of the dry valley densities in the same 76 small basins is shown in (b).

was then subdivided into 76 small constituent basins varying in order between first and third Strahler order, and representing some 72 per cent of the total basin area. The basins were not selected according to stream order because the order of basins changes according to prevailing conditions,[53] and because drainage density, which is being investigated, is largely independent of order. The area of each basin was measured with a polar planimeter; the lengths of mapped stream channels, of dry valley length, of the basin parallel to the principal drainage line, and of the perimeter of the basin were measured with an opisometer, and the relief of each basin was estimated to the nearest 10 feet from 1:25,000 maps. This basic data allowed the calculation of the drainage density of the stream network (Dds), the density of the valley network representing the stream plus the valley network (Ddv), the relief ratio and a measure of basin shape.

The frequency distributions of drainage density values from these 76 basins are shown in Figure 3.5a which illustrates the two distinct populations obtained. The difference between the two histograms (Fig. 3.5a) is shown in Figure 3.5b where the frequency distribution of dry valley densities is plotted. The bimodal distribution (Fig. 3.5b) separates two types of basin: those where the density of dry valleys is low and those where the density of dry valleys is greater than 1.5. An alternative expression of the nature of the two densities is obtained by plotting total stream or valley length against basin area (Fig. 3.6) and this demonstrates the way in which, under the conditions prevailing in the Otter drainage basin, length increases as area increases. The two relationships have a similar gradient, and as this gradient is influenced by the sum total of catchment characteristics, it may indicate that the total network is controlled in a similar way to the present stream density. Inevitably, rock type is an important control and this may be examined by grouping the 76 basins into three categories. Although it is not possible to separate the 76 basins according to single rock types, three fairly distinct groups may be differentiated. Catchments underlain by Keuper Marl (Table 3.1, Group 2) with some Upper Greensand have the highest stream densities but the lowest valley densities. Catchments on the fringes of the east Devon plateau (Table 3.1,

TABLE 3.1

Group	Predominant Rock Type in Basins	Number of Basins	Relationship between total stream length and area	Relationship between total valley length and area
1	Upper Sandstone Pebble Beds Lower Marl	28	$\Sigma L_s = 2.41A^{0.74}$	$\Sigma L_v = 4.37A^{0.87}$
2	Upper Greensand Keuper Marl	31	$\Sigma L_s = 2.70A^{0.90}$	$\Sigma L_V = 3.66A^{0.88}$
3	Upper Greensand Keuper Marl Upper Sandstone	17	$\Sigma L_s = 2.78A^{0.79}$	$\Sigma L_V = 5.04A^{0.76}$

Group 3) at present have high stream densities but include a more substantial dry valley element than does the previous group. Catchments in the south west of the Otter basin, developed on more permeable rock types (Table 3.1, Group 1), have the lowest present drainage densities but include a substantial dry valley component. In figure 3.6 it is evident that there is a greater scatter of the data derived from the present stream network (Σ LS) than in the case of the data based upon the valley network (Σ LV). This contrast may be ascribed to that fact that, whereas the valley network is a more permanent feature relevant at the graded time scale, the present stream network is more easily affected by a variety of controls operating at the level of the steady time scale (Fig. 3.3).

Further insight into the difference between the stream and the valley networks (Fig. 3.6) may be gained by examining the relationships between drainage density and other catchment characteristics. Utilising the data collected for each of the 76 small basins, it is possible to indicate the correlation between stream density (Dds), valley density (Ddv) and dry valley density (Ddv-s) with measures of relief and of basin shape (Table 3.2). The difficulties

TABLE 3.2

Spearman rank correlation coefficients between morphometric properties of up to 76 small basins within the Otter drainage basin. Coefficients are shown only where significant at 95% level. Basin shape is expressed as L^2/A where L is basin length (miles) and A is basin area (square miles).

	Basin Area	Dds	Ddv	Ddv-s	Relief Ratio	Basin Shape
Basin Area	1.00	—0.46	—0.56	—	—0.81	—
Dds		1.00	0.39	0.27	0.50	0.27
Ddv			1.00	0.72	—	0.34
Ddv-s				1.00	—	0.29
Relief Ratio					1.00	—
Basin Shape						1.00

confronting the interpretation of this simple correlation matrix are emphasised by the high correlation coefficients between basin area and density, and between basin area and relative relief (Table 3.2). However, the density of dry valleys is largely independent of area, and the low correlation coefficient between dry valley density and present stream density may indicate that different groups of factors are responsible. There is some relationship between dry valley density and drainage basin shape (Table 3.2). which is interpreted to indicate that dry valley density is highest in the basins which possess the least efficient shape. The difficulty of attempting to relate measures of basin shape and relative relief to density of the three networks derives from the fact that the 76 constituent basins extend over a range of rock types each operating in a distinctive way. The three groups recognised in Table 3.1 are distinctive in that group one includes mainly permeable, and group two largely impermeable catchments, and group three a combination of both attributes. When the 76 basins are grouped into these three categories, the dry valley density is significantly related to relative relief in group three, and the catchments with the greatest density of dry valleys are found in the catchments with the highest relative relief. One further parameter—distance of the outlet of the constituent basin from the mouth of the Otter basin at Budleigh Salterton— was related to dry valley density, and this showed that the density of the dry valleys was generally greatest in the basins near to the coast. The conclusions from morphometric analysis are, therefore, that the two frequency distributions based upon populations of present stream densities and present valley densities (Fig. 3.5a) are distinct, and that the difference between these two distributions (Fig. 3.5b) is a bimodal frequency distribution possibly indicating the existence of two populations of dry valley. Although the two relationships between area and length (Fig. 3.6) are similar, further subdivision of the total population reveals that dry valleys are unevenly distributed over the drainage basin of the Otter, that their incidence is closely related to rock type, and that they are generally most frequent in the basins with the highest relative relief, with the least efficient shape, and in basins near the coast.

Morphological Relations

Field examination confirms the existence of two types of dry valley in the Otter basin. The large ones are up to 30 metres (100 feet) deep, up to 1 kilometre (1,100 yards) in length and are characterised by steep sides up to 20 degrees. The smaller ones are much shorter; they have a convexo-concave cross section, and frequently bifurcate near the head and have two heads (Fig. 3.5, B). Both types may have a steep headwall, especially on the permeable rocks, but the larger ones are distinct in that they frequently possess a flat floor and in this and other respects they are similar to the valleys which contain streams at the present time (Fig. 3.5, H). The depth of the infill of head and slope wash deposits is as much as 3.5 metres (11.5 feet) (SY 093890), but more typically of the order of 1.5 metres (5 feet) (SY 086936).

The larger ones, typically developed on the Pebble Beds and on the Keuper sandstones, merely extend the line of the present stream network but in some cases are found hanging above stream-occupied valleys to which they are tributary. Several large dry valleys terminate on terraces of the Otter valley (Fig. 3.5, E) and particularly on the lowest terrace which grades to the mouth of the Otter at approximately 7.5 metres (25 feet) above present sea level; the large dry valleys do not cut below this level either towards the present Otter flood plain or towards the buried rock channels of the Otter. The position of the large ones is also notable in that, although some merely extend the line of the headwaters of the present stream network (Fig. 3.5, F), others which are tributary to existing valleys, occur in definite dip and strike locations. The strike dry valleys represent a series of stages which has culmin- ated in two dry valleys coalescing and isolating one of the small cuestas indicated in Figure 3.5. Thirty small cuestas have been identified in the Otter basin and 70 per cent of these are developed on the Upper Sandstone. This pattern is especially well-developed on the western side of the Otter (Fig. 3.5, between F and D) but it occurs on a smaller scale on the

E

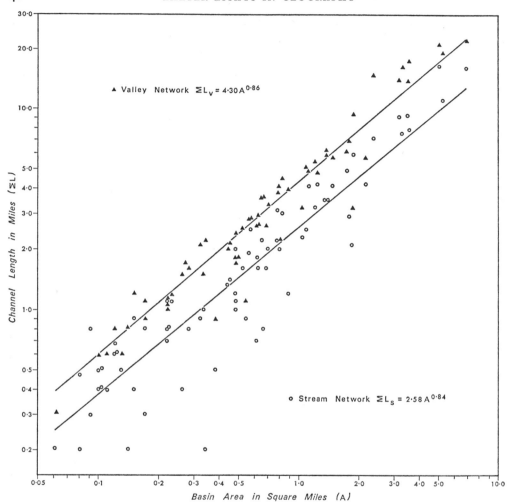

Fig. 3.6   The relationship between stream length and valley length and area for 76 small basins within the Otter drainage basin. Compare with Figure 3.2 for South-West England.

eastern side (Fig. 3.5, H). The pattern of the smaller dry valleys is notable in two ways; it is more dendritic than that of the larger ones, and the small valleys may terminate in a broad basin-like area (Fig. 3.5, D), in a fan of material (D); or they may end with no apparent continuation towards the nearest valley or stream (A). Unlike the larger variety, they frequently dissect the lowest terrace of the Otter (E) and cut down towards the infill deposits.

One striking characteristic of the distribution of the dry valleys is that the large ones decrease in frequency towards the head of the basin while they are most numerous where the interfluve is narrow or non-existent. Thus dry valleys occur in area G (Fig. 3.5) where the original capping of Upper Greensand has been removed by cliff recession and lowering, and they are also numerous in areas like H where the plateau surface (J) is very narrow owing to the extension of the tributaries of the Sid. On the western side of the River Otter (F, E) the dry valleys occur in an area where the minor interfluves are very narrow, although they may not have been breached completely to form a minor cuesta such as Baker's Brake (SY 062870); in the upper part of the basin they occur where the spurs (C) have been breached and the Upper Greensand has been removed. The smaller dry valleys occur throughout the Otter basin but are particularly frequent on or immediately below steep slopes.

Dating of the dry valleys as a whole is difficult. That they are later than middle Pleistocene is indicated by the facts that the large ones dissect the highest terrace fragments of the Otter basin which grade to the present coast at approximately 60 metres (200 feet) O.D., and that some cut into the middle terrace of the Otter valley (Fig. 3.5). Some of the large dry valleys, particularly in the south-western part of the drainage basin, terminate on the lowest terrace level but do not cut through it, although valleys which contain streams at the present time have done so. This therefore suggests that whereas the large dry valleys operated in the middle and late Pleistocene, they ceased to function after the last interglacial; more precise dating, however, must await an agreed Pleistocene chronology derived from the coast. The deposits which infill the floors of the dry valleys are difficult to interpret because only where flint and chert material on the eastern side or Pebble Beds and terrace gravel material on the western side have been incorporated, can head deposits clearly be distinguished from slope wash material. In the floors of the large dry valleys there are often two layers of material which are probably head deposits, whereas the smaller dry valleys often possess only one layer of distinctive head material (Fig. 3.5, South of F). The valleys dissecting the eastern side of the Otter basin (Fig. 3.5, G, H, J) are frequently infilled to a depth of 3 metres (10 feet) by head material containing flint and chert which is not present in the overlying hillwash. When a stream occurs in these valleys it has dissected the infill, but elsewhere either a part, or the whole, of the valley has not been reoccupied by a stream. In these valleys there are occasional traces below the scarp of hollows which may originally have contained springs but have since been abandoned (SY 102890). It is likely that, if not both, at least one of these head deposits in south-east Devon is the product of the Wurm. Dry valleys of both types possess one or both of these head deposits on their floors and sides, and so it would appear that the valleys have not functioned since the head material was emplaced.

The larger type of dry valley, found well-developed on the permeable rocks in the south-west of the Otter basin and to a lesser degree below the east-Devon plateau (J), appears to have originated prior to the last phase of solifluction in the area. The way in which these dry valleys are identical in form, size and character to the neighbouring valleys which at present contain streams indicates that they may have had a similar composite origin and have developed during interglacial and glacial phases. The position of some of the major ones, terminating on the low terrace of the Otter valley, may indicate that they have not been profoundly modified since the last cold phase when some solifiual material accumulated on their floors. The position of the major dry valleys, adjacent to narrow or breached interfluves or below narrow portions of the east-Devon plateau, suggests that these valleys may have become dry as a result of a lowering of the water table consequent upon reduction in width of the aquifer. This suggestion is supported by the facts that the dry valley density is greatest in catchments where the relief is greatest; that although permafrost may have characterised earlier phases it may not have occurred extensively in south-east Devon during the last cold phase;[54] and that the valley network densities can be accommodated within the range of stream densities that exist at present.

The smaller depressions, grooves and valleys present a rather different picture. Their position, their relationship to the present valley and stream network, and their morphological features all indicate that they are a more recent phenomenon in the landscape. That they functioned during the last cold phase is proved by the presence of head deposits on their floors and slopes, while their discontinuous nature and their position on steep slopes indicate that they were developed by solifluction under periglacial conditions. Solifluction is now conceded to be a complex process and, particularly on outcrops of sandstones and marls, the last cold phase must have seen a complex assemblage of processes. It is possible that in the late winter and early Spring these small depressions were occupied by snow patches but in summer they were the lines along which soliflual material moved towards the larger valleys and some slight deepening may have occurred as a result. Such features are therefore common on steep slopes such as those fringing Buckerell Knap (Fig. 3.5, A) and Cheriton Hill (B). Where two large dry valleys occurred in a strike position at the back of a terrace remnant, solifluction and the development of the small dry valleys may progressively have lowered the col between the two original valleys and thus led to the inception of a small cuesta. The small dry valleys have the characteristics of cradle-like dells and are usually quite distinct from the larger dry valleys.

THE PROSPECT

During the Quaternary the Otter basin was deepened and opened-out to give a broad valley which stimulated the question posed by De la Beche in 1829. The opening-out has been achieved by gradual reduction in the area of the Upper Greensand and of the east-Devon plateau. The east-Devon plateau, which must have been a more prominent element in the landscape of later Tertiary times, has been reduced to its present area (Fig. 3.5) as a result of the contrasting processes operating during glacial and interglacial phases of the Quaternary. Against the background of the model depicted in Figure 3.3, it is inevitable that changes in the density of the drainage network should occur, and on permeable rocks these changes are recorded by the persistence of large dry valleys in the present landscape. The character of particular rock types, which is an important influence upon stream density, was also a significant control influencing the subaerial processes that operated under periglacial conditions. Such periglacial processes in the Otter drainage basin have produced a second and smaller type of dry valley which persists in the present landscape. The recognition of these two types of dry valley within the Otter drainage basin may be relevant to the explanation of the presence of dry valleys within larger areas of South-West England (Fig. 3.1), but whereas changes in the extent of the drainage network, and hence of the drainage density, may be apparent on permeable rock types, the equivalent changes on impermeable rocks may be reflected in the function rather than in the extent of the drainage network. Morphometric analysis offers a promising approach towards this problem but a final solution must be achieved by utilising evidence from landform and sedimentological analyses interpreted in the light of an increased understanding of contemporary processes[55] and set into the framework of geomorphological time. Such problems which depend for their solution upon the reconciliation of data and methods from a variety of fields of geomorphology are amongst the most challenging for future investigation.

REFERENCES

1 Horton, R. E. 'Drainage basin characteristics' *Trans. Am. Geophysical Union* 13 (1932), 350–61

2 Woodruff, J. F. 'A comparative analysis of selected drainage basins' *Professional Geographer* 16 (1964), 15–19

3 Chebotarev, N. P. *Theory of stream runoff* Israel Program for Scientific Translations (Jerusalem 1966) 15, 115–6
Benson, M. A. *Factors influencing the occurrence of floods in a humid region of diverse terrain* US Geol. Surv. Water Supply Paper, 1580-B (1962)

4 Dury, G. H. 'Contribution to a general theory of meandering valleys' *Am. Journ. Sci.* 252 (1954), 193–224
Dury, G. H. *Principles of underfit streams* US Geol. Surv. Prof. Paper 452-A (1964)

5 Schumm S. A. 'Quaternary Palaeohydrology' in *Quaternary of the United States* ed. H. E. Wright and D. G. Frey (Princeton 1965), 783–94

6 De la Beche, H. T. 'Notice on the excavation of valleys' *Phil. Mag.* 6 (1829), 241–8

7 Waters, R. S. 'The geomorphological significance of frost action in South-West England' In *Essays in Geography for Austin Miller* ed. J. B. Whittow and P. D. Wood (Reading 1965), 39–57

8 Shorter, A. H., Ravenhill, W. L. D., Gregory, K. J. *Southwest England* (London 1969), 30

9 Jukes-Brown, A. J. 'The origin of the valleys in the Chalk Downs of north Dorset' *Proc. Dorset Nat. Hist. and Antiq. Field Club* 16 (1895), 5–13

10 Arber, E. N. A. *The coast scenery of North Devon* (London 1912)
Simpson, S. 'The development of the Lyn drainage system and its relation to the origin of the coast between Coombe Martin and Porlock' *Proc. Geol. Ass.,* London 64 (1953), 14–23

11 Stephens, N. 'Some Pleistocene deposits in north Devon' *Biuletyn Peryglacjalny* 15 (1966), 103–14

12 Hendricks, E. M. L. 'The physiography of west Cornwall, the distribution of Chalk flints, and the origin of the gravels of Crousa Common' *Geol. Mag.* 60 (1923), 21–31

13 Brunsden D. 'The Ashburton valley—an example of the study of river capture' *Trans. Devon Ass.* 100 (1968), 85–100

14 Clayden B. and Manley D. J. R. 'Devonshire' *Soil Survey of Great Britain Report* 15 (1962), 22–4

15 Kidson, C. 'The denudation chronology of the river Exe' *Trans. Inst. Brit. Geographers* 31 (1962), 43–66

16 Gregory, K. J. 'Dry valleys and the composition of the drainage net' *Journ. Hydrol.* 4 (1966), 327–40

17 Waters, R. S. 'Dartmoor Excursion' *Biuletyn Peryglacjalny* 15 (1966), 125

18 Gregory, K. J. 'The composition of the drainage net' *Morphometric Analysis of Maps.* Occasional Paper No. 4 of the British Geomorphological Research Group (1966), 9–11

19 Warwick, G. T. 'Dry valleys in the southern Pennines' *Erdkunde* 18 (1964), 116–23

20 Lamplugh, G. W., Hill, J. B., Gibson, W., Sherlock, R. L., Smith, B. *The Geology of the country around Ollerton* Memoirs of the Geol. Surv. (1911)

21 Schumm, S. A. and Lichty, R. W. 'Time, space and causality in geomorphology' *Amer. J. Sci.* 263 (1965), 110–19

22 Cotton, C. A. 'The control of drainage density' *New Zealand Journ. of Geol. and Geophys.* 7 (1964), 348–52

23 Chorley, R. J. and Morgan, M. A. 'Comparison of morphometric features, Unaka Mountains, Tennessee and North Carolina, and Dartmoor, England' *Bull. Geol. Soc. Am.* 72 (1962), 17–34

24 Brunsden, D. *Dartmoor* British Landscape through maps, Geographical Association, 1968, 9–13

25 Haggett, P. and Chorley, R. J. *Network analysis in geography* (London 1969), 147–50

26 Johnson, E. A. G. 'Land drainage in England and Wales' in *River Engineering and Water Conservation Works* Ed. R. B. Thorn (London 1966), 29–46
Brown, E. H. 'Man shapes the earth' *Geogr. Journ.* 136 (1970), 80–1

27 Brierley, J. 'Flooding in the Exe valley' *Proc. Inst. Civil Engineers* 28 (1964), 151–70

28 Sedgwick, A. 'Anniversary Address' *Proc. Geol. Soc.* 1 (1830), 187–212

29 Taylor, A. 'Action of denuding agencies' *Geol. Mag.* II (1875), 437–76

30 Prestwich, J. Presidential Address *Quart. J. Geol. Soc. Lond.* 28 (1872), lx–lxiii

31 Greenwood, G. *River Terraces* (London 1877)

32 Dury, G. H. *The East Midlands and the Peak* (London 1963), 42

33 Manley, G. 'The evolution of the climatic environment' in *The British Isles* Ed. J. Wreford Watson and J. B. Sissons (London 1964), 152–76

34 Anon. 'Occasional flow in a Chalk dry valley' *Nature* (1940), 466

35 Te Punga, M. T. 'Periglaciation in southern England' *Tijdschrift van het Koninklijk Nedelandsch Nardrijkskundig Genootschap* 74 (1957), 401–12

36 Fagg, C. C. 'The recession of the Chalk escarpment and the development of the dry chalk valley' *Proc. Croydon Nat. Hist. and Scientific Soc.* 9 (1923), 93–112

37 Small, R. J. 'Geomorphology' in *A survey of Southampton and its region* Ed. F. J. Monkhouse (Southampton 1964), 37–50

38 Lewin, J. *The Yorkshire Wolds: A study in geomorphology* University of Hull, Department of Geography Occasional Paper (1969)

39 Lewin, J. 'The formation of Chalk dry valleys: The Stonehill valley, Dorset' *Biuletyn Peryglacjalny* 19 (1969), 345–50

40 Small, R. J. 'The role of spring-sapping in the formation of Chalk escarpment valleys' *Southampton Research Ser. in Geog.* 1 (1965), 3–30

41 Reid, C. 'On the origin of dry Chalk valleys and of Coombe Rock' *Quart. J. Geol. Soc. Lond.* 43 (1887), 364–73

42 Rudberg, S. 'Geomorphological processes in a cold semi-arid region' *Axel Heiberg Island Research Reports McGill University Preliminary Report* 1961-62, Ed. F. Muller, 139–50

43 Schmitthenner, H. 'Die enstehung der dellen und ihre morphologische bedetung' *Zeitschrift für Geomorphologie* I (1926), 3–28

44 Dylik, J. *Guide Book of Excursion C.* INQUA VIth Congress (Poland 1961)

45 Marosi, I. 'On the "derasional" valleys' *Földrajzi Ertesitó* 14 (1965), 229–42

46 Pecsi, M. 'The role of derasion in modelling the earth's surface' in *Ten years of physicogeographic research in Hungary* Ed. M. Pecsi, (Budapest, 1964), 40–7
Pecsi, M. 'The dynamics of Quaternary slope evolution and its geomorphological representation' *Evolution des versants* Ed. P. Macar (Liege, 1967), 187–99

47 Brown, E. H. 'Some aspects of the geomorphology of south-east England' in *Guide to London Excursions* Ed. K. M. Clayton, (London 1964), 115

48 Jones, J. A. A. 'Morphology of the Lapworth Valley, Warwickshire' *Geog. Journ.* 134 (1968), 216–26

49 Kerney, M. P., Brown, E. H., Chandler, T. J. 'The late-glacial and post-glacial history of the Chalk escarpment near Brook, Kent' *Phil. Trans. Roy. Soc. Ser. B.* 248 (1964), 135–204

50 Klatka, T. 'Flat-floored dry valleys in the foreland of the Lysogory Mountains' *Biuletyn Peryglacjalny* 2 (1955), 79–89, 216–19
Klatkowa, H. 'Bowl-shaped basins and dry valleys in the region of Lodz' *Acta Geographica Lodziensia* Sec. 3 (1965)

51 Markgren, M. 'Geomorphological studies in Fennoscandia' Vol. II Chute slopes in northern Fennoscandia *Lund Studies in Geography* 27, 28 (1964)

52 Winslow, J. H. 'Raised submarine canyons. An exploratory hypothesis' *Ann. Ass. Am. Geogr.* 56 (1966), 634–72

53 Gregory, K. J. and Walling, D. E. 'The variation of drainage density within a catchment' *Internat. Assoc. Sci. Hydrol. Bull.* 13 (1968), 61–8

54 Williams, R. B. G. 'Permafrost in England during the last glacial period' *Nature* 205 (1965), 1304–5

55 Gregory, K. J. and Walling, D. E. 'Instrumented catchments in south-east Devon' *Trans. Devon. Ass.* 100 (1968), 247–62
Walling, D. E. 'Streamflow from instrumented catchments in south-east Devon' *Exeter Essays in Geography* Ed. K. J. Gregory and W. L. D. Ravenhill (Exeter 1971), 54–81

4

Streamflow from Instrumented Catchments in South-East Devon

D. E. WALLING

In recent years geographers have shown a growing interest in catchment studies. This interest has been stimulated by the development of studies in quantitative and process geomorphology; it has been facilitated by the adoption of the systems approach within physical geography; and it has been accompanied by an increasing interest in hydrology. The International Hydrological Decade (1965-75) has encouraged catchment studies, and a recent publication[1] summarising catchment research in the United Kingdom indicates that geographers are active in this field of hydrological study.

It is becoming increasingly apparent that the drainage basin provides an ideal unit on which to base studies of the physical landscape. In Exeter, one topic upon which interest has focussed has been the relationships between catchment characteristics and water yield from a drainage basin. This aspect of the hydrologic cycle seems particularly worthy of study because a knowledge of the controls exerted by catchment characteristics should assist in the understanding of catchment dynamics and of areal variations in catchment response, and will therefore allow the extension of hydrologic data in both space and time. Although many successful studies have been carried out in North America relating drainage basin characteristics to streamflow[2, 3, 4, 5, 6, 7] when attempts are made to apply similar techniques to South-West England no conclusive results are readily obtainable. This arises because of the general problems of isolating the controlling characteristics of a catchment that functions as a system, and of selecting parameters that adequately characterise the pattern of runoff. Furthermore, different catchment characteristics may control the various aspects of the pattern of water yield. Several further problems result from the paucity of long records of streamflow; the comparatively small number of accurate stream gauging stations; the large and diverse character of most of the gauged catchments; and the difficulty of obtaining from the available topographic maps meaningful measures of catchment characteristics.

Convinced of the value of such studies which relate catchment characteristics to hydrologic parameters, and in an attempt to further their application within South-West England, a series of small catchments were instrumented by the author in south-east Devon. Small instrumented catchments were selected in order to afford a greater degree of control of the catchment characteristics and in order that the resultant measurements of streamflow would be more easily related to the restricted range of catchment characteristics. Moreover, streamflow parameters derived from a small catchment should reflect the overall catchment character rather than in the case of a large river basin the modifying influence of the river channel or the flood plain. In order to effect a simple comparative study within the framework of the multiple watershed approach,[8] a small area was sought that would provide several small catchments for instrumentation and would also embrace a considerable variety of catchment characteristics.

With these considerations in mind, a small area of the east Devon Plateau was chosen (Fig. 4.1, a, c). This area was particularly favourable, for when viewed at the local scale it included a variety of catchment characteristics, yet its terrain types were representative of a fairly large area of south-east Devon to which the data could possibly be extended. The general physique of south-east Devon and of the study area in particular is illustrated in Figure 4.1. The study area, covering the Gissage, a northward-flowing tributary of the Otter, and the headwaters of the River Sid, consists of part of the clay with flints-capped east Devon Plateau that has been dissected to reveal the under-lying Upper Greensand and Keuper Marl (Fig. 4.1, d). The topography includes the flat plateau surface; steep bounding slopes with angles of up to 21 degrees developed on the outcrops of Upper Greensand; and, in the lower parts of the valleys, gentler slopes of 4-11 degrees developed on the Keuper Marls. These topographic elements are closely paralleled by the pattern of natural vegetation and land use within the area. The plateau surface mantled with the deposits of clay with flints is mainly an area of unenclosed heathland and thin soils, although some reclamation has taken place. The steep slopes developed on the Greensand are again dominantly unenclosed and support rough pasture, woodland, and gorse, whilst the gentler slopes of the Keuper Marl have been utilised for farming with a predominance of permanent pasture. The Pleistocene legacy in the area is well-evidenced by the layer of head, several feet thick and composed of Cretaceous debris, that covers the slopes below the outcrop of Greensand. The surrounding area already possessed a network of rain gauges installed as part of the Devon River Authority Hydrometric Scheme;[9] a permanent river gauging station on the River Otter at Dotton (SY 087884) with records dating back to 1962; and a temporary river gauging station on the River Sid at Sidmouth (SY 128879). Some basic hydrological data was therefore available for the area. The average annual rainfall of the study area (1915-60) is between 889–1,016 millimetres (35–40 inches) (Fig. 4.1, c) and is fairly well distributed throughout the year, although November, December and January each receives more than 10 per cent of the monthly average.

The choice of the individual catchments for instrumentation was governed by accessibility; freedom from the possibility of interference with any equipment; the availability of suitable sites for a stream gauging station; and the range of catchment characteristics. The five catchments selected for instrumentation range in size from 0.111 sq. kilometres (0.043 sq. miles) to 6.40 sq. kilometres (2.47 sq. miles) and their dominant characteristics are indicated in Table 4.1. The three smallest (Fig. 4.1a, Nos. 1, 2, 3) were chosen as representative of three distinct terrain types within the area. Catchment 1 consists of a small

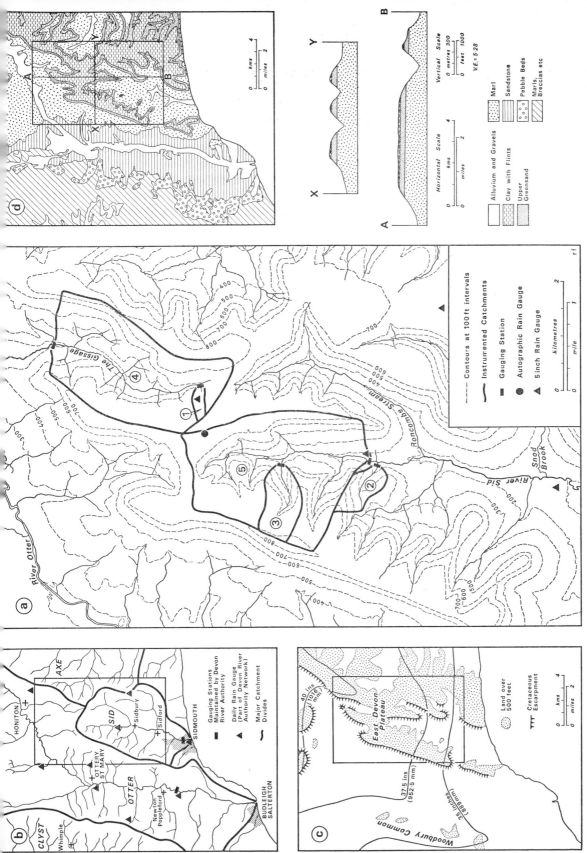

Fig. 4.1   The location and physique of the instrumented catchments (a), and the setting of the study area within south-east Devon showing source of hydrometric data (b), physique and approximate average annual rainfall isohyets (1915–1950) (c), and Geology (d). Geology is adapted from Geological Survey maps: Crown Copyright, by permission of the Controller of HM Stationery Office.

stream draining the clay with flints-mantled plateau surface; its lower portions are formed by a small gulley developed into the Upper Greensand and the dominant land use is un-enclosed heathland. Catchment 2 is located mainly on the Keuper Marl of the lower valley slopes and is largely farmland. Catchment 3 is a steep-sided valley, deeply entrenched into the clay with flints and Upper Greensand, with a limited outcrop of Keuper Marl exposed in the valley floor; this catchment is dominantly forested with deciduous woodland and recently planted coniferous plantations. The two larger catchments, catchments 4 and 5 (Fig. 4.1a) provide different combinations of these major terrain types. Catchment 4 is dominantly agricultural in its lower areas, whereas catchment 5 possesses a considerable proportion of woodland (Table 4.1).

A multiple watershed experiment should ideally include all combinations of topography, geology, vegetation and land use but this was not possible within the scope of this study. However, it was hoped that the five catchments selected would provide a useful basis for studying the influence of different catchment characteristics on the hydrologic response of small watersheds. Since the five catchments are included within the area described by a circle two miles in radius, it was hoped that the rainfall input to the catchments and the macroclimate could be viewed as uniform. The measured variations in water yield could therefore be attributed solely to the variations in catchment characteristics, thereby simpli-fying the task of comparative analysis within the framework of the multiple watershed approach.

CATCHMENT INSTRUMENTATION

Instrumentation of the catchments was dictated primarily by cost, the problem of access, and the limitations of single-handed installation. Since this study was not intended as a complete Water Balance study, nor as an intensive documentation of fluvial processes, instrumentation was limited to the major hydrologic parameters. An autographic natural siphon rain gauge, fitted with a weekly chart, and a check gauge were installed in the centre of the study area so that no part of an instrumented catchment was more than 3.2 kilometres (2 miles) from these instruments. It was originally intended to install a series of weekly and daily totaliser gauges within the catchments in order to study the extent of areal variations in precipitation, but the lack of suitable sites free from disturbance meant that reliance was placed upon two storage gauges within the catchments, one read daily and the other weekly, and three further daily gauges in the adjacent area. (Fig. 4.1a, b).

In the three smallest catchments, streamflow measurement stations were constructed, using sharp crested thin plate weirs. A 90 degree triangular notch was used in the smallest catchment (Fig. 4.1a, No. 1) and rectangular notches in the other two cases (Fig. 4.1a, Nos. 2, 3). These weirs were constructed from aluminium sheet with sharp brass edges to the notches, and were secured in concrete foundations and cutoff walls. Construction of gauging structures on the two larger streams (Fig. 4.1a, Nos. 4, 5) was impossible with the resources available, but fortunately pre-existing controls were found that could be utilised for discharge measurement, using the rated-section technique. In one case (Fig. 4.1a, No. 5)

TABLE 4.1
Characteristics of the five instrumented catchments

Geology

Catchment Number (Fig. 1a)	Proportion of Geological Outcrops			Proportion of Catchment above Greensand base
	Clay with Flints	Upper Greensand	Keuper Marl	
1	98.0	2.0	0.0	100.0
2	3.0	22.0	75.0	25.0
3	58.0	30.0	12.0	88.0
4	48.0	16.0	36.0	64.0
5	47.0	21.0	32.0	68.0

Topography

Catchment Number (Fig. 1a)	Area Sq. Miles	Basin Relief Feet	Basin Shape L^2/A*	Low Flow Drainage Density miles/sq. mile‡
1	0.043	130	4.0	2.2
2	0.180	490	4.1	1.9
3	0.300	405	2.5	2.5
4	1.920	435	2.8	2.7
5	2.470	560	1.9	2.9

Vegetation and Land Use

Catchment Number (Fig. 1a)	Land Use Percentage of Basin Area		
	Woodland	Unenclosed	Enclosed
1	1.1	92.2	6.7
2	5.7	20.8	73.5
3	77.0	2.1	20.9
4	11.0	19.7	69.3
5	39.5	11.7	48.8

* Basin shape is expressed as L^2/A where L is the length of the basin in miles and A is basin area in square miles.

‡ Low Flow Drainage Density is derived from Measurements of length of functioning stream channel within a catchment during normal low flow conditions.

the concrete sill of a waterfall was used and in the other case a concrete waterfall sill and a concrete-lined channel section. At each station water level above the crest of the control or weir was continuously recorded by Munro vertical-type recorders equipped with weekly clock-driven charts. Stage/Discharge rating was carried out by formulae for the thin plate weirs[10, 11] and by current meter rating using an Ott CI miniature current meter for the rated sections.[12] The stage recorder charts were converted to discharge records by using transparent conversion overlays and by digitisation of the stage record at hourly intervals and subsequent computer processing.

RESULTS AND ANALYSIS

The instrumentation described above was completed in July 1967. Analysis has initially been restricted to the period 7 July 1967 to 6 July 1968, since the disastrous floods that occurred in south-east Devon on 10 July 1968 damaged some of the instruments and disrupted the continuity of the record. This period of twelve months' record, although not as convenient as a water year, has proved satisfactory, since flow levels were low both at the beginning and at the end of the period.

Rainfall Input
Analysis of the rainfall data for these twelve months shows that, although there was some areal variation in rainfall input, the centrally placed autographic rain gauge provided records that could be extended over the study area without any great loss of accuracy. The annual rainfall total of 1,033 millimetres (40.66 inches) for the central gauge is very similar to the corresponding total of 1,041 millimetres (40.97 inches) for the daily gauge near the stream gauging station for catchment 5 (Fig. 4.1a). It is therefore suggested that the annual total of 1,033 millimetres (40.66 inches) is appropriate to the entire area of the catchments. Inspection and comparison of the daily rainfall totals from the same two gauges during the study period again suggest only limited areal variation. Correlation analysis of the daily rainfall totals from the two gauges assuming a unitary relationship gave the following results (Table 4.2).

TABLE 4.2

Correlation analysis of daily rainfall totals from two rain gauges.

Criterion for selection of observations included in correlation	Correlation Coefficient	Standard Error of the Estimate
All days with rainfall	0.99	0.035
All days with rainfall >0.1 inches	0.98	0.065
All days with rainfall >0.25 inches	0.98	0.065
All days with rainfall >0.50 inches	0.97	0.095

Since the peripheral rain gauge occupies a valley floor site two miles from the central gauge, it is suggested that this gauge exhibits the maximum extent of any areal variation in rainfall. However, the close degree of association indicated by the correlation coefficients demonstrates the limited extent of storm rainfall variation over the area. For the purposes of this study it has been assumed that the rainfall recorded by the central gauge is representative of the area covered by the catchments under consideration. A limited degree of correction has been applied to the rainfall record when the evidence suggested that areal variation might have been important. The general uniformity of rainfall over the area of the study catchments allows the application of the multiple watershed technique of analysis in its simplest form. Variations in water yield can be related directly to catchment characteristics without recourse to complex analysis to remove variations attributable to differences in rainfall input. A large number of catchments would be necessary to carry out a full statistical analysis of the influence of catchment characteristics, and with only five catchments under study the conclusions must be based, to a large extent, on subjective reasoning.

Simple Water Balances

Map analysis and field inspection suggested that four of the catchments were watertight and suitable for general water balance evaluation (Fig. 4.1a, Catchments 1, 3, 4 & 5). Using the simple hydrologic equation, Rain=Runoff + Evapotranspiration Loss + or — change in storage, i.e. Rain = Runoff + ET $\pm$ $\triangle$ St., annual water budgets were drawn up for the four catchments. Change in storage ($\triangle$ St.) could not be evaluated by the usual techniques of well-level analysis but, since flow levels were similar in form for all catchments at the beginning and the end of the budget period, it was assumed that this element was small and an approximation was derived from analysis of the general catchment recession curves (Appendix 1). The errors involved in the storage term are small. The water balance components for the individual catchments are listed in Table 4.3. The values of the loss components compare satisfactorily with the value of Potential Evapotranspiration calculated by the Penman Formula[13, 14] for Exeter airport (SY 003933) which is nine miles to the west of this area and the only adjacent location for which sufficiently detailed meteorological data was available.

TABLE 4.3
Water Balance components for four instrumented catchments
7 July 1967–6 July 1968.

Catchment No. (Fig. 4.1a)	Rainfall (inches)	Runoff (inches)	Loss (inches)	Storage (inches)
1	40.66 (1033 mm)	18.38 (467 mm)	21.69 (551 mm)	+0.59 (15 mm)
3	40.66 (1033 mm)	17.45 (443 mm)	23.21 (590 mm)	0.00
4	40.66 (1033 mm)	25.56 (649 mm)	15.10 (384 mm)	0.00
5	40.66 (1033 mm)	20.68 (525 mm)	19.22 (488 mm)	+0.76 (19 mm)

(Penman Formula Estimate of Potential Evapotranspiration   20.44 inches (519 mm)

Differences in the magnitude of the Runoff and Loss components for the individual catchments must reflect variations in catchment characteristics, since rainfall input and macroclimate can be accepted as uniform. In considering the loss components, simple daily budget calculations of soil moisture deficit were made, using the rainfall values and the Penman values of potential evapotranspiration. The calculated soil moisture deficits did not at any time during the study period exceed 89 millimetres (3.5 inches) and, since the root constant of the natural vegetation in the catchments is probably not less than this value, it was assumed that evapotranspiration loss took place at the potential rate over each of the catchments. A prime factor controlling variations in the runoff and loss components is considered to be variation in local microclimate conditioned by the topographic diversity within the five catchments. Penman[15] describes the case of a south-facing valley losing more water than a north-facing valley by evapotranspiration, and studies made by Lee[16] demonstrate the variation of potential insolation according to aspect. Variation in the receipt of direct solar radiation must influence the rates of evapotranspiration. Catchment 4, with a north-easterly orientation and the majority of its slopes possessing north-westerly and easterly aspects, exhibits a loss component appreciably below those of the other catchments. Underground inflow into this catchment might explain this reduction in losses, but the geological structure and the records from the nearby catchments do not support this conclusion. Catchment 1, located almost entirely on the plateau surface and fully exposed to direct solar radiation, exhibits a higher loss rate than catchments 4 and 5 that are much more incised. However, topography and its influence on receipt of solar radiation is not the only catchment characteristic controlling variations in the components of the water balance. The work of Law[17] has shown that forest cover can increase the loss from a drainage basin. Catchment 3 with the highest proportion of forest cover (77 per cent, Table 4.1) exhibits the maximum loss component. The topographic character of this catchment is not entirely favourable for receipt of full direct solar radiation, and this suggests that vegetation cover is as important as local topography in controlling the losses and the total runoff from a catchment. The higher loss rate in catchment 1 might also be ascribed to the presence of peat and marshy areas in parts of this catchment. Variations in catchment characteristics can be seen to have considerable influence on the water budget of a catchment.

Figure 4.2 illustrates in more detail the water balance components for the four catchments, by considering the monthly components. An approximation of the monthly storage component has been made by apportioning the annual loss component in proportion to the monthly values of potential evapotranspiration calculated by the Penman formula, and subtracting this estimate and the runoff component from the monthly rainfall total. Further contrasts between the catchments are demonstrated by this more detailed consideration. Catchment 3 is distinctive for having the smallest fluctuation in the magnitude of the monthly runoff component, and this can be attributed to the large proportion of Upper Greensand, a good storage aquifer, within the catchment, and to the forest cover which has often been shown to reduce the variability of runoff from a catchment. The storage graph for this catchment illustrates the considerable amount of storage available within the Upper Greensand aquifer and the thick head deposits in the lower parts of the valley. In contrast,

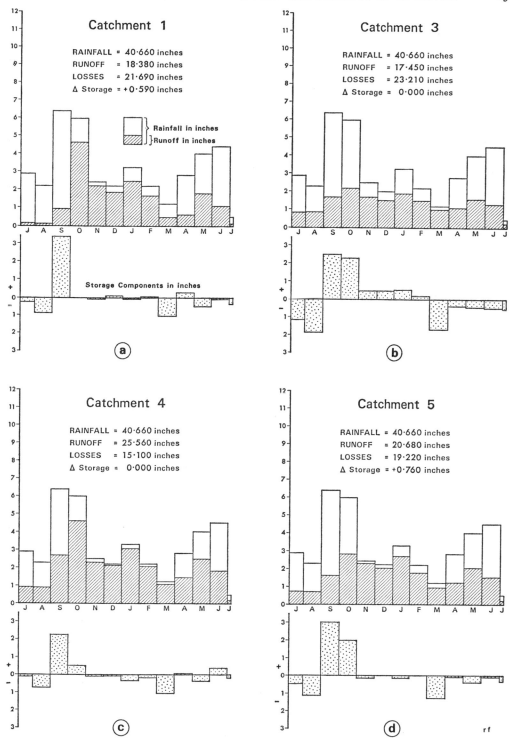

Fig. 4.2   Monthly water balance components for four of the study catchments.

F

catchment 1, which is primarily developed on the clay with flints—a poor aquifer lacking any extensive covering of head—exhibits marked fluctuations in monthly runoff, while a lack of long term storage is illustrated by the small amounts of runoff attributable to storage during the low flow period of August 1967. Catchments 4 and 5 are between the two former catchments in the extremes of variability of monthly runoff and of long term storage, although certain differences can be detected. The greater proportion of Upper Greensand, the greater dissection of this aquifer, and the larger proportion of forest-cover in catchment 5 result in smaller variation in the monthly runoff component and larger storage components. Catchment characteristics can exert appreciable influence on the precise nature of the water balance within a catchment. Overall losses and total runoff, variability of the monthly runoff components and variations in catchment storage appear to be modified by aspect, rock type and vegetation. Rock type and vegetation seem to be of greatest significance in accounting for variations in monthly runoff, whereas aspect and vegetation are more important in controlling the overall water balance. However, the physical characteristics of any drainage basin are closely inter-related and it is difficult to define the specific effects of any individual catchment characteristics.

Streamflow Duration curves

Consideration of the water balance components of a catchment provides only one viewpoint for assessing the effects of varying catchment characteristics. In many studies, parameters of the streamflow record have been used as dependent variables in order to demonstrate the influence of catchment characteristics, and in this project specific consideration has been given to the manner in which different runoff parameters reflect control by catchment characteristics. The streamflow duration curve is a useful means of characterising the stream-flow record; it may be thought of as the annual hydrograph with its flows arranged in order of magnitude. In Figure 4.3a the streamflow duration curves for the study period from the five catchments have been superimposed. A wide range of catchment characteristics influences the precise form of the duration curve, and comparative analysis provides further insight into the different hydrologic responses of the catchments and their underlying causes. One simple measure of the form of the duration curve is the Variability Index proposed by Lane and Lei.[18] This index, an approximation to the standard deviation of the flow record, has been shown to reflect many catchment characteristics and the authors postulated that it could be synthesised from a consideration of the nature of the catchment. Table 4.4 lists both this index and the 30/70 index for the individual catchments. The 30/70 index is another descriptive measure of the duration curve expressing the ratio of the flow level exceeded 30 per cent of the time to that exceeded 70 per cent of the time.

Geology appears to be a dominant factor in controlling the values of the Variability Indices. Catchment 1, with its high proportion of clay with flints, an impervious drift, covering the surface, has a high variability index associated with the high range of flows, whereas catchment 3, with the largest proportion of pervious Greensand aquifer, possesses the lowest variability index or lowest range of flows. In the case of the four catchments with varying proportions of Upper Greensand and Keuper Marl within their catchment areas

TABLE 4.4

Descriptive Indices of the streamflow duration curves for the five catchments

Catchment Number (Fig. 4.1a)	Variability Index*	30/70 Ratio
I	0.814	2.83
2	0.755	3.50
3	0.407	1.53
4	0.530	2.00
5	0.522	1.75

*See Appendix 2 for derivation of this value.

(Fig. 4.1a, Nos. 2, 3, 4, 5), the Variability Index seems primarily to reflect the proportion of Greensand outcrop within the catchment (Fig. 4.3b).

A catchment with a pervious aquifer will have increased infiltration, reduced storm runoff, increased baseflow and a smaller range of flows, compared to a catchment with impervious geology. However, vegetation and soil cover must exert a further influence on the Variability Index. In catchment 3 the low Variability Index must in addition be related to the large proportion of forest cover and associated soils with good infiltration properties. This catchment has a considerable proportion of clay with flints within its area, but the effects of this are modified by the forest cover. The 30/70 ratio is similarly controlled to a large extent by the geology of the catchments (Fig. 4.3c).

The minimum flow levels indicated by the duration curves—the flow levels exceeded 100 per cent of the time—reflect the long-term storage potential of the catchment under drought conditions and therefore the rock type. A good aquifer which stores a large quantity of groundwater will sustain comparatively high flows during a drought period, whereas a poor aquifer may even cease to be a source of streamflow. The clay with flints which predominates in catchment 1, and the Keuper Marl which occupies a large proportion of Catchment 2, are poor aquifers for longterm storage and therefore flows in these two catchments are appreciably lower than in the other three catchments where the Greensand aquifer maintains higher minimum flows. The Keuper Marl is not so poor an aquifer as the clay with flints, and the very low flow values found in catchment 2 are partly attributable to the topographic setting which causes groundwater outflow to the catchment on its south-west border. Within the four catchments (catchments 2, 3, 4 and 5) where different proportions of the three rock types occur, a general relationship can be found between minimum flow level and the proportion of the catchment above the base of the Greensand outcrop (Fig. 4.3d). The vegetation and soil character will also influence the minimum flow levels in that they determine the surface infiltration properties and therefore the extent of aquifer recharge and of soil moisture storage. Recent work[19] has shown that soil moisture drainage may provide a sustained source of streamflow during low flow periods

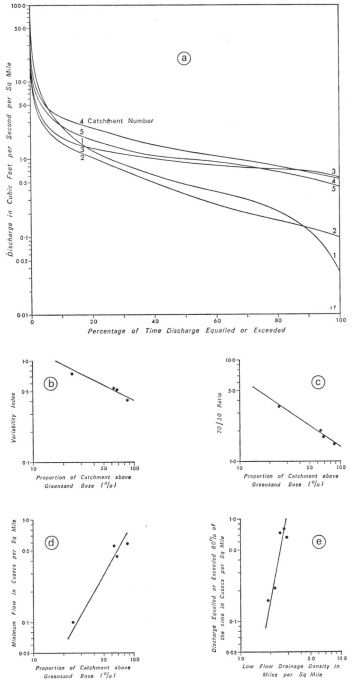

Fig. 4.3   Superimposed streamflow duration curves for the five catchments (a), and relationships between duration curve indices and catchment characteristics (b), (c), (d) and (e).

and that therefore soil character may be an important factor in controlling minimum flow levels. The large proportion of forest cover and the deep debris layer associated with the head deposits in catchment 3 both exert an influence which further explains why this catchment exhibits the highest level of minimum flow. Drainage density defined as the total length of functioning streams within a drainage basin per unit area (miles/sq. mile) is a characteristic that itself reflects control by the overall complex of catchment characteristics, and it is interesting to note that a clear relationship can be found between low flow drainage density within the five catchments and the 80 per cent flow level, the level associated with such functioning drainage densities (Fig. 4.3e).

The maximum flow levels of the duration curve result from storm runoff and these reflect many further drainage basin characteristics, especially those related to the surface character and the topography. High levels of storm runoff require impervious surface conditions and steep slopes to assist runoff formation. Geology still exerts a considerable influence over the pattern of peak runoff levels exhibited by Figure 4.3a. The impervious nature of the rock types which occur in large proportions within catchments 1 and 2 respectively results in maximum storm runoff levels. This situation contrasts with that of the minimum flows, for these two rock types produce the lowest levels of minimum flows. Similar general control of both peak flow levels and minimum flow levels by geology is noted by Giusti[20] in the Piedmont of Virginia where rivers with the highest peak flows are frequently those with the lowest minimum flows. Although many factors influence the exact form of the streamflow duration curve for a catchment, in the case of the five instrumented catchments geology seems to exert the dominant influence.

Runoff Components

In trying further to evaluate the influence of catchment characteristics on runoff, and especially on peak runoff, it becomes necessary to appreciate that runoff has many origins, ranging from the ground surface down to the deep groundwater reservoir, and that the different origins will reflect control by different sets of catchment characteristics. Genetic separation of flow into such components as surface runoff, throughflow, interflow and groundwater flow has often been attempted in the past,[21] but this type of separation is entirely arbitrary unless it is based on a sophisticated chemical analysis of the runoff itself and the likely chemical character of runoff from different sources, such as has been carried out by Russian workers.[22] Recent work by Nash and Sutcliffe[23] has realistically proposed that there is a continuum of different paths by which runoff reaches the stream, and this conclusion seems logical. It is, nevertheless, of value to sub-divide the flow record into certain components: the method of Hibbert and Cunningham[24] suggests the use of a time-based hydrograph separation into Quickflow and Delayed flow. This technique employs an arbitrary separation line projected upwards from the beginning of the hydrograph rise at a gradient of 0.05 cusecs per square mile (Fig. 4.4b) and involves a time distribution separation of runoff rather than any genetic division. Quickflow occurs during and in the short period following storm rainfall and may consist of surface runoff, throughflow or interflow,

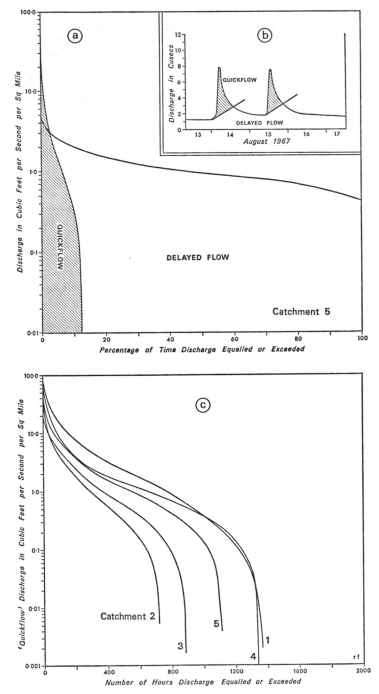

Fig. 4.4   Flow separation analysis, showing the basis for separation into Quickflow and Delayed flow (b), flow component duration curves (a), and superimposed Quickflow duration curves (c).

and is compatible with the ideas on storm runoff suggested by Kirkby and Chorley[25] and the T.V.A.[26] Graphical separation of runoff records into the above two categories is very time-consuming, and therefore a computer technique has been developed to perform the separation on the flow record of digitized hourly values. The results from individual hydrographs conform almost exactly to those obtained by graphical methods. The computer separation allows the hourly flow values to be tabulated into Quickflow and Delayed flow components and calculates daily, monthly and annual totals for the two categories. The proportions of Quickflow and Delayed flow for the five instrumented catchments are shown in Table 4.5.

TABLE 4.5

Annual flow separation for the five instrumented catchments.

Catchment No.	Quickflow (inches)	Quickflow %	Delayed flow (inches)	Delayed flow %	Response Ratio*
1	9.22 (234 mm)	50.15	9.16 (233 mm)	49.85	22.68%
2	2.53 (64 mm)	23.60	8.16 (207 mm)	76.40	6.22%
3	2.71 (68 mm)	15.50	14.73 (374 mm)	84.50	6.67%
4	5.32 (135 mm)	20.80	20.24 (514 mm)	79.20	13.08%
5	4.68 (119 mm)	22.60	16.00 (406 mm)	77.40	11.50%

*Response Ratio is defined as the ratio of the total Quickflow to the total precipitation.

The annual flow separation data provide a general description of the runoff record, and are a useful complement to the flow duration curves. The basic control exercised by geology, vegetation and soil character on the runoff pattern is again demonstrated. The clay with flints of catchment 1 produces a high proportion of Quickflow, since the thin soil and impermeable parent material promote rapid runoff and low values of infiltration, whereas the good infiltration properties of the forest soil and the considerable outcrop of Greensand in catchment 3 result in minimum proportions of Quickflow. The response ratio indicates the percentage of the total precipitation that resulted in Quickflow: again certain catchment characteristics exercise a control. Catchment 1 expectedly has a high response ratio as a result of its geological background, and catchment 4, although it has a lesser proportion of Quickflow than catchment 5, possesses a higher response ratio as a result of the smaller losses within the catchment and therefore smaller soil moisture deficits during the periods of storm runoff.

Separation of the flow record into two components means that flow duration curves can be derived for both categories of flow (Fig. 4.4a) and Figure 4.4c presents the Quickflow duration curves for the five catchments. These curves reflect the storm runoff dynamics of the individual catchments much better than do the duration curves of total flow. A striking variation between the catchments occurs in the total number of hours that Quickflow occurred; this ranges between 722 hours in the case of catchment 2 to almost twice that value, 1361 hours, in the case of catchment 1. The high total durations experienced by catchments 1 and 4 are not easily explained by any common factor, but are probably related to the impermeable surface conditions within catchment 1 and to the low overall loss in catchment 4, which must promote smaller soil moisture deficits. Both of these factors encourage storm runoff. Catchment 2 functions to produce Quickflow on fewer occasions than the other catchments, but the highest hourly values are in excess of those produced by catchments 3 and 5. Such a pattern suggests the importance of soil moisture status within a catchment, with very little runoff produced during dry conditions yet relatively high amounts during very wet conditions. Catchment 3, in which both the forest cover and the background of geology and soil promote rapid infiltration, exhibits a low overall Quickflow duration. When considering the maximum values of Quickflow it is interesting to note that catchments 1 and 4 respectively produce the highest values and the longest durations yet catchment 2, which produces the next highest rates of Quickflow, exhibits the lowest duration. Storm runoff is a complex process and it is difficult to ascribe variations in catchment response to specific catchment characteristics: different sets of catchment characteristics will be dominant during wet and dry conditions and during periods of heavy and light rainfall. In addition, certain catchment characteristics in their control of loss rates will have an indirect influence in controlling the soil moisture status contrasts between catchments.

Depletion Curves

The Delayed Flow record from the catchments can be studied in more detail by considering the time distribution as well as the duration curves. Streamflow depletion curves provide a useful index of the dynamics of Delayed Flow production within a catchment. Figure 4.5 illustrates streamflow depletion curves following small storm hydrographs for the five catchments during two periods when rainfall was negligible. Figure 4.5a refers to a period during the summer and Figure 4.5b to a period during the winter. The effects of catchment storage can be clearly seen when comparing the two seasons. During the summer, catchments 1 and 2 with their poor storage characteristics exhibit lower flow levels than the other three catchments, but this contrast is not so marked in winter when recharge has replenished the storage. Even in winter, however, the flow levels from catchments 1 and 2 rapidly fall below those of the other catchments, and these two catchments exhibit the most steeply sloping depletion curves during both seasons. The storage provided by the Greensand aquifer and the head deposits on the lower slopes in catchments 3, 4 and 5 results in much lower depletion rates. The very steep segments in the upper part of the depletion curve for catchment 1 (Fig. 4.5b) would appear to reflect the shallow surface storage that responds readily to storm rainfall but is thereafter rapidly exhausted. As in the case of other characteristics of low flow and Delayed Flow previously considered, geology and soil character seem to exert the dominant influence on the nature of the streamflow depletion curve, although the whole complex of catchment characteristics contributes to the precise form of the curve.

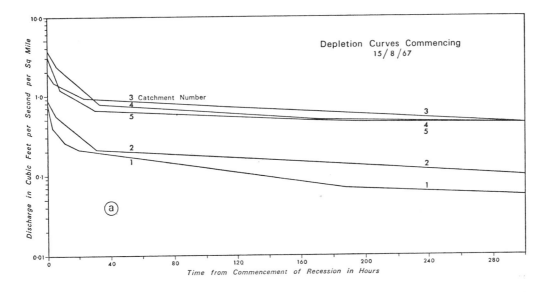

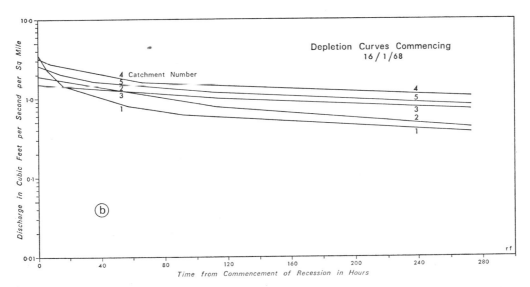

Fig. 4.5 Flow depletion curves for the five catchments for two periods with no significant rainfall.

Rainfall/Runoff Relationships

Duration curves give no indication of the time distribution of runoff and in order to study in more detail the pattern of storm runoff production within the catchments, the individual storm runoff hydrographs must be considered. A brief study of the storm hydrograph records from the five catchments reveals that there is no definite relationship between the catchments for either magnitude of peak discharges or storm runoff amount. On one occasion a catchment might provide the maximum peak discharge and storm runoff per unit area, whereas on another occasion it might produce the lowest values. It is impossible to categorise and to state that, because of a certain combination of catchment characteristics, one catchment responds most readily to storm rainfall. In order to understand fully the dynamics of storm runoff for each catchment, the manner in which they differ, and thus the influence of varying catchment characteristics, it would be necessary to derive complex runoff models for the catchments, as well as to optimise the parameters and to relate parameter differences to meaningful variations in catchment characteristics. Such a solution is not possible within the scope of this study, but simple descriptive Multiple Regression Models have been developed to describe storm runoff production. For each catchment, the nature of the separated Quickflow hydrograph as characterised by the Hydrograph Rise (increase in discharge above the preceding delayed flow level) and total Quickflow volume or runoff amount were related to the causative storm rainfall and an index of the moisture conditions within the catchment preceding the storm. The storm rainfall was defined by the rainfall amount, duration, and maximum fifteen-minute intensity, and the moisture conditions were defined either by the level of Delayed flow immediately preceding the hydrograph rise or by a general index of Soil Moisture Deficiency derived from a daily budget accounting of rainfall and the Penman estimates of potential evapotranspiration for the overall area (Appendix 3). A stepwise multiple regression computer programme was employed in order to analyse the variables defined above, and observations were available for between 65 and 92 storm runoff events for each catchment. Hydrograph Rise and runoff amount were used as dependent variables, and the rainfall and moisture condition parameters as independent variables. The stepwise programme accepts an independent variable into the regression equation if the ratio of the decrease in the Residual Sum of Squares to the new Residual Mean Square exceeds a certain acceptance F level. In this analysis an F level of 5 per cent was used. It was found, using both linear and logarithmic transformed relationships, that rainfall amount and an index of moisture conditions were the only significant independent variables. It is interesting to suggest that the reason for the non-appearance of both rainfall duration and rainfall intensity in the significant regression sets is that storm runoff production in these catchments is closely controlled by conditions of throughflow and saturated overland flow[25] where total rainfall amount is important. This contrasts with the Horton model of runoff production,[27] where the occurrence of overland-flow is conditioned by rainfall intensity; storm runoff only occurs when rainfall intensity exceeds the infiltration capacity of the soil; and infiltration capacity tends to decrease during the duration of the storm rainfall.

The multiple regression equations relating Hydrograph Rise and Storm Runoff Amount to rainfall amount and the index of Soil Moisture Deficiency, an index common to all five catchments, can be used as descriptive equations to summarise the pattern of runoff production in each catchment. The following equations (Table 4.6) were derived and in each case the multiple correlation coefficients were approximately 0.90. These equations are used

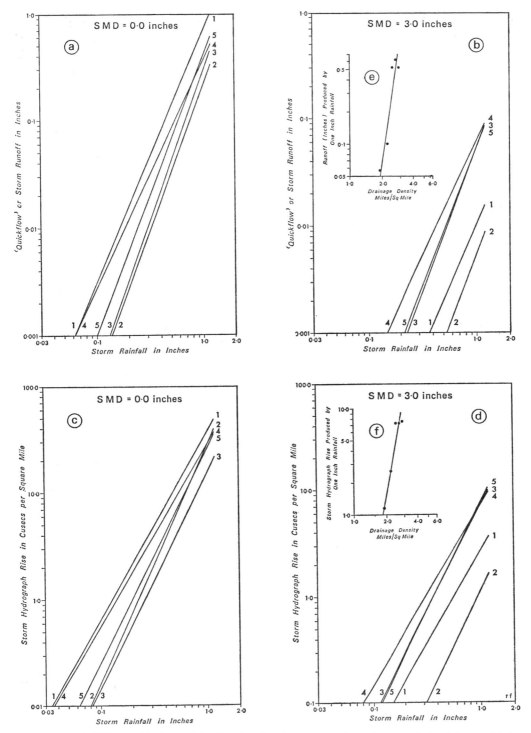

Fig. 4.6 Rainfall/Runoff relationships for the five instrumented catchments derived by multiple regression analysis.

solely as a descriptive least squares fit to the data from each catchment, and they should not be extended beyond the limits of the data from which they were derived. The patterns of response indicated by the individual hydrographs and summarised by the equations in Table 4.6 are portrayed graphically in Figure 4.6. Figure 4.6 illustrates Rainfall/Runoff

TABLE 4.6

Multiple Regression Equations describing storm runoff production in the instrumented catchments.

Catchment No.	Equation	No. of Observations	Correlation Coefficient
1	$\text{Log } Ra = -0.1751 + 2.3473 \text{ Log } R - 0.6116 \text{ SMD}$	92	0.91
	$\text{Log } Hr = 1.5515 + 1.7580 \text{ Log } R - 0.3739 \text{ SMD}$	92	0.92
2	$\text{Log } Ra = -0.7046 + 2.6668 \text{ Log } R - 0.5217 \text{ SMD}$	65	0.90
	$\text{Log } Hr = 1.2185 + 1.9867 \text{ Log } R - 0.3830 \text{ SMD}$	65	0.89
3	$\text{Log } Ra = -0.5638 + 2.7620 \text{ Log } R - 0.2290 \text{ SMD}$	72	0.93
	$\text{Log } Hr + 1.1720 + 1.9930 \text{ Log } R - 0.0990 \text{ SMD}$	72	0.90
4	$\text{Log } Ra = -0.4426 + 2.1141 \text{ Log } R - 0.2593 \text{ SMD}$	71	0.90
	$\text{Log } Hr = 1.4388 + 1.6877 \text{ Log } R - 0.1915 \text{ SMD}$	71	0.89
5	$\text{Log } Ra = -0.3937 + 2.6139 \text{ Log } R - 0.2890 \text{ SMD}$	74	0.90
	$\text{Log } Hr = 1.4042 + 2.0076 \text{ Log } R - 0.1745 \text{ SMD}$	74	0.91

The variable names can be explained as follows:—
    Ra = storm runoff or Quickflow amount in inches
    Hr = Hydrograph rise in cubic feet per second per square mile
    R = Storm rainfall amount in inches
    SMD = Soil Moisture Deficiency in inches

amount and Rainfall/Hydrograph Rise relationships for conditions of zero and 3 inches Soil Moisture Deficiency for the five instrumented catchments. These graphs can be studied, and an attempt made to ascribe the different relationships for the individual catchments to variations in catchment characteristics. It is evident that the catchments function very differently under wet and dry conditions. Catchment 1 produces the maximum values of both runoff and hydrograph rise under conditions of zero soil moisture deficiency, but among the lowest values under conditions of a 3-inch soil moisture deficit. However, catchment 2 produces low values under both wet and dry conditions. The differences between the catchments are best considered in terms of the variable source area concept of catchment dynamics,[26] which embodies extension and contraction of the network of functioning streams and of the areas contributing to storm runoff.[28] A previous study in two of the catchments (Fig. 4.1a, catchments 1 and 2)[29] has shown how the drainage net expands and contracts according to the level of flow from the catchment. Discharge values and drainage density were found to be related by a function approximately of the form

$Q \propto Dd^2$. During dry conditions the drainage net in a catchment will shrink, and, if subjected to rainfall, storm runoff will only occur from the areas of high soil moisture content in the areas bounding the streams. Under wet conditions, however, the drainage net will be considerably extended and there will exist a larger area of high soil moisture content bounding this network. If rainfall occurs under these conditions much greater amounts of storm runoff will occur, and if the storm is of long duration the area contributing to flow will be extended. These mechanics of runoff production are closely related to those of throughflow and its role in the production of storm runoff,[25] and differ considerably from the classic Hortonian concepts, in which the whole catchment is thought to produce storm runoff. When considering the influence of catchment characteristics on storm runoff production, one must take into account the characteristics that will control the magnitude and rate of extension of the drainage net and the contributing areas. Only when a large proportion of the catchment is contributing to storm runoff will the character of the total catchment area be directly influencing the runoff hydrograph. In most cases it will be the character of the contributing area that governs the form of the hydrograph. In any study of storm runoff, catchment characteristics must be viewed as dynamic in nature, for, if runoff is being produced only in the lower parts of a basin, then the characteristics of that area will differ considerably from those of the total catchment. However, catchment characteristics exert a direct influence on the precise portion of the catchment that will contribute to runoff.

In studying the patterns of runoff production indicated by Figure 4.6, consideration can first be given to the case of high soil moisture deficits (Fig. 4.6b, d). Catchments 1 and 2 both exhibit low summer flow drainage densities (Table 4.1). These values are related to the impermeable nature of the clay with flints in catchment 1, which under dry conditions stores little water to sustain flows, and to the low storage potential of the Keuper Marl and the topographic conditions, which cause outflow of storage to an adjacent catchment in catchment 2. Catchments 3, 4 and 5 which possess considerable proportions of Greensand within their watersheds maintain higher drainage densities under dry conditions. Since storm runoff occurs from the areas bounding the drainage network, catchments 1 and 2 produce low values of runoff and hydrograph rise whereas the larger contributing areas in the other three catchments produce greater values. Catchment 4 consistently produces the highest values under dry conditions and this may be related to the low overall losses for this catchment and the resultant greater extent of areas of high soil moisture content within the catchment. Conversely, in catchment 3, the deep soils and the high proportion of forest cover, with its increased losses, are unfavourable for the development of areas of high soil moisture bounding the stream network. There is a clear relation between low flow drainage densities and both runoff amount and hydrograph rise under conditions of high soil moisture deficiency (Fig. 4.6, e, f). Catchment area may be an important factor in further influencing runoff under dry conditions, since a large catchment will probably have a proportionately larger area of valley bottomland, the area most likely to contribute to storm runoff.

The graphs for zero Soil Moisture Deficit (Fig. 4.6a, c) reveal different relationships among the catchments. Under wet conditions the contributing area of the catchment is much larger and it reflects the overall character of the catchment. Catchment 1 with impervious surface conditions produces high amounts of runoff, whereas catchment 3, with a forest cover causing interception of incident precipitation; a large proportion of Greensand with good infiltration properties; and forest soils (again with good infiltration properties), produces minimum amounts of storm runoff. Whereas runoff amount mainly reflects the geology, vegetation and soil conditions within the catchment, the peak discharge, a reflection of the mode of delivery of that runoff to the catchment outlet, will reflect the topography and the surface roughness to a considerable extent. The graphs for zero soil moisture deficit indicate different patterns of peak discharge production from those of overall runoff amount. Although catchment 1 produces considerably more runoff under high rainfall than the other catchments, it does not exhibit such large increases for hydrograph rise; this reflects the lower relief and unenclosed land-use of the catchment which discourage high peak discharges. Catchment 2, with high relief and enclosed land-use (conditions which favour high peak discharges), produces the lowest values of runoff amount for high rainfall, yet some of the largest hydrograph rises. Catchment 3, with a woodland cover that reduces the hydrograph peak, exhibits a very low hydrograph rise for high rainfall, yet it produces runoff amounts similar to those of the other catchments. When considering the effects of catchment characteristics on storm runoff, it should be realised that the volume of storm runoff may reflect controls different from those on the peak of the runoff hydrograph.

Hydrograph Form

Any consideration of the overall form of the storm runoff hydrograph and its control by catchment characteristics must be highly complex, in view of the implications of the variable source area concept of runoff formation. Classic Unit Hydrograph theory assumes that the entire catchment contributes to runoff and that the storm hydrograph characterised by the Unit Hydrograph reflects the sum total of the characteristics of the catchment. However, this is not the case, for the hydrograph is produced by only a proportion of the total catchment, and this may under dry conditions be small, or, under conditions of low soil moisture deficits and high rainfall, large. Figure 4.7 illustrates for catchment 2, the maximum extent of the drainage net, the estimated contributing area, and the hydrograph response for two storms of five hours' duration. Figure 4.7a is based on a storm of 0.40 inches rainfall which occurred on 15 August 1967, when the conditions in the catchment were very dry, and the flow level immediately preceding the storm only 0.032 cusecs, whereas Figure 4.7b refers to a storm of 0.58 inches occurring on 1 November 1967, when the preceding flow level was 0.5 cusecs and when soil moisture levels in the catchment were very high. The hydrograph response has been portrayed by what we might term Unit Response Graphs, or the theoretical Quickflow hydrograph produced by 1 inch of effective rainfall and derived from the actual Quickflow hydrograph by assuming a linear extension such as is carried out in the derivation of simple Unit Hydrographs. Both these Unit Response Graphs are for a unit storm of five hours, but they exhibit different forms since

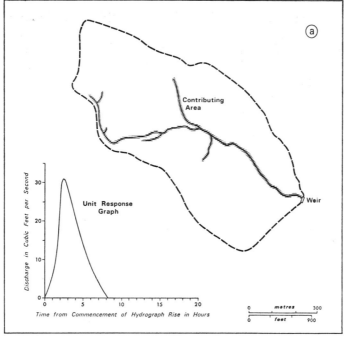

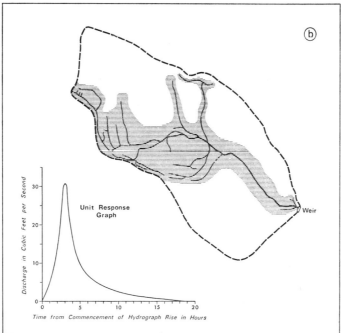

Fig. 4.7 The Unit Response graphs with approximate contributing area and functioning stream net during maximum discharge for two storms of five hours' duration on catchment 2.

they reflect control by the characteristics of the contributing area. The Response Graph for conditions of low soil moisture (Figure 4.7a) derives its character from the characteristics of the very narrow band of contributing area bordering the stream in the lower parts of the catchment; rise is rapid as there is little distance for runoff to travel before the maximum area is contributing to streamflow at the measuring weir; recession is equally rapid, since there is only a very small area from which storm runoff can drain. Conversely, in the case of Figure 4.7b the Response Graph rises more slowly since a longer time is required before the full source area is contributing to streamflow at the measuring weir, and the recession is more protracted as storm runoff drains and the functioning drainage density shrinks from a much larger area. The hydrograph response from a catchment will reflect the moisture conditions and the corresponding extent of the contributing area as well as the storm duration. When studying storm runoff, catchment characteristics must be viewed as dynamic parameters, for only under flood conditions will the streamflow hydrograph be produced by, and therefore reflect, the characteristics of anything approaching the entire catchment area.

CONCLUSION

Detailed study of the effects of catchment characteristics on streamflow from small instrumented catchments must necessarily emphasise the complexity of the relationships involved. However, a knowledge of the intricate control exerted by catchment characteristics is necessary before any worthwhile attempt can be made to apply studies of this topic to larger areas. When analysing the flow record from small catchments, one becomes aware of the problems involved in determining the origins and dynamics of runoff. Only when these are thoroughly understood will it be possible to determine the effects of catchment characteristics on runoff. Runoff from a drainage basin embodies a continuum of origins and it must be appreciated that the many different descriptive parameters of the runoff record will be controlled by different sets of catchment characteristics. Table 4.7 illustrates some of the many different facets of the runoff record that can be considered for these five catchments, together with the sets of catchment characteristics that appear to control them. The controls exercised by catchment characteristics on storm runoff are in particular very complex. If one accepts what has become known as the variable source area or partial area concept of runoff formation, then precise consideration should be given to the manner in which certain drainage basin characteristics influence the extent of the contributing area within a catchment and to the fact that the characteristics of the contributary area not of the overall catchment determine the precise nature of the runoff hydrograph. Amerman[30] has shown that any attempt to predict storm runoff from complex watersheds using data derived from small unit-source watersheds must involve consideration of the partial area concept of runoff production. The analysis of the complete streamflow record from a catchment, therefore, provides a much more effective basis for assessing the effects of catchment characteristics on streamflow from a catchment than the few runoff parameters listed

TABLE 4.7

Various streamflow parameters for the instrumented catchments
and associated dominant influencing catchment characteristics.

Streamflow Parameter	Dominant Influencing Catchment Characteristics
Water Balance Components	
(a) Annual Runoff	Topographic Aspect and Vegetation
(b) Monthly Runoff	Geology and Vegetation
Flow Duration Curves	
(a) Variability	Geology and Vegetation
(b) Minimum levels	Geology, Vegetation and Soil
(c) Maximum levels	Geology, Topography and Soil
Runoff Components	
(a) Component values	Geology, Vegetation and Soil
(b) Response Ratio	Geology, Vegetation and Soil
(c) Quickflow Duration Curves	Geology, and Aspect
Depletion Curves	Geology and Soil
Rainfall/Runoff Relations	
(a) Quickflow Volume	DYNAMIC CHARACTERISTICS and Geology, Vegetation and Soil
(b) Hydrograph Rise	DYNAMIC CHARACTERISTICS and Topography and Soil
Hydrograph Form	DYNAMIC CHARACTERISTICS

(It must be emphasised that the influence of any one catchment characteristic is difficult to isolate, for the characteristics are themselves closely inter-related).

for a gauging station in such publications as the Surface Water Yearbook.[31] Only when these effects are fully understood will it be possible to utilise the readily available published data.

ACKNOWLEDGEMENTS

The author is grateful to the Natural Environment Research Council who provided a research studentship during the tenure of which the research was carried out.

Thanks must also be expressed to the landowners in the study area who generously permitted the instrumentation of the catchments and allowed frequent access; to the Devon River Authority who provided advice and hydrometric data; and to Professor A. Davies and Dr K. J. Gregory, under whose guidance and encouragement the project was initiated.

G

APPENDICES

1   An approximation of the change in storage ($\triangle$ Storage) component of the **Water** Balance was made by extending the flow depletion curve at the end of the study period to the point where the discharge was equal to that at the beginning of the study period. Integration of the area beneath this extension provided a value of runoff storage which, added to an estimate of the likely evapotranspiration loss during the same period, gave a measure of storage increase. The extension of the recession curve was carried out by considering recessions for the summer period and estimating the likely form of the extension.

2   The Variability Index was derived slightly differently from that of Lane and Kai Lei.[18] The values of discharge at 10 per cent intervals from 0 to 100 per cent of the time were read off from the duration curve. The logarithms of these discharges were found and the Standard Deviation of these logarithms calculated to provide the variability index. Lane and Lei utilised the values at 10 per cent intervals between 5 per cent and 95 per cent of the duration, but these values do not take account of the extremes of the range of flows and the overall flow variability.

3   Estimates of the daily soil moisture deficit values were derived by using a daily budgeting procedure using the rainfall data from the central autographic raingauge and the values of potential evapotranspiration calculated by the Penman formula. Beginning with a period when the soil was at field capacity and hence possessed a zero soil moisture deficit, the cumulative effect of evaporation minus rainfall was calculated for each day. Since the maximum soil moisture deficit did not exceed 3.5 inches, no account was taken of the differences between actual and potential evapotranspiration rates.

REFERENCES

1 Natural Environment Research Council. *Hydrological Research in the United Kingdom* (1965-70) *Preliminary Report* (London 1970)
2 Benson, M. A. 'Factors influencing the occurrence of floods in a humid region of diverse terrain.' *US Geol. Survey Water Supply Paper* 1580-B (1963)
3 Bigwood, B. L. and Thomas, M. P. 'A flood-flow formula for Connecticut' *U.S. Geol. Survey Circular* 365 (1955)
4 Gray, D. M. 'Physiographic characteristics and the runoff pattern' in *Research Watersheds, Proceedings of Hydrology Symposium No. 4* (National Research Council of Canada 1965), 147-64
5 Lull, H. W. and Sopper, W. E. 'Factors that influence streamflow in the Northeast' *Water Resources Research* 2 (1966), 371-9
6 Schneider, W. J. 'Relation of Geology to Streamflow in the Upper Little Miami Basin' *Ohio J. Sci.* 57 (1957), 11-14
7 Striffler, W. D. 'Sediment, streamflow, and land use relationships in northern Lower Michigan' *U.S. Forest Res. Paper* LS-16 (1964)

8 Striffler, W. D. 'The selection of experimental watersheds and methods in disturbed forest areas' *Internat. Assoc. Sci. Hydrol. Pub. No. 66* (1965), 464–73

9 Shaw, E. M. 'The Devon River Authority Rain Gauge Network' *Weather* 21 (1966), 291–7

10 Kindsvater, C. E. and Carter, R. W. 'Discharge characteristics of rectangular thin plate weirs' *Proc. A.S.C.E. J. Hyd. Div.* 83 (1957), 1–36

11 British Standards Institution 'Measurement of Liquid flow in open channels; Thin plate weirs and venturi flumes' *B.S. 3680* Part 4A (1965)

12 British Standards Institution 'Measurement of liquid flow in open channels; Velocity area methods' *B.S. 3680* Part 3 (1964)

13 Berry, G. 'The evaluation of Penman's natural evaporation formula by electronic computer' *Austral. J. Appd. Sci.* 15 (1964) 61–4,

14 Meteorological Office '*The calculation of Evaporation from Meteorological Data*' (Met. Off. 1966)

15 Penman, H. L. 'Evaporation over the British Isles' *Q.J.R. Met. Soc.* 76 (1950), 372

16 Lee, R. 'Potential insolation as a topoclimatic characteristic of drainage basins' *Internat. Assoc. Sci. Hydrol. Bull.* 9 (1964), 27–41

17 Law, F. 'The effect of afforestation upon the yield of water catchment areas' *Jour. Brit. Waterworks Assoc.* (1956), 489–94

18 Lane, E. W. and Kai Lei 'Streamflow variability' *Trans. A.S.C.E.* 115 (1950), 1084–1134

19 Hewlett, J. D. 'Soil Moisture as a source of base flow from steep mountain watersheds' *U.S.D.A. Forest Service S.E. For. Expt. Sta. Paper* 132 (1961)

20 Giusti E. V. 'A relation between floods and droughts in the Piedmont Province in Virginia' *U.S. Geol. Survey Prof. Paper* 450 C (1962), C128–C129

21 Barnes, B. S. 'The Structure of discharge recession curves' *Trans. Am. Geophys. Union* 20 (1939), 721–5

22 Voronkov, P. P. 'Hydrochemical bases for segregating local runoff and a method of separating its discharge hydrograph' *Meteorologiya i Gidrologiya* 8 (1963), 21–8

23 Nash, J. E. and Sutcliffe, J. V. 'River flow forecasting through conceptual models. Part I—A discussion of principles.' *Journ. Hydrol.* 10, (1970), 282–90

24 Hibbert, A. R. and Cunningham, G. B. 'Streamflow data processing opportunities and application' *International Symposium on Forest Hydrology* ed. Sopper, W. E. and Lull, H. W. (Pergamon Press 1967)

25 Kirkby, M. J. and Chorley, R. J. 'Throughflow, overland flow and erosion' *Internat. Assoc. Sci. Hydrol. Bull.* 12 (1967), 5–21

26 T.V.A. 'Bradshaw Creek—Elk River: A pilot study in area-stream factor correlation' *T.V.A. Res. Paper No. 4* (1964)

27 Horton, R. E. 'Erosional development of streams and their drainage basins: hydrophysical approach to quantitative morphology' *Bull. Geol. Soc. Am.* 56 (1945), 275–370

28 Hewlett, J. D. and Hibbert, A. R. 'Factors affecting the response of small watersheds to precipitation in humid areas' *International Symposium on Forest Hydrology* ed. Sopper, W. E. and Lull, H. W. (Pergamon Press 1967)

29 Gregory, K. J. and Walling, D. E. 'The variation of drainage density within a catchment' *Internat. Assoc. Sci. Hydrol. Bull.* 13 (1968), 61–8

30 Amerman, C. B. 'The use of unit source watershed data for runoff prediction' *Water Resources Research* I (1965), 499–507

31 HMSO *Surface Water Yearbook of Great Britain* Published Annually.

5

Former Farms and Fields at Challacombe, Manaton, Dartmoor*

D. J. BONNEY

The significance of the extensive area of cultivation-remains surrounding the former hamlet or vill of Challacombe (now a cottage and a farm) in the parish of Manaton was first realised some thirty years ago and formed the subject of a pioneer study.[1] The following is primarily a consideration of the historical evidence relating to the settlement and its fields and largely complements the earlier study, which, understandably, concentrated on a description of the remains on the ground. These deserve attention as a remarkably complete example of what was once essentially an open-field layout—one largely isolated on the margins of cultivation high on Dartmoor and, because of the hill-slopes involved, consisting almost entirely of terraced strips commonly known as strip-lynchets. Whether or not the remains represent a 'common-field' arrangement as recently defined by Dr Joan Thirsk,[2] the documents which have so far come to light do not tell us. In fact, no clear information from any period appears to have survived as to the working of the land or as to what system or systems of crop rotation, manuring and fallowing were practised.

Challacombe is situated on the eastern side of Dartmoor on the lower slopes of the eastern of the two valleys which make the headwaters of the West Webburn River. It lies over three miles from Manaton village towards the western end of the long, narrow arm of the parish which extends into the granite area of the Moor proper. The field remains lie between 1,100 and 1,350 feet above Ordnance Datum on the lower valley slopes, between and east of the headwaters of the West Webburn; at present they are mostly under rough pasture, often with a thick cover of heather, bilberry and bracken (Fig. 5.1).

With few exceptions the remains consist of strip lynchets arranged end-to-end in furlong blocks and generally parallel to the contours. Some lynchets have almost certainly been destroyed within the walled closes immediately east of the north-south road through the valley, while other lynchets have been removed to facilitate ploughing in the fields north

*This essay was to have formed part of a wider study of field patterns and cultivation remains on Dartmoor. The more general account, which was to have been written by the late Dr A. H. Shorter, had reached only an early stage at his untimely death.

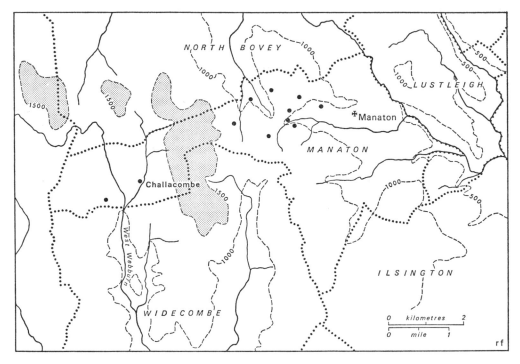

Fig. 5.1   Manaton Parish. The relationship of Challacombe and the other West Land settlements (marked by dots) to the main village.

of the present Challacombe Farm. Furlongs vary in length from 130 to 300 yards but the majority are under 200 yards. The longer ones are generally found on the gentler slopes where a slight reversed-S or aratral curve is often evident in plan. The risers or faces of the lynchets vary in height from $1\frac{1}{2}$ to 7 feet but most fall in the middle of this range. They are often very much spread, especially on the higher slopes, and, though heavily overgrown, they are frequently found to contain much stone, from large granite boulders to small blocks. In some instances the stones appear to be evenly laid, suggesting a deliberate bank or revetment built either before the lynchets had formed or during their accumulation. The treads, or cultivated surfaces, of the lynchets vary in width from 8 to 30 yards and a few are even wider, though in such cases later ploughing appears to have removed intermediate lynchets. In general, individual treads vary little in width along their length, except where a steepening slope forces them to narrow, but they do vary considerably within furlongs and are by no means always directly related to the degree of slope, i.e. the narrowest treads are not necessarily found on the steepest slopes.

Examination of the lynchet ends shows that in addition to the normal ramped, run-out and cupped forms many of the strips, in fact whole furlongs, now end abruptly at dividing banks crossing the lynchets at right angles. In the four furlongs which extend southwards from the Chagford/Manaton boundary on the east side of Challacombe Common, most of the strips end at low, spread banks extending up and down the hillside or at a sharp return upslope of the lynchet risers much reduced in height. But ground observation and air photographs (Pl. 6) indicate that the furlong-ends were formerly interleaved, as is common elsewhere in end-to-end arrangements of furlongs, though the evidence has largely been obscured by subsequent ploughing. South of these furlong-ends, the furlongs are divided by substantial banks, with a vertical stone face on one side fronted by a ditch, running up the hillside, while on the west side of Challacombe Common the furlongs are divided by low, grassy banks with a jumble of stone, including some orthostats, along them. In both these latter areas some of the banks clearly overlie the ends of strips and, therefore, represent a revision of the original furlong-ends. This revision cannot be dated with any certainty but may well be associated with the narrow ridge and furrow (narrow rig) which covers most of the lynchets and which represents a ploughing technique generally attributed to the late eighteenth or earlier nineteenth century. Certainly much of the narrow ridging appears to conform to the banks dividing the furlongs.

Remains of a different nature occur in the field south-west of Challacombe Farm. Here strips, up to 200 yards long, run up and down slopes across the contours in a north-south direction, narrowing towards the north. They are divided by low, spread banks often set along the edges of low lynchets falling towards the west. Faint traces beneath them of earlier strip lynchets which follow the contours suggest that they are not part of the original layout.

The vill of Challacombe—the settlement and its associated lands—consists of a clearly defined and largely isolated unit within the parish of Manaton. Only Soussons, once two farms but now deserted, flanks it on the west beyond the headwaters of the West Webburn, while on the east the large unenclosed tract of Hamel Down isolates it from the remainder of the parish. The settlement has attracted little attention, either historical or archaeological, but in a recent study of deserted sites on Dartmoor Mrs C. D. Linehan has provided a brief description of the remains of the former hamlet and alluded to some of the earlier documentary information attributable to it.[3]

The origin and early history of Challacombe eludes us. It was probably in existence at the time of Domesday Book and the Rev. O. J. Reichel suggested that it might possibly be identified in that record with the one virgate held by a knight, Roger, 'of Nicholas the crossbowman as of his manor of Buckland-in-the-Moor.'[4] This suggestion, and it can be no more, was prompted by the frequent appearance together, in feudal documents of the period 1242 to 1428, of Buckland and a place which Reichel tentatively identified as Challacombe. The name forms, however,—*Cherleton, Cherlecumb* 1242/3; *Therlecumbe* (sic) 1284/6; *Cherlecombe, Churlecombe* 1303; *Churleton* 1346; *Charleton* 1428—do not altogether inspire confidence in Reichel's identification and, significantly, have not been accepted as early forms of the name, Challacombe, by the English Place-Name Survey.[5] The Survey gives *Chalvecombe,* from an unpublished Court Roll of 1481, as the earliest form of the name and one certainly more acceptable etymologically. Challacombe would thus appear to emerge undisputedly into history in the late fifteenth century and from 1498 onwards it occurs frequently, in the form *Chalnecombe,* among the *fines villarum* included in the accounts of the Foresters of Dartmoor. It was a 'venville' settlement,[6] one of a number of villages and hamlets on and around Dartmoor, but lying without the Royal Forest, whose inhabitants had rights of common on the Moor. Venville, venfield, vyndefelde etc. is apparently a corruption of *fines villarum,* the fine representing a rent paid for the common rights. The accounts[7] show that Challacombe was paying a fine of 6d., presumably per annum, between 1498 and 1528, although totals are recorded for only four years. By 1532 this payment had increased to 10d. which was the amount continued at least until 1565.

Some indication of the size of the settlement is given in a copy of a rate levied in 1613 for the repair of Manaton church.[8] This lists what appear to be all the tenements within the parish and divides them into two groups headed East land and West land respectively. Under the latter twenty-one tenements are listed, among them South, South Middle, North Middle, North and East Challacombe. These same five tenements appear in a lease of 1880 and, with the exception of two which had been merged, were clearly definable at that date. Thus, whatever size the vill may have reached at an earlier period, it would appear that by 1613 it had stabilised at five tenements, each presumably with its own farmhouse and attendant buildings and each supporting at least a family unit. The rate levied on the tenements in the West land varied from 3s to 1s 4d per tenement. Two of the Challacombes paid the lowest rate and none exceeded 1s 8d. In fact their payments were among the lowest in the parish, since in general the tenements in the East land paid a higher rate than those further west on the Moor.

An estate survey of the Courtenays (Earls of Devon), undated but of the early eighteenth century, sheds further light on Challacombe and the activities of its inhabitants.[9] It relates to the Manor of Kenton which lay in two distinct parts—one, Kenton itself, along the western side of the Exe estuary adjacent to Powderham Castle, the seat of the Courtenays and the other 'in the manor of Manington near Dartmore in Devon west, from the former part 12 miles and is in one perifery.' The latter part consisted of 22 tenements—those of the West land in the 1613 rate together with a mill—all specified by name except the mill and '5 tenements in the small village called Challecombe'. The survey continues 'This part is very poor, cold and hungry grounds, full of rocks, and naturally heathy, but by the extra-ordinary pains and costs of its owners, produces good rye, some wheat, but more oats and barley. Here are some meadows between the hills, not sufficient to maintain their cattle in Winter were it not for the help of clover grass. Their Commons in this part are Heathy Downs . . . Hamble (Hamel) Downe is in common to all his Gracis tenements in this part as well as Tutebarro' where the said tenements cut turf for their present supply.' The survey then lists the tenements with their respective tenants, acreages and, in all but one instance, number of parcels into which they were divided. What can only be the Challa-combes appears as follows:—

tenants		tenement	acreage	parcels
John Langsworthy John, son	}	A tenement	55—3—37	8
John Pethebridge		A tenement	45—0— 2	10

tenants	tenament	acreage	parcels
John Pethebridge	A tenement	30—0— 1	5
William Willock			
William ⎫ Willock Peter ⎭	A tenement	72—1— 1	
Alexander Lemand	A tenement	67—2—25	13

A further Kenton survey of 1787[10] contains more detailed information relating to Challacombe, but only in respect of two tenements, each referred to as 'part of Challacombe' and otherwise unspecified by name. Their identity, however, may be established virtually beyond dispute by comparing them with the Land Tax Assessment of 1782. The latter shows that William Ponsford (sic) and Joan Burnelt (sic) held, though did not occupy, South Middle Challacombe and North Challacombe respectively. Further confirmation is provided in the case of South Middle Challacombe by the striking similarity between the field-names of the 1787 survey and those given in the Manaton tithe map and apportionment of 1842. No field-names are recorded for North Challacombe in the latter document but they do appear in the lease of 1880[11] and exhibit a certain, though less marked, similarity.

The survey gives further support for the evidence provided by the ground remains that some form of open-field cultivation was formerly practised at Challacombe, though precisely how much of the land was being cultivated on a regular basis by the late eighteenth century is not known. For each of the two tenements a list of *landscores* is given in addition to the names and acreages of a number of enclosed fields or closes (see below). The latter represent meadows, probably long enclosed and rarely cultivated, whose improved grazing formed a decided contrast to the rough herbage of the surrounding moorland. The term landscore (O.E. *land-scearu*) means generally a boundary, or a share or division of land and it has been shown elsewhere[12] that in Devon it is found in association with strip cultivation. In the present context there seems little doubt that it refers to divisions in the form of strips within the essentially open (? common) arable fields of Challacombe. Although the area of the landscores is unspecified, it is represented presumably by the discrepancy between the total acreage of each tenement and that of its closes. In both cases, out of a total of about 67 acres some 37 would appear to be in landscores and it is noticeable, and perhaps more than mere coincidence, that in the one instance where the total number of landscores is given their number is 37. We may be forgiven for comparing these with the classic acre strips which figure so prominently in the literature of agrarian history.

The landscores are variously grouped within a series of ten named units and the fact that each tenement has landscores in all the units indicates some intermingling of holdings; this is a further feature frequently, if not inevitably, associated with open-field cultivation. It would seem reasonable to compare these units, eight of which are termed *wares*, to the bundles of strips or lands, known as furlongs or shotts, which are a normal constituent of the open-fields elsewhere in England. The term *ware* is of some interest and would appear to be connected to *wara/werra*, 'a measure of land or unit of geld' and *warecta/waretum*, derived from *vervactum*, 'fallow or fallow-land'.[13]

'Mr Paunsford for part of Challacombe'
[South Middle]

'House, outhouses etc.,   16p.

1	Langscore	in	Overgang Ware	
2	Landscores	in	Roe	,,
2	,,	,,	Well	,,
3	,,	,,	Little	,,
5	,,	,,	West	,,
6	,,	,,	Middle	,,
7	,,	,,	Long	,,
4	,,	,,	Mill	,,
2	,,	,,	Hellens	
5	,,	,,	Casebury	

[37   ,,   Total]

	a.	r.	p.
*Stoney		2r.	1p.
Higher Park	2a.	1r.	17p.
Laver Park	1a.	1r.	5p.
Croffs			
Moorey	1a.	1r.	29p.
*Brook Meadow	1a.	1r.	10p.
Nearer Brook Meadow	2a.	2r.	33p.
*Lower State	2a.	2r.	33p.
*Catchit		3r.	7p.
*Cost Lost	3a.	3r.	29p.
*Broad Park	3a.	2r.	1p.
*Foot Land Field	2a.	2r.	26p.
*Foot Land	2a.	0r.	16p.
Gradnor	1a.	2r.	8p.
*Broad Meadow	2a.	2r.	12p.
Total	66a.	2r.	27p.

Total of closes	29a.	1r.	27p.
,, ,, landscores	37a.	1r.	0p.

A right of Common upon West Town
Coombe and Hambledown belongs to
this Estate.

West Down	125a.	
Coombe	58a.	1r.
Hambledown including		
Grims Pound	325a.	1r.

[*Names appearing under South Middle
Challacombe in tithe apportionment 1842].

'Joan Burnal for part of Challacombe'
[North]

'Scite of a house, barn and Linhay,
  Smallhay etc.,

3	Landscores in	Overgang Ware	
4	,, ,,	Roe	,,
3	,, ,,	Well	,,
2	,, ,,	Little	,,
		West	,,
		Middle	,,
4	,, ,,	Long	,,
2	,, ,,	Mill	,,
3	,, ,,	Hellens	
2	,, ,,	Casebury	

	a.	r.	p.
Haye		2r.	7p.
*Pound		3r.	13p.
Pits	2a.	3r.	24p.
Broad Park	1a.	1r.	22p.
Grimms Lake	1a.	3r.	25p.
Broad Park Moor	1a.	2r.	35p.
Moor		2r.	20p.
Willow Meadow	1a.	3r.	38p.
*Berry			
(Moor Suggs	10a.	0r.	34p.
*(Higher Moor Soggs	3a.	0r.	32p.
(Lower ,, ,,	5a.	1r.	9p.
Total	67a.	3r.	31p.

Total of closes	30a.	2r.	19p.
,, ,, landscores	37a.	1r.	12p.

A right of Common upon Coombe West
Down and Hambledown belongs in this
estate.

[*Names appearing under North
Challacombe in a lease of 1880].

Comparison of the 1787 survey with the tithe map and apportionment is instructive. For South Middle Challacombe, where a substantial number of the fields named in the survey occur in the later document, it is noticeable that they are all enclosed fields and that there is no mention of *landscores* or of *wares*. In fact *landscores* are not mentioned at all for Challacombe in the tithe apportionment and the term *ware* occurs only three times, each in the name of an enclosed field—Close Ware, Great Close Ware and Little Close Ware. It is significant, however, that of all the enclosed fields on the tithe map for which names are

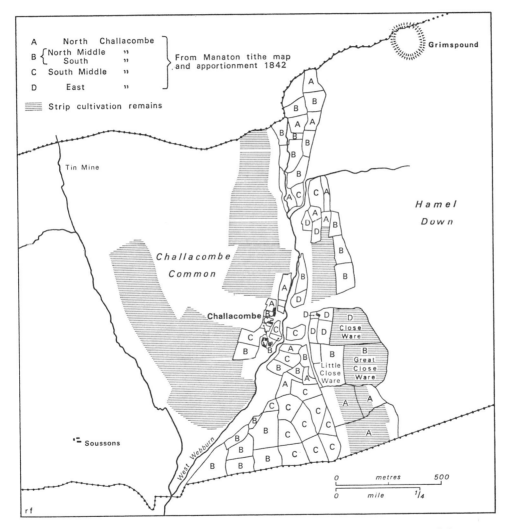

Fig. 5.2 Challacombe. The pattern of land holding in 1842 and the distribution of the surviving remains of strip cultivation.

given, these are the only ones which now contain, or appear ever to have contained, substantial remains of former strip cultivation, thus adding support for the idea that the *wares* and their *landscores* were essentially units of arable. (The fact that these names do not occur in the 1787 survey cannot be taken as evidence that the fields were enclosed after that date since the survey does not cover the tenements to which the fields belonged). Most of the area occupied by the strip lynchets is shown as unenclosed commons forming part of no one tenement and probably no longer arable, although unfortunately the column headed 'state of cultivation' in the tithe apportionment is left blank. But it must be observed that tithes of grain and corn for Challacombe were payable to a lessee of the Dean and Chapter of Exeter; this indicates that these commodities had once been grown there, even if this was not currently the case. One further point to be noted from the tithe documents is the somewhat scattered nature of even the enclosed fields belonging to each tenement; they do not consist of single, compact blocks (Fig. 5.2) as might have been expected.

By the mid-nineteenth century, whatever the position earlier, the inhabitants of Challacombe were occupied not only in agriculture but also in tin-working. The numerous overgrown hollows and spoil-heaps (Pl. 6) along the valley bottom as well as the scars in the valley sides (which in places cut the strip lynchets) and the abandoned tin mines to the north and west today bear eloquent if not elegant testimony to this former activity. To the north and north-west, within the radius of a mile, lay the Golden Dagger, the Birch Tor and Vitifer and the Headland tin mines, all long since abandoned. The Census returns of the mid-nineteenth century, however, provide clear evidence of the activities and social composition of the inhabitants of Challacombe and indicate their involvement in tin mining. The return of 1841 shows that from the five households four adult males were occupied in farming and two in tin-working, but a decade later the respective totals were six and ten, and in 1861 four and eight. The search for tin continued and in 1880 Moses Bawden, mine agent of Tavistock, leased for 21 years a parcel of land consisting of the enclosed fields of the five Challacombes together with Challacombe Commons and West Down 'with licence to sink pits etc.' But by 1906 (Ordnance Survey Six inch map 2nd ed.) the settlement had shrunk to its present proportions and today the extensive area of strip lynchets and the less obtrusive remains of the deserted farmsteads are the chief reminders of the former existence of the small farming community which once engaged in communal agriculture in this high and relatively remote corner of Dartmoor and by its means wrested a modest living from a difficult if not hostile terrain.

ACKNOWLEDGEMENTS

My thanks are due to the Royal Commission on Historical Monuments (England) for permission to use unpublished material in its archives.

REFERENCES

1 Shorter, A. H. 'Ancient Fields in Manaton Parish, Dartmoor' *Antiquity* 12 (1938), 183–9
2 Thirsk, J. 'The Common Fields' *Past and Present* no. 29 (1964), 3–25; also ensuing discussion in nos. 32 (1965), 86–102 and 33 (1966), 142–7

3 Linehan, C. D. 'Deserted sites and rabbit-warrens on Dartmoor, Devon' *Medieval Archaeology* 10 (1966), 113–44

4 Reichel, O. J. 'The Hundred of Haytor in the time of "Testa de Nevil" A.D. 1244' *Trans. Devonshire Assn.* 40 (1908) 110–37

5 Gover, J. E. B., Mawer, A., and Stenton, F. M. *The Place-Names of Devon* (Cambridge 1931–2), 481

6 Dartmoor Preservation Association *Dartmoor* (Plymouth 1890), 40; Yates, E. M. 'Dark Age and Medieval Settlement on the Edge of Wastes and Forests' *Field Studies* 2 (1965), 143–8

7 In Duchy of Cornwall Office. I am indebted to my colleague Dr B. E. A. Jones for consulting these records and others in the Devon County and Exeter City Record Offices.

8 Devon, C.R.O. 2B/6/4

9 Devon, C.R.O. 1508M/Surveys/Kenton/6

10 Kenton Survey Books 1787 2, 61–5: Devon C.R.O. 1508M/Estate Volumes/Surveys

11 Exeter City R.O. 56/1/1

12 Shorter, A. H. 'Landscore, Stitch and Quillett Fields in Devon' *Devon and Cornwall Notes and Queries* 23 (1949), 372–80

13 For these terms see Latham, R. E. *Revised Medieval Latin Word-List* (London 1965)

6

The Missing Maps from
John Norden's Survey of Cornwall

WILLIAM RAVENHILL

John Norden's maps of Cornwall, which were drawn for the *Speculi Britanniae Pars, A Topographical and Historical Description of Cornwall,* were until recently known only from their appearance in the version printed by William Pearson for the bookseller Christopher Bateman. It was published in London in 1728 and is, as far as the setting of the print allows, a page for page copy* of John Norden's manuscript in his own handwriting; this was dedicated and presented to King James I of England. The manuscript is still preserved in the Harleian Collection (Harl. MS 6252) in the British Museum, where the catalogue[1] describes it as 'A book in folio fairly written, entitled *Speculi Britanniae Pars . . .* Dedicated to James I. The title illuminated, the maps engraved with several coloured views etc. not dated, but apparently a copy presented to the King in MS.' The presence of several coloured views in Norden's own hand interlined in the text together with the absence of his manuscript maps —the engraved maps of the printed copy being inserted into the manuscript instead—has for many years presented an enigma; one deepened by Edward Lynam's provocatively ambiguous statement[2] in 1950, claiming that when the printed version was produced in 1728 the manuscript maps 'were missing, so Bateman substituted excellent contemporary maps.' The first question therefore that needs to be answered is whether Norden did actually produce any maps of Cornwall and if so at what date, and whether they were included in the manuscript presented to King James I. In the preliminaries to the manuscript after the dedication, Norden wrote that he was illustrating his description with a 'generall Charte or Mapp of Cornwall' and 'Maps . . . of the perticuler Hundreds' and proceeded to give two lists of conventional signs, followed by instructions on the use of his grid-reference system. Furthermore, the use of catchwords, as for example on the bottom of page 42 of the manuscript 'the Map of Kirrier,' is additional evidence in support of the former presence of maps. That maps of Cornwall were drawn by Norden was a view certainly held by Richard Carew of Antony, an eminent and knowledgeable contemporary,

---

*All page references are to the pagination in the printed edition of 1728. A reprint was made in 1966 by Frank Graham, Newcastle upon Tyne, but the pagination is different from the 1728 edition.

who, when revising his *Survey of Cornwall* for a second edition, wrote to Camden[3] from Antony on 13 May 1606 'if I wist where to find Mr Norden, I would also fain have his Map of our Shire: for perfecting of which he took a journey into these parts.'

The manuscript presented to King James I bears no date; nevertheless the period during which Norden was carrying out his 'perambulation, view and delineation' of the topography of Cornwall can be circumscribed with reasonable accuracy. In the Dedication, Norden refers to the occasion when 'under Your Majesties fauoure' he 'traveyled certayne dais journies on London waye in companie of Don Antonie' after the latter's arrival 'in the weste partes of this realme for refuge.' It seems, therefore, to have been in the early 1580s, when Norden was around 36 years old, that he was undertaking work for the Crown in the West Country.[4] The writing of the text must have taken place some years later than this, as the description of Mousehole (page 37) includes a reference to the burning of 'this litle village by the Spaniardes in anno 1595' and on page 14 Norden mentions 'the tynners beinge assembled at a courte at Lostwithiel in anno 1600.' Furthermore, the statement on page 9 that James's son had been invested Duke of Cornwall immediately after the decease of her late Majesty puts the date of final compilation after 1603. Norden had been in Cornwall to the certain knowledge of Richard Carew, who, as noted above, mentioned his maps in correspondence with Camden in 1606. It is known that Norden was out of favour with the Queen's ministers in the last years of Elizabeth's reign and it is on record that he wasted little time in trying to regain his former position after her death. In a complimentary address upon his majesty's accession in 1603, Norden pleaded for the King's support to continue 'the re-description of the shires of England, wherein to my great impoverishment I have travelled . . . And if it stand not with your gracious pleasure to employ my poor service in the former Descriptions, that your Highness would be pleased to employ the same in the survey of some of your Majestie's land.'[5] Norden was soon afterwards employed as a surveyor of Crown lands—by the end of 1603 if this is what he meant by his moan in 1619 about receiving only £500 for 'all my travayles both for Prince Henry and Prince Charles' over a period which, from the context, is sixteen years.[6] He appears to have received no support for his other request and so finally must have perished his vision of the *Speculum Britanniae*. Was it this realisation that finally led him to make available his materials to others? William Kip engraved the map of Cornwall for Camden's *Britannia* in 1607, and subsequently John Speed, with due acknowledgments, included a map of Cornwall in the *Theatre of the Empire of Great Britaine* in 1611. It is then most probable that Norden completed his manuscript and presented it to the King sometime between 1603 and 1607.

Although there is sufficient evidence to suggest that Norden did include his maps of Cornwall in the manuscript presented to the King, the mystery of their disappearance has, until recently, remained unsolved. The subsequent binding into the manuscript of the engraved maps, in place of the manuscript maps, is even more cartographically mysterious, particularly as Norden's map references in the manuscript text are incompatible with those of the engraved maps. The extent and distribution of this incompatibility for the General Map and the Hundred maps are shown in Table 6.1.

TABLE 6.1

Collation of the map references in Harleian MS. 6252,
the printed edition and the engraved maps of 1728.

	1. Total number of map references in text	2. Number of references changed in 1728 text	3. Number of references still incorrect on 1728 maps	4. Number of references in text not on 1728 maps
General Map	589	449	29	81
Penwith Hundred	87	1	19	0
Kirrier Hundred	83	1	36	2
Powder Hundred	103	19	9	1
Pyder Hundred	70	16	1	0
Trigg Hundred	59	11	0	2
Lesnewth Hundred	33	29	2	0
Stratton Hundred	35	0	5	0
West Hundred	54	8	3	0
East Hundred	80	12	1	3

Column 1 lists the total number of map references and column 2 gives the number of map references in the 1728 printed version which are different from those in the manuscript. Column 3 lists the number of references in the printed text which are incorrect for the printed map. Note that of the total of 589 map references for the General Map, 449 have been corrected to fit the 1728 engraved map. To have concocted the 1728 General Map from the manuscript references alone, or from a 'contemporary' map, would have been a labour of immense magnitude, but, if it were possible, then agreement between manuscript references and engraved map would follow as one would be derived from the other. Clearly therefore, some General Map must have existed between the manuscript text and engraved map. What is particularly striking about the figures for the Hundreds is the change which occurs after the first two Hundreds. In the cases of Penwith and Kirrier few changes have been made to the printed text and consequently a large number of wrong map references persists. In the rest of the Hundreds a number of changed references has been made and few references remain incorrect. How then are these incompatibilities between manuscript text and engraved maps to be accounted for? Why was the need for correction detected in the case of some Hundreds and not in others? Why was such an extensive and complicated editorial revision necessary and what is its cartographical significance? It may be that the different treatments accorded the Hundreds can be partly attributed to editorial carelessness, of which there must be some. A plausible explanation for the need of editorial correction is that the engraving from the original manuscript maps on to copper plates necessarily involved certain adjustments, but the adjustments required for each map were not necessarily the same and so no universality of treatment can result

H

or indeed be expected. In the order of engraving it can be seen that the inscribing of the grid lines comes late, almost last in fact, and certainly after the insertion of the place names. In the case of Penwith and Kirrier, the two Hundreds are so packed with place names that it is unreasonable to expect them—or the symbols representing them—to fall exactly within the same grid squares as in the original and in any case a certain engraver's licence must be allowed for. In support of this argument is the less crowded map of Stratton (only 35 references in all) where the engraved grid was made to coincide with that on the original, no corrections to the references being made. What is more, the arrangement of the references in this Hundred (and in East Hundred) indicates that the original maps were transversed to put north facing the right-hand side of the page, as is the case in the printed version. From this it may be inferred that Norden did not merely construct a map of the whole of Cornwall and then draw off the Hundreds on a larger scale. In Lesnewth nearly every reference has needed to be changed, but the nature of the corrections is peculiar, in so far as only figures have been changed by the addition of two digits, the letters remaining unaltered; for example, Botreaux Castle b6 in the manuscript becomes b8 in the printed text. Apart from this numerical change, the grid must lie coincident with the grid on the original manuscript from which we assume that it was copied. It would seem then that each Hundred received the treatment appropriate to its eventual placing on the copper plate—a further argument in favour of there having been maps bound in at their proper place in the manuscript text.

So overwhelming was the evidence that maps were drawn by Norden and that they had survived and were available to the engraver in the 1720s that further research seemed to be called for among any papers left by the personalities concerned with the printing in 1728.

The clue which led eventually to the solution of the problem of the missing maps was given by the frontispiece in the 1728 printed edition; it is an engraving of the 'West Prospect or Front' of St Germans in Cornwall and is in honour of Richard Rawlinson, DCL, FRS; this, with the other dedication to Edward, second Earl of Oxford (1689-1741), apparently acknowledges those to whom Bateman was indebted. By the late 1720s Richard Rawlinson was engaged in the administration of the estate of his bibliophile brother Thomas Rawlinson (1681-1725). Thomas had been a life-long antiquarian and in his day was known as the 'leviathan of book-collectors.' After Thomas died in 1725, Richard bought much of his late brother's library, but he, in his own right, was also a collector of printed books and manuscripts. 'Not a sale of MSS occurred, apparently, in London, during his time, at which he was not an omnigenous purchaser. But history in all its branches, heraldry and genealogy, biography and topography, are his specially strong points.'[7] On his death he willed most of his collection to the Bodleian—it is the largest donation that the library has ever received. Search through the catalogue[8] of this vast collection of manuscripts gave no hints that the maps might be concealed there but it did bring to light that in London in 1720, Richard Rawlinson published *The English Topographer or an Historical Account of all the Pieces that have been written relating to the Antiquities, Natural History or Topographical Description of any part of England*.[9] For Cornwall he provides, on pages 28–30, this pertinent bibliographical information. 'In the Hands of Roger Gale of Scruton in Yorkshire, Esq;

is a fair Manuscript Survey of Cornwall, wrote by Mr Norden, adorn'd with curious Miniatures of the greatest Remarkables; and another Copy of the same Manuscript is in the Possession of Mr Benjamin Cowse of London, Bookseller, who has long promis'd this Piece to the world; and one would imagine his own Interest, a prevalent Argument, would induce him to have perform'd it before this Time. One of the Copies of this Survey, viz. the best, was presented by the Author to King James I and after the Dispersion of the Royal Library fell into private hands.' From this extract by Rawlinson and from the mention of the names of Cowse and Lord Oxford, the search led backwards and forwards in time; names of others who had handled Norden's manuscript came to light, particularly in the Diaries of Thomas Hearne,[10] and, although no claim is made that all has been discovered about the transmission of the manuscript, enough is known to make possible an attempt at a chronological outline of the bibliographical provenance of both manuscript text and maps (Fig. 6.1).

John Norden completed his *Description of Cornwall* and sent it with the maps bound into the manuscript to King James I—hereafter referred to as manuscript A. It found a place in the Royal Library and acquired the Arms of England and France on its binding. It was included in a list of manuscripts at 'Whitehall',[11] 'made soon after 1641.'[12] According to the later testimony of the Cornishman, John Anstis (1669–1744), Heraldic writer and Garter King at Arms, 'an officer of the King's, during the Civil War time, got into the Library, and into the Jewel House, and divers offices, and carried away many of the Office-books, and other fine books from the Library: that these books do yet remain in Yorkshire, under six locks: that Mr Thoresby of Leeds has seen them; and that they will be sold.'[13] It is a well-recognised fact that wars and rumours of wars bring to the fore the need for maps and topographical literature. The presence of a King's officer would suggest a deliberate mission to collect such important material not only for the impending campaign but also in order to deprive the Parliamentarians of such valuable military information. It is possible that among these books which were removed could have been Norden's Cornwall and if this was the case then it could have been kept in a safe place for several years. Eventually, at some date before 1720, it must have come on to the booksellers' market and was then acquired by the London bookseller Benjamin Cowse.

In the year 1711 and again in 1714, Thomas Hearne was seeking information about Norden's Cornwall. Hearne (1678–1725) was employed in the Bodleian Library for many years of his life and maintained a constant correspondence with the antiquaries and literary men of his day. From 1705 to within a few days of his death, he kept an elaborate diary, giving lengthy entries about the books he read or those which came under his notice. Hearne wrote to John Anstis on 23 November 1714 'I hear you are giving us an Edition of Norden's Descr. of Cornwall with curious improvements of your own. There was a MS. of it formerly at St James's; but 'twas stole out with many MSS. besides.'[14] Hearne was in possession of this information because the 'Whitehall' list of manuscripts had been acquired by him some years previously in 1711. To Hearne's pointed sentence about a theft, Anstis in reply on 23 November 1714 was informative in another, but important, context. 'Norden's book came into the hands of the Earl of Aylesbury, was sold in the auction of his Lds. books,

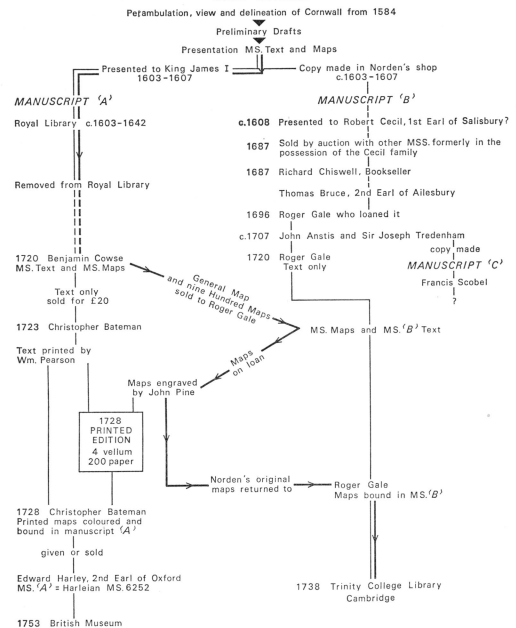

Fig. 6.1   Norden's Speculi Britanniae Pars: Cornwall, the transmission of the manuscript texts and maps.

and is now in the hands of Mr Gale the Younger, who intends to print it . . . The book is in the manner of Hertfordshire and Middlesex with some fine draughts of rocks etc.'[15] 'Norden's book' which was referred to in this letter was not manuscript A, but a copy of it which was acquired by Roger Gale—hereafter designated manuscript B (Fig. 6.1).

Manuscript B is a scribe's copy, in an early seventeenth-century hand, of manuscript A and not a copy of any preliminary drafts of A. This is evident as the scribe faithfully copies the page numbers of the list of contents of manuscript A and, since the scribe's hand is much larger than Norden's handwriting, twice as many pages are filled in manuscript B as are needed for manuscript A; therefore the page references in the list of contents are at variance with those in the text. As yet the early provenance of manuscript B is not known for certain but there is some evidence to suggest that after manuscript A was completed a copy was made, probably by a scribe in Norden's workshop, and this copy may subsequently have been sent to Robert Cecil, the first Earl of Salisbury, who was Norden's one time patron and employer. In 1687 an auction was held at which manuscripts formerly in the possession of the Cecil family were sold.[16] The sale catalogue includes 'Norden (Jo.) Speculum Britanniae, A Topographical and Historical Description of Cornwall.'[17] It was purchased by the bookseller Richard Chiswell and when next heard of, it was in the possession of Thomas Bruce, the second Earl of Ailesbury; at an auction of his books manuscript B was purchased by Roger Gale who is reported as having it in his library by 1696.[18] Some time between 1696 and 1707 manuscript B was probably on loan in the hands of John Anstis, according to the testimony of the Cornishman Thomas Tonkin,[19] who, many years later (1733) wrote, 'John Norden, whose Description of Cornwall, dedicated by him to King James the First was lately printed; which, though but a mean performance, full of many egregious mistakes, with most defective and eroneous maps of every hundred: yet as there are several things in him hardly to be met with elsewhere, I have not scrupled to cull them out of his heap, always mentioning from whence I had them. This book of his I had many years since seen in MS. with Mr Anstis: and there is a copy of it taken by the late Sir Joseph Tredenham, . . . now in the hands of his son-in-law, Francis Scobel, Esq.'[20] Tonkin's testimony is of value in providing the background to the correspondence between Anstis and Hearne, quoted above for the 23 November 1714. It should be noticed that the same letter speaks of 'fine draughts of rocks etc' but no information is given about any maps. Manuscript B, at this stage, had no maps; this is made clear by Rawlinson who, in his attempt to keep his personal copy of The English Topographer up to date, wrote a marginal annotation alongside 'Roger Gales copy' 'This wants the maps.'[21]

Benjamin Cowse, who had acquired manuscript A, was in business at the Rose and Crown, St Paul's Churchyard and a frequent visitor at his shop was Humfrey Wanley. Wanley was Library-Keeper to Robert Harley, the first Earl of Oxford, and Edward, his son, the second Earl. From 1715 to 1726 Wanley kept a diary[22] in which he recorded the visits of, or to, booksellers as well as negotiations with them. In his diary on 30 March 1720 Wanley says that he visited Cowse and 'disposed him to trade with my Lord for . . . his MS of Nordens Survey of Cornwall, now printing.' There is no subsequent confirmation in the diary that Wanley succeeded in effecting a purchase but both Hearne and he provide other evidence that Benjamin Cowse held on to the manuscript some time longer but was induced to remove the maps from manuscript A and sell or give them to Roger Gale, who inserted them in manuscript B. 'Mr Cowse hath Norden's Original Book from whence the Maps were taken and putt into Dr Gales' wrote Wanley in the margin of his personal copy of Nicolson's *English Historical Library*.[24] Benjamin Cowse gave up his bookselling business in 1723 and by 1726 had sold manuscript A, now minus the maps, for £20 to his friend and business associate Christopher Bateman, whose bookshop was at the Bible and Crown, Paternoster Rowe, London. Bateman was a highly respected and noted bookseller, renowned for his honesty and fair dealing. By September 1726 he seems to have fallen on hard times and, assisted by friends, hoped to redeem himself by printing Norden's Cornwall.[23] Already by this date the miniatures in manuscript A had been engraved and the printing was 'very forward' by 12 October 1727.[25] For some years past the manuscript maps had been with Roger Gale, but he was quite willing to lend them to Bateman so that they could be engraved and published. The manuscript maps, therefore, were separated temporarily from manuscript B and were on loan to Bateman, who arranged for the engraving to be done—probably by John Pine at the Print Shop in St Martin's Lane. Now, with hindsight, it can be said that both the General Map and the nine Hundred Maps were carefully handled both by the engravers and by Bateman. On 13 May 1728 Hearne[26] wrote in his diary 'Norden's Chorographical Description of Cornwall is printed pompously at London in 4to. Four were printed on Vellom, one for the Earl of Oxford, the Patron, who gave £50 to poor Christopher Bateman under the notion of Editor, another Dr Rawlinson hath, and two others are in private hands.'[27] These gifts of vellum copies to those who had helped to see a volume through the press were a typical eighteenth-century gesture on the part of map publishers but the diary entry is also valuable in providing an explanation for the two dedicatory engravings and preliminaries of the printed version as well as the next move of manuscript A. It is fortunate that Hearne uses the phrase 'under the notion of Editor' with regard to the Earl of Oxford, because the 1728 printed volume contains four pages entitled 'Some Account of the Author, by the Editor.' In this account both the style and information are similar to that found in *The English Topographer* and Hearne is able to confirm that this account of Norden was penned by Richard Rawlinson.[28] In addition, Rawlinson must have helped by generally encouraging and supporting the publication and so deserved the dedication which is attached to the engraving of 'The West Prospect of St German's in Cornwall.' In some copies this engraving is placed, not among the preliminaries, but facing the alphabetical entry for St Germans on page 39. For the patron and subscriber, Lord Oxford, what recognition and recompense for such timely largesse could Bateman make? Hearne, who claimed to have known Bateman for nearly 30 years before 1731, remembers him as a person 'regardless of money'[29] and one 'who cannot be prevailed upon to take it.'[30] A sumptuously engraved dedication was printed and bound in the 1728 edition but it would have been in keeping with Bateman's personality to do more than this. Could it have been he who arranged for a set of the engraved maps to be coloured with the same hues as those on the original maps and inserted into manuscript A, afterwards presenting it, cartographically complete, to Lord Oxford? In his library it became catalogued with the number 6252 and in 1753 was transferred to the Harleian Collection in the British Museum, where it now is. Meanwhile some 200 copies[31] of the printed edition were produced but Bateman did not live to enjoy the receipts, if indeed there were many, for 'he died but poor and was buried on Monday night July 26 1731 at the Church of St Gregory, near St Paul's.'[32]

The engraving of the maps for the printed edition having been completed, Christopher Bateman returned the original manuscript maps to their owner. On 30 May 1728 Hearne heard of this and was able to record in his diary[33] 'The mapps in Norden's Cornwall, lately printed, Mr Bateman borrowed of Roger Gale, Esq. They were returned to Mr Gale again, who had also in lieu of his lending them three Copies. These Mapps without doubt belonged originally to the MS. that Mr Bateman hath and printed from, it being, as appears by the Royal Arms on the Cover on each side, the very book the Author presented to the King. And I make no question, but 'tis that very MS. that was formerly in the Royal Library in St James's, tho' gone since.' From this date nothing more seems to have been heard specifically about the manuscript maps. It will be remembered, however, that Roger Gale had manuscript B; the subsequent transmission of this was clearly the next stage calling for the present investigation. Roger Gale died in 1744 but six years previously, on 21 July 1738, he wrote from Scruton near Bedale, Yorkshire, that he was despatching to Trinity College, Cambridge, by the Richmond carrier, a load of manuscripts. 'In such a collection' he informed the 'gentlemen' at Trinity 'there must be some that may be lookt upon as trifles, but when you examine the whole, I am confident you will allow more of them to be of value, and some to be very rare and curious . . .'[34] Included in this collection was manuscript B and bound into the text in their appropriate places were Norden's original manuscript maps. On the return of the maps from Bateman, Roger Gale had seen to their preservation for ten years and then arranged for both them and manuscript B to be conveyed into the safe keeping of Trinity College, where he, and his father before him, had been scholars and fellows.

In all there are ten maps, as indeed Norden said there were in his 'Rules of Direction towching the Use of the Booke' (page 5 of manuscript A, Harl. MS. 6252)—'the general Charte or Mapp of Cornwall, and therein all the principall townes, parishes, chiefe hamlets, howses of name, Castles, Ryvers, Brookes, Rills, Harbors, Hauens, Coues, Creekes, principal Hills, Rockes, Mynes, and other necessarie obseruations. All which are more at large expressed in the Maps . . . of the perticuler Hundreds'—'Penwithe, Kirrier, Powder, Pyder, Trigg, Lesnewth, Stratton, Weste, Easte.' That these maps were originally in Harl. MS. 6252 there can be no doubt, for in addition to the documentary sources already referred to, there is supporting evidence to link the maps and the text: both are in Norden's hand and style; both have watermarks of identical variety, while the map references of the text fit the maps. That these original maps by Norden were available to the engraver in 1728 is also proved, not only by the overall similarity of detail but also by a wax-rubbing on their backs associated with the tracing process. What is more, the engraver has copied Norden's errors. One of the most glaring of these is placing the title 'Part of Powder Hundred' to the west of East Hundred where in truth West Hundred should be.

At an earlier stage in this essay it was pointed out how the incompatibilities in the grid references between the engraved maps and Harl. MS. 6252 directed the course the research should take and how they led to certain inferences being drawn. Now that the manuscript maps have been located it is possible to compare the originals with the engraved maps and to replace inference by visual observation. On the original manuscript maps the grid northings and eastings (designated respectively by lower-case letters and numbers) are boldly and clearly shown on the divided map borders. In contrast, the grid lines extending from these across the map are made in extremely fine and faint pencil but, in view of the clarity of the border divisions, there is no great problem presented to the engraver in making a copy by tracing, if this were the only detail to be copied. In association with all the other information to be shown, however, there certainly was a problem and as the insertion of the grid came late in the order of copying it was probably not traced but ruled in after the divisions were set out by dividers. On the General Map there are 33 easting squares in a distance of 387 mm and 23 northing squares were required to be inserted in 270 mm; as a result of ruling rather than tracing, the engraved grid lines are very nearly, but not quite, in the same places as on the manuscript maps. This very small lack of coincidence in such a closely-set mesh of squares is sufficient to account for the need of making the 449 changes in the printed text (Table 6.1).

On the maps of Penwith and Kirrier, Norden's original manuscript maps cover more extra-hundredal ground than the engraver put on his copper plates and the grids on the respective maps are not in coincidence. On the Penwith maps the northings are different; on the Kirrier maps the eastings are misplaced. Why the need for editorial correction was not detected is a mystery. Was it just an oversight or was it that the type for these two hundreds had been set and that the cost of printer's corrections was more than Bateman's resources could pay for? On the respective maps of Powder the eastings are not quite in coincidence but the need for checking the references was noticed and as Table 6.1 shows, a number of changes was made. On the maps of Pyder and Trigg Hundreds both eastings and northings are not in coincidence but in these two hundreds very successful editorial emendations were made. The inference made earlier for Lesnewth can now be confirmed as fact; Norden started his number references further east than the engraver did and this explains the need for every reference to be changed by the addition of two digits, the letters remaining unaltered. Less confusion would probably have arisen if the engraver had copied Norden's format more closely and placed the numbers in the middle and not in the corners of the squares. The grids coincide on the maps of Stratton and no changes of reference were made but this is not the same as saying that all the references are thereby correct. Of further interest is the confirmation that Norden did transverse the map of this hundred and that of East to put north facing the right-hand side and not, as is the case in all the other maps, at the top of the page. On the maps of the two remaining hundreds, West and East, there is only a small lack of grid coincidence but the need for editorial adjustments was seen and these were undertaken.

Norden was a pioneer in the use of grids on maps but it was a very much simpler matter for him to draw them in faint pencil lines on his manuscript maps and then cover them with other symbols in ink and colour than it was for the engraver to cut them in copper plates without impairing the clarity of other details. It is not surprising therefore, to find that on most of the maps the engraver did not make a perfect copy of Norden's grid lines—an engraver's inconsistency which, the author hopes, Arthur Davies will regard with indulgence, for without that inconsistency this particular essay in his honour could not have been written.

ACKNOWLEDGMENTS

For their kind co-operation and assistance the author wishes to thank Dr Philip Gaskell, Trinity College Library, Cambridge; R. Fairclough and E. A. B. Owen, University Library, Cambridge; Miss Susanna Guy, Exeter University Library; Miss Lancaster, Devon and Exeter Institution and Dr R. A. Skelton who, in addition to commenting on an early draft of the essay, has significantly contributed to the author's knowledge of John Norden.

REFERENCES

1 Catalogus Librorum Manuscriptorum Bibliothecae Harleianae 1808
2 Lynam, E. 'English Maps and Map-makers of the Sixteenth Century' *Geog. Journ.* 116 (1950), 20
3 Gulielmi Camdeni Epistolae Epist. 58 (London 1691), 72
4 Norden seems to have used the opportunity when surveying manors to prepare his county maps and descriptions 'I tooke occasion in my travayle in those parts to performe it after this poore sort, being otherwise imployed in surveyes theare.' Dedication in *Speculi Britanniae Pars altera: Northamptonshire.*
5 British Museum Royal MS. 18 A xxiii.
6 Duchy of Cornwall, E.M. 5, Courts of Survey Minutes, fo. 178b.
7 Macray, W. D. *Annals of the Bodleian Library* (Oxford 1890), 234
8 Madan, F. *A Summary Catalogue of Western Manuscripts in Bodleian Library at Oxford* 3 (Oxford 1895), 177–556
9 Rawlinson, R. *The English Topographer* (London 1720)
10 Hearne, T. *Remarks and Collections of Thomas Hearne* 1–11 various editors (Oxford 1889–1915)
11 Bodleian Library Smith MSS. 34 (olim 25), 105
12 Madan, F. op. cit. 458
13 Wanley's Memorandum Book, British Museum, Lansdowne MS. 677
14 Hearne, T. Diary 56 Bodleian Library, Rawl. MS. 15179
15 Bodleian Library, Rawl. MSS. Letters 19, 33
16 The author is indebted to Dr R. A. Skelton for the information about the transmission of manuscript B through the Cecil Library.
17 Mattingley, H., Burnett, I. A. K., Pollard, A. W. *List of Catalogues of English Book Sales 1676–1900* (British Museum 1915), 124. f. 17 and 821.i.8 (i)
18 Nicolson, W. *The English Historical Library* (London 1696), 29
19 See his letter among the preliminaries of Lord de Dunstanville, *Carew's Survey of Cornwall* (London 1811), xxxiii
20 In order to maintain bibliographical clarity, the copy made by Sir Joseph Tredenham is designated manuscript C.

21 Rawlinson, R. *The English Topographer* (London 1720) Bodleian Library Gough MS. 17669 Gen. Top. 193, 29

22 *The Diary of Humfrey Wanley* British Museum Lansdowne MSS. 771 and 772 but may be consulted more conveniently in Wright, C. E. and R. C. *The Diary of Humfrey Wanley* (London 1966).

23 Hearne, T. *The Remarks and Collections of Thomas Hearne* 9 ed. Salter, H. E. (Oxford 1914), 189

24 Nicolson, W. *The English Historical Library* (London 1714) Bodleian Library, H 9 5 Art

25 Hearne, T. op. cit. 9, 355

26 Hearne, T. *Remarks and Collections of Thomas Hearne* 10 ed. Salter, H. E. (Oxford 1915), 13

27 Ellis, H. ed. *Speculi Britanniae Pars: An Historical and Chorographical Description of the County of Essex by John Norden, 1594* (London 1840), xxi

28 Hearne, T. *Remarks and Collections of Thomas Hearne* 10 ed. Salter, H. E. (Oxford 1915), 131

29 Hearne, T. Ibid. 441

30 Hearne, T. Ibid. 102

31 Hearne, T. Ibid. 17

32 Hearne, T. Ibid. 441

33 Hearne, T. Ibid. 17

34 James, M. R. *The Western Manuscripts in the Library of Trinity College Cambridge* 3 (Cambridge 1902) xii

7

The Ordnance Survey and the Origins of Official Geological Mapping in Devon and Cornwall

J. B. HARLEY

Devon and Cornwall were among the earliest counties to be mapped by the newly established Ordnance Survey in the opening years of the nineteenth century. In the 1830s they also became the nursery of official geological mapping in England and Wales, and, although separated by over twenty years, the two developments were an integral part of the continuous development of official map-making at a regional and national level. Far from being separate historical strands, topographical and geological mapping were often delicately interrelated and this essay describes the nature and causes of the interaction as well as its consequences for the development of the Ordnance Survey maps of South-West England. The history of cartography, like the history of science in general, is concerned, not only with impersonal technical developments, but also with an interplay of people and policies at a national and local level, set in the context of general social and economic history. The unpublished correspondence of Sir Henry de la Beche, the founder of the official geological survey, together with Ordnance papers in the Public Record Office and at Southampton, enables us to appreciate the contribution of such human factors to a regional chapter of the history of map-making—the origins as well as the repercussions of which extended far beyond the boundaries of Devon and Cornwall.

I

One of the more striking aspects of the history of the Ordnance Survey in the first half of the nineteenth century was a rapidly growing recognition of the value of its maps both in the practical implementation of plans for social and economic improvement and in the systematic field study of sciences such as archaeology and geology. If the original *raison d'être* of the Trigonometrical Survey of England and Wales was to further geodetic science, and if, during the Napoleonic War, the strategic uses of maps were often uppermost in official thinking, the years after 1815 brought new vistas to the Survey. Demands for the speedy publication of the First Edition one-inch maps, primarily with their utility in civilian affairs in mind, came from counties stretching from Lincoln to Shropshire. In 1818 Thomas Colby, the deputy director of the Survey (after 1820 its Superintendent) could ask rhetorically '. . . to what more proper object can the survey be directed in time of peace, than to aid the general improvement of the country.'[1] He was commenting on a request by the gentlemen of Lincolnshire to have the Ordnance maps of their county surveyed out of turn in order to facilitate schemes for drainage and enclosure, but maps were also recognised as tools in the process of industrial expansion, in the planning of towns and in the engineering of new forms of inland transport. At a more academic level, the Ordnance Survey made a notable contribution in the nineteenth century to the mapping and recording of field antiquities, to the study of local orthography and to geological mapping—the central theme in the present essay.

In the first three decades of the nineteenth century the policy of the Board of Ordnance towards geological mapping tended to be ambivalent. The first deliberate step by the Survey to involve itself in geological work was the appointment, in May 1814, of Dr John Macculloch as Geologist to the Trigonometrical Survey.[2] His assignment, however, was not to prepare a geological map of the country, but rather to locate areas in Scotland where abnormal deflections of the plumbline might be expected, so that they could be avoided in the geodetic measurements for establishing a meridian for the construction of the one-inch map.[3] Not until 1826 was he officially employed in the systematic mapping of the geology of Scotland and then only after a period (from 1820) when the Treasury had refused to sanction expenditure on the project.[4] Even when the Survey was established, the lack of an accurate base map—Macculloch had to plot on the out-dated and unreliable map of Arrowsmith—was a primary handicap to his work in Scotland. As he was to point out later, a geologist able to work on the Ordnance Survey maps of England was uniquely fortunate:

> 'It would require but a small geologist indeed to lay down the rocks of any part of England on the Ordnance Maps; he is to be envied on whom such a duty may hereafter fall.'[5]

In England, however, where the publication of the one-inch maps had reached as far north as the Midlands by the late 1820s, the Government was apparently reluctant to become financially committed to a programme of geological mapping. By 'Government' it should be stressed that this does not imply the officers directing the Survey, nor even the Master General and the Board of Ordnance, but the Lords of the Treasury to whom the Board was finally accountable for its expenditure. Had it been left to Colby and some of his officers, the Geological Survey might well have been founded sooner. In the survey of Ireland Colby had advocated 'that the topographical survey should be considered a foundation for Statistical, Antiquarian, and Geological Surveys' and, in 1832, J. E. Portlock was charged with the organisation of a geological branch.[6] In England Colby, it was said, had encouraged his surveyors 'during their labours in the field' to keep a 'register of the mineral changes accompanying variations in the outlines of the land'[7] and he was a conscientious

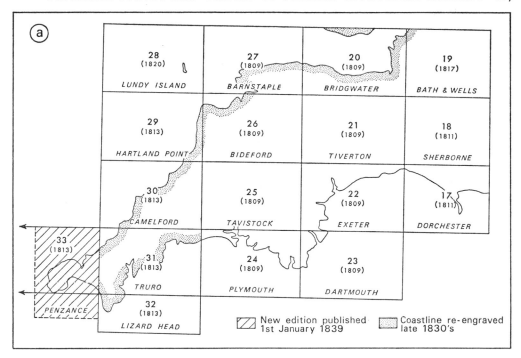

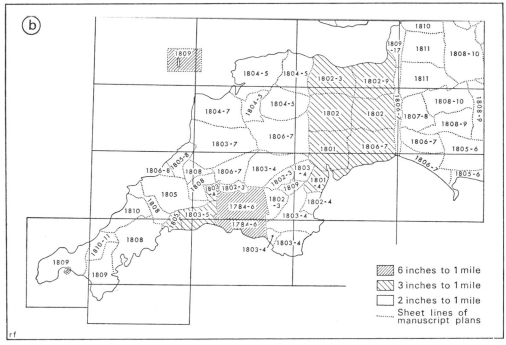

Fig. 7.1 The *Old Series* Ordnance Survey One-Inch Maps for South-West England.
(a) Dates of first publication and of re-engraving. The original sheet names and numbers are indicated.
(b) Scales and dates of topographical survey. Based on an index map in the British Museum, Maps Ref B. 4a.

member of many of the scientific societies of his day—including the Geological Society of London from 1814.[8] Several of his officers were also keen students of the geological phenomena encountered in the course of their regular work and indeed the problem was to ensure that this activity did not interfere with the normal progress of the topographical surveying. Something of Colby's dilemma is illustrated in February 1832, on the eve of the events in South-West England to be described later. John R. Wright, an assistant surveyor, had sent Colby the NE quarter of the Leominster sheet (Ordnance Survey, *Old Series,* sheet 55), with geological annotations and when Colby forwarded it with an enthusiastic letter to R. I. Murchison, the President of the Geological Society, he made a special point of stressing that 'Mr Wright has not injoyed the leisure to Study these progressive improvements of Geology which are gradually advancing it towards the state of an exact science.'[9] In his reply to Wright, on the other hand, approval had to be tempered with official caution:

> 'An intimate knowledge of the stratification and of the Geological features of a Country is highly useful in the delineation of the form of the hills; and I have always been of opinion that this knowledge might be collected in passing over a country for the formation of a map, without any sacrifice of time. But I know there are persons who look upon Geological examinations as a distinct labour which interferes with the operations of the Survey and retards its progress: it will therefore, be requisite to make the Geological examinations so subservient to the Map that no delay whatever may be imputed to the Department.'[10]

In this, as in other instances, Colby's scientific leanings were inhibited by financial restrictions. Geology, in Portlock's words, was at best 'permitted, not commanded', and, had it not been for powerful outside pressures, the Board of Ordnance might have been even slower in lending its formal co-operation to the work of geological mapping than it was.

Outside the Ordnance Survey, the principal advocates of a national geological survey fell into two main groups. First, there were the quickly growing ranks of the amateur and professional geologists, whose forum was the Geological Society of London, founded in 1807; and, secondly, a broader group of organisations and individuals who recognised the considerable practical use of geological maps. Both professionals and laymen were unanimous in regarding the one-inch maps of the Ordnance Survey as a means by which their aims might be accomplished. As early as 1805—when the Ordnance Survey had produced maps of only Kent and Essex—Sir John Sinclair, erstwhile President of the Board of Agriculture, had suggested that William Smith, the pioneer geologist, might be 'attached to the corps of engineers who are surveying the country, with a view to recording the results of his geological examination upon the maps then in course of preparation.'[11] Nothing was done, however, but, as they appeared, the Ordnance maps were a stimulus to other geologists. One of the earlier essays in plotting geological information on Ordnance maps was that of William Lonsdale of Bath, who on 6 February 1829 read his paper to the Geological Society of London 'On the Oolitic District of Bath . . . illustrated by the corresponding sheets of the Ordnance maps so far as they have been hitherto engraved, coloured geologically . . .'.[12] He was to comment later on 'the great advantage he possessed in having the Ordnance Maps for the base of his survey' and was supported by Dr W. H. Fitton, the President of the Society:

> 'to geologists who have travelled in England, I need not mention the benefits that our science has derived from the maps already engraved; nor dwell upon the misery of plunging from a tract that we have traversed with the advantage of this guide, into regions where the survey leaves us lost, as it were, and bewildered from the want of such assistance. . . . the want of adequate maps may cause the final and irreparable loss of much geological inform-ation.'[13]

The example of Lonsdale's work is not unique, but it epitomises the high esteem in which the Ordnance maps were held by the generation of geologists whose leaders were to influence the course of events in Devon and Cornwall.

II

Official mapping and amateur enthusiasm in geological survey were brought into per-manent harness in Devon and Cornwall. That the region can claim precedence was owing to several factors. First, the one-inch maps of the Ordnance Survey, praised so highly by contemporary geologists, were among the earliest in the country to be published—in Devon in 1809 and in Cornwall in 1813 (Fig. 7.1a). Secondly, South-West England was not only an area of considerable intrinsic geological interest, but also (a critical argument to the political economists of the day) a region with an important mining industry which might benefit considerably from accurate geological survey. Thirdly—and closely related to the second point—there was a long tradition of geological research in Devon and Cornwall: when Henry de la Beche published his memoir on the geology of the region in 1839 his bibliography was extensive and included contributions by many of the most eminent geologists, both past and present.[14]

Such auspicious conditions did not in themselves give birth to the official geological survey, but found a catalyst in Henry de la Beche (1796–1855), a forceful personality and an outstanding pioneer of geology.[15] Although he had been born in London, De la Beche had spent part of his childhood in south Devon and went to school at Ottery St Mary. He had been a Fellow of the Geological Society since 1817 and when he returned to work in South-West England after 1830 he had considerable geological experience in the field—in England and Wales, in Jamaica (on the occasion in 1824 of a visit to the paternal estates), and more particularly in the West Country (in November 1827, for instance, he had read a paper before the Geological Society of London on the geology of the south Devon coast, near Babbacombe and Torbay). He was not a rich man, but had sufficient means to allow full-time devotion to his geological pursuits. By 1832 he was well qualified and doubtless felt confident as he formulated a scheme to enlist the support of the Board of Ordnance in his plan to apply geological colouring to the eight sheets of the Survey covering Devon.

His initiative, the first step in the founding of an official geological survey under the wing of the Ordnance Survey, is most easily understood from the words of his letter to the Master General of the Board of Ordnance, dated 28 March 1832:

'Having applied myself to the Study of Geology for many years and having directed much of my attention to the Geological relations of this my native country (as may be seen in several published works & in various memoirs published in the Transactions of the Geological Society, and in the different Scientific Journals of this country) and being convinced of the great practical utility of what I am about to propose, I offer no apology for intruding myself on the notice of your Hon.[ble] Board with a view to obtain the completion of an undertaking which has for some time past occupied much of my time and attention; one that I had set out with the intention of accomplishing at my own proper cost, but in which I am defeated by the failure of certain funds I had intended to apply to that purpose. I am induced therefore to offer to your Hon.[ble] Board the fruits of my labours at a price that I am well assured will be considered *very moderate* knowing as I do that it will be much below the sum they will have cost me when completed. As I really have not the slightest intention of deriving pecuniary profit from this undertaking but merely seek a reimbursement of the extra expenses it must necessarily entail upon me; I shall hope to receive your support to the extent I propose, should I make it appear that my terms are likely to prove advantageous to the Ordnance.'[16]

The 'price' suggested by De la Beche was £300. For this sum he offered to add geological information, within the space of two years, to the Ordnance Survey maps covering Devon (*Old Series* sheets 20 to 27 inclusive) and to 'lay down the detail accurately to scale and properly coloured upon each of those sheets, in so clear and intelligible a manner as to admit of its being readily transferred upon the Ordnance Copper Plates.'[17] The case was prepared astutely. As well as securing the support of his friend Adam Sedgwick, the Professor of Geology at Cambridge, De la Beche had analysed the probable cost of the work in a business-like fashion, resulting in a selling price for the maps, with added geological information, which would bring a profit to the Board. The letter ended with a peroration on the value of the enterprise

'conferring a great benefit on a Science that is every day increasing in interest and importance, the Government will convince the public that it is disposed to assist the progress of Science in this country, and would forward a work which would be of great practical utility to the Agriculturalist, the Miner, and those concerned in projecting and improving the Roads, Canals, and such other public works, undertaken for the benefit and improvement of the Country.'[18]

The proposal was warmly received, and cleared its bureaucratic hurdles with remarkable speed. Colby reported to his superior, Major-General Sir Alexander Bryce, Inspector General of Fortifications, on 9 April that, although he could not accept 'responsibility for the accuracy of the Geological information proposed to be inserted on the Ordnance Maps' he felt the offer was 'highly advantageous to the Public' and, moreover, set a good example as 'a matter of general political economy for the benefit of the Empire.' The main conditions he wished to see stipulated were, first, that the scheme of colours employed on the maps should be approved by the Council of the Geological Society and, secondly, that De la Beche should 'undertake, at his own cost and risk, to publish all ... indexes of Colors, Geological Sections, Memoirs,' ancillary to the main work.[19] By 2 May, the Secretary of the Board of Ordnance was able to write to De la Beche, indicating acceptance of his offer, subject to the provisos made by Colby, and stating that payment of the £300 would be made in eight equal instalments, after he had delivered each of the sheets 'Geologically coloured for engraving.'[20]

De la Beche's acceptance was not unqualified and 'though excellent in theory', he felt the suggestion that the Council of the Geological Society should discuss his scheme of colours to be sadly impracticable. The 'worthies' of the Society were not 'men of business and dispatch'; he feared interminable delays and accordingly urged Colby, in his capacity as Superintendent of the Survey, to ask for a quick answer.[21] Colby's prompt reaction was that the geological survey should not wait on the Council's decision. He would accept De la Beche's judgment in the matter of colouring as far as the work in the field was concerned: 'when we have engraved the lines of demarcation on the Copper, a Copy can be coloured according to the decision of the Council'.[22] The compromise was acceptable to De la Beche. It was already May and he was impatient at 'Losing the best part of the year for Geological Work': he intended to 'proceed forthwith into Devonshire: there is work enough for two years.'[23]

After 1832 there is a gap in the surviving Ordnance Survey letter books until May 1835,[24] so that we are denied the insights they doubtless once provided into De la Beche's relationships with Colby and the Board of Ordnance. From external sources, however, we learn that he was able, in accordance with his proposed timetable, to complete the mapping of Devon within two years. In his 1834 presidential address to the Geological Society, G. B. Greenough was able to report that

'Mr De la Beche, one of our Vice-Presidents, acting under the Direction of the Board of Ordnance, has produced a geological map of the county of Devon, which, for extent and minuteness of information and beauty of execution, has a very high claim to regard. Let us rejoice in the complete success which has attended this first attempt of that honourable Board to exhalt the character of English topography by rendering it at once more scientific and very much more useful to the country at large.'[25]

And, in the following year, he thought the subject deserved a further eulogy:

'The researches of your Vice-President (De la Beche) in the counties of Devon and Somerset have been carried on this year with increased energy. Of the eight sheets of the Ordnance Map upon which he has been engaged, four were published last spring, three others are complete, the eighth is nearly complete, and an explanatory memoir with sheets of sections applying to the

whole are to be published before our next anniversary. Let us hope that
a work so admirably begun may not be suffered to terminate here.'[26]
    In May 1835, when the record of the Ordnance correspondence can be examined again,
the question of the extension of De la Beche's work into a national undertaking came to
the fore. In fact, the Board of Ordnance took the initiative and, on 25 May, referred the
maps of Devon to the 'President of the Geological Society, Dr Buckland and Professor
Sedgwick' in order to obtain 'the best information the Country can afford before they
come to any decision as to the extension of Mr De la Beche's labours upon this service.'[27]
Buckland's reply was as unambiguous as it was prompt: on 30 May he wrote of the 'very
high opinion I entertain of the value and extreme accuracy of the colouring placed on eight
sheets of the Ordnance Map by Mr De la Beche comprehending my native county with
great part of which I am minutely acquainted.'[28] The arrangement was that Buckland
and Sedgwick should appear before the Board of the Ordnance to put the case more fully
and a report, embodying their arguments, is dated 12 June 1835. This is an important
founding document of the Geological Survey in Britain and offered cogent intellectual
and practical justification for the expansion of De la Beche's work:

> 'Our opinion is that the execution of the geological survey of Devonshire is
> the result of great labour combined with great skill, and that no geological
> Map of such extent has been published in Europe to equal it in the minute
> accuracy of its details. We regard its publication as reflecting great honor on
> the Board of Ordnance, with whom it originated, and at the same time as a
> benefit to European Science.
>
> We are further of opinion, from this evidence, but still more from our
> personal knowledge of the unusual combination of qualifications which are
> united in Mr. De la Beche, that it would be highly honourable and useful to
> the Nation to continue his services, in the extension of a geological survey on
> one uniform system over other parts of great Britain.
>
> We believe that the promotion of such a work would have an important
> effect on the progress of physical geography, and many departments of
> Natural History—that it would most essentially aid in fixing geology on a
> permanent basis—and that it would be also connected with the advancement
> of some important questions in exact science. These however are views on
> which we do not feel ourselves called to dwell, though we cannot doubt of
> their importance; and know that they have given rise to great works on the
> continent, among which we may mention a geological map of France under-
> taken at the expense of Government, and just on the point of being published.
>
> We therefore more particularly submit to the attention of the Board of
> Ordnance an outline of some of the economical advantages to be expected
> from such a labour as we recommend . . . '

These 'economical advantages' were arranged under six headings—to aid the search for
coal and metals; to locate the best materials for making and repairing roads; to point out
'the situation in which water may be obtained at the least expense in sinking wells'; to

assist in the construction of canals, railways and tunnels; to provide a knowledge where 'good limestone, brickearth and building stone are to be met with' and to indicate the 'juxta-position of lime, marl, gypsum and other materials for the artificial improvement of soils.' The cost to the Ordnance Survey of raising a small team of geologists under De la Beche was trifling, the report argued, compared with the capital cost of public works where geological knowledge was essential.[29] The arguments were convincing. On 13 June Colonel Colby wrote to the Master General with a statement of the estimated cost of implementing the proposal—£1,000 a year exclusive of De la Beche's salary; on 15 June the Board's minute on the subject was submitted to the Master General and received his approval and, on 30 June, the Treasury—the final arbiter—added its agreement in principle, undertaking to 'cheerfully give their sanction to any measure which may facilitate so desirable a result, if it can be obtained at a moderate expense.'[30] They required an estimate of the time it would take to complete a geological map of the whole country; the question was referred to De la Beche, who replied on 4 July that

> 'depending as it must do upon the amount of competent aid which I may receive, if that aid be such as I have reason to suppose it will be from conversations with Col. Colby on this subject, I consider that the Geological Map will keep pace with the Geographical Map, and consequently that both Maps will be completed at the same time.'[31]

Faced with this clever, if rather evasive answer, the Treasury still felt the total expenditure was 'insufficiently ascertained', but as the season when field work could be undertaken was already 'far advanced' (it was mid-July), a go-ahead was given for the work in Cornwall, with the promise to review a national undertaking, once the cost of completing the work on this one county was known.[32] It seems likely that their caution was rooted in the experience of the geological survey of Scotland, where Macculloch had claimed large sums of money – over £5,500 from 1826 to 1829 – without actually producing a map.

III

Such were the events in Devon which led to the foundation of an official geological survey on a semi-official basis and later, in Cornwall, developed into a small organisation which was integrated into the Ordnance Survey. It is well known from the writings of historians of geology such as Bailey, Flett and Woodward[33] that this pioneer activity in South-West England was subsequently extended to South Wales and put on a national footing. Less well known is the effect of the acquisition of a geological branch on the conduct of the topographical survey and, in particular, on the one-inch maps which were a basic tool of the field geologist. It has been argued that the Ordnance Maps were a significant stimulus to geological work in the field: the corollary is that the needs of the geologist helped to impose a new discipline on the work of the topographical surveyor. The first theatre for this interaction was Devon and Cornwall. De la Beche's work, albeit in the context of a national policy for the Survey, was intimately related to a major geographical revision of large areas of the original Ordnance maps, including the whole of the Penzance sheet (33) and most of the coastlines of Cornwall, North Devon and Somerset. Moreover, the re-engraving of the original copper-plates in these areas accompanied the revision (Fig. 7.1a).

To put these events in perspective it is necessary to describe briefly the original Ordnance Survey maps of Devon and Cornwall.[34] In a personal sense the South West had strong associations with the early years of the Ordnance Survey. William Mudge, the first effective Superintendent of the Ordnance Survey, was a Devon man—the son of Dr John Mudge, a celebrated Plymouth physician; Thomas Colby, who was the dominating figure in the history of the Ordnance Survey in the 1830s, was the victim of a near-fatal pistol accident at Liskeard in Cornwall, when he was engaged in trigonometrical survey, while several other surveyors, such as Charles Budgen, were also recruited in Devon.[35] But the main reason why Devon became one of the first English counties to be surveyed was that its south coast, especially Plymouth and the dock towns, was of great strategic importance.

A map of Kent, based on Ordnance materials (but not published by the Board of Ordnance), had appeared in 1801; four sheets covering Essex, the first Ordnance maps proper, were published in 1805, and were followed in 1809 by the eight sheets relating to Devon—the second part of the 'General Survey of England and Wales' (Plate 7). By 1811 some of the remaining parts of Dorset and Somerset had also been published, so that the appearance in 1813 of four sheets covering Cornwall meant that the coverage of South-West England was complete and, moreover, provided a representative cross section of the earliest—in some ways the still experimental—sheets of the Ordnance Survey.

The accuracy of this early work is especially germane to the interaction of geographical and geological mapping in the 1830s. For their date of publication, by comparison with the work of private map-sellers, and bearing in mind the one-inch scale, the early Ordnance maps were a model for the new century. By 1830, however, owing to the rapid development of the Survey's techniques, they had been surpassed and left as obsolete, so that the sheets on which De la Beche had to work—as Colby was quick to recognise—fell short of a desirable standard of accuracy. The general reasons for the inadequacy of the early maps of the Survey have been discussed elsewhere,[36] and in Devon and Cornwall a similar diagnosis can be made. A principal cause was the relative inaccuracy of the topographical survey as compared with the trigonometrical operations. The original purpose of the Survey, as founded in 1791, was to 'ascertain, by a Trigonometrical operation, the situation of all the Headlands on the Channel, and the Eminences and remarkable Objects throughout the Country, thereby preparing correct materials for a Geographical description of it.'[37] The decision to make a national topographic map was not taken until several years after 1791: 'The original survey', as J. E. Portlock put it, was 'grafted . . . upon an independent scientific work, was local, and detached in order of performance . . . and . . . the importance of a great national survey was at first only partly recognised.'[38] His words fit exactly the history of the sheets covering Devon and Cornwall. 'The independent scientific work' was the primary triangulation of England and Wales which, in 1795 and 1796, had been extended along the south coast of Devon into Cornwall and then along the north coast of the two counties. Its accuracy is not open to reasonable doubt and the official report records a major scientific operation conducted in accordance with the highest standards.[39] Observations were made with Jesse Ramsden's 'great' theodolite in order to locate the primary trigonometrical stations, but additional astronomical measurements helped to fix the meridians of St Agnes Beacon and Butterton Hill, as well as a series of latitudes and longitudes; altitudes were levelled and the precise distance from the mainland of a number of offshore landmarks—such as the Lizard and Scilly lighthouses—was meticulously calculated. The secondary triangulation was equally thorough and, in Devon, for example, bearings were taken by theodolite to no less than 600 local landmarks so that 'almost every steeple' (as Mudge claimed) had been incorporated in the trigonometrical framework.

The topographical survey, by way of contrast, matched Portlock's definition of being 'local, and detached in order of performance'. The varying scales, dates and accuracy of the original Ordnance Survey manuscript plans relating to South-West England (Fig. 7.1b) can be reconstructed from the surviving copies in the Map Room of the British Museum. These include elaborately coloured six-inch military plans in the Plymouth area (out of date by the time they were due for publication)[40]; a broad belt of countryside in east Devon surveyed at the alternative military scale of 3 inches to 1 mile, the rest of the region being surveyed at a scale of 2 inches to 1 mile. In places plans deteriorate into little more than compass traverses, executed rapidly and rendered incomplete by the reluctance of suspicious landowners to give access to their land in war time,[41] or inaccurate through the practice of employing civilian surveyors on a temporary piece-work basis.[42] Although the skilled engravers of the Board could impart an aura of uniformity to the published sheet, the lack of a standard specification for the detailed mapping prevented the production of a consistently accurate map. Notwithstanding the technical improvements which they embodied, the first Ordnance maps of Devon and Cornwall thus perpetuated some of the limitations of eighteenth-century county maps. In one respect they were county maps: the sheets for each county, although part of a national sequence, were issued separately—those for Devon on 11 October 1809 and those for Cornwall on 5 January 1813; the borders were omitted from the inside edges of the sheets so that the gentry could mount them as one and, for those who still preferred the format of a county atlas, a separate title page was engraved (Plate 7). And thus, owing to the strength of cartographic tradition, the county became a unit of early geological as well as of Ordnance mapping.

IV

The appointment in October 1820 of Captain Thomas Colby as Superintendent of the national survey was a turning point—almost a new beginning—in its history. Although the maps of Devon and Cornwall had been published before Colby assumed direction of the Survey, the improvements introduced by him exercised an important effect, especially on the work done during the period when De la Beche was engaged in the geological mapping of the two counties. The last years of Mudge's period as Superintendent of the Survey had seen the first serious attempt to improve the standard of the topographical survey. The instructions which he issued to field surveyors in 1816—insisting on regular progress reports, limiting the use of pre-existing private plans and of work by cadets in training and by civilian surveyors, and stipulating that archaeological sites should be systematically depicted[43]—were still regarded as standard in the 1820s. The extensive application of the principles which they embodied was left to Colby. He was under pressure from two directions: on the one hand, there was a clamour that sheets of the unpublished areas of England and Wales should appear more quickly; on the other hand, some of the older surveys were coming under fire as out of date and inaccurate. With the latter, the sheets containing coastal areas, such as those for Devon and Cornwall, which suffered, in any case, from normal obsolescence, came under rigorous scrutiny because of the work of the Admiralty hydrographers, whose chart-making activities followed the Ordnance Survey in parts of South-West England. Lundy Island (sheet 28), which had to be hastily re-engraved shortly after its publication in 1820, provides an extreme example of the shortcomings of an early Ordnance Survey sheet. A complaint was made by the Admiralty and, in August 1820, Admiralty surveyor L. R. Fitzmaurice reported from the Surveying Vessel *Hasty*, then in Appledore Pool, that he had

> 'completed that part of my instructions which relate to Lundy Island, and sent a tracing of the same by this Post to Captain Hurd—with the data from which the Chart is constructed, by which it will appear that the direction of this Island as given by the Ordnance Survey is quite incorrect.'[44]

The case was proven and Colby acted quickly, withdrawing the printed sheets and re-engraving the plate, with a sharp censure to the surveyor on the 'very considerable . . . disgrace and expense of this transaction' and hoping 'that when the Bills are sent in the Master General will not require an explanation so discreditable to this Department.'[45]

Other inconsistencies in the early Ordnance Maps may have been minor in comparison, but they pointed to an urgent need for a stricter control over the techniques of the field survey. Colby's remedy, involving both prevention and retrospective cure, exerted a major influence on the development of the *Old Series* maps of England and Wales throughout the 1820s and 1830s. The first real trial of his determination to improve the accuracy of the maps came in the survey of Lincolnshire. Despite the arguments for their early publication (they eventually appeared in 1824) he insisted that the existing manuscript plans be virtually resurveyed prior to engraving.[46] Such correction of old (but still unpublished) plans was extended to much of England and Wales in the next decade.

The second prong to his policy—and the one which is relevant to the maps of Devon and Cornwall—was an attempt to revise the detail of the older sheets. From the beginning, minor corrections had been made to the copper-plates of many maps (the earliest known version of the Plymouth sheet, for example, is distinguished by the absence of the Breakwater in Plymouth Sound and of the lettering 'English Channell,' both of which were added shortly after publication)[47] and, in addition, inner borders were engraved on the Devon sheets in the early 1820s. The *systematic* revision of selected topographical features, on the other hand, was only undertaken after 1820, under Colby's influence. A hint of its scope is provided by his report on the progress of the Survey, prepared for the Board of Ordnance in 1834 and containing a précis of its history, as well as recommendations for future expenditure. One recurrent item was the 'Annual cost of inserting new roads and other alterations on the published plates to prevent the Maps from becoming obsolete' and, among completed work in a number of counties, it was noted that 'a good deal has been done toward the correction of the Old Devonshire Map, which from original in-accuracy and recent local improvements had become obsolete'.[48] An index map of England and Wales, indicating the *Old Series* sheet lines and the 'State of the Revision of Imperfect Work', accompanied the Report. As well as Lincolnshire and much of the Midlands and Wales, the revised areas of 1834 included a strip of territory along the coast of Somerset, north Devon and a small area of Cornwall (O.S. sheets, numbers 19, 20, 27, 26 and 29), areas which were completely re-engraved later, in the 1830s.[45]

In 1834 a negative—even hostile—attitude of the Board of Ordnance (prompted by the Treasury) towards this revision of the older published sheets is particularly noticeable. Colby had apparently acted on his own initiative without consulting his superiors and the work in Devon was something of a test case:

> 'The question of revision was first brought under the Master General's notice in 1823; and authority generally seems to have been given for it, without knowing to what extent it might lead; and, the Committee apprehend, with-out any idea that it would be requisite to correct coastlines and localities of those Maps which had already been published. Lt.-Col. Colby, however, considered that he had a general authority not only to revise Errors, but to insert from time to time new lines of Canals, Roads, and other Improvements, which are constantly taking place; The Committee think it necessary to call the attention of the Master General and the Board to this subject. They think that in every case where a Revision is likely to occasion any great increase of Expense, it should be reported, and not undertaken without specific authority. The Committee is of the opinion that the Revision of the County of Devon, since 1832, the Map of which had been many years published, and was found too incorrect for Admiralty purposes, as well as for the Geological delineation undertaken by Mr Delabeche, ought not to have been com-menced, as it was without distinct reference to, and authority from, The Master General and Board.'[50]

This was the position in 1834. The geological mapping of De la Beche, together with Admiralty criticism of the mapping of the coastline, had provided Colby with an excuse to revise the maps of the coast of north Devon. But his unilateral action was censured. No immediate financial provision was made for revision in the new estimates and work in the field was presumably brought to a halt, although, as we shall see, within a year, he was to be allowed a 'Geographical Correction Account.'

V

In reaching its decision the Treasury could have foreseen neither Colby's stubbornness in pursuit of what he believed to be the right course of development for the Survey nor the result of their own decision to allow De la Beche's geological survey to be extended into Cornwall. The geological survey of Cornwall, once it was on an official footing with a regular grant, gave Colby the opportunity he needed together with some funds for the resumption of the topographical revision of the Ordnance maps of South-West England. The Ordnance correspondence is again invaluable in affording insight into the strategy employed by Colby—probably in collusion with De la Beche—in achieving an extension into Cornwall of the revision of the maps of north Devon.

On this occasion Colby made no secret of his intention. In a letter to the Master General of 13 June 1835 containing an estimate of the probable annual expense of continuing the geological survey as £1,000, he intimated

> 'When the Geological Survey of Cornwall shall be directed to be carried into effect I propose to attach to Mr De la Beche a practical Surveyor who has already some knowledge of Geology and who will correct the Geographical details of the Ordnance Map of Cornwall (of which the Survey is 30 years old) at the same time while he is proceeding with the Geological enquiries.'[51]

The 'practical Surveyor' was Henry McLauchlan (1791–1881), attached to the Ordnance Survey, but also a Fellow of the Geological Society of London. It is implicit in Colby's suggestion that the geological grant would bear the cost of geographical correction, but the idea, although adding to the cost of revision, does not seem to have provoked a hostile reaction in the Treasury or the Board of Ordnance. An important factor was probably De la Beche's insistence not only that the existing Ordnance maps of Cornwall were inadequate for his purpose but also that geological work required especially accurate maps. He had certainly passed such an opinion to Colby, who wrote to him on 14 July 1835 (only a month after the continuation of the Cornish work had been sanctioned) that,

> 'I like your proposal of letting Mr. McLauchlan do the Coast of sheet 29 and of employing Mr. Still with yourself in getting over the Penzance sheet which requires much correction, both for the sake of the Geological Map and of the Ordnance Map; it will be necessary to make the New Edition of the Geographical Map of Cornwall correct in all essential matters:—It will not have the perfection of an absolutely new Ordnance Map, but it ought to be superior to any other map of the county. We cannot be content with a low degree of accuracy.'[52]

At the same time, Colby tells us that he had advised against continuing the geological survey in Cornwall 'where the geographical map was old and required much correction' and

> 'this misfortune was increased by the Circumstance of my having, at the same time, to propose a resurvey of a part of the Essex Map, which made me anxious to avoid such a simultaneous application for the Land's End Sheet. In fact, all I can do for you, is to pay Mr. Still on the Geographical Correction account.'[53]

There was then, in the revision of Cornwall, a sharing of costs: Still was to be paid by the Ordnance Survey and McLauchlan from De la Beche's geological grant. On 18 July, Colby instructed Captain Robe to

> 'Let Mr. McLauchlan be directed to proceed to Cornwall to go on with the Coast and Correction of the Cornish Map and Geology of it under Mr. De la Beche's direction.'[54]

It may be noted in passing that, in De la Beche's quarterly account of his field expenses, the cost of geographical correction usually exceeded that of the geological work.

It is clear that, as the work in Cornwall proceeded, the provision of two surveyors was barely adequate to prosecute the revision in a proper manner. It was of necessity selective. In February 1836 Colby wrote of the need

> 'to ascertain what portions of the Map require extensive alteration . . . some of the work as you have seen require only trifling alterations, and perhaps the extent of the work which cannot be used without a resurvey could be readily discovered by a casual examination on the part of Mr. McLauchlan, let him direct some of his attention to this object.'[55]

The result of this examination was to dispel any grounds for optimism. Individual maps and even different areas within them turned out to be of 'very different qualities', both because of their age and original inaccuracy, and, subsequently, Colby noted that the amount of correction necessary exceeded his 'anticipations'[56]: in September he 'was casting about to consider the possibility of doing something to expedite the geographical corrections in Cornwall'.[57] McLauchlan had revealed the 'deplorable state' of much of the work and Colby's solution was to confine Henry Still to the correction of 'one sheet until it is ready for engraving, and thus to proceed sheet by sheet, to afford employment for the engravers'; McLauchlan on the other hand was to continue working along the coast 'as long as the season permits'.[58] This instruction is the key to the extent of the 1830s Ordnance revision in Cornwall: the single sheet referred to was sheet 33 (Penzance), and, although the rest of the interior of the county was not systematically revised, McLauchlan was able to complete his correction of both the north and south coasts. These were the areas which were completely re-engraved in the late 1830s, with the Penzance sheet being published in 1839. (Fig. 7.1a).

The whole Cornish episode was something of a compromise for all parties concerned. The Board of Ordnance—apart from fearing that the costs of the geological work would escalate—were still suspicious that too much was being spent on the task of revision, but were manoeuvred into allowing its continuation Progress continued against a background of financial stringency, with Colby clearly accountable for any irregular expenses. In April 1836, for example, he informed De la Beche that he had 'strained a point to send a Surveyor to sheet 29 to complete the revision of the Coast which Mr McLauchlan has left incomplete'; in May he was questioned about his estimate for corrections.[59] He was careful to justify his actions and to point out that a by-product of the geological work would be 'an accurate edition of the Ordnance Map of Cornwall'. But this was only partly achieved, with the geographical revision coming to an end once the immediate needs of the geological work had been met. And thus for Colby also the result was a compromise. A perfectionist, he had to be content with a job half done. He re-emphasised later that he had 'objected very strongly to the Geological Survey being commenced in Cornwall'[60] and on these grounds had apologised to De la Beche that he 'should have been compelled to commence your geology on so defective a map . . . but the die is cast and we must do our best.'[61] The delays and inadequacies were frustrating to De la Beche also. In April 1836 he wrote from Redruth that 'the Survey has often been delayed from the geographical corrections' and later complained that he had

> 'frequently been compelled to pass twice over the same area; once when I found the Map too defective to enter my work upon it, and again after the Draftsmen had effected the necessary corrections. Hence had not the Map been so defective a much larger area might have been examined in the same time.'[62]

But despite the piecemeal and rather stop-gap nature of the revision of the Cornish sheets—the essential work was finished by the autumn of 1837[63]—De la Beche was able to complete the geological survey to his satisfaction.

Taking a broad view, it is not an exaggeration to assert that events in Devon and Cornwall exerted a lasting influence on the development of both Ordnance and Geological Mapping in England and Wales. De la Beche was allowed to continue his work—in the first instance in South Wales—as Director of a national Geological Survey, which remained until 1845 under the wing of the Board of Ordnance. The need to revise obsolete topographical sheets prior to their geological survey also seems to have been accepted by the Ordnance hierarchy. The old Pembrokeshire sheets were completely surveyed in advance of the geological work and later re-engraved and, in Derbyshire too, Colby was able to prevent the development of problems arising from simultaneous geographical and geological surveys. Moreover, the principle of selective revision of the *Old Series* maps, independently from the geological survey, was also extended, as in Essex, to other parts of the country. After the late 1830s Colby gradually won his battle on the question of national expenditure on the Ordnance Survey.

In Devon and Cornwall the effect of De la Beche's survey was that the *Old Series* sheets were partially revised in the 1830s—a significant consideration for scholars who use them as evidence of the early nineteenth-century landscape. The work was left incomplete when De la Beche moved on, but the maps were still less obsolete than sheets of similar age elsewhere. The progress of the geological survey also left a permanent record on the copperplates of the South-Western sheets. Again, with economy in mind, it was decided to engrave the geological symbols on the copper-plates of the topographical maps, rather than engrave separate plates. De la Beche was one of those who felt 'reluctance to make geological marks on the geographical map, considering that its application to geological purposes is merely a secondary object'.[64] This problem was not solved until after 1847, however, when the process of electrotyping made possible the easy duplication of the *Old Series* copperplates, both for separate purposes, such as the geological survey, and to replace the worn-out plates of the regular series. But the work in Devon and Cornwall preceded this innovation and the practical needs of the moment, as with the revision, over-ruled the doctrine of perfection. Geological data as well as geographical revision became a permanent feature of the Ordnance maps until they were finally withdrawn in the 1890s.

The Ordnance Survey sheets of South-West England are thus a memorial, not only to technical advances in the national survey during the 1830s, but also to the financial and political reefs through which surveyors and scientists had to chart a common course.

ACKNOWLEDGEMENTS

Any student who comes to write about the development of geological mapping in Britain will find himself deeply in debt to the scholarly researches of the late Dr F. J. North, whose published writings and manuscript collections have been drawn on freely in the present essay. I am also grateful to Dr Douglas A. Bassett, Keeper of Geology, National Museum of Wales, to E. F. Bunt, former Librarian at the Institute of Geological Sciences in South Kensington, and to Dr V. A. Eyles, for help in furnishing references and the locations of manuscript sources.

REFERENCES

1 Portlock, J. E. *Memoir of the Life of Major-General Colby* (1869)

2 Eyles, V. A. 'John Macculloch, F.R.S., and his Geological Map: an account of the first Geological Map of Scotland' *Annals of Science* 2(1937), 118

3 Close, C. *The Early Years of the Ordnance Survey* (1926: new edition, 1969, with an introduction by J. B. Harley), 61

4 Ordnance Survey Letter Book, 1817–1822, Ordnance Survey Manuscript at Southampton, *passim* contains much of the exchange of correspondence between Macculloch, the Board of Ordnance and the Treasury on this subject.

5 Macculloch, J. *Memoirs To His Majesty's Treasury Respecting a Geological Survey of Scotland* (1836).

6 Woodward, H. B. *The History of the Geological Society of London* (1907), 109–10

7 Murchison, R. I. in his address to the Geological Society in 1833 in *Proceedings of the Geological Society of London . . .* 1 (1834), 446

8 Woodward, H. B. op cit. 276

9 National Museum of Wales, Cardiff, Department of Geology: De la Beche papers 'Letters copied from a book in the possession of the Ordnance Survey . . . 1830 to 1841', 40. The copying of these letters—now in typescript—was initiated by F. J. North in 1934. The originals were subsequently destroyed by enemy action in the 1939–45 war. There is also a second sequence of manuscript original letters, addressed to De la Beche, many of them from Colby.

10 Ibid. typescript series

11 Phillips, J. *Memoirs of William Smith* (1844), 48; quoted by F. J. North in 'Further chapters in the History of Geology in South Wales' *Trans. Cardiff Naturalists Society* 67(1934), 36

12 *Proceedings of the Geological Society of London*, 1 (1834), 99

13 Loc. cit. 52

14 De la Beche, H. T. *Report on the Geology of Cornwall, Devon and West Somerset* (1839)

15 *Dictionary of National Biography* contains a good article on De la Beche, but his geological activities are particularly well described by North in the article cited above and also in his papers 'From the Geological Map to the Geological Survey, *Trans. Cardiff Naturalists Society* 65(1932), 41; and 'Geology's debt to Henry Thomas de la Beche' *Endeavour* 3(1944), 15-19

16 National Museum of Wales, De la Beche correspondence, typescript sequence, 44–5

17 Loc. cit.

18 Ibid. 48

19 Ibid. 52–3

20 Ibid. 56–7

21 Ibid. 61–5

22 Ibid. 66. In fact De la Beche seems to have reached some agreement at least with certain members of the Council of the Geological Society insofar as there is preserved in the Library of the Institute of Geological Sciences in South Kensington a table of the 'Colours to be employed in Colouring Geologically Sheets 21, 22, 23, 24, 25, 26 and 27 of the Ordnance Map of Great Britain . . .' and with the annotation that, 'These colours are copied from those deposited in this office by H. T. De la Beche, Esq.' after they had received the sanction of the Council of the Geological Society of London on the 16 May 1832. They are the same as those at present adopted by J. C. B. Greenough, Esq.' for the 2nd Edition of his Geological Map of England & Wales, preparing for publication. A. W. Robe Cap.' R. E., 22nd June, 1832, Ordnance Map Office Tower'

23 Ibid. 65

24 Ibid. 94

25 *Proceedings of the Geological Society of London,* 2 (1833–38), 51

26 Ibid. 154. On 25 May 1835 De la Beche wrote to the Board of Ordnance to report that the Devonshire Survey was complete; National Museum of Wales, correspondence, typescript sequence, 93

27 National Museum of Wales, De la Beche correspondence, typescript sequence, 94

28 Ibid. 96

29 Ibid. 98–102

30 Ibid. 103–7

31 Ibid. 113

32 Ibid. 117–8

33 Bailey, E. *Geological Survey of Great Britain* (1952); Flett, J. *The First Hundred Years of the Geological Survey of Great Britain* (1937); North, F. J. op. cit.; Woodward, H. B. op. cit.

34 A fuller description of the history of the individual sheets covering Devon and Cornwall will be found in the notes accompanying the *Reprint of the first edition of the one-inch Ordnance Survey of England and Wales ed. J. B. Harley* (1969–71)

35 Some account of this aspect appears in the works cited by J. E. Portlock and Sir Charles Close.

36 Harley, J. B. 'Error and Revision in early Ordnance Survey Maps' *Cartog. Journ.* 5 (1968), 115–24

37 *British Parliamentary Papers.* 1812, IV, 4

38 Portlock, J. E. op. cit. 161

39 Captain Mudge and Isaac Dalby, et al.*, An Account of the Operations carried on for accomplishing A Trigonometrical Survey of England and Wales . . .* 3 vols. (1799–1811) *passim.*

40 '. . . an accurate Survey and measurement of Plymouth and Dock Towns with their fortifications and the adjacent Country Surveyed by Order of his Grace, the Duke of Richmond, etc., Master General of the Ordnance, under the direction of Colonel Dixon, Chief Engineer, by William Gardner, Surveyor' 1784 to 1786.

41 Close, C. op. cit. 50; Simon Woolcot wrote from Devon in 1804 to say that especially on the coast he had been frequently subject to 'insults and interruptions' to his work.

42 *British Parliamentary Paper,* 167. The rate of supplementary piece-work pay was 32/6 per square mile.

43 Ordnance Survey Letter Book, 1817–1822, Manuscript at Southampton, 224–6.

44 Ibid. 112
45 Ibid. 177
46 Portlock, J. E. op. cit. 95
47 The earliest state is in the British Museum, Map Room, 2119. (30.); later copies with these details added include the BM Maps C.9.a.2 (Royal) and the Sir Joseph Banks copy BM Maps 148.e.27
48 P.R.O. W.O. 44/614
49 See the maps in J. B. Harley, op. cit. (1968)
50 P.R.O. W.O. 44/614
51 National Museum of Wales, De la Beche correspondence, typescript sequence, 104
52 Ibid. Manuscript letter from Colby to De la Beche, dated 14 July 1836
53 Loc. cit.
54 Ibid. typescript sequence, 127
55 Ibid. 144
56 Ibid. Manuscript letter from Colby to the Inspector General of Fortifications, dated 11 July 1837
57 Manuscript letter from Colby to De la Beche dated 15 September 1836
58 Loc. cit.
59 Ibid. typescript sequence, 152, 160
60 Ibid. 215
61 Ibid. Manuscript letter from Colby to De la Beche, dated 15 September 1836
62 Ibid. 155, 244
63 Ibid. 214
64 Ibid. 228

8

Demographic Trends in South-Devon in the Mid-Nineteenth Century

DAVID BRYANT

'Migration, whether seasonal or permanent, is a normal and universal feature of social life.'[1] This essay examines the effects of migration on the population composition of a small study area in the Dart Valley in the mid-nineteenth century and investigates the nature of the movements which were then taking place. It also considers the relative merits of different methods by which such movements may be identified and mapped for the purpose of analysis. The work is based upon the Reports of the 1851 Census, and the age, sex, and birthplace data (parish and county of birth) contained in the enumerators' schedules for 1851, which are available in the Public Record Office.[2] The study area (Fig. 8.1) includes the three towns of Totnes, Ashburton and Buckfastleigh, together with the rural parishes of Broadhempston, Buckland-in-the-Moor, Dartington, Dean Prior, Holne, Rattery, Staverton and Woodland, which make up a compact area extending from the southern margins of Dartmoor to the head of navigation on the river Dart.

Population Change 1801–1851

The total population of this area, excluding the 293 inmates of the Totnes Union Workhouse, was 13,781. According to the birthplace evidence in the census schedules for 1851, only 8,035, or 58 per cent, were natives of their parish of residence at the time of enumeration. Almost a half of the total population had moved from one parish to another between birth and enumeration and, in view of the fact that many more may have moved away from their home parish and returned to it later, while many others may have moved within the boundaries of one parish, the total amount of movement taking place must have been very considerable. In order to appreciate fully the effects of the migratory behaviour of the population on its composition, demographic trends in the study area must be related to those elsewhere and particularly to two main demographic developments which were taking place contemporaneously between 1801 and 1851 (Table 8.1). In the first place the population of England and Wales was increasing very rapidly. No decade in the first half

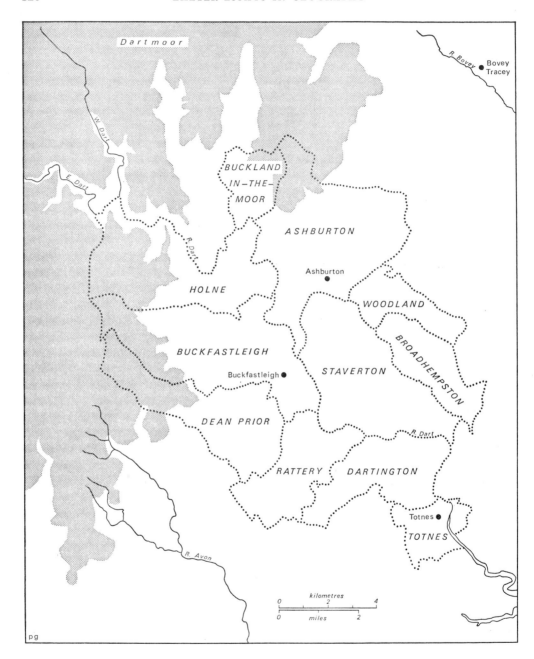

Fig. 8.1   The study area: eleven parishes in the Dart valley. Parish boundaries from Ordnance Survey one-inch-to-the-mile map (1961). The location of the study area within Devon is shown in Figure 8.3.

of the nineteenth century showed less than a 13 per cent increase in total population compared with the previous decade: the total population recorded in 1851 (18,054,170) was twice that of 1801 (9,156,171).

TABLE 8.1

Population of Study Area, Devon, and England and Wales by Decennial Periods 1801-51

Date	Study Area	Devon	England and Wales
1801	10,937	342,223	9,156,171
1811	11,606	384,893	10,454,529
1821	13,104	441,329	12,172,664
1831	14,277	497,470	14,051,986
1841	14,436	537,270	16,035,198
1851	14,074	572,330	18,054,170

The second important development was the rapid urbanisation of the population during this period. The census of 1851 recorded for the first time in Britain an urban population whose number exceeded that of the rural communities.[3] The chief reason for the rapid growth of the towns at this time was the steady inflow of migrants from the rural areas, attracted by the prospect of higher wages and better and more varied opportunities for employment. The movement was not new but in the second half of the eighteenth century the pace had quickened and the absolute growth of the rural population was, as a result, much slower than that of the towns. By the second quarter of the nineteenth century the rural outflow had begun to affect the absolute size of the rural communities and at some point between 1821 and 1851 a considerable proportion of the villages and rural parishes of England and Wales passed their peak of population and entered into decline.[4] W. G. Hoskins[5] has described the situation in Devon where, apart from the growth of Plymouth, Exeter and the seaside towns, the county was characterised after 1831 by a steady decline in the rate of population growth compared with that of the country as a whole. Between 1841 and 1851, especially, hundreds of rural parishes and small market towns lost people to the larger towns. Depopulation in Devon most severely affected those parishes whose population was less than 500 and which were almost entirely rural. Larger parishes frequently had craft industries serving local markets; this helped to keep the numbers stable for a longer period.

The population of the study area increased steadily until 1841, although during the decade 1831-41 the rate of increase had slowed appreciably. The return for 1851 recorded the first actual decline, with a fall in population from 14,436 to 14,074—a fall of about 2.5 per cent. This trend continued and by 1861 the total was only 12,699. Even in the earlier decades of the century, when the population of the study area was still increasing, the rate of growth was less than that for England and Wales, and, with the exception of the decade 1811-21, less than that for Devon. Within the area it is difficult to identify a general pattern

K

of population change (Fig. 8.2a). Except in the cases of Ashburton and Staverton, the populations of the towns and rural parishes in the area increased between 1801 and 1811. This was a period of prosperity for these rural areas, as war-demands stimulated agricultural production. Many districts experienced a sharp increase in population between 1811 and 1821 and this trend is particularly noticeable in Totnes, Ashburton, and Buckfastleigh, and in the parishes of Broadhempston, Rattery, Holne and Buckland-in-the-Moor. The period after 1815 is thought to have been one of acute rural depression, for the coming of peace meant the loss of important markets in the Fleet and the Army, as well as the collapse of corn prices and competition from imported wheat, butter, eggs and poultry.[6] During a period of rural depression one would expect the pace of rural depopulation to quicken. The population of the three towns, particularly that of Buckfastleigh, did increase and it is

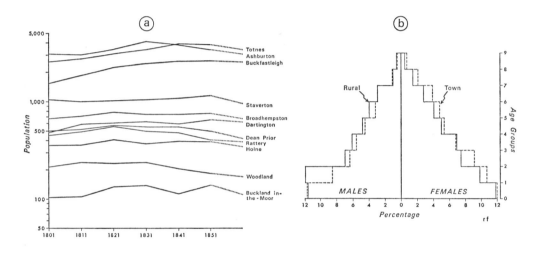

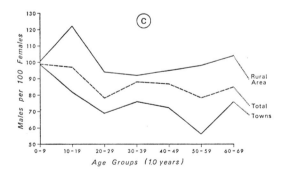

Fig. 8.2　(a) Population changes within the study area, 1801–1851.
(b) Superimposed population pyramids for the urban and rural sectors of the study area.
(c) Sex ratios for each 10-year age group in the urban and rural populations.

reasonable to assume that many of the immigrants came from the surrounding parishes. The 'vacuum' left in these areas of dispersal might well have been filled, however, by people moving back from more remote, 'deep', areas—the marginal lands, cultivated during the war years (which would have been the first to be evacuated). After 1821 the pattern is very confused, with very little similarity among the different parishes. Only the decennial totals for Buckfastleigh show any consistency; its population continued to increase, although at a diminishing rate, throughout the period. The population of Ashburton fell sharply during the decade 1831–41 and again in the decade 1841–51, by which time Totnes is also shown to have been losing population, having reached its nineteenth century peak in 1841. The fall in the population of Totnes was only slight at this stage (21 persons) but the loss is much more significant when related to the continuing national trend of rapid population growth. The natural increase over ten years, together with probable immigration, had been more than compensated for by emigration. This first decline in the population of Totnes occurred during a decade which saw the arrival in the town of the South Devon Railway. Totnes now had to compete as a centre of absorption with other more distant yet more attractive centres.

The earlier and more rapid decline of Ashburton is particularly interesting, since in this case the causes can be fairly surely determined. The period 1831–51 was particularly critical in the town's development. Its prosperity had depended, after the decline of the mining activities in the neighbourhood, on the manufacture of serges and on its function as a coaching centre on the main Plymouth–Exeter road. During the twenty years in question both activities suffered severe setbacks. The markets for serges declined rapidly in the eighteenth century and, after the Napoleonic Wars, only the Chinese market was kept open by an artificial monopoly exercised through the East India Company: when this monopoly was broken in 1833 many of the remaining mills rapidly closed down, and Ashburton, although still a wool manufacturing centre in 1851, was one of the towns chiefly affected.

White's Devonshire Directory of 1850[7] has the following entry:

'It (Ashburton) had 3,080 inhabitants in 1801, and 4,165 in 1831 but in 1841 they had decreased to 3,841, owing to the decline of the serge and blanket manufacture, formerly extensively carried on in the town and neighbourhood, where a few factories are still engaged in it.'

The second major setback was the non-arrival of the South Devon Railway in the 1840s. Again a reference is made in White's Directory:[8]

'Before the opening of the railways it was a great thoroughfare for coaches, vans etc., between Plymouth and London'.

The use of the word 'before' here tells its own story. The loss of its route situation meant also the destruction of the many allied trades, such as hostelry and saddling, which had depended upon it. Ashburton's importance as a market centre must also have been undermined by the competition of towns with rail connections. Of the three towns, only Buckfastleigh maintained a growing population throughout the period. The rate of growth slackened after 1831, however, for even in this 'large manufacturing village'[9] the effects of the decline in the woollen industry were being felt. Of the four blanket and serge mills only two were operating in 1851, employing four hundred hands. The 1861 census recorded a slight decline in the population (2,613–2,544), although the remainder of the nineteenth century saw a steady growth to 3,009 in 1891.

The difficulty of determining population trends in the rural areas is largely due to the fact that their populations were often so small that insignificant events attain a disproportionate importance. If any trend is evident at all, however—and the lack of an obvious pattern perhaps emphasises the relative prosperity of this region, which was probably one of transmigration rather than dispersal in the normal sense—it is that populations tended to increase slowly from 1801 to 1821, and that after 1831 only minor and irregular fluctuations occurred. Certainly, the rural parishes of the middle Dart Valley showed little sign of the drastic decline in numbers experienced later by many of the more remote Devon parishes, some of which lost as many as 60 per cent of their population during the second half of the nineteenth century. By 1861, however, a pattern of diminishing numbers was evident in all the towns and rural parishes in the area. An interesting exception to the general pattern was Staverton where, between 1841 and 1851, the population increased by 83 from 1,069 to 1,152, an increase of nearly 8 per cent. The probable explanation is that between 1840 and 1850 the Penn Recca Slate Quarries, which had been worked on a small scale for centuries, were greatly enlarged and modernised. £30,000 was spent on equipping the quarries with 'facilities for economical working possessed by no other quarries in the West of England',[10] and by 1850 about 100 hands were employed in the getting and preparation of slate. The attraction to the district of slate-workers and their families was probably responsible for much of the 1841–51 population increase. After 1851 the population of Staverton declined as the slate quarries were worked out, and by 1890 the Penn Recca quarries were exhausted.

Migration and Population Composition

There can be no doubt that migration from and within the study area was taking place on a large scale. Thomas Shapter[11] in his book 'The Climate of South Devon' published in 1862 gives figures for 1847–56 which show that the birth rate for the area in this period was rather more than 28 per thousand, while the death rate was 19 per thousand. Even allowing for a slightly higher death rate in the towns, a natural increase of 9 per thousand per year should have produced a considerable population increase, if migration had not taken place. In Totnes, as we have seen, the population would have increased by about 400 between 1841 and 1851. In the parish of Holne (population 394 in 1841) the figure would have been about 50. For the study area as a whole a population increase of between 1,300 and 1,400 might have been expected. It is surprising how often rural depopulation is only recognised in areas showing an actual decline in absolute numbers. During this period of rapid natural population increase, even a steadily maintained population is one that must have been subject to fairly heavy losses, and the extent of a decline when it occurs must be reckoned not only in terms of the absolute loss, but also in terms of the loss plus the natural increase that would have taken place.

The migratory behaviour of the population and its effect upon certain aspects of the population composition with which this essay is chiefly concerned must be seen in the light of the general picture of numerical trends which has been outlined above.

Those who migrate are not usually a cross section of the whole population, and the movement of people from rural to urban areas produced important demographic changes in the sending and receiving populations, particularly with regard to the age and sex characteristics of the population. Unfortunately the census surveys of the period did not include questions about age/sex differentials in relation to migration behaviour but a good deal can be inferred from the study of anomalies in the age and sex structure of the urban and rural communities. The superimposed population pyramids in figure 8.2b show clearly that the population structure of the area is typical of an area with a relatively high birth rate and a high rate of natural population increase. A very high proportion of the population is found in the lower age groups. 59 per cent of the population of the study area was less than 30 years of age, and 43 per cent was less than 20 years of age. Perhaps the most striking feature of figure 8.2b is the imbalance between the male and female populations for the urban and rural areas in the 10 to 30 age groups. There is a sharp reduction in the proportion of females in the rural parishes, particularly amongst the teen-age group, and this clearly reflects the migratory activity of females moving to the towns in search of more suitable work than that which was available in the rural areas. Correspondingly the proportion of teen-age males in the rural areas is very high, but this becomes less marked amongst the 20–30 year olds, as male migratory activity increased. Figure 8.2c, comparing the sex ratios of different age groups in the rural and urban populations, emphasises the points already made. It is well known that the number of male babies born usually exceeds the number of females and in the period 1841–51 the ratio was about 104 males to 100 females. This was more than compensated by the higher rates of infant mortality amongst male children and by a number of social factors, including the fact that young men were liable for military service and were more likely to emigrate overseas, and also that death rates for men were marginally higher than those for women. Women, therefore, generally outnumbered men and the sex ratio for the study area in 1851 was about 90 males to 100 females.

It is clear from figure 8.2c that a much higher proportion of women of all ages was to be found in the towns, although this was less marked amongst the very young and the middle-aged groups. The greatest difference between the urban and the rural sex-ratios occurred amongst the 10–19 year-olds. For this group the sex ratio in the rural areas is 122 males per 100 females, while in the three towns the corresponding figure was 82. Once again the implication is that migratory activity was most marked among the young adults and particularly among young women. The situation was essentially the same among the 20-year-olds, with a much higher proportion of females in the town populations, although by this time the male preponderence, which had been so evident in the previous age group in the rural areas, had been whittled away as the young men began to follow the girls to the towns and to take advantage of opportunities of employment in other parts of the country. The situation is more balanced in the middle-age sector, although there was still a higher proportion of women in the town population. This tended to become more marked amongst the oldest groups. When the sex ratios of the eleven parishes in the study area are studied individually the same general trends are observed. Throughout the first half of the century, the three towns each consistently recorded high ratios of females to males. This was most noticeable in the case of Totnes, where, in 1851, there were only 78 men to every 100 women. The range of employment opportunities available in Totnes, particularly in the service trades, would have been very attractive to young girls who could find little suitable employment in the rural areas. The eight rural parishes, on the other hand, tended to have high proportions of men in their populations, although the ratios fluctuated widely between 1801 and 1851; this was largely because of the small populations involved. The chief exception to the general trend was the parish of Broadhempston. In 1851 the sex ratio in Broadhempston was 94 males per 100 females and in 1831 the proportion of males had been as low as 79. The occupational evidence in the schedules suggests that there was a thriving shoemaking trade in the parish at this time and it is significant that a number of its processes are eminently suited to female labour.

To return to the original measure of mobility, only 58 per cent of the population of the study area were enumerated in 1851 in their parish of birth. It can be seen from Table 8.2 that in general the population of the three towns, taken as a group, was more 'stable' than that of the rural areas; that is, the percentage of persons resident in their parish of birth at the time of the census was greater in the towns than in the rural parishes. The figures are 60 per cent and 57 per cent respectively. With the exception of those for Dean Prior, the figures for Buckfastleigh Town and Ashburton Town are the highest (Table 8.2)—72 per cent and 62 per cent respectively. Either the native population of these towns was less ready to migrate than that of the rural parishes in the area, or these high values reflect a small level of in-migration into Ashburton and Buckfastleigh in relation to the size of their populations. This is probably the explanation of the high stability index for Ashburton, where population and economic activity were in a declining state at this time. In view of the greater economic and social opportunities which the towns provided, one would expect these to retain a higher proportion of their native population. In addition, because of their much greater number of homes and jobs, they could accommodate a considerable amount of 'concealed movement', that is, movement between one job or home and another, without there being any need to go into another parish. The evidence suggests that there is a relationship between the size of a parish and the apparent stability of its population, as expressed by the proportion of its residents who were born in that parish. The larger the parish the more stable was the population. It will be argued later that there was a constant shifting of the population. The larger the parish the greater the amount of movement that could be accommodated without the necessity of settlement beyond the parish boundaries. If a rural area could be defined as having a 'movement absorbency' equal to that of the towns, the rural-urban relationship in this respect could well be reversed, so that rural populations would appear more stable than urban populations.

In Totnes only 51 per cent of the town's population is recorded as having been born within the parish. Totnes was the administrative and commercial focus of the region, with good rail, road and water connections which facilitated wider and stronger links with the

TABLE 8.2

Native Population of Towns and Parishes in the Study Area in 1851

Parish	Total Population	Natives	Per Cent
Totnes	3,535 (excl. T.U.W.)	1,795	51
Ashburton	3,432	2,030	59
Ashburton Town	2,623	1,628	62
Ashburton Rural	809	402	50
Buckfastleigh	2,613	1,811	69
Buckfastleigh Town	2,170	1,561	72
Buckfastleigh Rural	443	250	57
Broadhempston	754	433	57
Buckland	141	70	50
Dartington	660	337	51
Dean Prior	507	373	74
Holne	386	208	55
Rattery	413	217	53
Staverton	1,152	685	60
Woodland	188	76	40
Rural Areas	5,453	3,051	56
Three Towns	8,328	4,984	60
TOTAL	13,781	8,035	58.5

rest of the country. It was not only an attractive destination for migratory movement in the area, therefore, but also a point of departure for longer distance movements to London and the industrial north. The figures given in Table 8.3 emphasise this wider range of contact. They show the percentages of the populations of the three towns derived from origins

TABLE 8.3

Percentage of the Population of the Three Towns from Outside Devon

Town	Population	Number Born Outside Devon	Per Cent
Totnes	3,535 (excl. T.U.W.)	333	9.4
Ashburton	2,623	198	7.5
Buckfastleigh	2,170	89	4.1
Rural Areas	5,453	258	4.7
Study Area	13,781	883	6.4

(birthplaces) outside Devon. The percentage for Totnes is much the highest at 9.4; Ashburton is next with 7.5, reflecting its function as a staging post on the main Exeter-Plymouth road. Buckfastleigh, with few of the social amenities and historical and physical advantages of the other two, included in its population only 89 people (4.1 per cent) who were born outside Devon. In comparison with the larger towns the rural parishes were very much isolated. Only 4.7 per cent of their population was born outside the county. In all about 6.4 per cent of the population of the area had been born outside the county of Devon and the majority of these, 422 out of a total of 883, came from the neighbouring counties of Cornwall, Dorset, Gloucestershire, Somerset and Wiltshire.

The bulk of the immigration into the study area was local in character; 85 per cent of the total immigration into the towns and parishes of the area (4,848 out of 5,746) was from recorded birthplaces in Devon. Figure 8.3 shows the distribution by parish of the birthplaces of these immigrants. The distribution pattern has three main features: a pattern of decreasing numbers with increased distance from the focus of movement; a marked grouping of migrants' birthplaces to the south and east of Dartmoor; and a number of striking secondary groupings and alignments within the general pattern already described.

The general principles of migratory behaviour which are responsible for this sort of pattern (Fig. 8.3) were first formulated by E. G. Ravenstein in 1885[12]. He had studied the birthplace data of the 1881 Census and in the light of his enquiries he made the following general observations regarding the migratory behaviour of the population:[13]

> "1   The great body of our migrants only proceed a short distance, and there takes place consequently a universal shifting or displacement of the population, which produces 'currents of migration' setting in the direction of the great centres of commerce and industry which absorb the migrants.
>
> 2   It is the natural outcome of this movement of migration, limited in range, but universal throughout the country, that the process of absorption would go on in the following manner: The inhabitants of the country immediately surrounding a town of rapid growth, flock into it; the gaps thus left in the rural population are filled up by migrants from more remote districts, until the attractive force of one of our rapidly growing cities makes its influence felt, step by step, to the most remote corner of the kingdom. Migrants enumerated in a certain centre of absorption will consequently grow less with the distance proportionately to the native population which furnishes them."

This trend is clear enough (Fig. 8.3), although before too many inferences are drawn it is advisable to note the extent to which the main distributional features are only a reflection of the distribution of population in the county at that time. Parishes of origin are most frequent in those areas of Devon where population densities are greatest, that is, their distribution is closely associated with the more fertile soils and the more accessible parts of the county. Even though the economic pressures encouraging emigration were greater in the more remote upland areas, these are less important as places of origin of migrants because of the small populations involved. The largest numbers of migrants, therefore, are from areas to the south and east of Dartmoor. The cities of Plymouth and Exeter and the rapidly growing

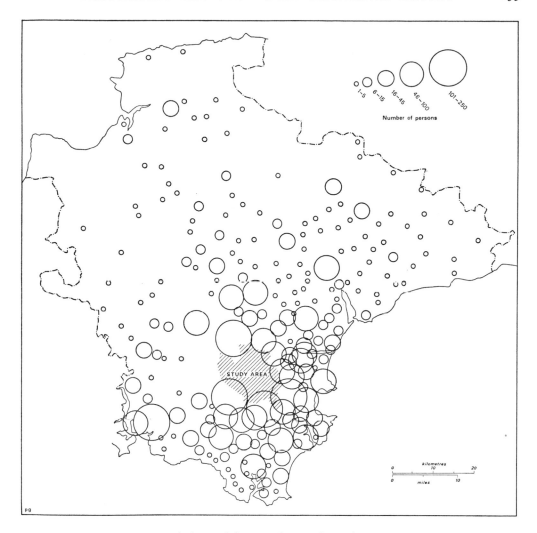

Fig. 8.3   Birthplaces of those resident in the study area in 1851.

coastal towns and resorts of Torquay, Dartmouth, Teignmouth and Kingsbridge all stand out as important contributors to the immigrant population of the area. Lines of more marked migratory contact also follow the large villages and small towns situated in the fertile valleys of the Culm, Clyst, Exe, Otter and the Axe. In north Devon two distinct groupings of birthplace origins are associated with the population concentrations around the estuaries of the Taw and Torridge. Another interesting alignment can be traced NW–SE between the Exe estuary and Barnstaple Bay, as lines of origin follow the more densely populated 'corridor' linking the Creedy Valley with those of the Yeo, Taw and Torridge.

Finally, alignments are suggested following the valley of the lower Dart and the main Exeter–Newton–Totnes and Ashburton Road.

It is clear, however, that the absolute numbers of migrants entering the study area from particular parishes in the county are not in themselves a particularly clear indication of the relative intensity of migratory activity between the various parts of the county and the study area.

In figure 8.4 the number of migrants from each parish of origin in Devon has been expressed as a percentage of the population of that parish. A generalised isopleth map has

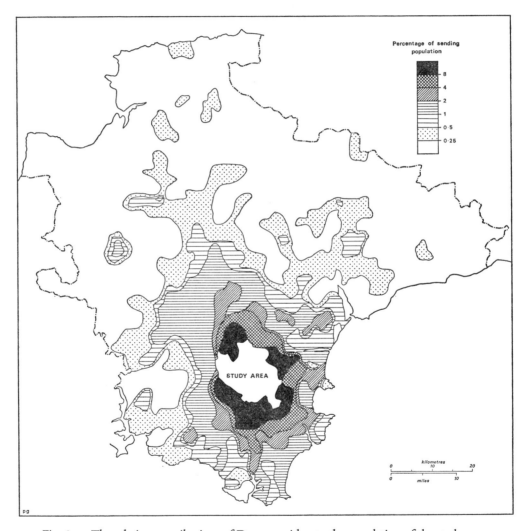

Fig. 8.4   The relative contributions of Devon parishes to the population of the study area.

been constructed on the basis of these figures in order to show the relative contribution of parishes in Devon to the population of the study area. This produces a picture of the intensity pattern of migratory activity focusing upon the area during this period. The map clearly supports Ravenstein's suggestion that "Migrants enumerated in a certain centre of absorption will grow less with the distance proportionately to the native population which furnishes them." There is a clear pattern of diminishing levels of movement into the study area with increased distance from it. More important is the fact that Exeter, Plymouth and the coastal towns no longer appear as important sources of immigrants. The number of migrants from each of these centres has now been related to the greater migratory potential of their large populations and this is a measure of the significance of the movement from these places. The information from which these maps have been constructed can easily give a misleading picture of the true migratory situation. The movements tend to be considered from the point of view of one absorbing centre. The Middle Dart Valley was not a major centre of attraction and, although Totnes was an important local focus, it would be wrong to think of migration in this area as being only one-way. For example, the birthplace data in the schedules for Broadhempston show that 54 of the inhabitants had been born in the neighbouring parish of Staverton. 58 persons enumerated in Staverton, however, were natives by birth of Broadhempston. The balance of movement in this case was in the opposite direction to that which would have been assumed if only Broadhempston had been studied.

Discussion

There are obvious problems in the use of the birthplace data in the census schedules as a means of analysing inter-parish migration; its traditional use can give only a very generalised picture of the range and direction of the complicated movements which were taking place. It cannot be assumed, for instance, that in each, or even in a majority of cases, the migrant travelled directly from the place of birth to the place of residence at the time of enumeration. Equally, a middle-aged man, enumerated as a resident of his parish of birth, may have travelled widely in the interim. A thorough search through successive census schedules (and at the moment this information is only available for 1851 and 1861) might be expected in theory to reveal the movements of all individuals at ten year intervals, but it is easy to see that, as the schedules give no information about destinations, once a migrant has left a parish it could be very difficult to trace him in the returns for the next census. In the light of this deficiency, the method described below is simply a variant on the more orthodox use of the birthplace data provided in the enumerators' schedules. Its object is to fill some of the gaps in our knowledge of a person's whereabouts between birth and enumeration. While birthplace is the only direct information given about the previous whereabouts of the population, there is one group for whom additional information can be inferred. In the case of women with children living at home, the place of birth of the mother is known; the place of birth of the children is known; and the place of residence of the mother at the time of the census is known. The knowledge of the place of birth of some or all of a mother's children provides valuable information about the whereabouts of the mother herself between her own birth and enumeration. The assumed line of movement of a mother identified in this way may be termed a 'trace' and the pattern of these 'traces' around any parish may be easily reconstructed and mapped (Table 8.4). The birthplace of the mother is given in the enumerator's schedule. Her location at the time of her confinements can be seen from the recorded birthplaces of her children, and her place of residence at the time of the census is known. The 'traces' in figure 8.5 have been constructed in this way from examples 1 (A–B–C–Broadhempston), 2 (X–Y–Z–Broadhempston), and 3 (1–2–3–4–Holne) in Table 8.4. In the first of these the 'trace' has been drawn from Paignton (A), the place of

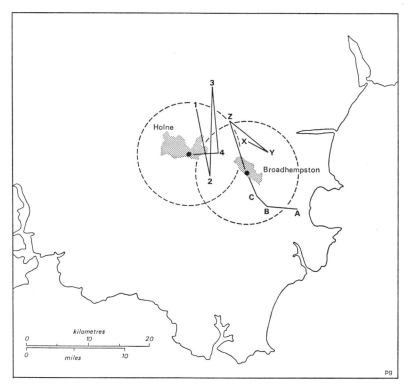

Fig. 8.5 Birth–confinement–residence–traces for 3 women enumerated in Broadhempston and Holne in 1851. Circles with radius of 8 km (5 miles) to scale.

birth of the mother, through Berry Pomeroy (B) and Littlehempston (C), where the earlier confinements occurred, to Broadhempston, where the mother was resident at the time of the census, and where the youngest of her children was born. In the same way additional 'traces' may be added to the map to complete a flow diagram of mothers' movements around the parish. It can be seen from the map for Broadhempston (Fig. 8.6a) constructed in this way

TABLE 8.4

The Places of Birth of Three Women Enumerated in Broadhempston and Holne in
1851 and the Birthplaces of their listed Children

	Place of Birth	Location of Confinements	Residence in 1851
1.	Paignton	Berry Pomeroy Berry Pomeroy Littlehampston Broadhempston	Broadhempston
2.	Bickington	Ogwell Ilsington	Broadhempston
3.	Widecombe	Buckfastleigh Manaton Ashburton Ashburton Ashburton	Holne

that movement was largely confined within a radius of 8 kilometres (5 miles) from the centre of the parish, and of this by far the greatest volume of movement took place between Broadhempston and Staverton. The pattern of 'traces' around Holne (Fig. 8.6b) appears to be less concentrated, probably because of the smaller number of women involved. Again, however, movements were clearly localised, and in this case two main axes predominated, one between Holne and Widecombe to the north, and the other between Holne and Buckfastleigh to the south-east. The degree to which Dartmoor was a barrier to short-distance migration in this area is suggested in both maps by the small number of 'traces' to the north-west.

There are a number of points to be considered in the evaluation of this method of identifying and depicting population mobility. In the first place, there is ample evidence of fairly large-scale local population movement at this time, especially amongst the lower classes of rural society. Employment was frequently seasonal and in order to find new employment it was often necessary for the labourer to look outside the parish in which he had been previously employed. Any regular movement of families from parish to parish in search of work would clearly be reflected in birthplaces of the children of those families. W. M. Williams[14] found that the population of Ashworthy, a small rural community in Devon, was "surprisingly mobile". Only 37.4 per cent of the farm labourers and their families remained in the same dwelling between 1841 and 1851. In addition, many people who left between 1841 and 1851, particularly farming families, reappeared in Ashworthy within the next 20 or 30 years, having returned from neighbouring parishes. Frequent references to inter-parish movements occur also in the notes included in the Reports of the

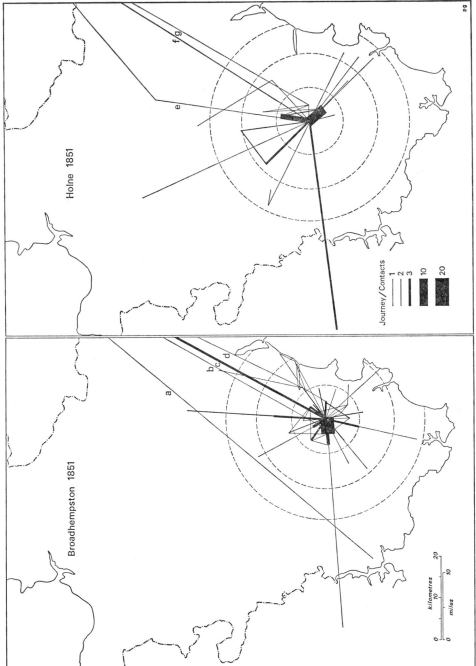

Fig. 8.6 (a) Birth–confinement–residence–traces around Broadhempston. (b) Birth–confinement–residence–traces around Holne. a, b, c, d, e, f, g indicate 'traces' which include a birthplace or confinements outside the county of Devon. The concentric circles in each case are drawn at intervals of 8 km (5 miles) from the focus of movement.

Census, like those for the parishes of Widworthy, Southleigh, Offwell, Cotleigh and Monkton, where the 1841-51 decrease in population was "ascribed to the amalgamation of small farms, which has lessened the demand for labour and induced many to emigrate, or to seek employment in adjoining parishes".[15] In addition, the Poor Law Reform Act of 1834 brought relief from many restrictions on movement imposed by previous laws, especially where movements between parishes within one Poor Law Union were concerned. It does seem likely, therefore, that, in view of the limited material possessions which might otherwise tie a labouring family to any one residence and in view of the evidence given above, families were moving frequently about the countryside. It is significant that, of all the married women with children listed in the schedule for Broadhempston, only 42 per cent show no evidence of movement. The corresponding figure for Holne is 36 per cent.

The principal weakness of the birth-confinement-residence-trace can be easily illustrated in the case of example 1 in Table 8.4. It was assumed that the mother moved from Paignton, where she was born, to Berry Pomeroy where the first 2 children were born. She is then thought to have moved to Littlehempston, where a third child was born, before settling in Broadhempston. The data is capable of other interpretations, however. It is quite possible, that while living at Broadhempston, the mother visited friends or relatives at Berry Pomeroy and later at Littlehempston and that the births took place during the course of these visits. The schedules give no reliable guide to the circumstances of a mother's presence in the recorded places of birth of her children. On the other hand, there are many instances where the pattern of confinement-locations for any one mother suggests very strongly that movement did in fact occur along the line of the assumed 'trace', or, at least, that the mother was resident in some of the confinement places for a considerable period. In the example from Holne, the mother gave birth to three of her children in Ashburton, suggesting that she was resident in that parish for several years. It might also be argued, however, that births may have occurred which are not recorded in the census and which might, if they were known, alter the line of a 'trace'. Similarly, the method does not take account of the possibility of 'fostering' and 'adoption' and of the presence of step-children, although these are sometimes explicitly designated. Finally, many of these possible shortcomings would be of less significance if, instead of 'traces' (that is, suggested lines of movement) only 'contacts' were identified and shown on the map. Maps showing the direction and extent of social contact around villages and parishes are of great interest and value, particularly in the degree to which they reveal the level of social isolation of rural communities. There is a close parallel here with the work of Peel,[16] Constant[17] and Perry,[18] all of whom used records of marriages recorded in parish registers to measure the extent and direction of social contact around rural communities in Northamptonshire, Huntingdonshire and Dorset.

REFERENCES

1 Redford, A. *Labour Migration in England, 1800-1850* (Manchester 1964), xiii

2 Armstrong, W. A. 'Social Structure from the Early Census Returns' in *English Historical Demography,* ed. E. A. Wrigley (London 1966), 209–237

Beresford, M. 'The unprinted census returns of 1841, 1851, 1861 for England and Wales' *The Amateur Historian,* 5 (1963), 260–269

Interdepartmental Committee on Social and Economic Research: *Guides to Official Sources, No. 2, Census Reports of Great Britain, 1801-1931* (HMSO, 1951)

3 Census of 1851, Report 1, Part 1, xlviii

4 Saville, J. *Rural Depopulation in England and Wales, 1851-1951* (London, 1957), 5

5 Hoskins, W. G. *Devon* (London 1954), 175

6 Fussell, G. E. 'Four Centuries of Farming Systems in Devon; 1500–1900' *Trans. Devon Ass.* 83 (1951), 179–204.

7 White, W. *History, gazetteer, and directory of the County of Devon, 1850* (Sheffield 1850), 462

8 Ibid. 461

9 Ibid. 515

10 Ibid. 442

11 Shapter, T. *The Climate of South Devon* (London 1862)

12 Ravenstein, E. G. 'The Laws of Migration', *J. Roy. Stat. Soc.* 48 (1885), 167–227

13 Ibid. 198–199

14 Williams, W. M. *A West Country Village, Ashworthy.* (London 1963), 129–131

15 Census of 1851, Report 1, Part 1, 40

16 Peel, R. F. 'Local intermarriage and the stability of rural population in the English Midlands' *Geography* 27 (1942), 22–30

17 Constant, A. 'The geographical background of inter-village population movements in Northamptonshire and Huntingdonshire, 1754–1943' *Geography* 33 (1948), 78–88

18 Perry, P. J. 'Working Class Isolation and Mobility in Rural Dorset 1837–1936: A study of marriage distances'. *Trans. Inst. Brit. Geographers* 46 (1969), 121–141

9

Recreation and Land Use—A Study in the Dartmoor National Park

MARK BLACKSELL

> . . . shalt thou—alone—
> Dartmoor—in this fair land, where all beside
> Is life and beauty—sleep the sleep of death,
> And shame the map of England?
> N. T. Carrington: *Dartmoor—a descriptive poem* London 1826

Contrary to popular belief, the landscapes of Dartmoor are exceptionally varied. The conception of a bare, wild granite dome, surmounted by imposing tors, so often bandied around, is far from giving a complete picture, and the lush woodland of the steep valleys with their fast flowing streams, the large Forestry Commission plantations and the reservoirs are just as characteristic of this part of Devon. Every year thousands of visitors are drawn to Dartmoor and its varied wilderness. However, despite its attractions and despite the fact that it was designated as a National Park more than twenty years ago, very little public effort or money has been devoted to educating a curious public as to what is available. For most people—certainly those living outside Devon—the moor remains an enigma isolated in a remote part of the country and, when visitors come to see it, they usually have little idea of what to look for or how to find out about it. The main aim of this study is to develop a generalised approach for assessing how Dartmoor could be used to its fullest possible extent for the benefit of the nation, without destroying its essential character and resources.

This is a problem that to some degree affects all the National Parks. The unimaginative and inefficient use at present made of most of these areas is a direct result of the elements of compromise which characterise the legislation leading to their initial designation as National Parks. The 1949 National Parks and Access to the Countryside Act insisted, against the advice of two earlier White Papers[1, 2], that these areas be administered by local authorities, rather than as separate entities. Finance was also to be the responsibility of the local authority, although certain expenses could be reclaimed from central Government funds. Indeed,

143

the only direct National control was through the National Parks Commission, but as this was a purely advisory body its influence, at both national and local levels, was strictly limited. The results were predictable and unfortunate. On the one hand local authorities took very little interest in the National Parks, except to impose rather negative restrictions on development, in order to appease conservation organisations; on the other, Government Departments found that, in general, they were easily able to overcome any objections to development which they wished to sponsor in these areas, even though it was often totally at odds with the idea of a National Park as an area preserved as part of the national heritage for public enjoyment. This situation persisted for nearly twenty years, until, in 1968, the Countryside Act was passed. It was a major step forward, but by no means the complete answer to the problems of the National Parks. Although the Countryside Commission, which replaced the National Parks Commission, has much wider executive powers and is able to argue on an equal footing with other Government interests, most of the administrative and financial dilemmas remain. The Countryside Commission has used its influence to bring considerable pressure to bear on local authorities to take a greater and more active interest in the Parks under their jurisdiction, but the responsibility is still basically a local one. Even after the strong recommendations of the Maud report,[3] there is still only a suggestion, set out in the recent White Paper on Local Government Reform in England and Wales[4] of more autonomous and powerful bodies, to replace the present system of advisory boards and sub-departments of planning offices. The idea that the Parks should fill a national need and therefore ought to be nationally administered still seems a long way from being fully accepted.

    And so a study such as this of the potential of the landscape resources of a National Park must be framed in a national, not a local context. For this reason the evaluation of opinions about Dartmoor and of its resources must use techniques that can easily be applied to Parks elsewhere in the country, otherwise meaningful comparisons will be impossible. Three basic sets of information were vital for achieving this goal. First, one had to find out what the community at large wanted from Dartmoor and what it thought it had to offer; secondly there was a need for a detailed inventory of the amenities that already existed; and finally, since suggestions must be practical, it was essential to investigate fully any constraints on development and change.

The public need

Generalisations about the public are notoriously inaccurate and hard to substantiate, but for planning purposes information is essential and attempts to improve its quality must continue unabated. Although limited residential accommodation has meant that Dartmoor has compared rather unfavourably with most of the coastal resorts in the South-West,[5] every year thousands of visitors come on day outings and the number is steadily increasing.[6] To find out how these people used the National Park and how they felt about its future development, a questionnaire survey was carried out in the week 12th–19th June 1968. Ideally this should have covered a representative cross-section of all visitors, but sampling problems made this impossible.[7] Since the statistical significance of the survey for the whole population of visitors was, as a result, strictly limited, it seemed sensible to complete a relatively small number of questionnaires in depth. Only 150 people at six separate sites were interviewed, but even so the information collected was most revealing. The suggestion so often made, that Dartmoor is appreciated chiefly by a small number of enthusiastic minorities and that the bulk of tourists have little interest in it or its future, seems to be completely unfounded. The sample included people from all over Britain and every age group and major social class was well represented; the chi-squared test showed only nominal differences[8] between the various groups in their attitudes towards the National Park and the use made of it. Much could be read into these results, but further circumstantial evidence from the survey indicated that few of the visitors knew much about the National Park before they came and this lack of information strictly limited the scope of their activities, no matter what their background.

The survey first tried to find out more precisely just how much people knew about Dartmoor before they arrived. Nearly everyone (90 per cent) was aware that Dartmoor was a National Park and that they themselves were in it, but for the majority this was the full extent of their awareness. Only a minority (38 per cent) had with them a map, other than a small scale road map. The time was opportune for asking whether visitors possessed a map, since at that time the Ordnance Survey had only just published the one inch Tourist Map of the National Park. The lack of maps was of considerable importance, since without them the area accessible was effectively limited to the immediate vicinity of the major roads. When other sources of information were investigated there was even less response. Although over half the visitors interviewed said that at one time or another they had consulted a book on Dartmoor, only 30 per cent had actually seen, let alone used, the official guide to the Park. In a similar vein, nearly half the people knew about the National Park Information Centre at Two Bridges, but less than 5 per cent had ever actually visited it. It is an indictment of the Centre itself that the rate of response to this question was only marginally better here than the average for the survey as a whole. In fairness, however, it should be added, that since 1969 the site has been changed to a more prominent one on the main road, A384.

In general there was a much greater awareness of the restrictions to movement on the moor. Most people (85 per cent) knew of the limitations imposed by military training; over half (54 per cent) realised that all the land in the National Park was privately owned and that right of access was, therefore, strictly limited. The important point to emerge from these questions was that, when further asked if they had been impeded in any way by these or other restrictions, only a very small minority (12 per cent) admitted to noticing them at all. Military training and farming did not in any way prevent the majority of visitors from enjoying Dartmoor. Indeed, if there were any complaints, they were from the farmers and military, irritated by the influx of tourists.

What people did once they reached Dartmoor was obviously limited by the lack of information demonstrated above. Aside from wanting to catch a glimpse of the prison at Princetown, the majority of visitors come to the moor with only the most vague aims. Over three-quarters (76 per cent) of those interviewed gave as their main reason the wish for a quiet drive in the open country. Most, when pressed, agreed that they would park their car, picnic, sunbathe and perhaps have a short stroll. However, they were emphatic that they would not be trying to reach any sites or places of particular interest, such as the ancient monuments, tors or special view-points for which Dartmoor is famous, nor did they want to take part in any outdoor activities such as swimming, riding and boating. Indeed, in the sample as a whole the only open air pursuits to figure at all prominently were walking and swimming. Nearly a third of those interviewed (32 per cent) said that they intended to walk more than a mile over the open moorland and 12 per cent wanted to go swimming, but only a handful had any desire to go climbing or to visit the Nature Trail at Bellever (SX 654773) and even fewer were interested in riding, boating or canoeing. These results are in no way surprising and the pattern conforms very broadly to the national picture described by Sillitoe[9] in his nation-wide survey of the use of leisure time, but they do high-light two important points for future development in the National Park. First of all, even if there were more extensive provision for open air pursuits, it is doubtful whether demand would grow very rapidly, unless this expansion were also accompanied by commercial development to service the day tripper in his car. Secondly, the parts of Dartmoor where heavy demands are made on the land by tourists are limited, at the moment, to those where there is free and easy access by car and there is no indication that this is likely to change in the near future.

At the present time the provision of services for the vast number of visitors to Dartmoor is extremely meagre. In fine weather during the summer public-houses, cafés and car parks are all hopelessly overcrowded, yet it emerged from the survey that only a minority of visitors use these facilities. Despite the fact that nearly everyone had come to the moor by car (96 per cent), less than half had at any time during their visit parked their car in an official car park, either free or paying. Only a third had bought anything from a shop or kiosk since entering the National Park and only a quarter had used a public convenience. The proportion of people interviewed using filling stations, public houses and cafés was even smaller than this. Clearly it is nonsense to talk of the commercialisation of Dartmoor: the National Parks Committee has obviously kept a very tight rein on this type of exploitation. On the other hand, it is also clear that there is very little organisation of either activities or facilities. It will be suggested later in this study that it would be possible and even desirable to expand some of these amenities in a planned fashion and, by judicious charging, to raise some much-needed income for future investment. If a proper programme were worked out, it could, in the long term, considerably enhance Dartmoor.

Most of the people interviewed were greatly concerned about the future of the Park. They felt, rightly or wrongly, that it was potentially threatened by commercial exploitation and they welcomed any measures to protect and maintain it in its present state. The vast majority (over 85 per cent) were vehemently against such things as the provision of play-grounds for children, even if they were properly landscaped and cared for, and most people were even against developments like the signposting of paths across the moor. More car parks were also looked upon with considerable disfavour, despite the fact that during the weekend most of the verges on the roads over the open moorland were jammed with vehicles. Given this solid resistance to any sort of change in the amenities and facilities offered, it was rather surprising to find that the majority of people (62 per cent) were in favour of more stretches of open water and woodland with public access. Indeed there was only minimal criticism of these more recent additions to the Dartmoor landscape. Overall the sympathetic appreciation of the future problems of the National Park was considerable and most people were prepared to back their words with action. Over three-quarters said that they would welcome more restrictions on traffic and over two-thirds said that they would have no objection to paying an entry fee to the National Park.[10] However, very few of those interviewed really had sufficient information to make practical suggestions for future development and most had only the haziest notions of the cost of maintaining Dartmoor as a National Park and of where the finance came from.

Taking the survey as a whole, there were three conclusions of importance for this study. First of all it was clear that the attractions of Dartmoor had a very wide appeal; it seemed that there was no major section of the population that did not come in large numbers. Secondly, even though there was a wide basis of support for the National Park, most people had very little idea of what it had to offer or what it had to administer. Lastly, it was absolutely clear that the attempts made so far to introduce people to the amenities of Dartmoor and to help them enjoy them had been unsuccessful. The majority of visitors interviewed wanted things left just as they were, but one was left with the distinct impression that this was largely because they had no conception of the range of possibilities.

Amenity in the National Park

Having established some measure of what people wanted, it was necessary to find out to what extent the need was satisfied. In order to do this, a full-scale comparative survey of amenity within the Dartmoor National Park had to be undertaken and the results had to portray what Jean Forbes has called "the spatial distribution of locational attractiveness".[11] This could have been achieved by categorising all Dartmoor's many tourist attractions and then displaying these in a series of maps. However, besides being a laborious exercise, such results would have been very hard to interpret. Assigning weightings to the variables chosen would have been virtually impossible, but this is essential if such factors as public attitudes and accessibility are to be taken into consideration. It was decided, therefore, to use the kilometre grid to divide up the whole of Dartmoor and then to assign to each square a value, based on a pre-determined index. Although it was fully appreciated that kilometre squares were a rather crude unit of measurement, this system still produced 1,020 separate areas for consideration. The final results of the exercise are shown in Figure 9.1 and, even though this end product is a considerable simplification of the original field survey, it highlights some most interesting points. For instance it is quite clear that there is a large amount of variation in the recreational value of land on Dartmoor and also that the most valuable areas are both limited in extent and grouped closely together. Such results are of the utmost significance for future development. However, one must thoroughly understand the survey method, before one can examine the results in detail.

The first step in this exercise was to make an inventory of all the amenities which might conceivably attract people to the moor. Once this had been done and relative values had been assigned to each category, some composite index could be arrived at. It was therefore decided to use a scale of numbers from 1–5 and to give each amenity a score, which, although entirely subjective, would be weighted as far as possible in accordance with the results of the questionnaire survey of public attitude discussed above. The problems involved in drawing up the initial list were of course enormous and it was decided that the only practical method was by using a combination of field survey and information from the one-inch Tourist Map of Dartmoor. The results, together with the weightings, are set out in Table 9.1. The data was all discrete and could therefore be recorded on the grid simply by

TABLE 9.1

Tourist attractions		Recreational facilities		Accommodation		Other Services	
Viewpoints (marked on map)	5	Fishing	4	Caravan sites	5	Information centre	5
Dartmoor Prison	5	Riding School	4	Camping sites	5	Car Park	4
Tors (named)	5	Golf Course	4	Youth Hostels	5	Railway station	3
Historical sites	3	Footpaths and untarred roads	3	Hotels	4	Bus Stop	3
Archaeological sites	3			Inn	4	Telephone	2
Nature reserves	3					Public convenience	1
Woods	3					Shop	1
Tors (unnamed)	2					Post Office	1
National Park letter boxes	2						
Areas of special scientific note	2						
Triangulation point	1						
Churches	1						

the presence or absence of a particular amenity in a given square, but for some sorts of data a continuous form of recording was deemed to be more satisfactory. Roads and open stretches of water are both so attractive and so ubiquitous in their influence that it was felt that, wherever they occurred in the National Park, their presence or absence would be of importance. For this reason the following scales were worked out to accommodate them. If an A, B or C road passed through a grid square, it was given a score of 5, 4 or 3 respectively. If a square had no road in it, the distance to the nearest one of any class was measured and the following values assigned: up to 2 miles distant 1; 2–3 miles 0; 3–4 miles —1; and 4–5 miles —2. It was found that there was nowhere on Dartmoor more than 5 miles from a road. A similar system was employed for water, except that here the definition of a body of water was more difficult. The problem was overcome by including only reservoirs, lakes and ponds and those reaches of river shown on the one-inch Tourist Map by a double blue line. A value of 4 was given if there was open water shown within a grid square and then 2 if the nearest stretch was under a mile distant, 1 for 1—2 miles; 0 for 2–3 miles, —1 for 3–4 miles and —2 for 4–5 miles. Once again nowhere on the moor was more than 5 miles from open water.

The only other data which needed to be incorporated in the index, were those things which positively debased Dartmoor's value for the majority of visitors. From the survey it was clear that there was very little about which people actively grumbled, and most felt that the restrictions on movement impeded them only minimally. Only two non-attractions had, therefore, to be included: the military training ground was an obvious case and was awarded a value of —1; the other was marshland, which, while varying a great deal in character and in the value attached to it, was given a general rating of —2.

Once the numbers had been computed for the whole of the National Park, they produced

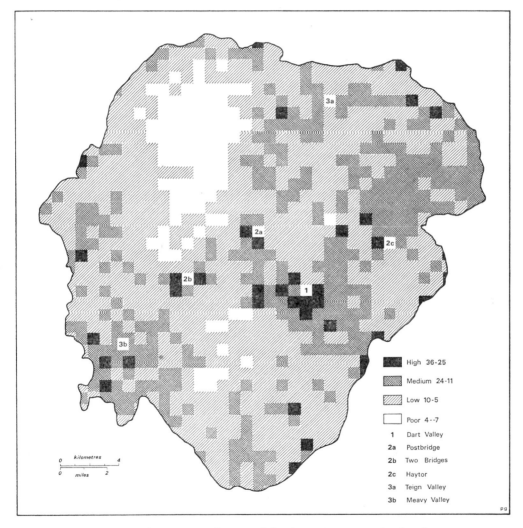

Fig. 9.1   The recreational potential for the Dartmoor National Park.

values for the grid squares ranging from 36 to —7. However, for the purposes of appreciating the main results of the analysis, such detail was quite unnecessary and the mass of information was reduced to the four categories shown in Figure 9.1. The map reveals a definite pattern in the distribution of amenities and shows the preponderance of development in the eastern third of the moor. Besides being the area where there is the greatest amount of enclosed farmland, this is also the section of Dartmoor where the landscape is most heavily dissected. The countryside here is much more varied than on the higher open moorland and it therefore presents a much greater range of possibilities for the visitor. Indeed, the areas of high moorland away from the roads in the north-west and the south, which contain the most characteristic landscapes of the National Park (Plate 12), emerge as having very little to offer the vast majority of tourists.

This conclusion is important, since any discussion of the problems of preserving the landscape can now start to concentrate on those areas that are really threatened by crowding and over-exploitation. There are three groups of area that potentially fall under this heading. The first is the Dart valley between Durrabridge (SX 747646) and the A38 trunk road (SX 668742). This area shown in Plate 13, besides being one of outstanding beauty, is both accessible and, by Dartmoor standards, heavily settled. As a result it has attracted more than its fair share of tourists and commercial growth. Even so it has yet to be singled out as an area where planning and development controls should be applied with the utmost stringency in order to preserve and take full advantage of the existing amenity. The second group, (Postbridge (SX 653792) (Plate 14), Two Bridges (SX 610750), Widecombe (SX 719769) and Haytor (SX 758771)) are all areas where the attractions are fairly concentrated. At Postbridge the combination of the clapper bridge, the nature trail and the hamlet itself encourage the casual visitor driving across the moor to stop; the same sort of attractions characterise the village of Widecombe. At Two Bridges the crossroads and above all the National Park Information Centre inevitably are going to draw increasingly large numbers of people to this point. Haytor is in a slightly different category, in that its attractions spring almost entirely from the scenery. Its high rating is due to a combination of factors: it is a typical example of a Dartmoor tor; it is easily accessible and also it commands an unsurpassed view of south-east Devon. Although there is dense traffic at these three points throughout the summer, the fact that each of them is fairly isolated means that there is considerable scope for future expansion and improvement of amenities. Haytor, for instance, has no proper facilities for coping with the influx of cars, which occurs every weekend in the holiday season, yet it would be relatively easy and inexpensive to deal comfortably with even larger numbers. The situation at Postbridge is similar. Despite the attractions of this hamlet, the first official car park was not opened until 1969.

The third group of areas has a slightly lower level of amenity than the first two. It is not that the areas are any less attractive in terms of natural beauty, but that their charms are in general less compact, less accessible and have, as yet, experienced less commercial development. The Teign valley and Fernworthy reservoir (SX 665840) in the north-east and the Meavy valley and Burrator reservoir (SX 560685) in the south-west are typical of this type of area. It would seem that there is a strong case for restricting development in some or all of these areas. The reasons are basically twofold: first of all it is important, for the sake of the natural landscape and ecology, that some valleys be left remote and inaccessible. Secondly, it is better from an economic point of view to try to concentrate economic development at a few well chosen sites. As has already been shown, the Dart valley would be ideal for accommodating some future growth and the development of another valley along similar lines would be something of a duplication.

Constraints on development and change

One of the main justifications for this study has been to try to put the case for recreational

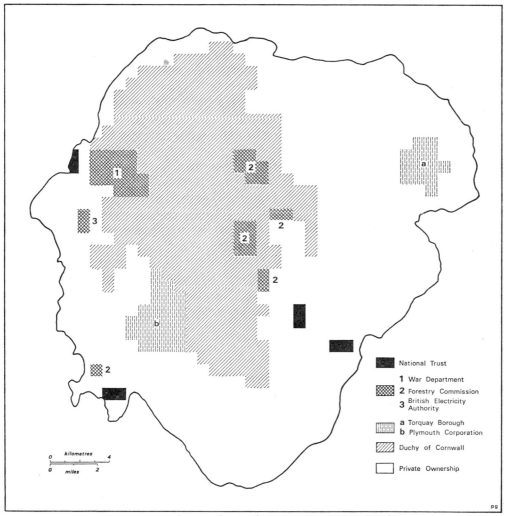

Fig. 9.2   Land ownership in the Dartmoor National Park.

development, so that it can compete with more vocal, organised, but often less well-founded claims on land. So far the emphasis has been on what people like and what the National Park has to offer them. However, despite the fact that Dartmoor is a National Park, recreation has to compete with a number of other uses, among them military, agricultural, forestry and water boards. However, the most serious conflicts are on two fronts. First there is the very serious difficulty that all the land in the National Park is privately owned, with the exception of some small areas which have been bought by government agencies and local authorities for non-recreational purposes; second there is the fact that tourists have to compete with other interests for the small amount of land that is available.

The private ownership of land has been the single largest stumbling block to development and change on Dartmoor. It has unfortunately meant that, instead of guiding the area into a programme of planned change, the powers of the National Parks Committee have largely been limited to placing restrictions on the activities of land owners. It is fruitless to talk about expanding amenities here and preserving the natural landscape there, unless one has the active and willing co-operation of those controlling the land. As can be seen from Figure 9.2 the only areas of the moor that are managed solely for recreation and conservation are the four small enclaves owned by the National Trust. The rest is all in private hands, with the exception of the limited areas owned by the Forestry Commission, the War Department, the British Electricity Authority and the Corporations of Torbay and Plymouth. Of the private owners, by far the largest is the Duchy of Cornwall. Since these are Royal lands, there would probably not be much difficulty in getting reasonable requests for development accepted in this estate. Unfortunately, however, all the Duchy lands cover the high open moorland and, as has been shown, this is the area with the least promise at the moment for tourism. The picturesque and easily accessible valleys on the periphery of the granite dome are all owned by completely private individuals. Thus any large-scale planning in these areas demands the acquiescence of a large number of persons.

The conflict of recreation with other uses of the land on Dartmoor has emerged in the course of this study as being less of a problem than it is often made out to be. It has been shown that both forestry plantations and reservoirs add to rather than detract from, the tourist potential of the Park, while military training impedes only a small number, and then relatively slightly. Unfortunately the question of agriculture is less easily solved. As can be seen from Figure 9.3, the areas of enclosed land extend right round the periphery of the National Park while in the east they penetrate right into its heart. The problem is not only that agricultural land limits the movement and access of visitors: if agriculture is to remain healthy, it must move with the times. New farming methods are going to necessitate changes in the rural landscape and this will mean changes in the traditional face of Dartmoor. This is not the place to examine this metamorphosis in detail, but one striking example might be considered. Dry stone walls are characteristic of upland Devon and Dartmoor in particular. Modern farming, however, demands that labour costs must be kept to a minimum and this means larger fields surrounded by easily erected barbed wire fences. The farmer recognises as well as anybody else that this is against the spirit of the National Park, but he is unable to bear the crippling extra cost of eschewing change. Here is the nub of the whole

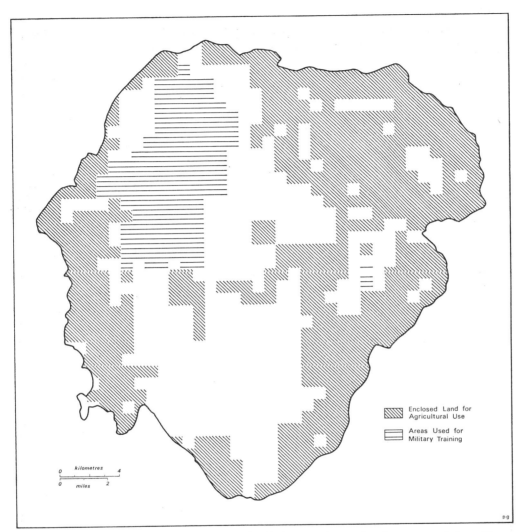

Fig. 9.3   Areas of the Dartmoor National Park which are either enclosed or reserved for military training.

problem; if agriculture and tourism are to exist side by side it cannot be at the farmer's expense. It is not a question of doing the farmer down; he will simply go out of business and the landscape one is trying to preserve will decay anyway. The same argument can be extended, in modified form, to the other conflicts in land use on Dartmoor. Unless tourism and recreation are accepted as integral to the National Park, and existing users are allowed to take advantage of their presence, they will never be able to fuse harmoniously into the landscape.

Conclusion

Dartmoor is one of the wildest and most stark of the National Parks and its cultural land-scape highlights as well as any in the country man's continuing struggle to come to terms with the natural environment. Every possible effort must be made to preserve this area for the national posterity, but, at the same time, as many people as possible must be given the chance to share in the experience of the moor. Up to the present time planning policy has concentrated on keeping the mass of visitors at bay, in order that nothing in the National Park shall be destroyed, rather than trying to introduce people to an exciting new world. As a result, although visitors come every year in their thousands, they are hide-bound by a lack of information and the majority are merely spectators, not active participants, in what the moor has to offer. If the National Park is to survive successfully, this must be changed. Tourism must be accepted as an integral part of Dartmoor's landscape and active co-operation must be developed between it and other uses of land. In order to achieve this result it is essential that the spectre of conflict be removed and one of active partnership be put in its place.

This study has highlighted some of the problems and possibilities. The questionnaire survey showed that the visitors to the moor have a wide range of tastes and backgrounds and in most cases they are unsure of what to expect from the National Park. It would be futile to try to satisfy everyone, but that is no excuse for trying to satisfy no one. Greater publicity and effort spent on advertising the moor's major attractions could add immeasur-ably to people's enjoyment. One of the main objections to this kind of development has been that it would produce over-crowding in an already congested area, but the amenity survey showed that real overcrowding is only likely to occur at a few easily defined points and even there the problem may be far from insuperable. In their classic work on outdoor recreation, Clawson and Knetsch[12] forcibly make the point that amenity does not necessarily increase with fewer people. Proper planning can accommodate high densities even in areas with the most fragile landscape and indeed the presence of other people in the right numbers is often an essential catalyst for proper enjoyment. One of the main points of this study has been to show the need for such growth and development and to point out how the most suitable areas can be logically selected.

The critical misconception perpetrated about the Dartmoor National Park is that there is an irreconcilable conflict between the land and the people who want to use it. The opposite is the case: the people who use the land are in fact responsible for the landscape. Tourism, like agriculture before it, can make a great contribution to the moor and it should be allowed to do so. The isolationism of the South-West is notorious: it will be a tragedy if this is allowed to continue and spill over into its National Parks.

ACKNOWLEDGEMENTS

I should like to thank Devon County Council and the many students who gave me invaluable help with this study.

REFERENCES

1 National Parks in England and Wales (The Dower Report), Cmd 6628, 1942
2 National Parks Committee (England and Wales) Report (the Hobhouse Report), Cmd 7121, 1947
3 Royal Commission on Local Government in England and Wales 1966–1969, Vol 1, Report, Cmd 4040-1, 1969
4 Reform of Local Government in England, Cmd 4276, 1970
5 F. M. M. Lewes. A. J. Culyer and G. A. Brady. 'The holiday industry' in *Exeter and its region* ed. F. Barlow (Exeter, 1969) 245
6 It is estimated by Devon County Council that nearly 2 million visitors came to the National Park in 1969
7 The cost of undertaking a survey of all visitors to the National Park was prohibitive and no attempt was made to draw a statistical sample. The sample chosen was, however, checked against the national population and the chi-squared test showed the correspondence to be significant at the 95 per cent level
8 In all cases the null hypothesis was accepted (95 per cent level)
9 Ministry of Housing and Local Government, Government Social Survey Individual Studies 1969 *Planning for leisure* by K. Sillitoe, Report No SS 388, London HMSO 1969, 38
10 In the questionnaire an entry fee of 12½p was suggested
11 Jean Forbes. 'A map analysis of potentially developable land' *Regional Studies* Vol 3, 1969, 179
12 M. Clawson and J. Knetsch. *The economics of outdoor recreation* (Baltimore 1966)

IO

The definition of Factors influencing Spatial Variability in Gross Output per acre on farms in South Devon

W. J. ARMSTRONG

Economic geographers are interested in the answer to two basic questions. The first concerns the spatial distribution of the particular forms of economic activity and the second considers why the spatial distribution appears in a particular form.

Research in economic geography until the last decade tended to pursue the descriptive approach embodied in the first question, but during the last ten years there has been an increased amount of interest in the functional approach embodied in the second. At least part of the reason for this broadening interest seems to be the growing awareness of the need to plan the use of our natural resources in order that the maximum satisfaction may be derived by the community as a whole. Once the question arises as to where a certain type of economic activity should be located in the future, it is apparent that a description of its present location is of limited use. Only by knowing *why* that activity is located where it is can we decide whether that location is the most desirable one and where it should be located in the future. The answer to "why" involves the determination of the factors responsible for the present distribution, while the extension of this information to the planning stage requires mapping of the spatial variations in these factors.

The need to determine the spatial distribution of the value of land for different uses is an important example. Increasing demands for land for urban and industrial development, recreation, water conservation, forestry and agriculture, coupled with the inadequacy of the free market to obtain an acceptable distribution among these various uses, emphasises the need to plan the use of land in Britain and this is now readily accepted by most sections of the community. If planners are to carry out this task successfully, then they will need considerable information on the spatial variations in the value of land for these uses.

This line of thought provides the *raison d'être* for land classification. The classification of the value of land for any one particular use must rely on an assessment of the spatial variations in factors known to have a significant influence on the utility of land for that use.

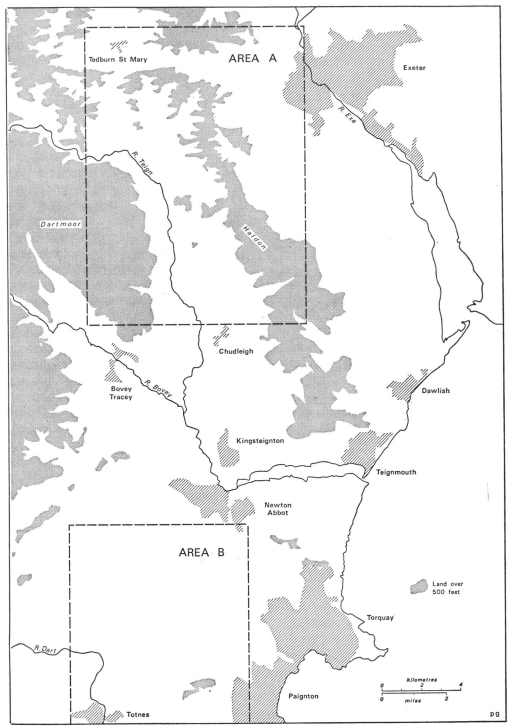

Fig. 10.1   South Devon.

The definition of the causative factors and the answer to the question "why" becomes all important, therefore, since it must be obtained before the relevant pattern of land values can be established.

Most agricultural land classification schemes have tended to use an approach similar to that outlined above. There has been a tendency, however, to make *ad hoc* assumptions about the influence of various factors on agricultural productivity. It has been common procedure, for instance, to assume that soil is the principal determinant of agricultural productivity and many agricultural land classification systems are based on this assumption. It is certainly true that, in most cases, soil has an important influence on agricultural productivity, but many other factors such as farm structure, type of farming and level of management, are also important. Furthermore, it should be recognised that "soil" is a term which includes many characteristics of the uppermost crust of the earth's surface, and the agricultural significance of each one of these characteristics varies from crop to crop, from one farming system to another and also between regions. It would seem, therefore, that there is a need to define those factors which are important in creating variations in agricultural productivity in the area concerned; having defined these factors, one can then proceed to classify land in the normal fashion.

With these considerations in mind the present research has been undertaken. The primary objective is to discover whether, using data collected from a sample of farms, it is possible to define some of the more important factors responsible for the variability of agricultural land values in south Devon.

It is considered that the basic unit of investigation should be the farm. At this level the various combinations of factors which influence the value of land for agricultural use can be assessed in terms of the interactions between the farmer and his economic and physical environment. The outcome of this interaction on each farm is a unique system of farming from which a particular output per acre will be obtained and it is contended that only by examining the variations in the productivity of land at this scale can a true assessment of the relative influence of each factor be made. Since a farming system can be composed of so many possible types and intensities of land use, it is necessary in a quantititive study of this nature to devise a single quantitative criteria of value which can be used to indicate the output of the system as a whole. The criteria chosen in this case is gross output per acre. The gross output per acre is defined simply as the total monetary value of all produce, divided by the total farm acreage.

In practice there are considerable difficulties involved in defining the influence of all possible factors on the spatial variation in gross output. There is the problem of the very large number of factors which could be considered. Fortunately access to a high speed computer considerably reduces the computational problems associated with such a large scale project. It is the time and expense involved in the collection of data which present the greatest difficulty. It is virtually impossible without long-term investment in expensive equipment to acquire sufficiently detailed information on farm to farm variations in physical factors such as climate. With the economic factors involved, one of the principal problems is that of gaining access to information such as levels of capital investment or the net return

M

obtained on each farm. On the social side probably the greatest problem of all arises in the assessment of a farmer's managerial ability.

For several reasons, therefore, it is obviously impossible to explain all of the variations in gross output per acre, but this should not deter an attempt to derive some explanation from the information which is readily available. In this study, the influence of the following nine factors on variations in gross output per acre was examined:

(a) texture of the farm's soil,
(b) drainage qualities of the farm's soil,
(c) distance of the farm from the sea,
(d) altitude of the farm,
(e) size of the farm,
(f) distance of the farm from the market,
(g) age of the farmer,
(h) number of years he has been manager of that farm,
(i) degree of specialization attained on the farm.

Factors (a) and (b) have been chosen to represent all of the various soil characteristics which could be taken into consideration, since the nature of so many of the agriculturally significant soil properties are dependent on these two factors. In the absence of any detailed information on the variation of climate from farm to farm, factors (c) and (d) were chosen. They were chosen because they are commonly held to be important factors responsible for variations in agriculturally significant climatic properties. According to economic theory the two variables (e) and (f) should have a significant influence on the intensity of production. Small farms should have a higher gross output per acre than have large farms, while farms close to the market should have a higher gross output per acre than those located farther away. Factors (g) and (h) are used as expressions of some part of the farmer's managerial ability. Factor (h) is chosen because of the high rate of turnover in farmers in the area. It was also felt that, since the farms which have become increasingly specialized over the past 15 years have also increased their intensity of production, there could now be a considerable variation in gross output per acre obtained on these farms as compared to the less specialized or mixed farms. Factor (i) was included for this reason and the degree of specialization obtained on each farm was measured by calculating the percentage of total income derived from the main enterprise.

The collection and preliminary processing of field information

A random sample of 40 farms was selected from two areas in south Devon (Fig. 10.1). Area A lies on the north-eastern margin of the South Hams in the environs of Paignton, Newton Abbot, and Totnes. Area B occurs in the Middle Teign valley and extends from Chudleigh in the south to Tedburn St Mary in the north. Both areas are underlain by varied lithologies. In the southern area there are parent materials of Upper, Middle and Lower Devonian age, and on the eastern margin, some farms are located on New Red Sandstones. In the northern area the principal parent materials are granite and Culm slates and cherts.

In this unglaciated part of Britain, parent material has such a strong influence on the development of soils and topography, that it could be argued that, at least in these respects, the two areas contain a representative spectrum of physical farming conditions in south Devon. The 40 farms in the sample were visited and information on land use and livestock numbers was collected. This information was used to calculate the gross output per acre of each farm. To complete these calculations it was necessary to make use of the standard gross output figures for the South West, as published annually by the Provincial Agricultural Economics Service. These standard output figures are effectively an expression of the average gross output per acre (yield × price) obtainable from any crop enterprise, or the average gross return per animal obtainable from any livestock enterprise.

The following three steps were used to calculate the gross output per acre for each of the 40 farms:

(1) Estimation of gross output from crops,

$$Y = \sum_{i=1}^{i=N} X_i S_i$$

where Y = gross output from crops,
$i_{1....N}$ = crops grown on farm
X_i = acreage devoted to that crop
S_i = standard output per acre for that crop.

(2) Estimation of gross output from livestock,

$$Z = \sum_{i=1}^{i=N} L_i S_i$$

where Z = gross output from livestock,
$i_1 \ldots N$ = types of livestock
L_i = number of animals of that type
S_i = standard output per animal for that type.

(3) Estimation of gross output per acre,

from $\dfrac{Y + Z}{A}$

where Y and Z are as in (1) and (2) above and A = total acreage of the farm.

Information on soil texture, state of soil drainage, size of the farm, age of the farmer and the number of years he had been on his present farm was also collected by questionnaire. The information on soil texture and soil drainage was checked with soil maps and memoirs, where available. The altitude of the farm, the distance from the market, and the distance from the sea were all calculated from O.S. maps.

The Statistical Analysis of the data

The definition of the independent influence of one of several factors on the spatial distribution of any phenomenon, when this distribution is itself an expression of the interaction of many factors, always presents a considerable problem to the research worker in geography. Spatial variation in the value of land for agricultural production is certainly the product of such a complex interaction of factors. The remainder of this paper is devoted to the application and assessment of a statistical technique whereby it may be possible to determine the independent influence of some of the many factors involved.

The basic aim of this analysis could be described as being to produce a production function for the variation in gross output per acre on farms in south Devon. This function would take the following general form:

$$Y = a + b_1X_1 + b_2X_2 + b_3X_3 \ldots \ldots + b_8X_8 + b_9X_9$$

where Y is the gross output per acre

a is a constant

$X_1 \ldots X_9$ are the 9 factors involved

$b_1 \ldots b_9$ are coefficients which indicate how the level of Y increases, or decreases, as the level of the relevant causative factor changes.

Such an equation would provide all the necessary information and if multiple regression analysis were to be applied to the data an equation of approximately the same form would be obtained:

$$Y = a + b_1X_1 + b_2X_2 + b_3X_3 \ldots \ldots + b_8X_8 + b_9X_9 + e$$

where the Y, a, the X's and b's are the same as above. The expression e represents that part of total variation in Y which could not be explained by the nine factors taken into consideration.

Since e is known, the amount of total variation in Y which is explained by this equation can easily be calculated. The statistical significance of the b coefficients can also be readily obtained. However, in its present form the technique has one major disadvantage. In multiple regression analysis, the X's are referred to as the independent variables and the Y as the dependent variable. If there *are* correlations between the independent variables, then the results are not valid, because the b coefficients are not indications of the *independent* influence of any one of these factors. If there were a significant degree of association between X_2 and X_3 for instance; then the regression analysis would indicate that these two variables are more important than they really are. It is also probable that the estimate of the amount of variation in Y explained by variation in the X's will be an over-estimate.

The degree of correlation between the nine factors under consideration is shown in Table 10.1. There are nine pairs of factors which show a significant degree of correlation. Some of these correlations, such as those between soil texture and soil drainage, or farmer's age and the number of years he has spent on that farm, would seem to be logical enough; but others, such as that between the distance of the farm from the sea and the number of years spent on that farm, are not. However, 8 of the 9 factors are associated with some other factor, and a method of making these factors independent of each other must be found before the relationship between them and gross output acre is examined.

Mathematically, the problem can be solved by using principal components analysis, which aims to divide the total variation in a set of observations into components which will be uncorrelated with each other. The analysis is performed on the correlation matrix obtained for the variables under consideration. The principal features of the analysis can be explained as follows. The correlation matrix is transformed into an identity matrix in which the original total variance is retained, while the covariance elements (i.e. those elements due to correlation between the variables) is removed. The latent roots of this matrix are then calculated and the number of latent roots will be equal to the number of original variables. Each one of these latent roots (or eigenvalues as they are commonly called) refers to a component of total variance, these components all being uncorrelated. The relative importance of each component (i.e. the proportion of total variance accounted for by that component) is indicated by the size of the eigenvalue. The proportion of total variance accounted for by each one of the principal components will be due to the influence of all the original variables. The relative weighting of each variable (i.e. the importance of the contribution made by that variable) in each component can be derived by the calculation of eigenvectors. There will be an eigenvector for each variable in each component. With this information it is often possible to identify certain components as being due to the influence of a small number of variables of the same type or even that of one variable.

This technique is very useful for economy of description. In the present context it also has the advantage of allowing the determination of the relative and independent influence of a set of variables on the variation present in a set of observations. The technique still does not provide a complete answer to the problem in hand, however, since, although one could obtain a good estimate of the most important sources of variation in farming conditions, one could not say whether the variables were significantly related to gross output per acre.

This goal can be achieved by carrying the analysis one stage further. Using the eigenvalues and eigenvectors from the principal components analysis, it is possible to utilise the original observations in such a way that there will no longer be any correlation between the nine variables. Consequently one can proceed to examine the relationship between the variables and gross output per acre using regression analysis. The principal features of this procedure are as follows. The data is standardized in the sense that the original difference between the observations with respect to units of measurement is removed. Using the eigen values for the principal components, it is then possible to define the principal components of the data for each individual farm. There will be 40 values for each principal component and these can be used in a regression analysis as observations of nine independent variables. The relationships between gross output per acre and each one of these independent variables are examined individually. By using the eigenvector weightings of each original independent variable on each component in this analysis, regression coefficients describing the relationship between each of the nine original variables and gross output per acre can be derived. The nine regression coefficients obtained for each variable (i.e. one for each principal component) are additive and so one can obtain an overall regression coefficient for that variable. In this way, therefore, it is possible to describe the relationship between each one of the original variables and gross output per acre.

TABLE 10.1

Matrix of Correlation coefficients for all possible combinations of the 9 factors.
Those significant on or above 95 per cent level of confidence are marked with an asterisk.

	Age of the farmer	Size of the farm	Distance to the sea	Altitude of the farm	Distance to the market	Soil Texture	Soil Drainage	No. of years on that farm	Degree of specialization
Age of the farmer	1.0000	.0039	-.0538	-.1137	-.0193	-.4662*	.2693	.8013*	-.0319
Size of the farm	.0039	1.0000	-.0115	-.0994	-.1597	-.1667	.1973	.0452	-.2740
Distance to the sea	-.0538	-.0115	1.0000	.5856*	.5283*	-.2719	-.1209	-.3846*	.0442
Altitude of the farm	-.1137	-.0994	.5856*	1.0000	.6618*	-.1170	.0024	-.1727	-.1297
Distance to the market	-.0193	-.1597	.5283*	.6618*	1.0000	-.2473	-.1206	-.1179	-.0372
Soil texture	-.4662*	-.1667	-.2719	-.1170	-.2473	1.0000	-.4393*	-.2076	-.3105*
Soil Drainage	.2693	.1973	-.1209	.0024	-.1206	-.4393*	1.0000	.3126*	.0400
No. of years on that farm	.8013*	.0452	-.3846*	-.1727	-.1179	-.2076	.3126*	1.0000	.1809
Degree of specialization	-.0319	-.2740	.0442	-.1297	-.0372	-.3105*	.0400	-.1809	1.0000

TABLE 10.2

Components

	(1)	(2)	(3)	(4)	(5)	(6)	(7)	(8)	(9)
Age of the farmer	.0077	.0008	.3054	.9339	.1550	.0027	.0631	.0417	.0687
Size of the farm	.1296	.4471	.2703	-.2157	.5002	-.4753	.3748	.0431	.2191
Distance to the sea	-.5241	.0386	.0035	.0173	.0061	-.4721	-.6012	.3286	.1565
Altitude of the farm	-.5214	.0518	.2302	-.1207	.0802	.5457	.2835	.4943	-.0780
Distance to the market	-.5448	.0518	-.1054	.0057	-.3083	-.0454	.2654	-.6305	.3498
Soil texture	.1061	-.6400	.2897	-.1790	.2358	.1610	-.0591	.0862	.6083
Soil drainage	.1378	.5387	-.0481	-.0004	.1967	.4694	.5000	-.2374	-.3478
No. of years on that farm	.3281	.2472	.2521	-.0086	-.7258	-.0717	-.0535	-.3469	-.3356
Degree of specialization	-.0446	.0258	-.7872	.1852	.0562	-.0017	.2948	.2500	.4366
EIGEN VALUES	2.3923	1.6882	1.3414	.9746	.8813	.6749	.4171	.3641	.2661
CUMULATIVE PROPORTION OF TOTAL VARIANCE	.27	.45	.60	.71	.81	.88	.93	.97	1.00

The technique was applied to the data and the remainder of this paper is devoted to a discussion of the results obtained and to an assessment of the usefulness of the technique in the present context. The correlation matrix showing the association between the factors is given in Table 10.1 and has already been discussed. A principal components analysis was performed on this matrix and Table 10.2 gives the eigenvalues and eigenvectors obtained for each component. There has been considerable discussion between statisticians and research workers about the size of eigenvalues and eigenvectors required before one can define a component as being worthy of consideration, or a variable as having a significant influence on a particular component. It should be noted that, in fact, the interpretation of these results must largely be a subjective one. It is considered that this lack of standards for comparison of results is one of the major drawbacks of using principal components analysis by itself as an analytical procedure. However, since in this case all of these values are used in the regression analysis it is felt that there is no need to do anything more than discuss the results in general terms.

The first component accounts for 24 per cent of total variance, and the factors of distance from the sea, altitude of the farm, and distance from the market have the highest weightings on this component. The first two factors are used to assess the variations in climate and it should be noted from the correlation matrix that there seemed to be a significant correlation between these factors and distance to the market. The second component, which accounts for 16.8 per cent of total variance, could almost be described as the soil component since the two factors of soil texture and soil drainage have the highest weightings. A considerable part of the 13 per cent of total variance accounted for by component 3 could be attributed to the effects of degree of specialization found on the farm. In similar fashion the fourth component (accounting for 9 per cent) could be called the farmer's age component. Farm size has its highest weighting in component 5 but even here it is overshadowed by the weighting for the number of years spent on that particular farm. All of the first nine factors have high weightings in at least one of the first five components and the cumulative proportion of total variance accounted for by these five components is 81 per cent. The remaining four components account for 19 per cent, while the variables with the highest weightings are distance to the sea, altitude, distance to the market, and soil texture.

When we have defined independent components of total variance, some of which can be attributed to the influence of particular types of factor, the next most logical question is whether these factors have an important influence on the gross output per acre obtainable. A multiple regression analysis, similar to that outlined above was carried out, using the principal components of the standardized cases as observations of independent variables, and gross output per acre as the dependent variable. As explained above, by using the factor weighting on each component it was possible to derive regression coefficients which would illustrate the influence of each variable, within each component, on standard output per acre. For each variable, therefore, there were nine regression coefficients and these were additive, so that an overall regression coefficient could be obtained for each variable. These regression coefficients are shown in Table 10.3.

Since this regression analysis was performed on standardized data, the relative importance

TABLE 10.3

Variable	Regression Coefficient
Age of the farmer	59.111
Size of the farm	21.177
Distance to the sea	−44.424
Altitude of the farm	−43.070
Distance to the market	−40.603
Soil texture	−73.820
Soil drainage	47.827
Number of years on that farm	37.046
Degree of specialization	12.906
CONSTANT	65.382

of each variable as a predictor of gross output per acre is shown by the difference in the size of the regression coefficients. From these results it can be seen that soil texture is the most important variable in this respect, followed by farmer's age, soil drainage, distance to the sea, altitude of the farm, distance to the market, the number of years on that particular farm, the size of the farm and the degree of specialization obtained on the farm. It is interesting to note that those factors which, according to the principal components analysis, seemed to give rise to the greatest degree of variation in farming conditions are not necessarily those with the greatest influence on gross output per acre.

The regression coefficient for farm size is a positive one (i.e. as the size of the farm increases so too does the gross output per acre). The size of the regression coefficient would also suggest that less emphasis should be placed on farm size as a factor controlling intensity of production. The importance of managerial experience is shown by the fact that the two factors of farmer's age and number of years spent on that particular farm, are positively related to gross output per acre. It would seem that the greater the percentage of clay and silt present in the soil, the lower the gross output per acre, whereas the greater the depth of free drainage the higher the gross output per acre. There is, of course, a great contrast between the textural and drainage qualities of the soils overlying the Culm measures and of those that are found elsewhere in the area, and no doubt the size of the two regression coefficients is an expression of the meaning of this contrast in terms of land value. If one can assume that altitude and distance from the sea will cause climatic variations, then one could conclude from this analysis that, as the two factors increase, the climate deteriorates from the agricultural point of view. The negative relationship between gross output per acre and distance to the market is what one would expect according to economic theory. The fact that the soil factors have a very important influence on the gross output per acre obtainable would suggest that these are basic factors which should be taken into account in attempting agricultural land classification in the area. Indeed, the results given in Table 10.3 show adequately the amount of emphasis which should be attributed to each one of the nine factors considered here.

The use of these regression coefficients beyond this broadly descriptive role is, however, quite restricted. It is not possible to say whether these regression coefficients are statistically significant or not. Consequently, if one were interested in using these results as a guideline for the approach to agricultural land classification, one would not be able to use any objective criterion in order to select relevant factors: the lowest regression coefficient could be as significant as the highest in the statistical sense. Moreover, these coefficients do not have any value as predictors in real situations since they are derived from standardized data. Consequently one could not extrapolate these equations to other farms in the area or use them to define the point at which any of these factors becomes an important limiting factor.

Conclusion

Regression on principal components is a useful descriptive technique which can be used to assess the relative importance of a large number of variables with respect to their influence on the value of land for agricultural production. Unfortunately it cannot be used to reduce what is potentially a very large number of variables down to smaller numbers which could be used to clasify land according to its value for agricultural production. In this respect it would certainly seem to be less useful than regression analysis. The results obtained are, however, much more reliable than those obtainable from regression analysis when there are significant correlations between the causative factors. Since this will almost certainly be true of the factors influencing the agricultural value of land in any area, it is felt that the technique is the more valid one in the present context. Finally, it should be remembered that it does allow one to select the factors which have the most important influence on the value of land for agricultural production and so at least to determine the basis of an agricultural land classification system in an objective way.

REFERENCES

Gould, P. R. 'On the geographical interpretation of eigenvalues' *Trans. Inst. Brit. Geographers,* 42 (1967), 58–86

Henshall, J. 'The demographic factor in the structure of agriculture in Barbados' *Trans. Inst. Brit. Geographers,* 38 (1966), 183–195

White, E. J. 'The relationship between height increment during the growing season and meteorological parameters, with reference to 3 tree species.' University College of Wales, Aberystwyth. Memorandum No. 13 (1970). *Aspects of Forest climates,* I, 1–12

I I

The Redevelopment of the Cornish Tin Mining Industry: Its Problems and Prospects

J. R. BLUNDEN

The Cornish tin mining industry produced 1,540 tons* of tin in 1968.[1] This may seem rather a small amount, but it saved the United Kingdom about £2,200,000 in foreign exchange. Since it is currently being suggested that Cornwall stands at the beginning of a 'considerable renaissance'[2] in this once important industry, the prospects for the national economy and that of South-West England could be exciting indeed. Yet any visitor to the Duchy cannot but be impressed by the large number of derelict engine houses scattered across its cliffs and moors instead of the surface accoutrements of a present-day dynamic extractive industry. In fact, out of the 250 active tin mines in 1840,[3] the only producers of tin ore until very recently were the mines of South Crofty, between Camborne and Redruth, and Geevor, near Pendeen on the Penwith peninsula, though tin from mine effluent has been recovered in the Red river and Carnon river valleys for some time.

The industry declined through a combination of technological, economic and managerial factors and found itself unable to compete with the alluvial ore fields of Malaya, Indonesia and Bolivia after their discovery in the nineteenth century. Most Cornish mines were worked on a 'cost-book' system, or as unlimited liability companies, often reaping from a trifling outlay enormous dividends which were shared out at once, leaving little capital in reserve to survive a recession or to carry out improvements. In many cases, the narrow and steeply inclined shafts and working tunnels prevented improved haulage techniques or mechanized working.[4] Further, the significant fact that tin can exist in quantity below copper ores, but separated from them by a barren zone,[5] only became generally known in the second half of the nineteenth century; consequently many companies merely exploited the copper, failing to appreciate that tin might exist in the veins at greater depths.[6]

Thus the knowledge that there may still be large reserves of tin ore left in Cornwall, as

*Since most of the figures refer to the past, English tons have been used in this essay. To convert to metric tons multiply by .9842.

169

well as the stimulus of the current excess of demand for tin over supply, have led to renewed interest in the possibility of expansion and redevelopment. Certainly the ore fields of Malaya, Bolivia and Indonesia, now accounting for 76 per cent of the world output, are gradually being worked out.[7] Labour and freight costs have also been rising. Additional reserves must become increasingly difficult to find. Indeed, it was calculated in 1961 that, at the then current rate of consumption, the known reserves of tin could only last another 30 years.[8] All these factors have been reflected in world markets where the price of tin has soared from below £900 per ton in 1961 to an average of well over £1,500 per ton from 1965 to 1969.[9] Meantime the short fall in production has been met from the fast-diminishing United States' strategic stockpile.[10] The impetus so given to Cornwall has been reflected in the share prices of one of the major current producers, Geevor Tin Mines Limited. In January 1954 the 25p (5s) ordinary shares stood at 49p (9s 9d). A recent quotation (1970) from the London Stock Exchange has put them as high as £4.62½ (92s 6d). The impetus has also made itself apparent in the impressive number of British, Canadian and American companies that have been considering the possibilities of the old mines of Cornwall, concentrating their efforts in districts which the Cornish Mining Development Association recommended as worthy of closer investigations in a series of reports entitled *Mineral Areas in Cornwall Worthy of Investigation,* the first of which was published soon after the last war.

Immediately to the south of Camborne in the area of Troon are the old Grenville mines, situated in a valley which separates the granite masses of Carn Brea and Carn Menellis. The Grenville United mines, which closed in 1920, in their time had produced 31,500 tons of black tin,[11] mostly from the rich Great Flat Lode.[12] Promising parallel lodes are now thought to exist and planning permission was given at the end of 1961 to Camborne Tin Limited, a company formed to prospect and work these by the Siamese Tin Syndicate.[13] Siamese Tin were later joined in the project by the Union Corporation (UK) Limited, who have since taken over control of the company. Camborne Tin Limited have also been prospecting and drilling in the Godolphin area about 11.3 kilometres (7 miles) south-west of Camborne,[14] where the West Godolphin and Godolphin mines were in production in the nineteenth century.

Between Redruth and Scorrier lies the Great North Downs mine and, separated from it by a major fault, Wheal Peevor. Great North Downs, an early copper working, was exploited for tin between 1861 and 1870, and between 1871 and 1873, but was abandoned because of a major slump in the metal market. Wheal Peevor, on the other hand, to the west and on a different lode, had enjoyed a period of high production from 1872 to 1885. Together with West Wheal Peevor, it was reopened in 1911 and worked until 1915 when wartime difficulties put a stop to operations below adit level, though all operations did not cease until 1920. As far as this district as a whole is concerned, one writer has suggested that beneath the existing workings lies 'one of the largest untapped sources of tin' in Cornwall.[15] Certainly when this was written, Camborne Tin also had 'high hopes' of the area, but the drilling which they undertook at Great North Downs after this seemed to belie any such optimism and they abandoned the concession.

More recently, however, the Barcas Mining Company, a subsidiary of Barnato Brothers Limited, which is itself a wholly UK owned subsidiary of the Johannesburg Consolidated Investment Company Limited, began preparations for the dewatering of the Peevor mines at Mitchell's Shaft, West Peevor. Although at first serious difficulties were encountered with an extensive choke in the main shaft, this was being cleared and at the end of 1967 good progress was being made.[16] However, the company had not reconditioned the deep adit system and the mine was flooded as a result of a cloudburst on the night of 1/2 July 1968. This has resulted in the cessation of work on this project, at least for the present.[17]

South of Camborne lie the old mines of Tolcarne and South Tolcarne which, as part of Pendarves United mines, survived only until the 1880s.[18] Today a consortium of the Union Corporation (UK) Limited, Guggenheim Exploration of Cornwall Incorporated, Tehidy Minerals Limited and other partners[19] are looking at the potential of this group of mines. As a result of diamond drilling, they have established the presence of lodes with between 1 and 2 per cent ore at depths of less than 91.4 metres (300 feet), and in May 1965 planning permission was given for a trial shaft. By January 1969 this had reached 259 metres (850 feet) and tunnelling had begun from it at two horizons.[20] This is the first major shaft to be sunk in Cornwall for more than 40 years. The nearby old Tryphena mine will shortly be dewatered not only to prevent flooding but also to provide a second access to the new working.[21]

The most interesting of the proposals to rework old tin mining areas is that in the Gwennap/Baldhu area. This district, formerly important for copper mining, consists of the tributary valleys that converge to form the valley of the river Carnon. Near Baldhu, Wheal Jane and West Wheal Jane, which amalgamated with a number of other mines in 1905 to form Falmouth Consolidated Mines,[22] were once important. Beyond these mines, and westwards across the Carnon valley, are the old Mount Wellington mine and a very large group of abandoned copper and tin mines extending over a large part of the parish of Gwennap and St Day. International Mine Services Limited, a Canadian company, are now showing interest in this area.[23] On their behalf Cornwall Tin and Mining Corporation of New York (one of the Hirshorn group of companies) announced in 1969 that they would sink a new 4.5 metre (15 foot) diameter circular shaft, following successful diamond drilling which began in 1968[24] on the Mount Wellington lode. Providing that the developments are satisfactory, it is thought that the mining operation will eventually yield 500 to 1,000 tons a day.[25] It is interesting to note that attempts to investigate the potential of the Mount Wellington lode were made close to the village of Twelve Heads even before the last war and exploration and development were in progress from 1935 to 1941.[26] Now, Prado Explorations Limited, an associate company of International Mine Services Limited, have begun further diamond drilling to the west of Mount Wellington.

It is in the neighbouring area of the old Janes mines, however, that the major developments are at present taking place. Here, now that planning permission has been granted, Consolidated Goldfields are spending £6,000,000[27] on a new mine which J. H. Trounson, chairman of the Cornish Mining Development Association, recently described as 'a really major mine—the biggest thing Cornwall has seen'.[28] The first encouraging results from geo-chemical investigations and diamond drilling were reported early in 1967[29] but it was not until 1969 that, with laboratory and pilot scale tests carried out on the ores obtained and with the detailed engineering studies completed,[30] it was decided to go ahead and bring the mine into production. This new mine should rank as a producer second only to one of the two currently working mines, South Crofty, when it begins production late in 1971 at a capacity of 150,000 tons of ore per year.[31] Reserves of ore are thought by Consolidated Goldfields to be, at a conservative estimate, about 5 million tons. With a percentage of tin of about 1.25, the mine should provide between 1,500 and 1,600 tons of tin in concentrate a year. Against the total investment of £6,000,000, profits could be about £350,000 a year. Because of its location in a Development Area, the government will be contributing up to £2,400,000 in grants; this must be a factor in the success of the mine. The mining rate will be built up in the early years and both high and low grade tin concentrates may be produced. The company has leased about 607 hectares (1,500 acres) with mineral options purchased for £6,000, but royalties will amount to about £60,000 a year. It is expected that the Janes will employ over 300 men,[32] expanding eventually to 500,[33] and as a profit earner the Janes mine could in fact take first place from South Crofty, a mine with a long and continuous productive history.

South Crofty began operations in 1854 and worked the southern half of the old East Wheal Crofty sett which had been rich in copper in the 1830s. By 1894, with 154 men in its employ, it had sunk to a depth of 314.5 metres (1,032 feet). In 1902 the company took over the adjacent but small and abandoned undertaking, New Cook's Kitchen mine, and then in about 1916 it pushed northwards, into what had been the sett of North Wheal Crofty. By the outbreak of the First World War, workings had reached a depth of 567 metres (1,860 feet) with some 480 men employed. It is interesting that South Crofty managed to survive the early 1920s, when the price of tin fell to record low levels and when heavy expenditure on drainage was incurred as a result of the closure of the adjacent Tincroft mine and the collapse of the engine shaft at the East Pool mine immediately to the northeast. By 1935 South Crofty had acquired a number of other old setts to the west, and more recently took over the old East Pool and Wheal Agar mines which closed in 1945. After the take-over, the newest section (Taylor's) was dewatered and in 1968 it was entered from South Crofty. Preparations are now in hand for the pumping out of the rest of the East Pool mine.[34]

Today the whole South Crofty undertaking is a thriving one, exploiting, in all, more than a dozen lodes of tin. It has reached a depth of 689 metres (2,260 feet) and employs some 470 men. In 1964 a modernisation scheme, which had taken six years to accomplish, was completed. In that year receipts totalled £828,489, with a working profit of £321,741. The mine had produced in the previous twelve months 994 tons of black tin from 88,410 tons of ore, representing a recovery grade of 2,518 pounds per ton of ore milled.[35] Up to the end of the year 1963, it had produced over 38,000 tons of black tin since its opening in 1854. In 1968, however, the board of South Crofty decided that the potential of the mines warranted even greater output and a programme of expansion is now geared to increasing production of ore from a total of 110,760 tons in that year to 200,000 tons in 1971,[36] 'doubling its output or thereabouts'.[37] In order to achieve this the company will need additional hoisting equipment and treatment plant. The rate of underground development will also need to be increased. All this will mean an expenditure in the two-and-a-half-year period up to 1971 of £650,000, to be met from internal resources;[38] it will also mean that South Crofty will keep in front of the forecast production of ore from the Janes by some 50,000 tons.

The other important tin mine with a long history of production is Geevor, about 9.05 kilometres (6 miles) north of Land's End, a mine which had made a long-standing contribution to the economy of west Cornwall and is currently a much needed source of employment in the area. The forerunner of this undertaking was the North Levant mine where work really began as early as 1810; its name was not changed to Geevor till 1905. In the twentieth century, in spite of minor recessions brought about by fluctuating tin prices and the trade cycle, output has expanded steadily, with the company acquiring adjacent setts. Two acquisitions have been of particular importance. One of these, the Boscaswell Downs mine, is situated in a half mile sett running south-east through Pendeen. But it is adjacent to, and to the immediate north-east of, the original Boscaswell lode that the main development work in this part of the Geevor company's holding has taken place. An old shaft (Treweek's) has been reconditioned to enable the further development of the Boscaswell main lode and a new lode, the Simms, to be worked efficiently. Over 1,524 metres (5,000 feet) of Simms lode has now been developed and it looks very promising for the future.[39] The Levant mine, the other notable acquisition, had been one of the major sources of tin and copper in west Cornwall. From 1820 to 1930 some 30,000 tons of black tin were produced,[40] but after the abandonment of the mine in 1930 the sea broke into the workings, a result of their having been unwisely carried up close to the sea bed. Nevertheless, it was the possibility of the seaward extension of Geevor into the lodes that had once been Levant's that suggested the acquisition of the latter and it was proposed that an attempt be made to seal the sea breach and drain the mine.[41] The first attempt to do this in 1961 failed and, after a review of Geevor's prospect, further efforts in this direction were postponed.

The focus of development at Geevor then switched to the other acquisition, the Boscaswell Downs mine. At the end of 1962, when the water level in this had been lowered to the 207 metre (678 foot) level, an entry was made from the parent mine. Shortly afterwards a new lode was discovered in the Boscaswell sett and exploitation of this began in 1964. Since that date the new Simms lode has been extensively developed and other lodes discovered.

It became clear, however, that, if further work was to be done on the other extension of the Geevor mine into Levant, additional finance would be needed. This was obtained by an arrangement with Union Corporation by which they share the estimated cost of £250,000[42]. So in July 1964 work on the Levant project began again. The breach was subsequently successfully plugged and the area sealed off from the rest of the mine by St Just Mining Services. Since then the process of pumping the water out of the mine has been in progress. A number of deep boreholes were drilled in 1966 in order to test the seaward extension of the known lodes south-west of Cape Cornwall and in 1968 exploratory diamond drilling south of Levant to 2,691 metres (8,828 feet) had been done.[43] These investigations, according to Geevor's managing director, Douglas Batchelor, have given 'some very good results[44].'

The future of Geevor does then look bright. Apart from the development of the potential of the adjacent Boscaswell and Levant mines, Geevor itself has undergone during the last ten years a comprehensive programme of rationalisation. In 1968, with a manpower total of 282 workers, the mine produced 747 tons of black tin worth £561,343 from 77,351 tons of ore,[45] and for 1969 output is reckoned to be up 30 per cent.[46]

Two other more modest undertakings have been recovering tin ore by streaming. Effluent deposits have been worked for years in the Carnon river valley at Bissoe, first by Hydraulic Tin Limited, and—after 1966—by the Continental Ore Company Limited, who acquired this business and who propose to develop its potential.[47] In 1967, the last year for which figures are available, about 100,000 tons of sand and slimes were treated, yielding 100 tons of 10 per cent concentrates and 110 tons of 52 per cent concentrates.[48] Meanwhile, to the north-west of Camborne tin streamers have for years worked the ore deposited in the Red river from the mines of Camborne and Pool. In 1966 the Cornish Tin Smelting Company Limited erected a tin concentration plant capable of dealing with 250 tons a day of residual materials from the Red river flats[49] and elsewhere. Two years later this dealt with 61,647 tons of material in a twelve-month period, giving 283 tons of concentrates.[50]

The same company was also actively pursuing underground sources of tin and has prospected in the last few years in the Camborne and Redruth district.[51] Twelve shallow diamond drill holes were made in 1966, as well as geo-chemical sampling, and in 1967 exploratory dewatering operations were carried out at Lyle's shaft of the old North Wheal Basset mine at Carnkie,[52] one of a group of five mines which closed in 1919.

Across the Penwith peninsula close to St Just airport, Penwith Mineral Explorations Limited have also been drilling and carrying out geo-chemical surveys. The results achieved by 1968 prompted the company to acquire further leases to the north of the present area, as well as in other parts of the St Just area and south-west Cornwall. This company has had to raise new capital to the extent of £30,000[53] in order to push ahead with developments.

But, in spite of all this activity, the redevelopment of the Cornish tin-mining industry has serious problems. First of all there is always the possibility of failure to find sufficient ore to justify commercial exploitation, even after heavy investment in exploration. Four examples of this spring to mind. At the historic Ding Dong mine some 4 kilometres (2½ miles) west of Penzance, Consolidated Goldfields Limited have recently carried out diamond drillings to estimate its future potential,[54] but results have been disappointing and it is unlikely that the mine will be reworked. At St Ives Bay, Coastal Prospecting Limited, a subsidiary of Union Corporation (UK) Limited, converted a motor vessel to extract tin from dredged sand and in 1967 completed a processing plant at Lelant.[55] This began to operate and shipments of tin were actually made[56] but for various reasons, including the low tin content of the sand in the bay and the problems of running the ship into the port of Hayle in bad weather, the project has since been abandoned. On Par Beach English Clays Lovering Pochin and Company Limited[57] began exploratory drilling for alluvial tin in 1968. The work was not expected to be completed until 1970[58] but it was prematurely abandoned in 1969 and it must be presumed that the results obtained were unsatisfactory. Another shore line exploration started in 1967 in Mount's Bay, where Amalgamated Roadstone Corporation Limited, Newlyn, worked at the end of a 52 metre (500 foot) steel-tube pier jutting out from the foreshore at Penzance. Drilling was carried out to evaluate the tin-bearing elvan dyke which proved so productive in the famous under-sea Wherry mine between 1778 and 1798[59] but the results of the drillings were poor. It is known, though, that these stanniferous elvan dykes do not necessarily persist over any great length or depth and so the chance of failure in this last case must have always been high.

Then, apart from the failure of investigations to live up to expectations, there is the problem of identifying the owner of mineral rights and of reaching agreement with him before extraction can be contemplated. In this connection, the experience of Baltrink Tin Limited can be cited. This company was formed by Rhodesia-Katanga, Kleinwort Benson and the Canadian Westfield Minerals in order to examine the extension of the lodes of the old Giew mine at Trink Hill, south-west of St Ives;[60] the mine had been worked inter-mittently until 1922 when the low price of tin on world markets finally caused it to close.[61] Baltrink Tin pursued an intensive programme of drilling and geo-chemical soil testing in order to confirm the nature of the easterly continuation of the old Giew mine's main lode, but found, because of cross faulting, that the prospects for development were not favourable. Perhaps this would not have been so unfortunate if Baltrink had been able to expand the boundary of their concession but the problem of identifying the owners of the mineral rights of the adjacent land was insoluble[62] and Baltrink has withdrawn from the field. A director of the company, Mr E. W. J. Tyler, is reported as saying of this venture, 'It is just too difficult, too impossible. You spend hours and hours just going round in circles. There is the rest of the world where people can go and look for minerals.'[63]

It is clear that Baltrink Tin is not the only company to have been frustrated in its efforts to identify the owners of mineral rights. There are, in addition, other companies who, having eventually discovered the mineral owner after a time-consuming search, find themselves further frustrated in their attempts to obtain a licence to work the minerals on reasonable terms. Certainly mining interests in Cornwall believe that there is a good case for government legislation to relieve these quite avoidable frustrations. As a writer in the *Financial Times* reported, following a visit with a large party of transatlantic and British mining men, to new mining fields in the Irish Republic, 'the visitors were as enthusiastic about Ireland's . . . far seeing legislation whereby it is reasonably easy to acquire land necessary for mining developments as they were unenthusiastic about the UK in (this) respect.'[64] The writer added that 'perhaps the Government might at least start taking steps to smooth the path of the miner in his often frustrating search for even who owns the mineral rights, let alone whether they are willing to part with them.'[65]

There are also other problems that have arisen which may best be described as those arising from land use competition. Here two particularly interesting cases spring to mind. The first involved the reworking of the old mine at Wheal Vor near Helston. This is situated close to the granite of Tregonning Hill and was not only a very ancient mine but also a rich one. During its most productive period from 1853 until 1877 the mine produced

N

9,620 tons of black tin[66] and profits reached over £99,000.[67] It is now thought, however, that the company which exploited this area failed to locate several ore bodies which may be commercially exploitable. Certainly Camborne Tin Limited thought it worth while to carry out a series of preliminary investigations, as a result of which they submitted an application for planning permission to re-open the mine. It seemed likely that this application would receive favourable consideration since the mine was in a Development Area and, if restarted, it might employ about 400 men in a locality where the unemployment rate was 6 per cent. Further, it was situated in a zone scheduled in the Cornwall Development Plan[68] for possible mining activities. A public enquiry into the proposed re-opening of the mine was held but, in spite of the application finding favour with the inspector, the Minister of Housing and Local Government refused to grant planning permission on the ground that the Helston and Porthleven Water Company obtained part of its water supply from the adit stream flowing from Wheal Vor. Permission for the water company to use this water had been given in 1956, and although this was strenuously opposed at the time by the Cornish Mining Development Association, they only succeeded in persuading the Minister to insert a saving clause in the order to the effect that nothing should prejudice the rights of the mine owners to resume operations. At the 1964 enquiry the water company pointed out that they could eventually replace the Wheal Vor source by pumping from the Looe Pool. The Minister did observe, therefore, in giving his ruling that it was without prejudice to a further application being made by the mining company when the alternative water supplies had been finally secured. He also expressed his hope that the water company would press on urgently with its scheme for obtaining alternative supplies and agreed that the reworking of the mine could be beneficial in an area of heavy unemployment.[69] However, when the water company eventually went ahead with their proposal to use Looe Pool as an alternative source, they were opposed by various local authorities on the grounds that the pool was polluted by sewage. This necessitated a further public enquiry which led to a prolonged wrangle over the costs of a scheme to treat the source of pollution.

Meanwhile, other difficulties arose at Wheal Vor concerning the already mentioned problem of mineral ownership. The major part of the area to be developed was in the hands of the Treworlis Estate, which was willing to co-operate with Camborne Tin. The Wheal Vor lodes, however, dip north at a fairly flat angle and in the deeper areas pass under the land of the Duke of Leeds. Negotiations started with Leeds Estates were prolonged, mainly because the latter had already begun discussions for the transfer of all mineral rights to another landowner in Cornwall. Just as matters seemed to be settling in favour of Camborne Tin, the Duke died, followed shortly afterwards by his successor to the title, thus leaving probate to be settled in two cases. There were further delays before the estate was finally sold. So it was that, after four and a half years, Camborne Tin were no nearer beginning their work at Wheal Vor. Meanwhile, the water dispute dragged on and the frustrated company applied to go ahead with at least a trial drilling in the area of the mine. Planning permission was given, provided that drilling in no way polluted the water supply. But unfortunately the Treworlis land borings were the only ones available until permission to work in what had been the Leeds land was obtained and it soon became clear that important finds were only likely in this last area. By this time, the delays had been so lengthy that Camborne Tin felt they could tolerate the difficulties of this situation no longer. They decided to concentrate all their efforts on their Pendarves concession now, apparently, the most promising of all the areas in Cornwall which they had been able to examine.[70]

Thus ended a sorry story, the details of which must cause concern to those who are anxious to see mining encouraged in Cornwall. It is ironical to note that Camborne Tin abandoned their schemes at Wheal Vor just before the negotiations for working the ex-Leeds estate could have been completed; more important, the local water company has now become part of the South Cornwall Water Board and the additional supplies to forego the Wheal Vor Source are piped in from another area altogether.

Another illustration of the problems of land use competition concerns attempts that were made, beginning in the spring of 1961, to re-open Carnelloe, one of a series of mines running along the cliff tops west from St Ives as far as Morvah.[71] This mine, situated close to an unscarred stretch of coastline of outstanding natural beauty, was closed nearly 90 years ago and the plan of Mr W. T. Harry to re-open it encountered the resistance not only of a 300 strong pressure group but also of the National Trust and the County Development Plan. Put briefly, the Objectors' case was that the mine, if exploration proved successful, would grow until the adjacent village of Zennor developed into a second Pendeen, the sprawling home of the Geevor mine. If it were unsuccessful, the damage to the landscape would be irreparable.[72] Mr Harry, however, forecast that the mine, for which he had already acquired the mineral rights and could raise £200,000 capital, would soon employ 200 to 300 men. He stressed that the mine was in any case well away from the village and that there was no question of spoiling the landscape. At the public enquiry set up on 11 May 1961, he stated that the mine would be developed in three phases. The first would be exploratory, involving little in the way of above-ground structures; the second would involve excavating one or two new shafts, and the final phase, the actual working of the mine, would be carried out under the sea.[73] The inspector agreed that a case for re-opening the mine had been made. The few buildings needed could harmonize with the landscape and the mine would provide local employment and a valuable source of tin for the nation. Nevertheless, the Minister of Housing and Local Government overruled this recommendation on the grounds that the intrusion of this kind of mining development into an area with an unspoiled coastline could only be allowed in quite exceptional circumstances and that in any case the success of the mine was uncertain.[74] In March 1963 a further application by Mr Harry to erect two huts and to begin prospecting work on the mine only was successful but by this time the original backers for his proposal, concerned over what they thought to be unreasonable delays, had withdrawn their financial support and invested elsewhere. Since then the planning permission granted to prospect has expired. However, at least one mining expert believes that in this area of highly altered slates and 'greenstone' resting on granite, rich tin ore is likely to be found, as the output of earlier mines between Pendeen and St Just bear witness.[75] It is known that the company working Carnelloe on a very small scale about a hundred years ago worked a narrow but rich tin lode there which 'came down on the grey elvan' (the greenstone sills) before it quite typically died out. The company were unable to

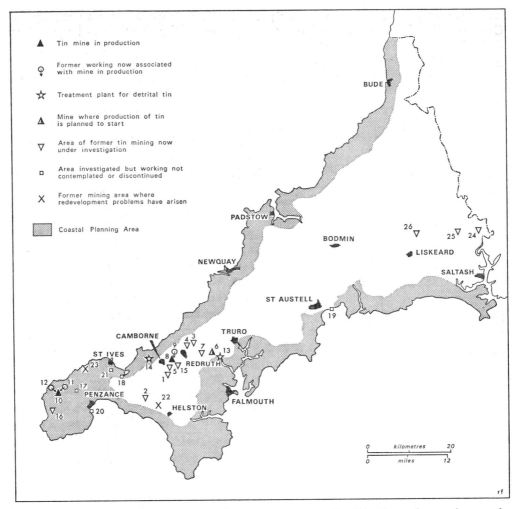

Fig. 11.1   Recent developments in Cornish tin mining. Key to localities shown by numbers on the map is:

1	Grenville mines	14	Red River (effluent deposits)
2	Godolphin mines	15	Basset and Frances mines
3	Great North Downs mine	16	St Just Airport area
4	Wheal Peevor mine	17	Ding Dong mine
5	Pendarves United mines	18	Lelant
6	Falmouth Consolidated mines (Janes)	19	Par Beach (alluvial deposits)
7	Mount Wellington	20	Newlyn
8	South Crofty mine	21	Giew mine
9	East Pool and Agar mines	22	Wheal Vor mine
10	Geevor mine	23	Carnelloe mine
11	Boscaswell Downs mine	24	Gunnislake area
12	Levant mine	25	Hingston Down area
13	Carnon Valley (effluent deposits)	26	Caradon Hill (Upton Cross) area

find the money to sink through the elvan,[76] which is a very hard rock. Indeed, it was only by sinking through the greenstone sills that the Levant mine, situated in a similar geological position, ultimately proved so successful.

From these two case histories, it is clear that tin mining development can conflict in certain instances with other land use interests and that these conflicts may obstruct viable mining projects, in that prospecting companies or financial backers will move their resources elsewhere if difficulties prove formidable. For the future the question of land use competition will most probably arise where mining expansion is attempted in areas which the local planning authority recently designated as part of the 4.8 kilometre (3 mile) deep coastal planning belt. This zone, with some exceptions, extends right round the county[77] and in it the County Council have attempted to inter-relate all land use demands, laying particular emphasis on tourism and the preservation of the coast.[78] However, it should be noted that the planning authority has for some time accepted the fact that, in many areas of Cornwall both on and off the coast, it may be necessary to consider planning applications for mining development. Such zones were identified and named 'Consultation Areas' in the County Development Plan, because it was believed that all interests would best be served if a decision to allow or reject a new mining development in these areas was made the subject of consultation between the County Council and the Cornish Mining Development Association. These consultation zones, originally defined on the advice of the Cornish Mining Development Association, are at present undergoing considerable revision, in view of the number of new mining developments now under way.[79] This system will be necessary if a properly planned expansion of the tin mining industry is to be achieved and reconciled with other land use interests. Moreover, the possibilities of conflict may be further lessened when it becomes more generally realised that the relatively few 'above ground' activities of this industry can be housed in buildings which blend with the landscape. Present day engineering methods mean that comparatively few shafts are required, a single one perhaps serving an area 3.2 kilometres (2 miles) or more in length underground.[80] In addition, modern technology means that mines may function without the environmental pollution characteristic of the nineteenth century.[81] Under these circumstances, it is increasingly likely that, in the future, planning permission for new developments will not be withheld.

The problems that have arisen over mineral rights, however, have no immediate prospect of being eased. The proposed legislation of the Labour Government, announced in June 1969, to assist mineral operators to gain access to land for exploration purposes and to acquire mineral rights, was unfortunately not implemented before the general election, though it is possible that the present Conservative Government will see fit to introduce a similar measure.

However, tin interests in Cornwall consider that the key to the ultimate prosperity of the industry must lie in a revision of the taxation system which will give concessions to prospecting and mining by means of some kind of 'tax holiday'. In this respect the United Kingdom strongly contrasts with Ireland. Until a few years ago, mining in Eire was moribund, but as a direct consequence of the adoption of a realistic tax code, culminating in 1966, when total tax relief for twenty years was granted, the industry was reborn and is expanding rapidly. The latest figures show that prospecting licences have been granted for about a third of the Republic's total area. Substantial discoveries have already been made and new mines are coming into production, whilst the output of lead and zinc from the Tynagh mine in County Galway is now the largest in Europe.[82] By 1973 it is expected that the annual mineral output of Eire will be worth £15,000,000.[83] It is interesting to note therefore that in 1961 Mr Harold Wilson advocated tax concessions in England similar to those available in Eire. In a debate in the House of Commons on the taxation of non-ferrous mines, he pointed out that a world shortage of tin—together with the problem of United Kingdom balance of payments—made it imperative for the nation to develop its own supplies. For this reason and 'because of the difficulties and risks of tin mining due to the disposition of the metal by nature, special tax concessions are required.'[84] He might also have mentioned the advantages to regional employment that might accrue from such tax concessions in an area of high unemployment and the fact that the savings in the outflow of currency would have amounted, even at that time, to £1,200 for every ton of tin produced at home.

Nothing was done to grant tax concession up to 1964, and if anything the situation deteriorated between that date and 1970. On 15 May 1970, however, details of tax concessions for owners of mineral rights were published in a new clause to the Finance Bill tabled by the Chancellor of the Exchequer. Hitherto royalties from mineral rights had been treated, for tax purposes, as income. The increasingly high-speed mining techniques, which have shortened the period during which minerals can be exploited, mean that landowners might be faced with the situation of receiving their royalties in a period so short as to make payments received more like a capital sum, a sum then taxed as income bunched together in a few years.[85] On top of this, there came in 1966 the betterment levy, as a result of which a landowner might find he was paying total taxes of £1.15 (23s) in the pound of his royalty income. In 1968 the law was changed so that the effective tax rate on mineral royalty income was cut to 94½p (18s 11p) in the pound, although the damage to land value as a result of mining would generally account for the remaining 5½p (1s 1d). By the new clause to the 1970 Finance Bill, these royalties were, for tax purposes, to be treated half as capital, half as income. This welcome change should have some beneficial effect on Cornish tin mining, although it does not go nearly as far as mining interests feel is necessary.

The excuse for making such a small tax concession—and that only to owners of mineral rights—seems to be that the scheme of Investment Grants (up to 45 per cent) given under Part I of the Industrial Development Act 1966 does in fact provide reasonable assistance to the mining industry itself. It should, however, be pointed out that not all of Cornwall has been designated as a Development Area to which this act applies; this leaves the potential mining districts in the east of the county ineligible for the full rate of grants. It is also fair to add that investment grants of the type provided by this act are not suited to an industry which needs to look far into the future. But perhaps even more important is the fact that the financial aids provided do not differentiate between the high risk business of tin mining, in which investment in prospecting is no guarantee of commercial success, and the manu-

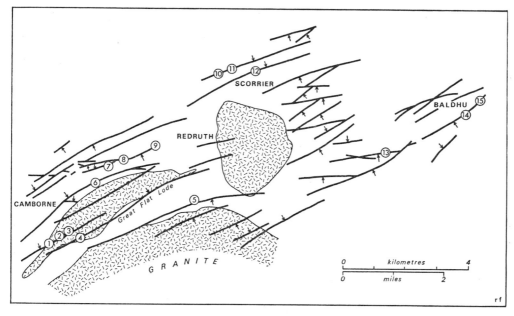

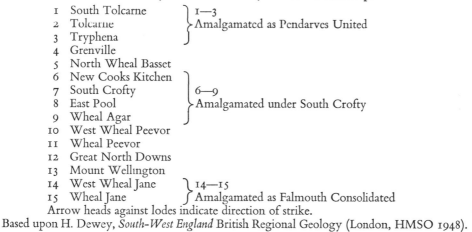

Fig. 11.2   Principal lodes in the Camborne, Redruth, Scorrier districts in relation to mines mentioned in the text. Key to mines shown by numbers on the map:

1	South Tolcarne	⎫	1—3
2	Tolcarne	⎬ Amalgamated as Pendarves United
3	Tryphena	⎭
4	Grenville
5	North Wheal Basset
6	New Cooks Kitchen	⎫
7	South Crofty		6—9
8	East Pool	⎬ Amalgamated under South Crofty
9	Wheal Agar	⎭
10	West Wheal Peevor
11	Wheal Peevor
12	Great North Downs
13	Mount Wellington
14	West Wheal Jane	⎫	14—15
15	Wheal Jane	⎬ Amalgamated as Falmouth Consolidated

Arrow heads against lodes indicate direction of strike.
Based upon H. Dewey, *South-West England* British Regional Geology (London, HMSO 1948).

facturing industries, where less capital is on the whole more safely invested. Given the balance of payments situation in Britain, the increasing long-term world shortage of tin, and the tax concessions offered to mining in Eire, as well as in Canada, Australia, the United States and elsewhere,[86] it is surprising that no decisive government action has been taken. Certainly the industry is making progress with a 10 per cent increase in output from 1967 to 1968, and a more than 10 per cent increase in 1969. Cornwall could indeed be poised for a rapid expansion of the tin industry. However, Dr J. F. McDivett has reported to the Organisation for European Economic Co-operation that 'Great Britain would seem to have the best developed negative attitude towards metal mining of the O.E.E.C. countries.'[87] 'Britain,' he added, 'would be one of the countries most likely to be rewarded by a thorough reappraisal of its mineral reserves, but the stimulus seems to be lacking.' Although these strictures, made in 1964, seem now to be less true than they were, he is perhaps still right to say of the United Kingdom that 'in order to attract the necessary capital, it is essential that investment should be granted a favourable and secure climate.'[88]

Undoubtedly, as far as tin is concerned, those involved in both exploration and the development of new mines in Cornwall are still looking to the government to provide such a climate. The limited provisions of the Industrial Development Act and the recent small tax concession to mineral owners are plainly not enough. Whilst the availability of new and efficient mining techniques and a growing shortage of tin may be sufficient to suggest to entrepreneurs that Cornwall has real possibilities for a mining renaissance, they will not be held there if other countries with exploitable resources of ore offer better financial incentives than does Britain. Their disillusionment and withdrawal from Cornwall could be unfortunate for the economy both of the county and of the United Kingdom.

REFERENCES

1 International Tin Council
2 Eglin, R. 'Mr Shore, the Miners' Friend' *The Observer* (29 June 1969)
3 *The Times* (23 March 1962)
4 Trounson, J. H. 'Practical Considerations in the Development of Old Cornish Mines' paper 18 in *The Future of Non-Ferrous Mining in Great Britain and Ireland* (1959), 371–82
5 Dines, H. G. *The Metalliferous Mining Region of South West England* (1956), 8
6 Dewey, H. *British Regional Geology, South West England* (DSIR, HMSO, 2nd edition 1961), 49–50
7 *Mining Magazine* 108 (1963), 39
8 Yates, Lamartine, P., Dewhurst, J. and Coppock, J. *Europe's Needs and Resources* (1961), 631
9 Mounter, J. 'Cornish Tin Mines Plead for Tax Relief' *The Times* (25 September 1967)
10 *The Financial Times* (20 April 1965)
11 From the company record of the Grenville United mines
12 Thomas, R. H. 'Observations on the Great Flat Lode' in *Royal Cornwall Polytechnic Society 44th Report* (1886), 184
13 *Cornish Chamber of Mines Report* (1966), 21
14 Ibid. 21
15 Barton, D. B. *The Mines of West Cornwall* (1963), 25
16 *Cornish Mining Development Association Annual Reports* (1966/67), 3 (1967/68), 3
17 *Cornish Mining Development Association Annual Reports* (1968/69), 4
18 Barton, D. B. op. cit. 27–8
19 Eglin, R. op. cit.
20 *Cornish Chamber of Mines Reports* (1967), 11 (1968), 13
21 *Cornish Mining Development Association Annual Report* (1968/69), 1–2
22 Barton, D. B. op. cit. 38–9

23 This company has also been exploring and drilling in East Cornwall, particularly in the St Ann's Chapel, Gunnislake area; the Upton Cross (Caradon Hill), Liskeard area; and in the area of Hingston Downs. The results have yet to be assessed.

24 *Cornish Chamber of Mines Reports* (1966), 17 (1967), 17

25 *Cornish Mining Development Association Annual Report* (1968/69), 1

26 Barton, D. B. op. cit. 39

27 *Cornish Mining Development Association Annual Report* (1968/69), 1

28 Eglin, R. op. cit.

29 *Cornish Chamber of Mines Report* (1966), 13

30 *Cornish Chamber of Mines Report* (1968), 14

31 *Cornish Mining Development Association Annual Report* (1968/69), 1

32 *The Times* (9 May 1969)

33 *Cornish Mining Development Association Annual Report* (1968/69), 4

34 *Cornish Chamber of Mines Reports* (1966), 19 (1967), 19 (1968), 19

35 Based on report and statement of the company for the year ending 31 December 1964

36 *Cornish Chamber of Mines Report* (1968), 19

37 *The Times* (9 May 1969)

38 *Cornish Chamber of Mines Report* (1968), 19

39 *Cornish Chamber of Mines Reports* (1966), 15 (1967), 15

40 From the company records of the Levant mine

41 Garnett, R. H. 'Divers Investigate the Levant Mine' *Mining Magazine* 104 (1961), 73–5

42 *The Times* (7 June 1965)

43 *Cornish Chamber of Mines Reports* (1967), 15 (1968), 16

44 Eglin, R. op. cit.

45 *Cornish Chamber of Mines Report* (1968), 16

46 Eglin, R. op. cit.

47 *Cornish Mining Development Association Annual Report* (1966/67), 4

48 *Cornish Mining Development Association Annual Report* (1967/68), 3

49 *Cornish Mining Development Association Annual Report* (1965/66), 5

50 *Cornish Chamber of Mines Report* (1968), 15

51 *Cornish Mining Development Association Annual Report* (1967/68), 3

52 From the company records of Bassett mine

53 *Cornish Chamber of Mines Report* (1968), 18

54 *Cornish Mining Development Association Annual Report* (1965/66), 4 (1964/65), 1

55 *Cornish Chamber of Mines Report* (1966), 21

56 *Cornish Mining Development Association Annual Report* (1967/68), 3

57 Part of the English China Clays combine based at St Austell in Cornwall

58 *Cornish Mining Development Association Annual Report* (1967/68), 4

59 *Cornish Mining Development Association Annual Report* (1967/68), 3

60 *Cornish Mining Development Association Annual Report* (1964/65), 1

61 Barton, D. B. op. cit. 10–11

62 *Cornish Mining Development Association Annual Report* (1966/67), 2–3

63 Ritchie, B. 'Cornwall's Old Industry is Teething Again' *The Times* (5 June 1967)

64 The Mineral Development Acts 1940–1960 have permitted not only the application of modern prospecting techniques but in addition they have facilitated the acquisition of land where the mineral developer cannot locate the owner of the minerals or where agreement cannot be achieved with the private mineral owner.

65 *The Financial Times* (17 October 1966)

66 Barton, D. B. op. cit. 22

67 From the company records of Great Wheal Vor United mine

68 Cornwall County Council Development Plan Survey (1952), Part I, Appendix 16 271–5
69 *Cornish Mining Development Association Annual Report* (1963/64), 1–2
70 Details of the conclusion of this venture were given by the Chairman of the Cornish Mining Development Corporation, J. H. Trounson, in a letter to the author (22 July 1969)
71 Barton, D. B. op. cit. 11
72 *The Times* (19 January 1961)
73 *The Times* (11 May 1961)
74 *Mining Magazine* 106 (1962), 3
75 Trounson, J. H. in a letter to the author (22 July 1969)
76 From the company records of the Carnelloe mine
77 Heck, H. W. J. 'Strategic Planning for the Coast—the Example of Cornwall' *Journal of Town Planning Institute* (1968), 395
78 Ibid. 396
79 *Cornish Mining Development Association Annual Report* (1968/69), 4
80 Trounson, J. H. 'Mining in Cornwall' *The Observer* (6 July 1969)
81 Walter, A. J. 'A Pattern for the Revival of Mining Exploration in the British Isles,' paper 32 in the Symposium on the *Future of Non Ferrous Mining in Great Britain and Ireland* (1959) 575–83
82 *Cornish Mining Development Association Annual Report* (1967/68), 1
83 *Cornish Mining Development Association Annual Report* (1966/67), 1
84 *Hansard* (HMSO 21 June 1961) column 1,514
85 *The Economist* (9 May 1970), 70
86 Truscott, S. J. *Mine Economics* (3rd edition 1962), 205–23
87 McDivett, J. F. *The Status of Mineral Exploration in Europe* (OEEC, 1964), 63
88 Ibid. 131

Attitudes to a Business Environment: The case of the assisted areas of the South West

PETER NEWBY

THE DEVELOPMENT OF MANUFACTURING INDUSTRY

The industrial structure of Cornwall and parts of Devon has undergone a fundamental change in the twentieth century. The collapse of the mining economy in the late nineteenth century resulted in the decline of fishing and agriculture and caused depression throughout the region. A new prosperity has, however, emerged based upon a tourist and retirement economy that has flourished during the post-war period.

Within the main stream of this recovery there has occurred quite rapid industrial growth. The local authorities in the region prepared sites for individual factories and developed industrial estates. Between 1950 and 1960, for example, Exeter received 183 enquiries about sites on the city's trading estates. Since then the applications for information have increased (Table 12.1). A similar pattern can be seen in the Government-assisted areas of the South West. In Cornwall in 1956 there were just nine enquiries about industrial sites. By 1967 there had been 620 such enquiries. Enquiries for industrial sites in Plymouth increased slowly until the late sixties, when, in both Plymouth and Cornwall, the number of enquiries suddenly grew.

Of course, not all of these enquiries resulted in a site being taken up. For instance, between 1950 and 1960 in Exeter only 45 sites on industrial estates were occupied. Between 1945 and 1968 25 medium and large industrial units established themselves in Plymouth, while, between 1956 and 1967, 92 manufacturing concerns established themselves in Cornwall. There is, however, a contrast in the structure of industrial development in the two areas. Of the sites which were occupied in Exeter, only nine were taken by manufacturing industry. In Plymouth and Cornwall, on the other hand, the emphasis has been upon manufacturing industry. This partly reflects the nature of the overall enquiries, for, as these were assisted areas, the majority of enquiries would be from manufacturing concerns, and

TABLE 12.1

Enquiries about Industrial Sites in the South West, 1961–1969

	Exeter	Plymouth	Cornwall
1961	23	20	*
1962	20	12	*
1963	24	10	*
1964	*	16	*
1965	*	20	*
1966	*	25	*
1967	*	23	90
1968	*	45	155
1969 (Jan.–July)	*	46	100

* Data unavailable.

Source of Data: Exeter City Council; Plymouth City Council; Cornwall County Council

partly it reflects the desire of the authorities to give their areas a stability based upon a diversity of manufacturing industry. The similarity between Plymouth and Cornwall is also apparent from the type of firm which has moved into them. In Cornwall a little over 40 per cent of the firms are concerned with engineering and metal processing, while in Plymouth 46 per cent of the firms are in this category. In both cases the next largest category was that of the production and processing of textiles, leather and clothing: this accounted for 14 per cent of the firms in Cornwall and 30 per cent of those in Plymouth. There was, in addition, a strong contingent of electronics and electrical engineering firms in both areas. The type of firm which has moved into the assisted areas of the South West is, according to the findings of Cameron and Clark[1] and Howard,[2] typical of the mobile elements of British industry. Very few firms had specific locational requirements, although the manager of one chemical firm did say that:

'the overall reason for siting the plant in the area was the considerable efficiency achieved in the extraction of bromine from sea water.'

One cause of industrial growth in Plymouth and Cornwall lies in the national policy of industrial decentralisation, in which Cornwall has shared from 1958 and Plymouth from 1958 to 1961 and, according to the report of the Hunt Committee, from 1969 onwards. This policy is double-edged. On the one hand development in the Midlands and the South of England is controlled through the restricted issue of Industrial Development Certificates; on the other hand there are positive incentives to tempt a firm to move into one of the areas assisted by the Government.

For a businessman the difference between a Development Area and an Intermediate Area lies in the amount of aid he can actually receive. As a generalisation, the Intermediate Areas, such as Plymouth, can offer 25 per cent building grants and a range of industrial training grants covering part of an employee's wage while in training, together with part of the cost of training courses. Assistance towards the cost of transferring key workers is also available. In addition, the Government can provide advance factories. Development Areas can provide an extra 10 per cent building grant, investment grants up to 45 per cent, and low-rate mortgages to cover the complete cost of capital or plant, while for every employee, the firm receives a financial rebate.

Once a firm has moved, however, what is its attitude to its new environment, an environment which, without the financial inducements, may be extremely sub-optimal? By posing this question, this survey goes beyond the brief which Cameron and Clark gave themselves:

'the analysis deals entirely with the initial causes of industrial mobility . . . No account has been taken of whether manufacturers ultimately felt, in the light of their production experience, that they had made the right decision.'[3]

The question of the 'right decision' is assessed, in this paper, in terms of a less than positive attitude towards location. The answer shows dissatisfaction with certain features of the location. However, as a brief this leaves an important aspect unstudied. If a firm has a negative attitude to its location, why did it choose the South West in the first place? The location decision has an important bearing upon changes in attitude and for this reason it is relevant to examine the favourable attitudes held by the development authorities and to contrast them with those currently held by manufacturing concerns which have moved into the area.

THE DECISION TO LOCATE

The favourable attitudes which the firms had towards their new business environment at the time of relocation must have reflected the positive attitudes held by the development authorities. These authorities are competing with all other assisted areas for a limited stock of mobile firms, but the financial and material inducements outlined above are common to all assisted areas. Consequently the attitudes adopted by the authorities, those features of the South West which are stressed, indicate the 'fringe' benefits, such as service and recreational facilities, on which the region bases its competition with other assisted areas.

What part, however, does this information play in the businessman's decision-making? If we take the process down to a very general situation, the businessman takes decisions with respect to various levels of information. On the one hand, he gathers data which is specific to his requirements: on the assistance which he can expect to receive and on the resources which are locally available for incorporation into the productive process. This specific information is sought from all alternative locations and is aimed at reducing uncertainty. On the other hand, the businessman is subject to general impressions and opinions about a location, which we can term background information. Such information can be seen as a function of a person's experience, personality and system of values.[4] In introducing this idea we are introducing a perceptive process, a filtering and distorting mechanism which affects both the quantity and quality of information.

To a large extent this idea of a background source of information appears to have been under-emphasised in studies of location decision-making, yet in the case of the South West this is the information level upon which its competitiveness is based. The total information upon which a decision is made results from the fusion of specific and background sources. Specific information can confirm general opinions or attitudes, while background information can influence the type of specific information which is sought and, in certain situations, the degree to which specific information is accepted.[5] The information obtained about a location varies in the degree to which it is, on the one hand, fact or, on the other, value judgment, and nowhere is this more true than of the information circulated by the south-western development authorities. The information which the business decision-maker gets from newspapers, professional journals and local authorities can be seen as a form of propaganda, mixing fact, which is essential for judgments between alternative locations, with qualitative opinions. By placing both together the aim is to influence background information and value judgments as a source, giving them a stronger structure and greater credibility, and consequently a greater ability to influence specific information. As a result of the juxtaposition of industrial logic which results from fact, with emotional appeal which stems from value judgments, background information appears to have been given an importance in decision-making which it ought not to possess.

ATTITUDES TOWARDS ASPECTS OF ENVIRONMENT

The attitudes of the development authorities were investigated by a survey of their informative literature,[6] while those of the industrialists were tested by a questionnaire submitted to 66 per cent of the manufacturing firms which established themselves in the region between 1945 and 1968, asking them to evaluate the extent to which their location in the geographic and business environment of the South West was satisfactory. The response rate to the questionnaire was 53 per cent (42 firms) and, as can be seen from Table 12.2, the sample reflects the type of firm which in Britain has been geographically mobile.

TABLE 12.2

Sample of Firms which have moved into Plymouth and Cornwall in the Post-war Period—by Manufacturing activity

Manufacturing Activity	Proportion of Sample
Engineering	32 per cent
Textiles, Clothing	27 per cent
Electronics, Electrical Engineering	11 per cent
Plastics	8 per cent
Others	12 per cent

Source: Personal Survey

The most important aspects towards which a negative or dissatisfied attitude prevailed on the part of the firms were the peripheral location of the South West and the employment environment. These are broken down further in Table 12.3.

TABLE 12.3
Elements of the Environment judged Unsatisfactory

	Proportion of Total Complaints
Roads	16.7 per cent
Distance from Raw Materials	16.0 per cent
Air Line Transport	11.1 per cent
Workers' Transport	11.1 per cent
Labour Availability	10.4 per cent
Distance from Major Markets	7.6 per cent
Railways	7.0 per cent
Labour Turnover	6.3 per cent
Port Facilities	3.8 per cent
Links with Other Firms	2.1 per cent
Links with Educational Establishments	2.1 per cent
Others	5.8 per cent

Source: Personal Survey

It is interesting to compare these negative attitudes to location in the South West with the major specific determinants of location choice as determined by Cameron and Clark (Table 12.4). The factors of labour and communications which industrialists deem to be important in making a location decision are those very same factors which industrialists in the South West find unsatisfactory. These unfavourable attitudes are, perhaps, an expression of the extent to which background information was accorded a greater importance than it deserved.

TABLE 12.4
The Most Important Determinants of Area/Site Choice

Factor	Per Cent of Firms Mentioning Factor
Supply of Trainable Labour	80
Local Authority Co-operation	58
Accessibility to Main Markets	44
Ready-Built Factory	38
Transport Facilities for Goods	37
Access to Supplies	32

Source: Cameron and Clark[7]

Attitudes Towards Communications

Almost inevitably the largest proportion of complaints were concerned with the road system and the difficulties of communication with the rest of Britain. Associated with the specific complaints about roads, airline services and British Rail was a reported sense of isolation from raw materials and markets. The majority of the complaints were concerned with the distance between the manufacturing plant and the source of the raw material, and with the inevitable high cost of transporting them.

There was, however, a contrast in the extent to which various types of firm perceived isolation as a problem. The small firms, employing between 1 and 50 people, making up 46 per cent of the sample, accounted for over 50 per cent of the total complaints about distance from raw materials and markets. The situation is not unexpected, since small firms lack the resources to overcome basic locational problems. A similar situation exists with those firms employing mainly unskilled labour, which formed 55 per cent of the sample and accounted for 75 per cent of the complaints about distance from markets and 61 per cent of the complaints about distance from raw materials. Another factor which affected this sense of isolation was the type of site which the firms occupied. Those firms which had moved their operations completely saw isolation as much more of a problem than those firms which had merely established subsidiary sites in the region, retaining a head office or manufacturing plant in the Midlands or South.

Against this genuine and very serious problem of a sense of isolation we have to set the positive attitudes which the firms felt and which are reflected in the attitudes expressed by the development authorities. Cornwall County Council attempts to dispel any sense of isolation by emphasising proposed improvements in the road system and the potential that exists for sea and air traffic. The attitudes adopted by Plymouth reflect its greater accessibility which is not the case with Cornwall. Here the emphasis is placed upon existing services rather than on extensions to existing services. Greater emphasis is given to the port, with its facilities for vessels of up to 15,000 tons, warehousing space and regular connections with major continental ports, even though the indications are that it is little used by the newer industries. Railway services are fully described, with emphasis upon the inter-city services, showing the feasibility of return travel between Plymouth and London in a day, and upon bulk transportation facilities which are being improved with the new freightliner terminal.

The attitudes of the industrialist towards communications facilities, however, seem justified. The Regional Development Report states that at peak periods the roads of the South West carry volumes of traffic far beyond their capacity, while, of the railway, it says that:

> 'on strictly commercial principles this line (from Plymouth to Penzance)
> would have stopped at Plymouth.'[8]

Much as proposed improvements may once have provided an inducement to locate in the South West, it is the existing situation which creates problems for the industrialist and results in unfavourable attitudes on his part.

The complaints about transportation facilities can again be isolated to particular types of firm. As might be expected, those firms which import over 50 per cent of their inputs by road produced a larger proportion of complaints about road conditions (76.0 per cent) than the size of their group might suggest (68.6 per cent of the sample). Another factor which affected the way in which a firm viewed road transportation was the length of time it had been in the region. 60.5 per cent of the firms had been there less than 7 years and they produced 74.0 per cent of the complaints about roads. Conversely, those firms which had been here over 22 years (6.1 per cent of the sample) found no problems whatsoever with the road system. The tendency, therefore, is for firms to overcome the limitations imposed upon them by their situation or to accept the situation as it exists.

The costs that road transportation entails are highlighted by a comment from one firm in Plymouth, that,

> 'each day raw materials are transported by road to Plymouth and finished products are taken back. With large articulated vehicles this becomes a major problem, particularly in the busy summer months.'

Several other medium and large firms reported the same communications problem, while others reported it in respect of the movement of executives, regretting the lack of an airport and emphasising that the difficulties of road and rail links between the South West and the major international airports cut down the number of visits to the region and restricted the number of trips abroad which could be made by executives. For those firms which exported a large proportion of their production, this was amongst the most serious of their problems. However, the fault does not lie solely with the public authorities. Facilities exist but companies do not make full use of them, though at least two Plymouth firms airfreight goods via Exeter airport. Since the summer of 1969 Westward Airlines have flown a daily shuttle service from Plymouth to London. In spite of the complaints about airline travel, especially from firms in Plymouth, Westward's managing director felt obliged to point out that

> 'the larger industrial concerns just do not accept that it saves time.'

This is an interesting comment, in view of the fact that the 8.0 per cent of the sample employing over 301 people were responsible for 11.8 per cent of all complaints about air travel. At the other extreme the small firms with under 50 employees also saw airline services as a problem. The former attitude is probably an accurate reflection of dissatisfaction with existing services, while the latter is rather a reflection of the greater sense of isolation which these firms tend to feel.

The problem of the railways is, in a sense, more acute. Uneconomic lines in the region have already been closed. This decline in facilities has caused industrialists to seek other forms of transportation and as a result it has placed greater pressure on the roads while at the same time decreasing the viability of the rail network. The facts transmit themselves to the business sector and become manifested as a feeling of insecurity. As one industrialist expressed it:

> 'Rumours of the termination of the rail service at Plymouth have alarmed industrialists in Cornwall and could, if brought into effect, kill any further industrial development in the County.'

o

Most of the complaints about railways came from specific classes of firm. Those which had settled in small towns, 25.0 per cent of the sample, accounted for 55.1 per cent of the dissatisfaction with the railways. This is a clear indication of the effect that the pruning of the railway network has had upon the business environment. Firms in such towns as Wadebridge, Camelford, Bude and Launceston now feel that they have less of a choice in transportation facilities following the withdrawal of train services. The size of a firm also has an effect on the perception of rail services as a problem. The firms with over 151 employees account for 22.0 per cent of the complaints about the railways and comprise 27.0 per cent of the sample. The group of firms which are badly hit are those 27.0 per cent of all firms which employ between 51 and 150 people; these produce 44.4 per cent of all complaints. This, however, is equally a reflection of the nature of their sites since many of them are found in the smaller urban centres whose problems with regard to rail transportation were outlined earlier.

Attitudes Towards Linkage

The dissatisfaction with local service linkages can be seen as an extension of the attitudes towards the distance from raw materials and markets. Service facilities, in terms of industrial linkage, are an example of agglomeration economies and as such are an important aspect of an adequate industrial environment. At the very simplest level, if a firm is near to its supplies then transportation costs are minimised. The very fact that industry complains about the distance from raw materials and markets point to the lack of linkage in the South West. However, of equal importance are the ease and cost of communications, which influence the flow of orders, ideas and techniques between firms. One manufacturer put it in the following terms:

> 'As the majority of industries are manufacturing for customers far removed
> from Cornwall, telephone expenses are heavy.'

He went on to imply that, because of the need to keep costs down, communications with others in similar fields of production were minimised, yet such communications were important in keeping him in contact with his total business environment.

It is a great advantage, therefore, if a firm can establish forward and backward links in the local area. Realising this situation, the Cornish authorities attempt to give their area the image of a cohesive business environment, stating that

> 'As a result of the growth of manufacturing industry, a number of firms
> providing services to industry, for example tool makers, have been attracted
> to the County.'

This authority's approach is particularly relevant in the evolving industrial situation. Small industrial units are being attracted to small pockets of unemployment and it is for these small firms that industrial linkage with an informal productive unit is so important.

However, the feeling of isolation, together with the perception of the distance from raw materials and markets as a major problem, indicates that local linkage is not well developed. One firm which suffered greatly in this respect processed wood, and its complaint indicates the importance of linkage in keeping up with innovations in production. The managing director of this firm wrote:

> 'The problem ... is in obtaining information and help on new materials and supplies. In 95 per cent of the cases where we required a new type of material or product we were informed that the company's representatives did not come further than Bristol. In the case of bulky materials we were informed that the company would rather not supply owing to transportation difficulties.'

Perhaps not every firm has this problem to the same degree, but it appears that costs are higher than necessary because of a lack of integration amongst the firms in the South West. Firms which did complain about linkage have located in a particular type of environment. Most of them (83.0 per cent) are engineering firms employing less than 150 people, which have been at their site for less than 7 years. All of them are located in Cornwall in towns of less than 15,000 people.

Many of the firms think that the lack of integration is due to a lack of opportunity, and certainly this must have been relevant especially in view of the diversity of expansion that has taken place in the South West. However, there is also a strong possibility that many firms are not taking full advantage of the potential for linkage. The majority of the manufacturing concerns have moved from the metropolitan area, where a strong pattern of linkage exists.[9] Many have left an administrative office in the parent area. Amongst such firms there may be an unwillingness to change sources of supply because of the uncertainty and the effort that is involved. Thus, while the location has changed the pattern of economic integration has often remained the same.

Attitudes Towards Labour

The other major aspect of the environment towards which the business community held a negative attitude was that of labour. In terms of labour availability many of the firms reported that this was a problem, particularly with skilled labour. An industrialist wrote that:

> 'highly skilled labour usually has to be imported. Local labour for semi-skilled and unskilled jobs is moderately satisfactory.'

And he went on to say that this was due, in part, to a lack of industrial atmosphere in which the young of the South West grew up. 'The result,' he said, 'is reflected in the slower tempo generally apparent in the area.'

One of the most interesting aspects of the labour problem was the way in which labour availability and labour turnover were seen as problems by firms in very different circumstances. Firms employing under 50 people produced a greater proportion of complaints than the size of their group would suggest, while the larger firms complained less than expected. On the other hand the very smallest and the very largest firms saw labour turnover as a negligible problem, complaints being concentrated in the firms employing between 50 and 150 people. Perhaps this can be explained by the higher wages and better fringe benefits offered by the larger firms, reflecting what is known as an 'industrial orientation' to work, in which labour is attracted by economic reward, and by the greater sense of community and the development of much closer contacts between management and labour in the small firms. Goldthorpe and others[10] have termed this 'solidaristic orientation,' in which work is seen as a group activity. If we examine the question of labour problems in terms of the employment environment in which the firms located themselves, a contrast can be drawn between the large and small towns on the one hand and the medium-sized towns on the other. Both labour availability and labour turnover were seen as greater problems in Plymouth and the Cornish towns under 10,000 than the proportions of sampled firms in each group would suggest. Conversely in the towns between 15,000 and 35,000 people they were significantly lower than expected. A factor which appears to be operating in this case is the attractiveness of Plymouth with its better than average growth rates for the region. This in itself produces a labour shortage, but it has been emphasised since most of the firms that have moved into the city have been engaged in engineering, or clothing-manufacture, or in electronics. In addition, the very size of the city means that it possesses a well-developed service sector which is also labour-hungry. Consequently, the wage-drift situation comes into its own and labour turnover is reported as a problem. With the small Cornish towns the problem is slightly different. The pool of labour is rapidly absorbed by one or two firms, and, as they are small firms in a small town, they command a small hinterland with small labour reserves. The problem for them becomes one of tempting female labour to enter the labour market for the first time. In this situation it is interesting to note that 46.1 per cent of all complaints about workers' transport came from exactly this type of town.

The type of labour which is employed again creates a pattern in the responses. 55.5 per cent of the firms in the sample employed mainly unskilled labour, 36.1 per cent mainly skilled labour and the rest employed about the same numbers of skilled and unskilled. The pattern of complaints about availability was broadly in line with these proportions, but in terms of labour turnover there was a significant difference. The unskilled firms accounted for 44.0 per cent of the complaints while the skilled accounted for the same proportion.

Having introduced the problem of transport to and from work it is worthwhile, at this point, to investigate the situations in which it is perceived as a problem. It is not a transportation problem in the sense in which this has been considered before; it is more closely aligned with labour problems. We have already seen that it is reported as more of a problem in small towns than in large, and in this respect it is a direct reflection upon the provision of bus services in these areas. Equally interesting is the way in which workers' transport is connected with the size of the firm and the length of time it has been at its site. Generally speaking, the smaller the firm the more this is seen as a problem. 46.0 per cent of the firms in the sample employed less than 50 people, yet these accounted for 56.2 per cent of the complaints. The large firms, on the other hand, had no complaints. This pattern could reflect the small firms' location in small towns, together with the fact that they just do not generate enough traffic for the bus company to provide an adequate yet profitable service. Complaints about workers' transport also tended to decrease with the length of time a firm had been at its site. 75.0 per cent of all complaints came from the 60.5 per cent of firms which had been in the region under 7 years, while the 12.2 per cent of firms which had been there over 15 years accounted for only 6.1 per cent of the complaints. Apart from indicating that many of the small firms have been in the South West for a short time, or that firms which have moved into the small towns have been there a short time, it shows that with the passage of time a firm overcomes the problem of workers' transport, by ignoring it, accepting the situation and limiting the firm's growth, or by becoming large enough to merit a bus service, perhaps by relocating on a trading estate.

The problem of skilled labour is recognised by all development authorities and all emphasise their willingness to aid in the accommodation of essential personnel. However, while they do not ignore labour difficulties, the development authorities do not give them the weight afforded by the industrialists. Cornwall, for example, states that:

> 'the supply of good labour is one of the outstanding advantages that Cornwall can offer to industry.'

In the past this has been very true, the labour situation appealing to firms employing up to 150 people. However, for the last two or three years business men have been encountering the problem of labour availability. The unemployed are often in the wrong location for the industrialist, while the figures themselves may be inflated by workers from the summer tourist industry claiming unemployment benefits during the winter months. In addition a low population increase, together with the ever-present loss of young people from the area, creates a situation in which the long term labour prospects are very little improved. The firms often feel that they have moved from a location where labour is short to one in which labour conditions are similar and the locational characteristics, in relation to their markets, are that much poorer.

Another aspect of the labour situation towards which the employers have a very definite attitude is the quality of labour. The problem which many came up against was the lack of industrial experience. Plymouth development authority agreed with this, but added that industrialists moving into the city had found labour highly adaptable. Cornwall, on the other hand, denied the lack of any industrial heritage, informing the prospective industrialist that:

> 'proud of his long industrial tradition, the Cornishman is loyal and hard-working.'

The creation of such a positive image appeals to the very type of firm suited to Cornwall on other counts, a firm with a small number of employees in which *rapport* can be established between management and employees.

A few firms mentioned the problem of seasonal fluctuations in their labour force, but these were not generally regarded as being very important. Industrial wage levels are now sufficiently high, and the basic working week sufficiently short, to provide a disincentive effect for labour to move into the summer tourist sector. Much more widely expressed was the fear that as the number of unemployed fell, the financial incentives that were given to encourage relocation in the South West would be withdrawn. Uncertainty over this situation was creating uncertainty over future investment decisions.

Attitudes Towards Living in the South West

So far we have examined those aspects to which the business community has strongly negative attitudes. Now we wish to contrast them with the strong, positive, favourable image which the development authorities attempt to create.

An important element in this image appeals directly to the feelings of the decision maker, emphasising what, in the decision process, should only be background or supplementary information. Cornwall County Council stress the virtues of living in a holiday area, saying that:

> 'If you have visited Cornwall you will know how pleasant a place it is for holidays. It is equally pleasant as a place in which to live; climate, coast and countryside combine for perfect outdoor recreation.'

With an obvious appeal to the executive, various types of outdoor recreation are described: sailing; horse-riding; golf; and flying. In addition the council states that:

> 'executives are able to obtain houses in one of the most beautiful counties in England',

while the statement that:

> 'there are also independent schools for boys and girls in several towns'

can only be meant for them.

The appeal, therefore, is not to the business instincts of the firm but to the recreational and social activities of the executive and his family. Plymouth adopts a more industrially logical approach, stressing its advantages to industry in terms of labour, education and training facilities, and the availability of sites in a large urban area; but it also capitalises on its location in South Devon. Plymouth's Estates Office, in a booklet sent to all prospective industrialists, states that:

> 'one of the city's main attractions to workers and executives alike is its wonderful situation,'

and the attractions of the local area are then listed.

These are, in fact, very powerful attractions for the industrialist and his key personnel. The financial incentives to move to the South West are no different from those of other assisted areas; therefore the region has to compete on the basis of its tourist facilities, its major fringe benefit. That the tourist-economy is one of the more important points of competition has emerged from other surveys. In her study of industrial development in Plymouth, Braithwaite concluded that:

> 'the fact that the city is situated in one of the pleasanter parts of the country seems to have been important.'[11]

Luttrell puts the situation from the point of view of the decision maker:

> 'a businessman, influenced by personal factors in his choice of location, will not be concerned with maximising the profits of the company but with other goals like increasing his own welfare or satisfaction.'[12]

This very point emerged from the managing director of a Cornish firm:

> 'I was brought up in the South West and, despite its drawbacks, would prefer to work here rather than in any other part of the country.'

This situation also results when corporate aspects of business activity are considered. The management wants, from the outset, to obtain the approval of those key workers who are being transferred. They are important because, to a large extent, the success of the new plant depends on their attitudes to, and their satisfaction with, their new environment. The importance of their preferences, based on preconceived ideas and attitudes, was noted, again by Luttrell:

> 'Both chose the South West of England, and it is significant that these choices were almost entirely dictated by the wishes of the key staff which were to move with the new plant.'[13]

Gould's and White's work[14] on children's preferences for living in various parts of Britain substantiates the view of the company that it is far easier to persuade key personnel to move to the South West than to many other assisted areas. This favourable attitude to the South West has largely been retained by those people who moved. One executive wrote:

> 'The area is beautiful to live in and from a family point of view there is nothing better.'

Asked if they were satisfied with retail and recreational facilities, only 24 per cent of the executives who completed the questionnaire complained about the former (most of these living in Cornwall) and only 29.0 per cent about recreational facilities (Table 12.5).

TABLE 12.5
Attitudes Towards Retail Services, Recreational Facilities and Personal Contacts

	Percentage of Respondents Reporting Feature Unsatisfactory	Percentage of Respondents Living in Cornwall
Retail facilities	24.4	90.0
Recreational facilities	29.3	66.0
Opportunity for personal contacts	31.7	77.0

Source: Personal Survey

Typically the complaints about retail facilities concerned higher order goods. One director from Redruth wrote that:

> 'from a personal point of view the problems have been in obtaining household furniture, etc., as all large displays are at Plymouth.'

Attitudes Towards Development Authorities

The second feature of the image which the development authorities attempt to emphasise is that of helpful public bodies, and by and large it is an image that they live up to. 70.6 per cent of the firms that replied said that the local authorities had been extremely co-operative. Apart from giving the obvious sources of financial aid, the local authorities aided the incoming industrialist by finding a site that was geared to his labour requirements, providing training facilities for local labour and housing for key workers. Of the firms which said that the authorities could have been more helpful, the largest source of complaints was concerned with housing for key workers and executives. One director's frustration expressed itself in the following words:

'only if a tenant dies or moves can we get a council house.'

Several firms with difficulties over labour supplies commented that the local development authority should have taken the growth prospects of an industry with mainly female labour requirements into account when advising on a site. One factory owner pointed out difficulties encountered with the management of the planning process, contrasting the help received from the local authority with the lack of interest shown by the central authorities. This industrialist said that, as a result,

'we are shortly moving our whole operation to a site in the Irish Republic.'

CONCLUSION

The image of the South West which the local authorities attempt to create is somewhat different from that held by such industry as has moved into the region. The attitudes adopted by the local authorities are, to some extent, a reflection of the advertising media through which they are expressed. The specific image which they create, of living in a holiday area, affects the attitudes adopted by the businessman. The growing advertising budget shows that local authorities have realised the need to create a particular image for industrialists. For instance, in 1958 Cornwall spent only £100 on advertising. By 1968 this had risen to £2,000 per year and this was responsible for two-fifths of all enquiries received about sites. The fact that so many firms experienced so many problems reveals the extent to which this image, based on what is essentially background information, has influenced an economic decision. While these firms almost certainly took the question of accessibility into account in their location decisions, many appear to have under-emphasised it. Equally important for the type of firm which has been attracted to the region is the sense of being isolated from an integrated business environment, while labour problems provide another focus for dissatisfaction.

However, it is in the way in which certain types of firm perceive these problems that a great deal of future interest lies. A firm's attitude is affected by its geographical location, the type of product which it manufactures and the employment environment in which it finds itself. These inter-relationships need to be examined more fully, for if certain types of firm see problems in areas or situations in which others do not, there is, perhaps, a need for greater control on industrial decentralisation.

ACKNOWLEDGMENTS

My thanks are due to Hendon College of Technology for assistance towards the cost of the survey and to E. W. Lewis who commented upon an earlier draft of the paper.

REFERENCES

1 Cameron, G. C. and Clark, B. D. 'Industrial movement and the Regional Problem' *University of Glasgow Social and Economic Studies, Occasional Papers No. 5*. Oliver and Boyd, 1966, 24–5

2 Howard, R. S. (for the Board of Trade) 'The Movement of Manufacturing Industry in the United Kingdom, 1945–1965.' HMSO 1968

3 Cameron, G. C. and Clark, B. D. op. cit. 19

4 This aspect of individual decision-making is examined further by Huff, D. L. 'A Behavioural Approach to the Theory of Business' in *Interdisciplinary Studies in Business Behaviour* ed. McGuire, J. W.

5 For a further discussion see Elbing, A. O. 'Perception, Motivation and Business Behaviour' in J. W. McGuire, op. cit.

6 See, for instance, *Expand in Cornwall* from Cornwall County Council (1960) and *Expand in Plymouth* from Plymouth City Council (1960)

7 Cameron, G. C. and Clark, B. D. op. cit. 162–5

8 Report of the South West Economic Planning Council *Region with a Future: A Draft Strategy for the South West,* HMSO 1967

9 Keeble, D. 'Local Industrial Linkage and Manufacturing Growth in Outer London' *Town Planning Review* 40 (1969), 163–88

10 Goldthorpe, J. H., Lockwood, D., Bechhofer, F., Platt, J. *The Affluent Worker: Industrial Attitudes and Behaviour* (Cambridge University Press 1968)

11 Braithwaite, J. L. 'The Postwar Industrial Development of Plymouth: An Example of the Effect of National Industrial Location Policy' *Transactions of the Institute of British Geographers* 45 (1968), 39–50

12 Luttrell, W. F. *Factory Location and Industrial Movement* NIESR 1962

13 Luttrell, W. F. op. cit.

14 Gould, P. R. and White, R. H. 'The Mental Maps of British School Leavers' *Regional Studies* 2 (1968), 161–82

13

Urban Design in Dawlish and Chelston

EWART JOHNS

This essay examines the influence of period style on townscapes in Dawlish and Chelston, both in Devon. These two 'towns' (Chelston is part of modern Torquay, but is a very distinct urban region) are somewhat alike in size and setting—both occupying coombes and hill-slopes facing their common neighbour, the English Channel coast—but they show very marked contrasts of style in their lay-outs and building forms.

Dawlish

The appearance of central Dawlish can be clearly seen from the air photograph (Plate 15). The principal feature is the central open space known as The Lawn, and there can be little doubt that some process of town-planning has been at work here. What is not known is exactly whose hand, or hands, guided the process, or in what order the buildings and spaces came into being. One very useful reference has recently come to light, however, which seems to confirm the generally expressed local opinion that a certain J. E. Manning played a major part in fashioning Dawlish. This source is to be found in a diary, or notebook, compiled by a Mr Cornelius (clearly the S. R. S. Cornelius who wrote the guide to Dawlish in 1869), where there appears a 'copy of a letter from J. E. Manning.' The letter is dated 29 September, and the year is not given, but it can be inferred from the reference to the published guide that it was written in the early 1870s. Here is the part of the letter[1] that is relevant to the present subject:

'Dear Sir,

I have received your book on Dawlish . . . You are wrong about the flood. It occurred in the silent hour of night, from the sudden thaw of an early snow at Haldon. I lost by it £11,000 in Canal and House property. The first formation of the Canal and Lawn cost me about £5,000, and the renewal £3,600. The Lawn (all washed away), was formed by me, covered by some feet of soil by excavating the two roads of Queen Street, and Exeter Hill by the London Inn. Two new built houses, which cost me £2,100, behind Cross Row, had not two bricks resting upon another by daylight . . . The damage was by my having a few days more only to complete the side walling by the stone bridge.

Yours,

J. E. Manning.'

Exeter Hill must have been the present Strand Hill, the only road out of the town on the Exeter side on the Tithe Map of 1840. Strand Hill is still quite steep, and it may be argued that, if it is the result of excavation, its original form was probably a cliff similar to that found on the south side of the valley—for example, behind the Mill.

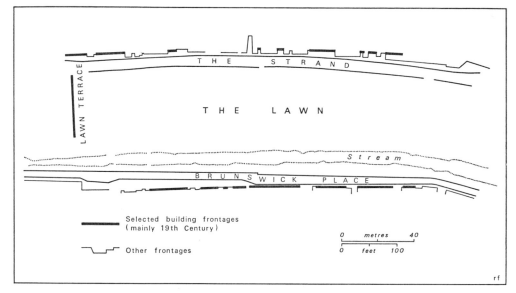

Fig. 13.1   Dawlish, The Lawn and its surroundings

Another useful document is the *Guide to the Watering Places on the Coast between the Exe and The Dart,* published in 1817.[2] The section from this guide which deals with Dawlish refers to the flood which is described above, and dates it in the year 1810 and so we can assume that some of the more important developments on and around The Lawn were taking place just before that date. It is interesting to read that 'The lower part of the village, particularly the bed of the river and the adjacent ground was considered by its proprietor to be much improved . . . the meandering of its stream through a thistled dale was changed to a course in a right line, broken by a multitude of petty falls, and bounded by a fine level lawn.'[3]

This clearly is a description of Mr Manning's work and, in the following references, the Guide helps us to appreciate some of the processes which created Dawlish (and, no doubt, other small wateringplaces and residential towns). 'On these new banks of the river, some daring adventurers had erected lodging houses . . . In the area in the midst of the lower part of the village all was order and neatness . . .', and there was 'in addition to the canal, planted on each side with trees . . . a row of houses crossing the vale at the head of the lawn.'[4] These words are brought to life in the engraving of The Lawn at about mid-century, reproduced in Plate 16 which shows the completed line of The Strand, with Lawn Terrace in the distance (though the trees have disappeared since the engraving was made).

Taken together, Manning's letter, the Guide of 1817 and the engraving of The Lawn are surely evidence of planning by a mixture of forces—the work of a small landowner with a taste for landscaping; the operations of 'adventurers' who presumably bought plots from Manning or other owners around The Lawn; and the common preference for orderliness and symmetry which marks both individual buildings and the general form of central Dawlish.

Attention to the details of the town-plan of Dawlish brings to light some further points concerning the origins of The Lawn. The levelling of The Lawn and the straightening of the stream were probably accompanied by the making of The Strand and Brunswick Place —the two streets on either side of The Lawn (though there seems to be no documentary evidence from which to date these streets). At first sight it seems obvious that some general building regulations have been imposed in central Dawlish, and this is especially clear in the case of Brunswick Place, where the house frontages form an almost perfectly straight line, changing direction very slightly at the public house (The Brunswick Arms), as can be seen in the 25 inch-to-one-mile Ordnance Survey map (Plate 17). The line of the housefronts is not, however, parallel to the street itself, but diverges slightly to the south as it extends upstream. On the north side of The Lawn, The Strand is built on a very gentle curve, and the building frontages make the kind of irregular line that is common in many a main shopping street in Devonshire. However, if we examine the alignment of the front walls of certain buildings which are set a little back from the street (some still retaining their original small front gardens), we discover something interesting not only about The Strand but also about its relationship to Brunswick Place and Lawn Terrace. Figure 13.1 shows that the line formed by selected parts of The Strand buildings makes a nearly perfect straight line, unlike the slightly curving street; furthermore, this line makes an exact right-angle with the frontages along Lawn Terrace, and forms a parallel line to the front walls of the buildings in Brunswick Place. In other words, the generally rectilinear form of The Lawn and its neighbourhood—obvious enough at a casual glance—was originally based on a very accurately designed layout, which was also, surely, the work of one person—probably J. E. Manning. With a symmetrical framework as a basis, developers were able to indulge in a certain amount of freedom in their individual choice of designs for their lodging houses, while still permitting that 'order and neatness' which was considered so proper in the early nineteenth century. The Lawn at Dawlish was not necessarily regarded as the height of fashionable sophistication in its day, for 'a confused and inelegant style of architecture predominates, in this, as well as in many other watering places, *chacun à son goût*. Every house, from the large mansion to the simple cottage orné, has no rival in point of similarity, though many in the field of taste.'[5] This rather acid comment by the stern critic in the Dawlish Guide seems to regret that rigidly formal regulations stopped short at the levelling of the meadow and the laying out of the rectangular building lines, but, to modern eyes, there is a good deal more of uniformity than of variety in the simple stuccoed houses, of Georgian proportions with their roofs all hidden behind a line of parapets and their doors and windows evenly spaced, while there seems just enough variation of height and frontal alignment to give visual interest and a feeling of intimacy to the scene. The grandiose terraces, pilastered and pedimented, that look so well in the city, would have been absurdly out of scale and harmony with the modest green vale and the buxom slopes.

In Dawlish, the straightened stream, the levelled Lawn and the rectangle of the building lines represent a small by-product of the 'Age of Reason'. Similar forms are still preserved, too, in other small Devonshire coastal towns—for example Sidmouth, Exmouth, Teignmouth and Shaldon. Yet at the very time when these places were being built, a new age was being born—the age of Romanticism—which was to express itself in a whole new set of preferences in the field of urban design.

Chelston

Although it is now a part of the continuously built-up area around Torbay, Chelston was developed along the coombes and over the hillsides which lie between the manors of Tormohun and Cockington, west of Torquay. Building at Chelston, apart from the original church, a mill, a small manor house and a few cottages, dates mainly from the last two decades of the nineteenth century. Interest is immediately aroused by the arrangement of roads and buildings as they appear on the O.S. 6 miles to one inch map (Plate 18). The branch railway line, which separates Torre and Chelston, also separates two kinds of urban plan: to the east are the villas of Torre, grouped spaciously and fairly formally around the narrow streets and dense blocks of buildings of the nucleus of Tormohun, (which includes Church Street, Laburnum Street and Church Lane); to the west, Chelston is made up of a low-density area of villas on curving drives to the south, and of mainly terrace formations to the north. It is this last area, generally known as Lower Chelston, which is to be discussed in the present paper. It is clear that the roads, buildings, and open spaces of Lower Chelston form some kind of cohesive plan; at the same time their arrangement is neither of simple Classical style, nor is it a curvilinear configuration such as is found in the famous Lincombe Hill and Warberry Hill estates at Torwood, on the other side of Torbay. In Lower Chelston the terraces and a few semi-detached or detached houses also avoid the 'parallel row' construction of much later nineteenth century townscape, and, although there is some relationship to be seen between street lines and former field boundaries, a careful comparison of the original enclosures of the area with the subsequent road system shows only a partial adaptation to the former network of fields (Fig. 13.2). Apart from Sherwell Lane and Old Mill Road, which have been built along the tracks of a more ancient communication system, most roads in the area ignore old boundaries and show a regard for the kind of layout which is in keeping with the rolling topography of the area. From this map evidence, then, it can be assumed that a plan of some kind was formulated by the developers of this part of Chelston, while a visit to the area reveals some unusual features, like the small playing-grounds at the rear of some of the terraces (Plate 19), the landscaped verges and the end-of-terrace plots (Plates 20, 21).

Exactly what factors influenced the choice of street system in Lower Chelston is not known, but this system was clearly intended to serve two ends beyond that of convenient access to property: these were a good appearance and the provision of public open space.

These two purposes, surely, have a logical connection with one another, since the adaptation of building plots to a deliberately asymmetrical street network produces an arrangement of small pieces of land of various shapes and sizes; these pieces can either be made to form private gardens of extreme irregularity or, as happens in Chelston, parts of them can be utilized as public land for verges, small ornamental corner plots, children's playgrounds and the like.

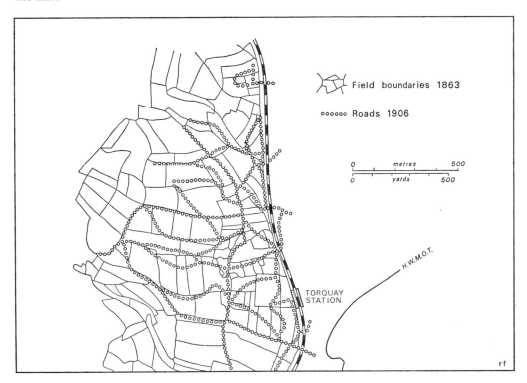

Fig. 13.2 The relationship between former field boundaries and the road system in Chelston. Based upon Ordnance Survey 1:10,560 maps, 1863 and 1906, with the sanction of the Controller of HM Stationery Office, Crown Copyright reserved.

Documentary evidence of the development of Lower Chelston has so far come to light only in small pieces. The relevant papers of the Mallock family, of Cockington Court, are said to have been destroyed in a fire, though copies of general plans of the Chelston area may yet turn up. In the meantime, some useful information can be put together from other sources, while the physical evidence in the field can, as we have seen, speak for itself. A large area of land west of Torquay Station, which had been the site of the Devon Agricultural Show in 1882 and which belonged to the Mallock family, was shortly afterwards split up into building lots. From various records, chiefly conveyances, it is clear that, in permitting development on their land, the owners were at the same time making provision for the general amenity of the district. Furthermore, evidence of the Mallocks' interest in the future of their land and in the prospects for the developing townscape on the periphery of their estate is provided before the time of the sale of land west of the railway line. Richard Mallock, the owner of Cockington Manor at that time, had leased land to a builder, William Vanstone, on 10 February 1880, and, in a memorandum attached to the deeds of No. 1 Woodland Terrace, and dated 12.12.81, the following agreement is described:[6]

> 'R. Mallock of Cockington Court agrees to let, and Mr F. R. Tapper agrees to take the strip of ground along the south side of the premises purchased . . . from Mr Wm Vanstone . . . (*this was a very narrow strip along the side of the house, and bordering a public right of way between two terrace rows*) . . . at the rent of one shilling per annum . . . Mr Tapper is to enclose the said Ground with a stone wall of similar description and height to that on the Eastern side of the Premises (the front garden wall) and to plant a Row of Evergreen Trees and Shrubs in the said Plot of Ground along the inside of the said Wall and at all times during the Term (99 years) to keep the said Plot of Ground so properly planted and the Wall in good repair in all respects.'

This scrap of information shows that Richard Mallock was a man who was prepared to lease land for little financial return, on conditions which maintained a high standard of appearance.

When the land was sold in Sherwell Valley, where the terraces and other houses and properties now constituting Lower Chelston were to be built, the Mallock family made various conditions in the deeds of conveyance, which show their concern for the provision of adequate open spaces in the district. In particular, there is an interesting list of pieces of land which 'shall at all times be used and maintained as open spaces in accordance with the Open Spaces Acts of 1877 and 1890 . . .'. This is contained in a *Conveyance of Parks* from the Trustees of E. Mallock and others to the Torquay Corporation on the 21 March 1907, which reads as follows[5] (words in italics are the author's):

> 'Corbyn's Head and Foreshore, and, 1. Two parks (*off Solsbro Road*); 2. Land opposite The Vicarage, Chelston; 3. Ashfield Gardens; 4. Goschen Terrace, etc. (*land behind the houses*); 5. Sandford Terrace, etc. (*land behind the houses*); 6. Fairfield Crescent (*triangle of land at end of playground between Mallock Road and Sherwell Lane*); 7. Lane near Sharon, Chelston (*triangle between Old Mill Road and Sandford Road*); 8. Land for widening, Torbay Road; 9. Strips of land fronting Paignton Road; 10. Pumping station, Cockington.'

Most of the places mentioned in this list are small patches of ground which are still preserved as public places and, in several cases, specifically as children's playgrounds, the most interesting and unusual being the small triangular places behind Goschen Terrace, Sandford Terrace and Mallock Road. It is such obvious good sense to make a playground out of land accessible to the backs of terraces, where children can gather, away from the streets, that it would hardly justify notice if such provision had been common at the time from which these examples date; as it is, it may not be too fanciful to suggest that Lower Chelston shows for its time some advanced thinking on the question of precincts and public spaces. (There are also a number of public footpaths linking the drives by short cuts, which show that the pedestrian had not been forgotten). It seems reasonably clear, therefore, that documents support the field evidence of some modest form of town planning at Chelston.

The planning process, if we accept it as such, seems to have been very similar in both Chelston and Dawlish: private landowners contrived to influence the layout of a significant part of the town, while leaving a good deal of the building in individual hands. The finished results in the two places are, however, quite different. While central Dawlish is laid out formally and symmetrically and The Lawn is a rectangle, Lower Chelston is built in harmony with the flowing lines of the landscape, and the main open space—the park in Sherwell Valley—retains the outlines of the original meadow, and preserves, prettified, the meandering brook. The buildings, too, are quite different in the respective towns. Dawlish's Georgian cottages are finished in stucco; they present an appearance of uniformity and have common proportions: the houses of Chelston are of red sandstone or red brick, or a mixture of both, and the emphasis is on variety of colour and form, and there is a relish for detail shown in the fretted woodwork, on the eaves, porches and verandas. A comparison between two such places as Dawlish and Chelston is, therefore, particularly useful as a means of measuring the place of design in urban morphology, and of introducing the question: 'Why were those designs preferred?' In Dawlish, where the straight lines of the streets and building-fronts ignore former boundaries, an urban shape was created to suit a social life which was making a break with the past, and in which people enjoyed showing themselves (and watching others) in public; the houses faced on to The Lawn, with little or no garden in front of them and even less behind them; from the many large front windows a choice view could be had of the principal place of promenade. At the same time stucco provided a refined mask for the 'too rustic' cob or rubble of the cottage walls, and the level Lawn and straightened stream completed a sense of orderliness and small-scaled urbanity, which quietly echoed the grander perfections of Brighton, Cheltenham and Leamington Spa. In Chelston, on the other hand, the kind of order preferred is that which was thought to be in keeping with the shapes of the environment into which streets and houses were—so to say—inserted: old lanes still weave through the district and climb and drop with the billowing hills; the brittleness and irregularity of the local red breccias, which provide the building stone, produce an extreme rusticity—only a strong conviction of the propriety of such a look could have persuaded a stone mason to carve material with such improbable outlines—and the whole district has a secluded feeling. The romanticism and naturalism may be discovered, at their secretive best, along the banks of the tumbling, winding brook, enclosed and shrubberied to the point of almost complete incarceration: few contemporary visitors to Torbay have seen it, in its little ornamental park, only half a mile from the place where its waters run to the sea beneath the pounding holiday traffic on the Marine Drive. Chelston was the product of an age in sympathy with England's rustic past.

Chelston was made up of middle-class residences and homes for artisans and people in

P

service-trades: Dawlish originally set out to attract genteel visitors to lodging houses. Yet these different functions were not so dissimilar as to explain, of themselves, the contrasts in the urban design of the two towns. The difference in time between the very early and the very late years of the nineteenth century brought with it a change in the ideas of what things *ought* to look like—whether they were streams or parks, flower-gardens or fences, doors or windows, eaves or roofs. Between the times when the urban landscapes of Dawlish and Chelston were made, new gospels of design according to Augustus Pugin, John Ruskin and William Morris had been proclaimed, and between them these prophets and their followers transformed the faces of many an English scene—not least the scenes in towns where to be in fashion was also to be 'in business.'

ACKNOWLEDGMENT

This essay was read at the 'Urban History Seminar' at Dartington Hall in May, 1969.

REFERENCES

1 From a volume called *Overseers and Apprentices, and Population and Ratement, in Dawlish* by a Mr Cornelius. The book is in the possession of W. J. Holman, Esq., The Moorings, The Strand, Dawlish, to whom the author is indebted
2 *A Guide to the Watering Places on the Coast between the Exe and the Dart* (Teignmouth 1817)
3 Ibid, 25
4 Ibid, 25
5 Ibid, 5
6 From the deeds in the possession of Miss Constance Ball of Woodland Terrace, to whom the author is indebted
7 Conveyance, in the Records Office, Torbay County Borough

14

A Case Study in Medical Geography, Wonford Ward, Exeter

MARY GRIFFITHS

Studies in medical geography are concerned with areal variations in disease and associated factors in the environment. The recognition of areal variations has in the past provided clues in the search for the causative agents in disease. Today, when most of the population in a developed country die from the degenerative diseases of old age, one would expect the areal variations to be small. That this is not so has been revealed by the National Atlas of Disease Mortality in the United Kingdom.[1] Differences in the level of mortality can be identified even within one city, as a study of Exeter has shown. Mortality in Exeter is similar to the national average and favourable in comparison with other county boroughs of similar size, yet some parts of the city have a mortality experience considerably better than average for the city, indicating the scope for increased longevity. In contrast, other areas may be identified, where mortality is high in comparison with the rest of the city. It is one of these areas of high mortality, Wonford Ward, that is the subject of this paper.

Wonford is one of seventeen wards in the city of Exeter; it is the second largest, with a population of 6,031 living in private households at the Census of 1961, compared with a total population in private households of 74,575. For the period of the study, 1958–64, both male and female mortality in Wonford Ward was significantly higher than that expected on the basis of the age/sex structure of the population. This became evident from a study of mortality in the wards of Exeter, based on an analysis of death certificates. The period 1958–64 was selected, as it is centred on the Census year of 1961 and, while a longer period of analysis would have been desirable, it was not possible to obtain detailed information on the age/sex structure of the wards for any year before 1961. It was necessary to confine the analysis to the wards, for this was the smallest unit for which standardisation for age/sex structure could be carried out and it is obvious that mortality in an area depends to a considerable degree on the age structure of the population. The study showed that there were some significant differences in mortality between the wards, and some possible reasons for these differences were put forward in terms of the physical and social environment of each ward. While most wards have some variety in the physical and social conditions within them, Wonford is a relatively homogeneous ward, the most distinctive in the city.

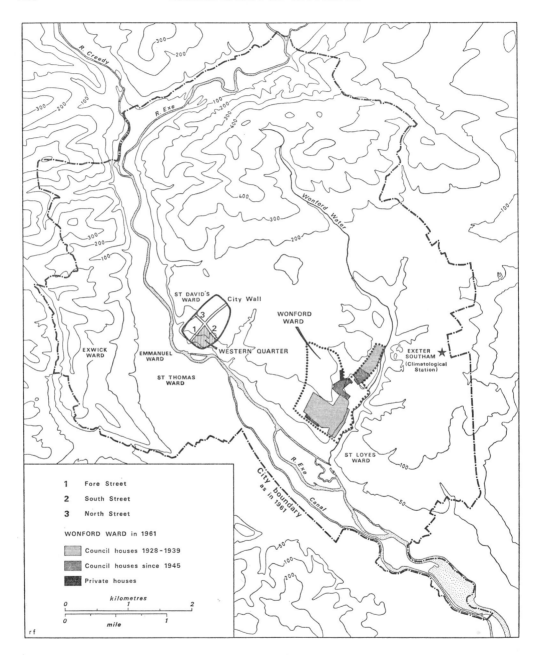

Fig. 14.1 Exeter.

Although the small village of Wonford had long existed on the south-eastern outskirts of Exeter, the main development came in the early nineteen-thirties when a slum area in the centre of Exeter was cleared and many of the people were rehoused here. Today over 90 per cent of the population of the ward live in council houses, many of them built in the interwar period (Fig. 14.1). Before proceeding with the description of present-day Wonford it is instructive to give closer examination to the area from which many of the people came.

Exeter has a tradition of interest in medical geography and this permits a brief historical study. An Exeter physician, T. Shapter, not only made a study of the cholera outbreak in the city in 1832 but was also among the first to illustrate his work with a map showing the location of deaths.[2] The early reports of the Medical Officer of Health for Exeter contained maps to show the place of residence of those dying from the principal infectious diseases (1896-1903) and the incidence of notified tuberculosis (1914, 1925).[3] There is considerable correspondence between the areas of the city which were shown to be less healthy in these works and those unhealthy in the eighteenth century as shown by R. Pickard's 'Population and Epidemics in Exeter in Pre-Census Times.'[4] The geographical variations in mortality within the city reflected differences in social conditions and some parts had remained the domain of the poor for several centuries. When these slum areas were cleared in the 1930s, many people were rehoused on the outskirts of the city. One of the poor parts was the Western Quarter—a section within the city walls to the west of Fore Street and South Street (Fig. 14.1). From this Western Quarter came many of those who were to inhabit Wonford Ward.

The first record of poverty in the Western Quarter is from the Hearth Tax Roll of 1671-72.[5] This tax was based on the number of hearths in the dwelling and people with only one or no hearths were exempt. Over 40 per cent of the population were exempt in the parish of St Mary Major in the heart of the Western Quarter. Only 4 of the 20 parishes were poorer than this and one of these also extended into the Western Quarter. Pickard's figures for baptisms and burials for the period 1690-1770 show a considerable excess of burials over baptisms in this area; this, according to his argument, indicates a decline in population. This decline was probably due primarily to the effects of epidemics in the eighteenth century: these were particularly disastrous in poor areas. The decline of nearly 20 per cent in the population of St Mary Major parish was exceeded by several other parishes, but it seems that this was one of the largest areas which was consistently poor.

The cholera epidemic of 1832-34 was more serious in St Mary Major and the two adjacent parishes to the north and west than in any other part of the city, killing between 3 and 4 per cent of the population (compared with 1.4 per cent for the whole of Exeter). The disease itself is waterborne but, as Shapter observed, the incidence of cholera was highest among 'persons who had no very settled business, whose habits were irregular and whose bodily comforts were badly provided for.'[2]

The same area appears on the maps in the early reports of the Medical Officer of Health for Exeter. The smallpox epidemic of 1896 was centred here. Again, in 1897, 24 of the 36 deaths from measles were in the area between North Street, South Street and the River Exe, which includes the Western Quarter; figures for the 1903 epidemic are similar. Other infectious diseases—scarlet fever, diphtheria and typhoid fever—also show a high concentration in this area, although, of course, it is not possible to give a full interpretation of the maps without knowing the population at risk. While the number of deaths from infectious diseases declined during the early years of the twentieth century, increasing attention was given to pulmonary tuberculosis, and tables and maps show that once again the population of the Western Quarter was badly afflicted. In 1925 the Medical Officer of Health for Exeter describes three areas where there was a high incidence of tuberculosis, the largest being the Western Quarter, and says: 'one is aware that there are often other factors operating amongst the population in these areas favourable to the occurrence of Tuberculosis, but nevertheless, one cannot ignore the bad housing conditions and overcrowding in these areas as being a most important factor in the causation of Pulmonary Tuberculosis.'[3]

Thus this area had experienced poverty for many generations and, but for the slum clearance schemes, would probably still be poor. Clearance of the Western Quarter slum area started in 1928; 129 houses were demolished and 242 houses had been erected by the Council in Burnthouse Lane, Wonford Ward, by the end of 1929.[6] By the mid 1930s the work was completed and a large proportion of the population from the Western Quarter was rehoused in new council houses on an open greenfield site at the edge of the city. The inhabitants had open spaces, modern sanitation and opportunities for new and better lives.

This new development was on the south-facing valley of Wonford Water, a small tributary of the River Exe (Fig. 14.1). As Exeter is in South-West England it has a mild, equable climate but there are local variations, and Wonford does appear to have a slight disadvantage in one respect. All houses in the ward are below 31 metres (100 feet) and records from the nearby climatological station (Exeter Southam) show that the Wonford valley receives more mists and fog than surrounding land. For example, during 1962 there were 40 days with fog at 0900 hours at Exeter Southam compared with only 7 occurrences at the Airport, which is beyond the valley mists. However, while the physical situation of this ward is not so favourable as that of some higher parts of the city, the environment is better than in the lowlying parts of the main Exe Valley. Houses in Wonford Ward have never been flooded, as have some homes in Emmanuel or St Thomas. Of the 17 wards of Exeter no less than six have a higher proportion of their population living in the valley at heights below 16 metres (50 feet) than has Wonford Ward. Moreover, as available records show, air pollution is everywhere low in Exeter but here, on the outskirts of the built-up area, it must be very low indeed.

On this site on the southern edge of the town the council had erected its new estate by the early nineteen-thirties. Semi-detached houses are neatly and spaciously laid out in broad crescents on either side of the central road, Burnthouse Lane. In the nineteen-thirties this must have seemed a city planner's ideal. The housing provision in Wonford Ward is, in terms of physical amenities, better than in any other ward in the city. In 1961 no less than 97 per cent of households in the ward had exclusive use of all household arrangements, hot and cold water, fixed bath and water closet. This compares with an average for the city (which is good compared with other county boroughs) of 77 per cent, although in 4 other wards the proportion is under 50 per cent. While the provision of physical amenities is exceptionally good, living conditions today have deteriorated, owing to overcrowding. Thirteen per cent of the population in the ward were living at an average density of over one and a half persons per room in 1961 (Exeter 4 per cent) and it is recorded that this is higher than for any other ward in the South West.[7] Despite the move from slums to a new environment, the old conditions of overcrowding developed once more.

A large proportion of the people who moved here were labourers and in the lower working classes. The 1966 Census (10 per cent sample) showed that the ward still had about 40 per cent (39$\pm$ 6 per cent) of its population in social classes IV and V, that is people in semi-skilled and unskilled occupations. This compares with a figure for Exeter of 24 per cent ($\pm$3 per cent). Not only does the area have a low social status but also the level of living is poor. The area is well known to social workers. One survey showed that this ward had 40 per cent of the city's juvenile delinquents in 1964.[7] The slum area of the city centre was cleared, but its way of life is perpetuated in the new estate.

There is also continuity in the pattern of death. The population of Wonford Ward has remained very stable, and about half the people who had council house tenancies in the nineteen-thirties were still living in the ward in 1958 (45 per cent of the original tenants, or 52 per cent if the widows of the original tenants are included). This proportion is undoubtedly an underestimate because of the difficulty of tracing changes of address in the records and it also excludes those who have at any time moved out of the ward, even for a short while. Nevertheless, the proportion living in the ward for at least 20, and up to 30, years after moving there is remarkably high. No less than 30 per cent of those dying in the ward between 1958 and 1964 had held a tenancy in the ward since the nineteen-thirties (or in a few cases were the widows of former tenants). As there would be on average about two adult occupants in each property it seems probable that about 60 per cent of those dying in the period of study had been resident in the ward since the houses were erected. Not all these came from the Western Quarter, but it seems that a majority of those dying in the ward had at one time been resident in the slum areas of the city centre. Mortality was high in those slum areas and mortality is still significantly above average in the rehoused population of Wonford Ward.

The level of mortality in Wonford is compared with that of Exeter by an index called a Standard Mortality Ratio (S.M.R.), which is a form of indirect standardisation taking into consideration the age/sex structure of the population. The S.M.R. is the ratio between the observed number of deaths and those expected if the age/sex-specific death rate were the same as those in a standard population, in this case the population of England and Wales. The 1960–62 average age/sex-specific death rates (Under 1, 1–24, 25–44, 45–54, 55–64, 65–74, and 75 years and over) for England and Wales are applied to the population of the wards of Exeter for 1961 and multiplied by 7 to give the expected number of deaths for the 7 years period, 1958–64. The study is concerned only with the population in private households, that is those living and dying in their own homes or resident in hospital for under 6 months (those living in aged peoples' homes, chronic sick hospitals and other institutions are excluded). The S.M.R.s are adjusted so that the S.M.R. for Exeter is equal to 100 for each cause of death, which permits ready comparison of all wards within the city.

The S.M.R. for Wonford (Table 14.1) is thus being compared with the S.M.R.s for other wards in the relatively homogeneous environment of Exeter and is not directly comparable with the national figures, although in most cases the S.M.R. for Exeter is close to the national average. The Chi-square (χ^2) test is used to discover whether the S.M.R. for Wonford Ward is significantly different from all other wards.

TABLE 14.1

Mortality in Wonford Ward, Exeter: 1958–64

Cause of Death	Males			Females		
	Observed Deaths	Expected Deaths	S.M.R. (Exeter= 100)	Observed Deaths	Expected Deaths	S.M.R. (Exeter= 100)
All Causes of Death	215	182	119*†	167	143	117*
Selected Respiratory Disease	28	18.5	151*†	18	10.3	175*
Pneumonia	11	6.5	169†	8	5.5	145
Bronchitis	17	10.5	162*†	8	4.1	195*
Cardiovascular Disease	104	85.7	121*†	94	73.4	128*†
Vascular Lesions of Central Nervous System	29	19.7	147*	37	24.5	151*
Coronary Disease	47	41.6	112	30	20.6	146*†
Cancer of All Sites	46	38.5	119†	25	31.4	80
Cancer of Lung—Males	18	13.3	135			

* S.M.R. for Wonford Ward significant at 5 per cent level.

† Difference between wards in Exeter significant at 5 per cent level.

The difference between the wards of Exeter for mortality from all causes in males is significant (0.1 per cent) with 2 wards having significantly low mortality. The S.M.R. for Wonford is 119 (that is, mortality is nearly 20 per cent higher than the average for Exeter), which is significant at the 5 per cent level. For females in Wonford the S.M.R. of 117 is again significantly high, even though the difference between the wards is not significant. Wonford Ward is the only ward in the city where both male and female mortality is significantly high. For all causes of death considered together, the total numbers are sufficient for an examination of deaths in three main age groups (45–64, 65–74 and 75 years and over). Although the number of deaths in males exceeds the expected in the three groups, the difference is most pronounced in the 45–64 age group. Here there is a significant difference between wards (at the 0.1 per cent level) and in Wonford 89 deaths were observed, which is 21 more than expected. In the 65–74 age group there were 54 deaths in males compared with the 45 expected, while there were only 4 more deaths than expected (45) at 75 years and over. This means that it is in the lower age groups that mortality in males in Wonford is especially high. Men are dying during their working life, which obviously creates a serious social and economic loss. For females the situation is not quite so serious. Although in the 65–74 category the number of deaths is significantly high, with 50 deaths observed compared with the 35 expected, the difference between observed and expected deaths is only 5 in the other two age groups. Thus the excess mortality in females is a decade later in life than for males.

What factors are responsible for this excess mortality in Wonford Ward?

'Most if not all illness is an expression of a basic unbalance in man's physiological adaptation to multiple physical and emotional stresses that are initiated for the most part in the conditions of his external environment.'[8] The occurrence of illness or death in an individual may be due to physical, biological or social circumstances, or, more probably, to an interaction of all three. This study can only be concerned with factors where some areal variation can be identified, and is thus concerned with aggregate conditions rather than separate individuals. Wonford Ward is looked at as a whole. The general physical and social character of Wonford may be examined, but it is not possible to investigate biological factors such as disease-causing viruses and vectors, the physiological characteristics of the population, or the response of individuals to their total environment. The recent Morbidity Survey undertaken as part of the Exeter Community Health Project will permit a more detailed investigation.[9]

It seems that the main reason for the high level of mortality in Wonford Ward is the extreme social class structure of the population. Social class is determined by the occupation of the deceased (or husband of the deceased) and each person is placed in one of the five social classes. 'The occupations in each category have been selected so as to secure that, as far as is possible in practice, the category is homogeneous in relation to the basic criterion of the general standing within the community of the occupation concerned. The criterion is naturally correlated with (and application of the criterion conditioned by) other factors such as education and economic environment, but has no direct relationship to the average level of remuneration commanded by particular occupations in the labour market.'[10] Thus while people in the social classes IV and V are only semi-skilled or unskilled, they are not necessarily poor. There is considerable evidence to show that social class is more than a mere classification of occupations. 'The whole mode of life, it has become evident, is implicated in "social class": type of family structure, methods of child rearing, language and way of speaking, aspirations, values and attitudes, expectations of health and concern with illness. It is not surprising that, very crude as it is, and blurring now in several respects, this distinction by "social class" is still providing a powerful tool in the diseases they suffer.'[11]

The association between social class and mortality is shown in national figures.[10] In Exeter there is a strong correlation between mortality from all causes and social class; this is seen when the wards are ranked according to the social class distribution of their population. Mortality is highest in those wards with a high proportion of their population in the lower social classes. No less than 55 per cent of deaths in Wonford Ward between 1958 and 1964 were of people who were ascribed to social class IV or V by the statement of occupation on their death certificate. This compares with 25 per cent for the rest of Exeter. The

1966 Census figures showed a smaller proportion of the population in these two classes in Wonford Ward (39 per cent ± 6 per cent). This probably indicates that the social class structure of the younger generation is not so adverse as it was for those who are dying at over 45 years, although the difference may in part be due to the higher death rate in the lower social classes.

There also seems to be some relation between mortality and the physical environment, as summarised by altitude, especially for deaths in males in the wards of Exeter. The contrasts in physical environment in Exeter are relatively small, and altitude is a very crude index of the difference. The association between male mortality and altitude is not so strong as that between mortality and social class, but the relatively lowlying situation of Wonford Ward may be an additional factor.

The relationship between mortality and the social and physical environment can be seen more closely by a study of the major causes of death. Mortality in Wonford is significantly high for the cardiovascular diseases and selected respiratory diseases (mainly bronchitis and pneumonia) in both males and females, while the S.M.R. for cancer in males is also above average. Cancer in females is the only major category where the S.M.R. for Wonford Ward is below that for Exeter.

The S.M.R.s in Wonford Ward are highest for deaths from the selected respiratory diseases, and it is this group which shows the greatest difference for males between the wards (significant at 0.1 per cent level). Mortality from pneumonia is associated with social class, as shown by national figures[10] and by the significant correlation between social class and mortality in the wards of Exeter. Nine of the 11 deaths from pneumonia in males in Wonford were of men in social classes IV and V. For bronchitis there appears to be an association with both the physical environment and social class for Exeter as a whole. A study of the place of residence of the deceased when death is ascribed on the death certificate to bronchitis as either a primary or secondary cause of death indicates an association with altitude. The χ^2 test does not quite attain significance at the 5 per cent level but there were more deaths than expected in the population living below 31 metres (100 feet) (155 deaths observed compared with 136 expected) and fewer in those living in higher parts of the city. The relatively low level of Wonford Ward may therefore be one factor in the higher mortality from bronchitis, but the association with social class is stronger and well-recognised. In Wonford, 6 of the 17 deaths from bronchitis were in men who had been unskilled workers and 6 had been transport workers. Female deaths from the selected respiratory diseases in Wonford are also significantly high, although there is no significant difference between the wards. The total number of deaths in this group among females in Wonford is only 18, but it seems that high mortality is associated with social class, for both pneumonia and bronchitis have a higher prevalence in the lower social classes, in Exeter as in England and Wales.

While the respiratory diseases discussed in the previous paragraph show the greatest excess of deaths over the expected number, the total number of deaths involved is relatively small. The cardiovascular diseases, on the other hand, account for nearly half the deaths in males and over half the deaths in females. For both males and females there is a significant difference between the wards, and in both cases Wonford has S.M.R.s which are significantly high. This is seen especially for vascular lesions of the central nervous system in males and for vascular lesions and coronary disease in females. This appears to be a reversal of the expected pattern, for mortality from these two causes has traditionally been higher in the upper social classes.[10] It seems from an investigation of the social class distribution of mortality from these causes in Exeter that the pattern is changing. This will probably be revealed for England and Wales when the Occupational Mortality Tables of the Decennial Supplement for 1961 are published. Provisional figures from the Registrar General indicate that in the 15–64 age group mortality from coronary disease and vascular lesions of the central nervous system is now considerably higher in the lower than in the upper social classes. This reversal in trend is seen for both males and married females. Once again it appears that the high level of mortality in Wonford is directly associated with the low social class of the population.

The S.M.R. for cancer for all sites is not significantly different from the average for the city for either males or females in Wonford Ward. The aetiology of cancer of different sites is so varied that cancer of specific sites should be studied, but cancer of the lung in males is the only category where the total number of deaths in Wonford is sufficient for even cursory examination. The S.M.R. for cancer of the lung is not significantly high, with only 5 more deaths than the 13 expected. The above average level is, however, in agreement with the known social class pattern of this cause of death; this shows higher mortality in the lower social classes.

Thus for each major category where the number of deaths is sufficient for the S.M.R. to have meaning, the level of mortality in Wonford Ward is in close agreement with the known social class pattern of that disease. It is unfortunate that the social class structure of each age/sex group is not known and that mortality cannot be standardised for social class as well as age. If this could be done, it seems probable that much of the excess mortality in Wonford Ward would be accounted for.

No doubt there are other isolated pockets in Exeter where conditions are similar to those in Wonford Ward. People from the later clearance of the Western Quarter (1934–35) were housed in St Loye's Ward in an estate adjacent to that in Wonford Ward. But St Loye's Ward also contains a large postwar council estate, a caravan park and a considerable number of upper class houses, so that the mortality conditions of the interwar council estate cannot be identified from the ward statistics. In Exwick Ward 60 per cent of the population lives in council houses. Many were built in the interwar period as they were in Wonford and they house people moved from other slum areas of the city centre. Here both male and female mortality is above average for the city although not significantly so (S.M.R. 111 for males and 110 for females). But no other ward is so homogeneous as Wonford and elsewhere those areas of above average mortality are masked in the average by more favourable parts of the ward. It is unfortunate that it is not possible to standardise for age structure for units smaller than wards.

Lest it be thought that all areas of high mortality appear in areas of council house property mention must be made of St David's Ward. Here mortality in males is much higher than in

Wonford (S.M.R. in St David's 141 for 1958–64, significant at 0.1 per cent level), although the S.M.R. for females is not above average (S.M.R. 109). This ward shows a great imbalance in the social class distribution of those dying. The proportion of deaths in social classes IV and V for males (43 per cent) is more than twice the female proportion (17 per cent). The high proportion of males of low occupational status is probably the reason for the high level of mortality.

The level of mortality in such wards as Wonford or St David's would not appear high in comparison with many other areas, but it is high for Exeter. It shows that even in a town where the level of mortality is favourable in comparison with that of other towns of similar size, there are still some areas where mortality is higher than it need be. Some elements of the population still have a much lower expectation of life than the rest. This study has also shown that it is not just the improvement of physical environment and amenities which is important. The inhabitants of Wonford Ward were moved from slums to new houses supplied with every necessity; but they inherited much from their past. Perhaps their health was impaired in their youth; perhaps they have maintained their former habits and way of life just as they have recreated overcrowded conditions in their new environment. All evidence seems to endorse other findings concerning rehoused populations and it seems as if 'the evil of slums could not be repaired in a period short of the life of one generation, if not several.'[12]

ACKNOWLEDGMENTS

The Author wishes to acknowledge the help and co-operation of Dr E. D. Irvine, Medical Officer of Health for Exeter, Mr M. H. D. Freeman, Manager of Exeter City Housing Department and their staff.

REFERENCES

1 Howe, G. M. *The National Atlas of Disease Mortality in the United Kingdom* (The Royal Geographical Society, Nelson, London 1963)
2 Shapter, T. *The History of the Cholera in Exeter in 1832* (Churchill, London 1849)
3 Medical Officer of Health for Exeter, *Annual Reports* for 1896–1903, 1914, 1925
4 Pickard, R. *The Population and Epidemics of Exeter in Pre-Census Times* (Published privately, Exeter 1947)
5 Hoskins, W. G. *Industry, Trade and People in Exeter, 1688–1800* (University College of the South West, now University of Exeter 1935)
6 Medical Officer of Health for Exeter, *Annual Report* for 1935
7 Bagley, C. 'Juvenile Delinquency in Exeter: An Ecological and Comparative Study' *Urban Studies* 2 (1965), 33–50
8 Rogers, E. S. *Human Ecology and Health* (Macmillan 1960)
9 Ashford, J. R. and Pearson, N. J. 'The Exeter Community Health Project' in *Computers in the Service of Medicine* I ed. G. McLachlan and R. A. Shegag (Nuffield Provincial Hospital Trust, OUP 1968)
10 Registrar General *Decennial Supplement for England and Wales for 1951, Occupational Mortality Tables* (HMSO 1958)
11 Morris, J. N. *Uses of Epidemiology* (Livingstone, Edinburgh 1964)
12 Martin, A. E. 'Environment, Housing and Health' *Urban Studies* 4 (1967), 1–21

15

The Residential Structure of Exeter

B. S. MORGAN

The purpose of this essay is to consider the success, both in relative and absolute terms, of the Burgess and Hoyt models of urban structure in explaining the residential structure of Exeter.

Both these classical models attempt to make generalisations about the arrangement of land uses in the city. E. W. Burgess in 1924,[1] on the basis of his experience in Chicago, introduced the notion that the main phases in the development of the city took place outwards from the central area, within a series of concentric zones. 'Encircling the downtown area there is normally an area of transition which is invaded by business and light manufacture. A third area is inhabited by the workers in industries who have escaped from the area of deterioration but who desire to live within easy access of their work. Beyond this zone is the "residential area" of high-class apartment building or of exclusive "restricted" districts of single family dwellings. Still further, out beyond the city limits, is the commuters' zone—suburban areas, or satellite cities, within a thirty-to sixty-minute ride of the central business district.'[2] The ecological concept of succession is central to the theory. Each zone expands into the one immediately outside it so that the city is undergoing continual change.

Hoyt, writing in 1939,[3] rejected this idea of the concentric zone. Using rent as a diagnostic variable in the study of the residential structure of American cities, he concluded that 'rent areas in American cities tend to conform to a pattern of sectors rather than concentric circles',[4] proceeding to show that the mechanism of sector formation depended upon initial differences at the point of origin. 'In all of the cities studied, the high-grade residential land had its point of origin near the retail and office centre, this is where the high income group work, and is the point furthest away from the side of the city that has industry and warehousing'.[5] Once initiated, the changes developed along mechanistic lines. 'High-grade neighbourhoods must almost necessarily move towards the periphery of the city. The wealthy seldom reverse their steps and move backwards into the obsolete houses they are giving up. On each side of them is usually an intermediate rental area, so they cannot move sideways. As they represent the highest income group there are no houses above them abandoned by another group. They must build new houses on vacant land. Usually, this vacant land lies available just ahead of the line of march of the area.'[6]

Recent studies of Belfast,[7] Oxford,[8] Sunderland,[9] and Edinburgh[10] have for the first time investigated the validity of these American models in the British situation. The general conclusion to be drawn from them is that neither the concentric or sectoral model can provide a total explanation of the patterns of residential segregation in the British city. In addition, evidence has been presented to suggest that the shortcomings of the classical ecological theories, dependent as they are on the free play of market forces, are increasing at the present time owing to their inability to assimilate local authority housing developments. Robson has gone so far as to conclude that 'the game of hunt-the-Chicago-model seems to be exhausted so far as the analysis of modern developments in British urban areas is concerned'.[11]

This essay on Exeter aims to broaden the base of British studies through the application of the classical models to an urban milieu different from those hitherto studied—that is, the small cathedral city. Alternate sectoral and concentric models of the city are advanced on the basis of house type and date of construction. Gross rateable value data, recognised to be a good diagnostic variable of social class, is employed in analysis of variance tests to assess the success of these models in explaining the distribution of social groups in the city. Attention is especially focussed on the breakdown of the simple residential structure during the last fifty years, which has been caused by the local authority intervening on an unprecedented scale in the housing market. The essay concludes with an assessment of the value of the models to the present-day urban geographer.

A SECTORAL MODEL

An examination of a map showing distribution of house types[12] in Exeter suggests that the residential parts of the city have a predominantly sectoral structure. The areas adjacent to the non-residential core are dominated by a wide variety of types of house—small terraces with and without front enclosures; large terraces; semi-detached and detached houses. To the east of the river Exe, a wedge of small terrace houses extends a mile or more in a north-easterly direction from the central area, separating two areas in which detached and semi-detached housing dominates. On the western, flood-plain side of the river, St Thomas consists of a large area of small terrace houses, after which semi-detached and detached dwellings attain pre-eminence on the valley side slopes. These morphological contrasts form the basis of the sectoral division of the city (Fig. 15.1) which is outlined opposite.

Northern sector

The river Exe forms the western boundary and the Southern Region railway line to London the eastern boundary of this sector. It is divided into two, spatially separate, parts by a belt of non-residential land-use extending outwards from the city centre; this includes the campus of the University of Exeter. It is represented in two parts in Figure 15.1. The morphological characteristics indicate that this is a high quality sector. Large terrace houses

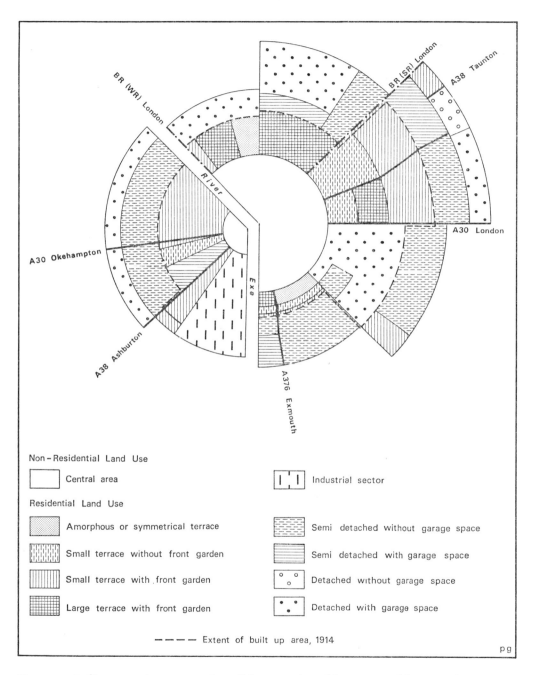

Non - Residential Land Use

☐ Central area

▥ Industrial sector

Residential Land Use

▦ Amorphous or symmetrical terrace

▦ Semi detached without garage space

▦ Small terrace without front garden

▦ Semi detached with garage space

▥ Small terrace with front garden

○ Detached without garage space

▦ Large terrace with front garden

• Detached with garage space

– – – – Extent of built up area, 1914

p g

Fig. 15.1 A diagrammatic representation of the sectoral model in terms of dominant house types.

with front gardens dominate the townscape adjacent to the central area, and are succeeded outwards by regions in which detached houses are the major element.

Two peripheral parts of the sector do not conform to this general pattern: these are to the west, where a belt of small terrace houses with front enclosures predominates, and to the east, where small semi-detached houses without space for a garage are the most common morphological element. This latter area, part of the Stoke Hill local authority estate, is included in this sector rather than in the north-eastern sector for two reasons: firstly, the estate, which dates from the 1950s, is similar in age to the adjacent areas, but contrasts with the late nineteenth century housing which is characteristic of the north-eastern sector at a similar distance from the central area; and, secondly, it is built on a continuation of the same south-facing slope as the rest of the northern sector, while it is separated from the north-eastern sector by a valley and cutting which is utilised by the Exeter—Honiton—London railway line. The other peripheral area, the belt of small terrace housing around Looe Road, is confined to the narrow floor of the Exe valley. It is separated from the higher ground (extending northwards from the valley of the Longbrook, a tributary of the Exe), on which the rest of the sector is built, by a very steep, and in some places almost vertical, river-cliff of the Exe. The Western Region railway line from Bristol and London enters Exeter along this eastern bank of the river, and St David's station, along with its extensive marshalling yards, is sited at the point where the flood-plain attains its maximum width. It is probably inevitable that the adjacent residential development, confined as it is to the little remaining flat land, consists of lower quality housing.

North-eastern sector

In the north this sector has common boundaries with the first. It is largely delimited to the south by the line of the old Roman road into Exeter from the east; this is the present main A30 Exeter to London trunk road, which in this section of Exeter includes Heavitree Road, Fore Street (Heavitree) and Honiton Road. The small area of Georgian building to the north of Heavitree Road around Bicton Place which is included in the eastern sector, and the new developments around Quarry Lane, to the south of Honiton Road, which are included in this north-eastern sector, are the only areas in which the sectoral boundary is not coincident with the A30 road.

This sector contrasts markedly with the northern sector in terms of morphology. There are 49 acres of detached houses without space for a garage, compared with 151 acres in the northern sector; 212 acres are taken up with small terrace houses, whereas this type of house is scarcely represented in the northern sector.

Terrace housing dominates the townscape of areas up to a mile from the central area. Small terrace houses opening directly on to the street in the inner zone—in Newtown and around Lion's Holt—are succeeded outwards in Heavitree by small terrace houses with front enclosures. To the south of the A38 Exeter—Taunton road, the larger terrace houses and villas on the Polsloe ridge intervene between these two zones of small terrace houses. This terrace area gives way to a zone in which semi-detached dwellings predominate.

Houses of this type are common in two areas—to the north of the A38 around Whipton village, where most of the houses have garage space, and in the vicinity of Sweetbrier Lane and Chard Road in Heavitree, where the majority of houses share a drive leading to a garage in the back garden. These two areas are separated by an extensive belt of land not used for residential purposes, which includes the grounds of a children's sanatorium, an area of allotments, and public playing fields. The outer zone of the north-eastern sector is made up of two contrasting parts—a southern section dominated by privately-owned detached houses dating from the inter- and post-war periods, and a northern section made up of terrace houses of the inter-war Widgery Road local authority estate, together with the post-war Whipton Barton estate.

Eastern sector

This sector, which is largely defined to the north by the line of the A30 road, has a complex south-western boundary. This is the only sectoral boundary that does not coincide with a well-marked natural or man-made feature. Its form, typically following first an individual plot line, then part of a street, then a plot line again, makes description virtually impossible. It must suffice to state that the boundary is an irregular one, running in an approximate line north-west to south-east, to the north of the A377 road to Topsham.

The inner part of the eastern sector is characterised by detached and semi-detached houses built for the most part at low densities. Many of these houses, particularly in the St Leonard's area, date from the late eighteenth and early nineteenth century and provide some fine examples of Georgian domestic architecture. However, late-Victorian villas and post-war small family houses are also common. A wide belt of non-residential land, including Topsham Army Barracks, the grounds of Wonford Hospital, the grounds of Exeter School, and a great deal of private open space, separates this inner zone with its many large houses from the meaner, semi-detached dwellings on the St. Loye's local authority estate. This estate represents all that is bad in inter-war public housing: monotony is the keynote, with all the houses built in a regular pattern at twelve per acre, all in the same style and using the same building materials. One of the least desirable residential areas in Exeter is thus situated in the same sector as one of the most desirable. The eastern edge of the St Loye's development still marks the boundary of the built-up area in this part of the city, as though it has had the effect of fossilising the sector.

South-eastern sector

This narrow sector, with the river Exe forming its south-western boundary, forms an axial development along the Topsham Road. Terrace housing is characteristic up to a mile from the central area. Two zones can be recognised: the inner dates from the late eighteen-early nineteenth century, and consists mainly of large terrace houses, including Colleton Crescent, one of the finest classical terraces in Exeter, while the outer includes the smaller, more standardised terrace houses of the Larkbeare estate, the construction of which began in the eighteen-nineties. The grounds of a small specialist hospital and a private open space separate this terrace area from a belt, a large part of which lies between Topsham Road and the river, in which privately owned semi-detached houses predominate. Most conform to the almost standardised style associated with the inter-war 'semi-d'. However, the one piece of good urban design dating from the inter-war period in Exeter is encountered to the south-west of Salmon Pool Lane. Here, Louis de Soissons, the architect of part of the original Welwyn Garden City, designed a scheme of streets and houses adjacent to the river. Only a few roads were completed at the outbreak of war in 1939 and the development was left unfinished.

The boundary with the eastern sector, although not following a well-marked natural or man-made feature, is clear-cut in these sections. The inner terrace area stands in strong contrast to the detached housing in St Leonard's, while the Devon County Hall in its extensive grounds and playing fields is interposed between the zone of semi-detached housing in the south-eastern sector and St Leonard's. However, beyond the Topsham Barracks, the Burnthouse Lane local authority estate—which is continuous with and morphologically identical to the St Loye's estate—extends to the Topsham Road, and poses a major problem of sector definition. If it were included in the eastern sector along with the St Loye's estate, the south-eastern sector would be confined to the ribbon development along Topsham Road in this section; on the other hand, if it were included in the south eastern sector, a morphologically homogenous area would be divided between two sectors. Again the siting of a local authority estate is causing the sectoral structure to break down. The Topsham Road acts as a focus for the south-eastern sector along the rest of its length, separating slightly contrasting townscapes on either side: and for this reason, for the purposes of testing the Hoyt model, the Burnthouse Lane estate is included in this riverside sector.

South-western sector

This sector is separated from the other residential parts of the city by the river Exe. Within the sector there is an almost classical development of concentric rings. The inner zone, which is largely coincident with the flood plain of the river, consists of street after street of small, bye-law terrace houses, built between 1870 and 1914: some of these have small front enclosures, some open directly on to the street. Inter-war semi-detached dwellings dominate the lower valley side slopes. Those to the south of the main A30 trunk road are in private ownership, but those to the north form part of the Buddle Lane local authority estate. After a period during which building was at a standstill, the development of small private estates, in which detached houses are the most common element, has begun during the last five years on the upper valley-side slopes. Some of the dwellings on these estates command exceptionally fine views over the Exe valley to the city beyond. To the east of the A38 (Ashburton) trunk road, a narrow wedge of terrace housing separates this south-western residential sector from an industrial sector with a large gas works, a collection of individual small-scale works, and, on the periphery, the post-war Marsh Barton industrial estate.

A CONCENTRIC MODEL

The distribution of house types presents little evidence to support a predominantly zonal distribution of social groups. Nonetheless, for the purposes of assessing the proportion of the total variation explained by a concentric structure, four zones are recognised which correspond very approximately to growth rings. The inner zone corresponds with the extent of the built-up area in 1880. It includes the area around Holloway Street; St Leonard's; Newtown; the area lying between Exeter prison and the river; and the older part of St Thomas. The second zone corresponds approximately to the area of 1880–1914 development, and includes the Larkbeare estate, the Polsloe estate, the lower Pennsylvania area, the lower Knightley estate in St David's, and the Parkhouse estate in St Thomas. The third zone approximates to the inter-war extensions to the built-up area. It incorporates the Buddle Lane, St Loye's, Burnthouse Lane and Widgery Road local authority estates, together with the private developments at Whipton, around Sweetbrier Lane in Heavitree and Broadway in St Thomas. The outer zone is virtually identical with the areas of post-1945 development.

TESTING OF THE PROPOSED MODELS

At the present time the ward is the smallest areal unit for which Census of England and Wales data is available for Exeter: this makes difficult the direct study, except in a most general way, of the distribution of social groups in the city, and these groupings have, therefore to be studied indirectly by utilising a diagnostic variable of social class. Rent has long been used in American studies for this purpose, notably by Hoyt[13] and Hatt,[14] and this provides a recognised variable for the student of urban social structure. Gross rateable value, which attempts to assess a fair rent for a property on the basis of its physical characteristics and location within the town, is considered the nearest published British equivalent to the rent indices adopted in America. The validity of this use of gross rateable value as a diagnostic variable is assessed in the work of Robson and Gordon: for Sunderland in 1961, Robson calculated the simple correlation coefficient between median gross rateable value and social class in each enumeration district to be $r=0.867$ for the private sector;[15] Gordon calculated $r=0.73$ for a similar correlation on the basis of the 1914 Valuation lists for Edinburgh.[16] Recent work on parts of Exeter[17] has shown the gamma coefficient[18] for the relationship between social class and rateable value to be —0.526. Although there must be some distortion in considering gross rateable value to be indicative of social class,[19] its use has some advantage over the employment of social class data taken directly from the Census. Rateable value data can be obtained for individual dwellings, and, as it is measured on an interval scale, it can be used directly in the whole range of parametric statistical techniques. Census data on social class is only available at best in blocks of 300 households. However, even if it were available on a household basis, it would have to be converted to an interval scale by aggregating the households in an area and expressing the number in each social class as a percentage of the area total before it could be used in parametric tests. Duncan, Duncan and Cuzzort[20] have convincingly demonstrated that work based on such

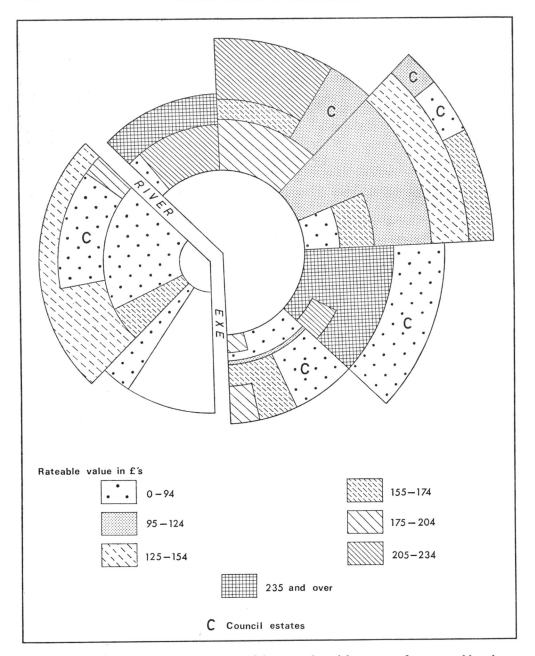

Fig. 15.2   A diagrammatic representation of the sectoral model in terms of gross rateable value.

areal data is likely to give misleading results. The distribution of gross rateable value in Exeter is represented diagrammatically in Figure 15.2. The northern sector is shown to be a high value sector, with the exception of the marginal areas; the north-eastern and south-western sectors as areas of lower value. The contrast between the high and low value parts of the eastern sector is well brought out, while the generally higher quality of the belt adjacent to the river Exe in the south-eastern sector is suggested. Again, there is little evidence of a concentric structure.

The applicability of the proposed models is tested in this article by carrying out separate one-way analysis of variance tests on a systematic sample of rateable value units. This involves assessing the significance of the difference between the sample means of gross rateable value—in the first instance between the sample means in the five sectors; in the second between the sample means in the four concentric zones. The technique also allows an estimate to be made of the variation that is explained and the variation that is left unexplained by the adoption of either model. For instance, if there were no variation in gross rateable value within the sectors, then the sectoral model would explain all the variation; the unexplained variation is the variation of gross rateable values within the sector.

The extraction of a sample from the Rate Valuation Books presents a problem which can best be illustrated with reference to the eastern sector. If the sample size in the sector were to be made proportional to the number of dwellings in it, then the local authority dwellings, built at a density of twelve houses per acre, would exert a greater influence on the sample mean of gross rateable value than the higher quality, low density, detached and semi-detached housing which makes up the greater part of the sector. As a result, a systematic sample is extracted, in which sample size in each of the segments formed by the intersection of the zonal and sectoral boundaries is related to its area.

TABLE 15.1

Analysis of variance test on the sectoral and concentric models of Exeter's structure

a. Sectoral model	Sum of squares	Degrees of freedom	Variance estimate
Between sample	607,734	4	151,933.5
Within sample	1,175,689	395	2,976.4

Variance explained by model   =   34.1 per cent
Snedecor's F   =   51.0 (significant at $P < 0.001$)

b. Concentric model	Sum of squares	Degrees of freedom	Variance estimate
Between sample	22,564	3	7,521.3
Within sample	1,760,859	396	4,446.6

Variance explained by model   =   1.3 per cent
Snedecor's F   =   1.7 (not significant at $P < 0.05$)

The results of the analysis of variance tests are listed in Table 15.1. As expected, the sectoral model is shown to be far more efficient in explaining variations in gross rateable value: the Snedecor F value is significant at $P < 0.001$ with 34.1 per cent of the sample variance explained by the model, whereas the Snedecor F value for the concentric model is not significant at $P = 0.05$ and only 1.3 per cent of the sample variance is explained. A two-way analysis of variance to investigate the percentage variation in rateable value explained by a combination of the two models is not possible. This test requires each of the concentric zones to be represented in all the sectors, whereas not all the stages of growth are characterised by residential development in the northern, eastern and the south-eastern sectors, owing to the boundary of the built-up area remaining at a standstill for considerable periods.

Nevertheless, the sectoral structure has broken down since the intervention on a large scale of the local authority into the housing market in the 1920s. This is illustrated by the results of separate analysis of variance tests to assess the efficacy of the sectoral model at three stages of the city's growth (Table 15.2): 63.7 per cent of the variation in the present-day rateable values is explained by the sectoral model in that part of the city corresponding to the built-up area in 1880, while in the area within the 1914 boundaries,[21] 55.3 per cent is explained. These high explained variances contrast with an explained variance of 34.3 per cent for those parts of the city within the 1939 boundaries; this is a figure similar to the one for the present-day city. The Snedecor F value in each case is significant at $P < 0.001$. Thus in the fifty years between 1880 and 1939, the efficacy of the sectoral model in explaining the residential structure of Exeter declined by almost 50 per cent.

SECTORAL GROWTH AND DECAY

This process of sectoral growth and decay merits closer attention by a study of, and an attempt to explain, the distribution of social groups through time. Old Census returns are of no more value in this respect than are recent returns for studying present-day distributions. However, until the last twenty-five years, Besley Directories of Exeter have included details of occupation on a personal basis. Although the information is not complete—the information in the later directories is less comprehensive than that in the earlier ones— and is sometimes of dubious accuracy, it does allow maps to be drawn which give a general picture of social class distribution on a house by house basis. The directories are used in the compilation of three maps showing the distribution of the residences of unskilled workers (social class 5 in the Registrar General's classification of social class) at three critical times— 1894–95, when the sectoral structure was best developed; 1923 when the influence of local authority housing schemes was beginning to be felt; and 1938, by which time the sectoral structure had largely broken down. The distribution of unskilled workers, which is indicative of the poorer parts of the city, is mapped rather than that of the professional class, for two reasons: firstly, it is impossible to distinguish in the directories between the office or consulting room and the residence of a professional person, and secondly, there is next

TABLE 15.2

Analysis of variance test on the sectoral model at three stages of Exeter's growth

a. Buildings dating from pre-1880	Sum of squares	Degrees of freedom	Variance estimate
Between sample	628,345	4	157,086
Within sample	355,830	115	3,094

Variance explained by model = 63.7 per cent
Snedecor's F = 50.7 (significant at P< 0.001)

b. Buildings dating from pre-1914	Sum of squares	Degrees of freedom	Variance estimate
Between sample	634,390	4	158,577
Within sample	513,540	211	2,434

Variance explained by model = 55.3 per cent
Snedecor's F = 65.2 (significant at P< 0.001)

c. Buildings dating from pre-1939	Sum of squares	Degree of freedom	Variance estimate
Between sample	524,189	4	131,047
Within sample	1,003,832	245	4,097

Variance explained by model = 34.3 per cent
Snedecor's F = 32.0 (significant at P< 0.001)

to no information regarding the occupations of the residents of the more select roads, possibly because they belong to the large class in receipt of unearned income. The map for 1894-95 (Fig. 15.3) shows unskilled workers to be largely resident in four areas. These are Newtown in the north-eastern sector; the Larkbeare area in the south-eastern sector; St Thomas on the flood-plain of the river, and lastly, what is now a largely non-residential part of the central area to the south-west of the North Street–South Street axis. This latter area was the only real slum in Exeter. On the other hand, there are no unskilled workers living to the east of the central area in St Leonards, while the few to the north of the city in the St David's and Pennsylvania area are living in small enclaves of lower quality terrace housing.

What is the reason for the growth of high quality sectors in the north and east of the city? Hoyt suggested that higher grade residential areas had their point of origin near the retail and office centre. He saw their subsequent growth as largely mechanistic, but went on to suggest that, among other influences, the following might be important:

(a) 'The zone of high rent areas tends to progress toward high ground which is free from the risk of floods and to spread along lake, bay, river, and ocean fronts where such water fronts are not used for industry.'

(b) 'The lure of open fields, golf courses, country clubs and country estates acts as a magnet to pull high grade residential areas to sections that have free, open country beyond their borders.'

(c) 'The higher priced residential neighbourhood tends to grow towards the homes of the leaders of the community.'[22]

These three factors (which concern the nature of the land immediately beyond the built-up area) rather than the differences at the point of origin, seem to best explain the situation of the high quality residential areas in Exeter; to be of primary importance, rather than of secondary importance, as implied by Hoyt. Topography exerts an undeniable influence. The St Leonard's area is made up of a belt of high ground adjacent to the central area; the northern sector, although separated from the central area by the Longbrook valley, is built mostly on a southward facing slope overlooking the town and the Exe estuary beyond. On the other hand, Newtown, the inner part of the north-eastern sector, is built on lower-lying land, while St Thomas is on the flood plain of the river Exe. High social values attaching to the land beyond the built-up area—the importance of which are implicit in Hoyt's work (factors (b) and (c) above) and which Jones[23] suggested as the best explanation of the situation of the better quality residential areas of Belfast—seem to act as an attracting force for high value sectors in Exeter.

Donn's map of Devonshire (1765), part of which is reproduced in Plate 22, reveals four country houses—Larkbeare, Mount Radford, Gower and Bellair—to the east and south-east of the central area, with the large Duryard estate to the north. (The Streatham estate, the present University campus, which is also north of the central area, post-dated the Donn map). These houses were for the most part the dwellings of the families of Exeter merchants, who were men of considerable local importance, for the city's commercial prosperity was at its height in the eighteenth century. Bellair, a Queen Anne house, was built in 1710 for John Vowler, a rich local grocer, while in 1765 the Baring family owned Larkbeare and Mount Radford. As a young man John Baring had come to Exeter from Bremen in north Germany, and was apprenticed to a serge-maker; he married Vowler's only daughter and heiress, and when he died in 1748 he was the most eminent merchant in the city. In 1737 he bought Larkbeare, which the family retained until 1832. His sons started a wool-importing business in London, but the elder, John, returned to Exeter to establish a private bank— the Devonshire Bank—and bought Mount Radford, converting the original Elizabethan house into a Georgian mansion. Almost the whole parish of St Leonard's became Baring property; this was sold off for a considerable sum of money after his death in 1816 to various builders who developed St Leonard's as we know it today, St Leonard's Road being originally the carriage-drive of the Barings, leading in from Magdalen Road along a graceful curve down to their mansion. Duryard was a hunting-park of the Anglo-Saxon Kings, and was eventually given to the city in the tenth century. It remained the city's property until it was sold off between 1700 and 1703. Two good houses were built on the estate—Great Duryard, built by Sir Thomas Jefford about 1686–90, and Duryard House, built about 1700.

At the time of Exeter's great growth in the early nineteenth century, residential sectors were those in which social values had partly replaced those of site. The map showing the distribution of unskilled workers in 1923 (Fig. 15.3) reveals essentially the same pattern as that of 1894–95. But whatever the reason for the growth of the sectoral structure, it was severely modified, during the inter-war period, by the development of local authority housing estates. Building activity since then concentrated in the north-eastern and south-western sectors, and this is reflected by the spread of unskilled workers to new houses on the periphery of these sectors. Few are resident in the northern and eastern parts of the city. The map for 1938 (Fig. 15.3) shows a very considerable change. The greatest concentrations of unskilled workers are now in the local authority housing estates—the Burnthouse Lane and St Loye's estates in the eastern and south-eastern sectors, and the Buddle Lane estate in St Thomas. There is corresponding reduction in the concentration in the area between North Street–South Street and the Exe, where the area's slum clearance programme is almost complete, but large numbers of unskilled workers still remain in Newtown and lower St Thomas.

The siting of the Burnthouse Lane–St Loye's local authority estates provides an interesting study of the new forces influencing residential development. In the earlier days of public housing there was considerable opposition from the residents of Exeter to local authority projects. As a result, the development of a large housing estate necessitated the Exeter City Council finding an extensive area of flattish land to which main facilities could be piped, but which was situated well away from the more desirable residential parts of the city. The site of these estates is separated from the high quality St Leonard's area by an extensive zone of non-residential land. On 15 December 1927, the attitude of the City Council was summarised in an extract from the City Architect's evidence to the Ministry of Health Enquiry on the Burnthouse Lane development:

'It is extremely difficult to obtain suitable land for housing purposes (in the city) owing to the following reasons:

(i)   Hilly nature of district,

(ii) No suitable land available near the centre of the city.

This site is particularly useful for our needs. It is comparatively level, can be economically developed, it adjoins a main road, yet is so placed that it will not affect the amenities of that road.

A glance at the map will show, that considering the Housing Requirements of the City, it would be impossible to select a tract of land that will less affect existing interests than this site.'

This policy of non-interference with existing interests was an undoubted success. In the early years of its development, Exonians nicknamed the new estate 'Siberia', so far was it from the rest of the city. On completion of the Burnthouse Lane development, the con-

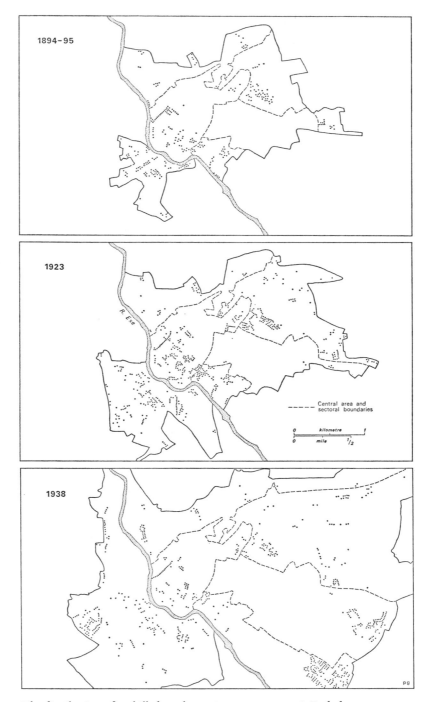

Fig. 15.3   The distribution of unskilled workers, 1894–95, 1923, 1938. Each dot represents one worker.
Source, Besley's Directory of Exeter.

struction of the St Loye's estate was begun on an adjacent site so that the anachronous situation has arisen whereby these large estates are situated in the line of advance of the eastern sector; this is the result of a conscious effort being made to keep them apart from the desirable St Leonard's area. Since the war, large local authority housing projects have been completed at Stoke Hill, Whipton Barton, Beacon Heath and Countess Wear; each new addition further modifies the sectoral structure developed under the 'free' land market conditions of the nineteenth and early twentieth centuries.

What has been the effect of this twentieth century growth on the older residential parts of the city? Hoyt suggests that the growth of high quality sectors in American cities leads to 'deterioration in the quality of areas in the rear of the line of march.'[24] The map showing the distribution of unskilled workers in 1938 reveals little evidence of such deterioration in the northern or eastern sectors. However, a large amount of good quality development has taken place to the north of the city since the war, and certainly at the present time the inner parts of the northern sector, mostly mid- and late-Victorian houses built for the middle classes, show considerable evidence of deterioration. Those streets adjacent to the central area have been partly taken over for low-grade commercial uses, cheap hotels and lodging houses; subdivision of the dwellings into partly self-contained furnished flats, without any attendant structural alterations, is common. Recent work by the author[25] has shown the existence of two social groups in the region who are in a situation of conflict. One group—of owner-occupiers of the unsubdivided houses remaining in the region— is an ageing group, with little residential mobility; its members were mostly employed, or are still, in the professional and intermediate occupations; the other consists of recently established households—young married couples or single persons sharing with a friend, renting partly self-contained furnished flats, and mostly finding employment in skilled, semi-skilled and unskilled occupations. This group also includes some students. A large proportion of this latter group are transients in the region. In other words, this area is developing into a classic rooming-house area, very much in accordance with Hoyt's ideas.

On the other hand, the St Leonard's area, immediately adjacent to the central area in the east, has maintained its high standards for more than 150 years. Some sub-division of the large houses has taken place, but in most cases self-contained unfurnished flats of high quality have been constructed, the residents of which are mainly young professional people. While the 'outward march' of this sector has been halted by the construction of the Burnthouse Lane–St Loye's local authority estates (with the result that it is in some ways an exceptional case) it is unlikely that this area, possessing the best examples of domestic Georgian architecture in Exeter, will be in any circumstances allowed to decline. The high social value attaching to areas of Georgian housing in any British city makes such areas very resistant to change and this is an important source of contrast between the British city and the American city of which Hoyt was writing. In North America highly valued neighbourhoods resistant to change are seldom encountered in the inner city area, which is generally of more recent growth than its English counterpart. Hoyt does not recognise the importance of social values in influencing the rate of neighbourhood change, but merely comments that 'Neighbourhoods in which houses are well constructed of enduring materials and with a stable architecture will maintain themselves for greater periods of time than areas of flimsily constructed houses.'[26] On the other hand Firey[27] has shown that the Beacon Hill area of Boston, probably the most historic of American cities, has resisted change as a result of action dictated by the sentiment of its inhabitants. In the British city and the older American city, at least, it seems that social values attaching to some older areas are likely to modify the process of the deterioration of neighbourhoods which would normally follow sectoral advance.

CONCLUSIONS

In the last ten years doubts have been expressed by British geographers concerning the value of the classical ecological models to the present-day student of urban social structure. These doubts have arisen partly because of the increase of local authority estates, together with the eroding of social differentials and the slowing-down of urban growth, and partly because earlier writers emphasised the isolation of the models themselves rather than the isolation of the important processes leading to residential segregation.

However, it is probably rather premature to dismiss the models as being completely without value. So far as Exeter is concerned, the sectoral model described in this essay has proved invaluable as a sampling framework for a social study of the city. The north-eastern and south-western sectors are very similar in their morphological structure, and samples taken in almost identical terraced and semi-detached housing areas in these sectors reveal contrasting social class characteristics. For instance, over half of the heads of house-holds interviewed in semi-detached houses in Heavitree in the north-eastern sector found employment in the professional or intermediate occupations, compared with less than 10 per cent in St Thomas.[28] The most likely explanation of these differences is that the sectoral division reflects differences in the social values attaching to areas. St Thomas, a large part of which is constructed on the floor-plain of the river, is locally considered to be an undesirable area in which to live, even though most of the twentieth century development has taken place on the valley-side slopes.

On more general lines, there is also much of value in the models. Elements of a concentric or sectoral structure have been recognised in many American and European cities, but few students of urban structure can be entirely happy with the very generalised explanations that have so far been advanced, whether they be 'deterministic mechanistic', as Jones labelled those of the early ecologists,[29] or whether they stress the importance of social values, as Jones himself did in Belfast.[30] In short, although the validity of the models has been adequately demonstrated, no completely satisfactory explanation has been forthcoming. And yet such explanation is far easier than an attempt to understand forces leading to a form which is itself not understood. Far more work is needed in this respect. However, because the classical models have to some extent broken down in the second and third quarters of this century, the implicit assumption seems to be made in some recent work that the processes that led to their growth under 'free' land market conditions are no longer operative and hence no longer relevant for study. This, at best, must be a dubious conclusion. Just as the form of the twentieth century city is more complex than that of the nineteenth century city, so the underlying forces that lead to this form must be more complex. Forces that may previously have largely explained the distribution of social groups in the city may now make up a much smaller part of the total explanation. Nonetheless, their study remains important. The application of the classical models of urban structure to individual cities can provide valuable insight into the functioning of these 'free' market forces.

REFERENCES

1 E. W. Burgess. 'The growth of the city: an introduction to a research project' *Proceedings and Papers of the American Sociological Society,* XVIII, (1924) 85–97

2 Ibid, 88

3 H. Hoyt, *The structure and growth of residential neighbourhoods in American cities* (Washington, D.C. 1939)

4 Ibid, 76

5 Ibid, 114

6 Ibid, 116

7 E. Jones. *A social geography of Belfast* (London, 1960), Chapter 16

8 P. Collison and J. M. Mogey 'Residence and social class in Oxford' *American Journal of Sociology,* LXIV (1959) 599–605

9 B. T. Robson. *Urban analysis: a study of city structure with special reference to Sunderland* (Cambridge 1969) Chapter 3

10 G. Gordon. 'The evolution of status areas in Edinburgh' *Report of the Liverpool Conference of the I.B.G. study group in urban geography, 1966* (duplicated)

11 B. T. Robson, op, cit. 132

12 B. S. Morgan. *A geography of the residential areas of Exeter.* Unpublished PhD thesis, University of Exeter (1970). Fig. 4.2

13 H. Hoyt. op. cit.

14 P. Hatt. 'The concept of the natural area' *American Sociological Review,* XI (1946), 423–427

15 B. T. Robson, op. cit. 105

16 G. Gordon. op. cit. 28

17 The gamma coefficient is a non-parametric measure of association developed by Goodman and Kruskal that can be used with two ordinal scales. It is interpreted in exactly the same way as the Pearson product moment correlation coefficient varying from $+1.0$ in the case of a perfect positive correlation to -1.0 in the case of a perfect negative correlation.

18 B. S. Morgan, op. cit. 57

19 This distortion is discussed in some detail in B. T. Robson, op. cit. 104

20 O. D. Duncan, R. P. Cuzzort and B. Duncan. *Statistical geography: problems in analysing areal data* (Glencoe, Illinois, 1961)

21 These explained variances are calculated on the basis of the present valuation of residences in that area of the city built before 1880, between 1880 and 1914, and so on. This may cause the estimate to be biased, although no large scale inner city redevelopment has taken place. If anything, the variation explained by the sectoral model is probably under-estimated.

22 H. Hoyt, op. cit. 117

23 E. Jones. op. cit. 278–80

24 H. Hoyt. op. cit. 82
25 B. S. Morgan. op. cit. 151
26 H. Hoyt. op. cit. 58
27 W. Firey. *Land use in central Boston* (Cambridge, Mass. 1947)
28 B. S. Morgan. op. cit. 141
29 E. Jones. op. cit. 270
30 Ibid, 278

16

Customer Trips to Retail Business in Exeter

PETER TOYNE

Location necessarily implies movement, since individual locations are separated by geographical distance. The analysis of location should, therefore, include the analysis of movement, but despite certain notable exceptions[1] it remains true that 'movement is an aspect of regional organisation that has been too lightly stressed in human geography'.[2] This is particularly the case in the analysis of retailing; the 'structural' relationships between the number of functions and establishments and the size, distribution, wealth and socio-economic characteristics of population have been closely investigated[3] but the patterns of customer movement generated by the location of retail outlets have, in comparison, received much less attention.[4]

Several kinds of customer movement may be identified according to their purpose. Clearly, the total possible number of purpose-combinations will vary from one shopping centre to another, depending on the number of different types of shop which each centre contains; and the formula

$$nCr = \frac{n!}{r!\,(n-r)!}$$

(where C stands for the number of combinations that can be made, when n = the number of shop types in a shopping centre and r = the number of shop types in each combination) can be used to estimate the total possible number of such combinations. Thus, for example, where eighteen different types of retail outlet are recognisable, as in Exeter, 262,142 different shopping-trip combinations are feasible. Many of these combinations, however, are merely minor varieties of a fewer major types, since the different shop types upon which the combinations are based can be grouped into broader categories: thus, the eighteen retail types in Exeter may be grouped into three main categories of food, fashion and household goods. It follows, therefore, that seven main groups of trip-combination may be identified, three of which may be described as single-purpose trips (shopping either for food, fashion or household goods); three as dual-purpose (shopping for food and fashion, fashion and household goods, or food and household goods); and one as all-purpose (involving shopping for food, fashion and household goods all in the same trip).

In order to assess the salient characteristics of each of these different kinds of customer movement in Exeter, a pilot survey was first made to gauge the total number of customers using each type of shop. The results were then used as a basis for establishing the proportional numbers of shoppers to be interviewed. The total number of shoppers in the city's central business district and the numbers visiting each of the different store types was found to vary with the time of week and day, making it necessary to take a stratified sample of all shoppers. Thus, the actual number of shoppers interviewed varied not only with the type of shop being used but also with the time of the survey which was conducted on the first Monday, Thursday and Saturday of each month of 1968 and 1969 between 0900 and 1800 hours. On each of the survey days, between 4,500 and 6,200 shoppers were interviewed, comprising approximately 8 per cent of the total population on each occasion. The results show that the relative importance of each of the different kinds of customer movement varies considerably, not only in general, but also according to the time of year. Application of Student's t test to the distribution shown in Table 16.1 reveals, for instance, that the overall trip structure in July and August is different from the structure in the period from October to January, and that the structure during the rest of the year is also rather different. Certain characteristic features of shoppers' behaviour are also found to be associated with each of the different trips.

Of the seven main types, all-purpose shopping accounts for the largest single proportion at all times of the year but becomes relatively most important in December when 36.8 per cent of all trips into the city are of this kind (Table 16.1 and Fig. 16.1). The proportion remains high during January (35.2 per cent) and then falls to its lowest level in February (24.2 per cent). Thereafter, it remains fairly static with the exception of a slight rise in July and August (31.0 per cent and 34.3 per cent respectively). The high December figures are

TABLE 16.1

Percentage of all customer movements formed by seven main trip types (by months)

Type of Trip	Jan	Feb	Mar	Apr	May	June	July	Aug	Sept	Oct	Nov	Dec
ALL PURPOSE	35.2	24.2	27.8	28.2	28.4	29.1	31.0	34.3	28.0	27.7	28.5	36.8
DUAL PURPOSE												
Food-fashion	13.8	13.7	13.4	12.9	13.1	14.6	15.9	17.9	18.3	17.9	13.0	11.4
Food-household	4.4	15.8	8.6	8.1	15.0	14.8	9.6	6.4	7.8	4.6	9.3	4.0
Fashion-household	6.0	6.3	10.5	11.0	7.9	6.3	6.9	7.1	9.5	8.3	7.2	6.4
SINGLE PURPOSE												
Fashion	20.2	19.8	16.4	15.7	14.0	13.2	16.0	12.2	15.2	21.1	19.0	16.8
Food	13.4	14.9	15.3	14.9	15.4	16.8	16.3	17.7	16.4	13.4	14.3	15.2
Household	7.0	5.3	8.0	9.2	6.2	5.8	4.3	4.9	4.8	6.8	8.9	9.4

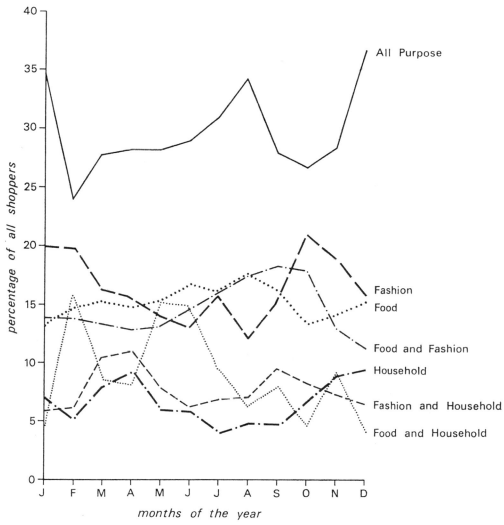

Fig. 16.1   Percentage of all customer movements formed by seven main trip types
(data from Table 16.1).

largely the result of seasonal Christmas shopping trips: at that time, 32 per cent of all shoppers interviewed had come to Exeter for Christmas shopping, of whom 81 per cent were making all-purpose trips.

In January, the winter sales appear to be the main shopping attraction: 35 per cent of all shoppers interviewed at that time had come to town for the sales, and, of them, 54 per cent were combining the trip with their normal weekly shopping trip, thereby classifying as 'all-purpose' shoppers. In contrast, the summer (July) sales appear to have little effect on all-

R

purpose trips for, as will be seen later, most shoppers at these sales make dual purpose trips for food and fashion goods. In fact, only 6 per cent of all summer sales shoppers make all-purpose trips (Table 16.2). The increase in all-purpose shopping in July and August is largely due to an influx of holiday-makers visiting Exeter for the day: in these two months, in both 1968 and 1969, holiday-makers accounted for 18 per cent of all shoppers in town, and of that 18 per cent the majority (78 per cent) were making what could be described as 'all-purpose' trips.

TABLE 16.2

Percentage of sales shoppers by seven main trip types

Type of Trip	Winter Sales (January)	Summer Sales (July)
ALL PURPOSE	52	6
DUAL PURPOSE		
Food-fashion	13	62
Food-household	5	3
Fashion-household	11	7
SINGLE PURPOSE		
Fashion	11	21
Household	8	1

In the course of such all-purpose trips, the customer visits an average of twelve shops: 80 per cent of all customers visit between eight and fifteen different shops, and only 0.5 per cent of the customers are able to get all they need by visiting less than four different stores (Table 16.3).

The next largest group of customer-movement is that which is for fashion goods and food, either on single or dual-purpose trips, and again the relative position varies throughout the year. As may be expected, there are marked increases in single-purpose fashion trips in

TABLE 16.3

Percentage of shoppers visiting given number of shops on all-purpose trips

No. of shops visited	Percentage of shoppers
1— 3	0.5
4— 7	16.1
8—11	39.2
12—15	41.0
16+	3.2

October when the new season's clothes are available; in the new year when the main annual sales are held; and again in July when the summer sales are on. Thus, in October and November such fashion trips account respectively for 21.1 per cent and 19.0 per cent of all customer movements; in January and February for 20.2 per cent and 19.8 per cent; and in July for 16.0 per cent, whereas during the rest of the year they form an average of 14.8 per cent of all trips (Table 16.1 and Fig. 16.1). In contrast, shopping for food only is relatively unaltered by seasonal changes, though there is a slight increase in the proportion of such trips in the middle of summer and again during November and December, after a sharp fall in October. In the period June to September, the proportion of holiday-makers shopping in Exeter solely for food provisions was of the order of 12 to 16 per cent, and this largely explains the summer increase in single-purpose food trips. The December increase, made particularly noticeable by the rapid decrease in such trips during October, is clearly a reflection of the approach of Christmas.

Dual-purpose food and fashion trips share certain characteristics of both the single-purpose food and the single-purpose fashion trips, and they become relatively much more important in the period from July to October when they form between 17 and 18 per cent of all trips (Table 16.1 and Fig. 16.1). Again, the influx of summer visitors, the attraction of the summer sales and the arrival of the new season fashions in October all contribute to this increase: 8 per cent of the shopping visitors and 62 per cent of all sales shoppers were making such dual-purpose trips. It is nevertheless surprising that the dual-purpose food-fashion trip is not relatively more significant at the time of the January sales. In fact, only 13 per cent of all sales shoppers in January were making dual-purpose food and fashion trips (Table 16.2). One reason for this difference between the proportions of shoppers on various trips at the two sales is, of course, that the summer sales tend to be much more fashion-good orientated than the winter sales, which include a far wider selection of reduced goods, particularly in the 'household' sphere. Shopping for household goods is consequently much more significant in January sales trips than it is in summer sales trips (Table 16.2).

Single-purpose food trips may involve shopping for five different types of goods—bread and cakes, fish, meat, general groceries and greengroceries, either singly or, more commonly, in combination. Shopping for greengroceries alone is the most common form of trip for any one of the five goods, while trips for bread, meat or groceries are of roughly the same importance (Table 16.4). The majority of such 'one-good' food trips (87.3 per cent) are made during weekday lunch hours by people working in the centre of town. It is only in trips for general groceries that supermarkets attract the largest proportion of shoppers; most shopping for single items of meat or greengroceries is done in smaller stores, though a moderate proportion of single purchases of bread and fish is made in supermarkets (Table 16.4).

The vast majority (79.3 per cent) of single-purpose food shopping involves more than just one of the five types of goods, and almost a third of such shopping involves three main commodities, usually bread, groceries and greengroceries (Table 16.5). Just under a quarter of all the trips are for two of the goods (usually bread and general groceries), while only

R*

TABLE 16.4

Percentage of single purpose food shoppers for one item only

Shopping for	Percentage of single purpose food shoppers	Percentage of which use supermarket
Bread	4.8	32.3
Fish	0.9	27.4
Meat	4.8	6.2
Greengroceries	6.4	5.4
Groceries	3.8	69.3

3.9 per cent are for all five commodities. The role of supermarkets varies slightly: fewer people shopping for two of the commodities use them than do people shopping for three or more commodities, and in turn this is reflected in the number of shops which are visited on the various shopping trips. Thus, for example, although most shoppers on any of the single-purpose food trips visit only two or three different shops, the proportion is smallest in the case of 'two good' trips where supermarkets appear to attract relatively less custom (Table 16.5).

Single-purpose fashion trips include shopping for clothing, shoes and jewellery, as well as visits to hairdressers or barbers, but the main kind of trip in this group is the one for clothing goods alone (accounting for 37.4 per cent of all single-purpose fashion trips). Very few customers shopping only for clothes find what they want in one shop (7 per cent), and almost half of the customers find it necessary to visit six or seven clothing shops on such trips. Shoppers looking for any two of the four fashion goods and services form the next most frequent type of customer movement (27.2 per cent of all fashion trips) and the most common combination is shopping for clothing and shoes. Trips involving any three or all four of the fashion goods and services are, however, the least numerous of all fashion trips,

TABLE 16.5

Percentage of single-purpose food shoppers by number and types of shops visited

Number of shop types visited	Number of shops visited					Percentage of which use supermarkets
	1	2	3	4	5+	
Any 2	6	31	38	17	8	56
Any 3	7	32	57	3	1	88
Any 4	1	30	56	2	1	93
All 5	3	28	52	10	7	84

and shopping just for shoes or jewellery, and trips to hairdressers and barbers, are all more important. The number of shops visited on each of the different trips varies considerably: as might be expected, most trips to hairdressers and barbers involve only one shop, and 83 per cent of the people coming out of hairdressers' shops maintained that they regularly visited the same hairdressers. Most people looking for shoes find it necessary to try four or five different shoe shops, whereas only 6 per cent of the customers looking only for jewellery had to visit more than three jewellers' shops. In contrast, most customers shopping for more than one fashion good or service find it necessary to visit between six and eight different stores (Table 16.6).

TABLE 16.6

Percentage of single purpose fashion shoppers by number and type of shop visited

Shopping for	Percentage of shoppers in this category	number of shops visited				
		I	2—3	4—5	6—7	8+
Clothing	37.4	7	16	20	49	8
Shoes	12.2	5	20	52	9	4
Hairdresser	10.1	99				
Jewellery	8.3	74	22	4		
		number of shops visited				
		I—3	6—8	7—9	10—12	13+
Any 2	27.2	18	68	11	2.5	0.5
Any 3	4.6	5	79	14	1.5	0.5
All 4	0.2	2	80	16	1.0	I

The greatest number of shops visited occurs on trips for food and fashion goods combined: almost half of such shoppers visit between twelve and fifteen stores, and nearly three-quarters visit between eight and fifteen stores (Table 16.7).

In general, taking the year as a whole, it can be seen that shopping for fashion goods and food, either singly or in combination, constitutes the main kind of customer movement in Exeter, for such shopping also forms a large part of the all-purpose trips (Table 16.1 and Fig. 16.1). In fact, 83 per cent of the 'all-purpose' trip customers said that the main purpose of their trips was to buy either food or fashion goods.

In comparison with trips involving food and fashion stores, those trips which are made to stores selling household goods are relatively less numerous, and form a smaller percentage of the total trip structure. In fact, the proportion of all trips formed by single-purpose household shopping and dual-purpose fashion-household shopping is, at all times of the year, much smaller than any of the trips already discussed, though again seasonal variations are apparent. For most of the year, single-purpose household trips are the least numerous of

TABLE 16.7

Percentage of dual purpose food-fashion shoppers by shops visited

number of shops visited	Percentage of food-fashion shoppers
1—3	9.2
4—7	15.2
8—11	24.5
12—15	48.7
16 +-	2.4

any kind and account, on average, for only 6.7 per cent of all customer-movements. During the pre-Christmas period, however, their importance is increased, since they include movements to shops selling children's toys and other gifts. This Christmas build-up is only slightly greater than the increase in such trips which takes place in March and April, corresponding with a period when 31.4 per cent of all shoppers in this category are shopping for materials connected with spring cleaning. Taking the year as a whole, however, it is found that trips to ironmongers, chemists or furniture stores, either singly or in combination, are the main kind of single-purpose household trip, since the two main kinds of trip involving any *two* types of stores in the household category are furniture-ironmongery trips (7.2 per cent of all household trips) and ironmongery-chemist trips (6.1 per cent of all 'household' trips) (Table 16.8).

The number of shops visited on the single-purpose household trips varies quite considerably and it is not without significance that the vast majority of shoppers to chemists,

TABLE 16.8

Percentage of single purpose household shoppers by number and type of shop visited

Shopping for	Percentage of shoppers in this category	number of shops visited			
		1	2—3	4—5	6+
Furniture	19.3	3	21	42	34
Ironmongery	22.6	2	57	39	2
Radio/TV	0.2	62	34	4	
Books	2.0	12	64	20	4
Confectionery/tobacco/ newspapers	6.4	94	6		
Chemist	21.1	93	7		
Any 2	23.4	1	7	23	69
Any 3 or more	5.0	1	4	22	73

confectioners, tobacconists and newsagents find what they are looking for by visiting only one such shop (Table 16.8). As is the case with trips to hairdressers, most customers tend to use the same chemist, confectioner, tobacconist or newsagent regularly. In contrast, an average shopping trip for furniture involves going round four or five shops, while a trip for either ironmongery or books will tend to involve visits to only two or three stores.

Dual-purpose food-household and fashion-household trips naturally necessitate visits to more shops, and it is found that in both cases roughly half of all customers on such trips visit between eight and eleven different stores (Table 16.9). It is interesting to note, too, that dual-purpose fashion-household trips become relatively more important in March and April but decrease in significance during the pre-Christmas season, when they form only 4.0 per cent of all customer movements. The most variable trips are those involving the dual purposes of shopping for food and household goods: over the year as a whole they account for 9.0 per cent of all trips, but they are relatively much more important in February, May and June when they respectively account for 15.8 per cent, 15.0 per cent and 14.8 per cent of all trips (Table 16.1 and Fig. 16.1). It can thus be seen that each of the seven main types of shopping trip varies not only in its relative contribution to the total customer-movement structure throughout the year, but also in its general characteristics.

The linkages which are made from shop to shop within the central business district are also a reflection of the overall shopping-trip structure. A stratified sample of shoppers was followed on their journeys through the main shopping centre of Exeter, and their shop-to-shop linkages recorded. The results of this survey show that movements from and to shops of a similar nature are the most common type of linkage, and that the two outstanding customer-links are those from one fashion shop to another (29.98 per cent) and from one food shop to another (24.77 per cent) (Table 16.10). Of the links between different types of shop, those between household and fashion stores are the most important (11.7 per cent). The number of links made between fashion and food shops is the smallest of all the different combinations, accounting for only 3.2 per cent of the movements: this figure may seem rather lower than expected in view of the fact that dual-purpose fashion-food trips account for 14.7 per cent of all trips, as has already been shown. The reason for this is that 86 per

TABLE 16.9

Percentage of dual purpose food-household and fashion-household
shoppers by number of shops visited

No. of shops visited	Percentage of food-household shoppers	Percentage of fashion-household shoppers
1— 3	8.4	5.1
4— 7	23.7	25.3
8—11	49.8	48.7
12—15	16.7	20.0
16+	1.4	0.9

TABLE 16.10

Shop to shop linkages: Percentage of all shoppers

from \ to	Food	Fashion	Household	Other	End of Trip	Total
Food	24.77	1.36	1.92	2.08	4.07	34.20
Fashion	1.83	29.98	4.59	1.95	1.15	39.50
Household	2.52	7.15	4.29	3.03	2.11	19.10
Others	1.18	2.10	0.78	1.21	2.02	7.20

cent of such dual-purpose shoppers were *primarily* shopping for fashion goods and included only *one* food shop on their itinerary. Proportionately, therefore, fashion-food linkages are less numerous than fashion-fashion links.

In detail, the pattern naturally becomes more complicated. Table 16.11 shows the total number of linkages that are made for every 10,000 customers in the shopping centre. It is clear that the greatest number of linkages is made between one clothing shop and another (1,200 per 10,000); one shoe shop and another (950 per 10,000); one clothing shop and a shoe shop (690 per 10,000); and between supermarkets and greengrocers (477 per 10,000). In general, like-linkages (i.e. links between two shops of a similar type) are made mainly by customers leaving grocers, fishmongers, clothing shops, shoe shops, furniture stores and cafés. It is in these groups, therefore that there is the greatest tendency to 'shop around.'

Customers' movements are, of course, affected by many factors, but particularly interesting is the way in which the customers perceive the opportunities and alternatives available to them. One simple indication of the significance of this factor can be inferred from the results of a survey in which shoppers were asked to list the shops which they felt might offer the goods they were looking for. The difference between the perceived and actual opportunities varies considerably, particularly between foodshops—where the differences are great—and clothing and shoe shops where it is less marked. In general, it is clear that customers have a very limited perception of the real alternatives available to them. Thus, only half or even less of the actual number of greengrocers, bakers, jewellers, hairdressers, chemists and confectioners, tobacconists and newsagents are known to most shoppers. In contrast, 9 out of every 10 clothing shops are known, and practically all shoppers knew the location of every supermarket in town (Table 16.12).

One reason why there are such apparent differences between the perceived and actual opportunities is that customer-allegiance to certain stores is more marked in certain types of shop than others. Mention has already been made of the importance of such allegiance in visits to hairdressers, confectioners, tobacconists, newsagents and chemists, where the majority of customers tend to use the same shop regularly, but it is also noticeable in other cases. In order to estimate the extent of this allegiance, shoppers were asked which shop they would tend to visit in order to obtain various goods. For certain goods, most people gave the name of just one shop which they normally visited, whereas for others, several

TABLE 16.11

Shop to shop linkages: number per 10,000 shoppers

from \ to	Supermarket	Grocer	Greengrocer	Butcher	Fishmonger	Baker	Clothing	Shoes	Furniture	Ironmonger	R/TV	Bookseller	Jeweller	C/N/T	Hairdresser	Chemist	Café	P.O Bank	End of trip	Total
Supermarket	276	230	463	418	69	276	46	24	3	5	2	1	—	92	—	24	92	23	276	2370
Grocer	87	186	93	40	12	28	17	23	2	1	—	—	1	35	6	—	17	23	10	580
Greengrocer	14	32	24	6	2	109	—	1	—	—	—	—	—	—	—	2	9	2	18	120
Butcher	7	19	6	17	4	8	6	11	—	1	—	—	—	15	—	9	19	9	68	190
Fishmonger	4	6	2	7	10	2	—	—	—	—	2	1	—	—	—	—	—	1	17	50
Baker	34	34	6	12	6	38	1	—	—	—	—	80	80	4	—	2	8	4	18	160
Clothing	40	—	—	20	—	20	1200	220	40	40	—	18	—	80	20	60	20	20	60	2000
Shoes	18	18	2	36	1	18	470	905	—	36	—	6	26	36	18	54	108	36	36	1810
Furniture	5	2	1	11	—	10	9	10	36	4	4	37	—	3	6	5	10	7	4	130
Ironmonger	17	8	2	8	—	3	100	50	12	46	8	—	10	8	16	42	25	25	12	420
Radio/TV	32	10	—	14	1	18	32	20	6	4	16	28	20	2	—	6	22	4	8	200
Bookseller	5	5	2	7	—	5	47	13	4	4	4	3	4	5	5	2	9	4	10	180
Jeweller	—	—	—	—	—	—	29	10	—	2	1	32	20	6	—	3	3	5	4	70
Confectioner/newsagent/ tobacconist	16	1	—	1	—	1	62	41	20	10	5	—	—	5	41	5	109	52	99	520
Hairdresser	6	1	—	—	—	3	29	13	—	—	—	18	9	—	13	13	1	2	15	70
Chemist	18	18	2	18	1	18	156	29	9	2	9	—	—	13	13	—	18	18	78	460
Café	7	—	—	—	—	—	53	56	7	—	—	6	13	12	3	4	67	30	136	380
P.O Bank	35	32	2	13	3	23	46	18	20	8	3	13	—	3	12	10	20	4	66	340

TABLE 16.12

Difference between actual and perceived shopping opportunities

Shop type	Mean number perceived for every ten shops of given type
Grocer	6
Greengrocer	5
Butcher	6
Fishmonger	6
Baker	5
Clothing	9
Shoes	8
Furniture	8
Ironmonger	7
Bookseller	7
Jeweller	5
Confectioner/newsagent/ tobacconist	4
Hairdresser	4
Chemist	4
Supermarket	10

shops were mentioned and in some instances people clearly had no real preference or allegiance and tended to 'shop around'. It very quickly became apparent that, although there was considerable variation in the shoppers' lists, not only between different shop types but also between younger and older people, certain patterns were unmistakeable (Table 16.13). The differences in allegiance between the under-30s and the over-30s were found to be significant at the 99.9 per cent Probability level where just one shop was named (Student's t = 5.32 against 12 degrees of freedom), and at between the 75 per cent and 90 per cent level where more than four shops were named.

The highest degree of allegiance is clearly felt towards butchers, fishmongers, ironmongers, hairdressers, chemists, cafés, confectioners, tobacconists and newsagents, although it is clear that this allegiance is always more noticeable in shoppers over the age of 30. Thus, for example, whereas 93 per cent of all shoppers over the age of 30 tend normally to visit the same butcher's shop, only 85 per cent of the younger shoppers do so: likewise, while 84 per cent of the younger shoppers normally use the same ironmongers, 96 per cent of the older shoppers do so.

It is clear that there is, in general, more customer-allegiance towards grocers, greengrocers, and supermarkets than towards other kinds of food shops but here again this pattern is more characteristics of the older shoppers. Thus, whereas only 12 per cent of the under-30 shoppers tend regularly to use the same grocery store, 80 per cent of them 'shop around' with no particular allegiance to any specific store. In contrast only 30 per cent of the over-30s 'shop around' in this way, while 39 per cent of them claim to get most of their groceries regularly at the same store. Similar behavioural patterns are clearly definable in greengrocery and supermarket shopping (Table 16.13).

Customer-allegiance to clothing and shoe shops is particularly interesting, for although the vast majority of shoppers, in both age groups, named only two or three such stores, the under-30s tended to 'shop around' much more for shoes than they did for general articles of clothing. The greatest differences between the two age groups is found in their allegiance to furniture stores: the under-30s tend to 'shop around' much more discriminatingly than do the over-30s, of whom the majority tend to use one store only.

Shoppers who claimed allegiance to one store of a given type gave a number of reasons for their choice, of which the five most common were connected with convenience, price, range of goods, quality and service. Naturally, there are considerable variations in the importance of the factors according to the kind of store being considered, but, in general price considerations seem to be the least important. The range of goods offered by a store generally appears to be the most important factor in determining customer-allegiance (Table 16.14). Prices, for instance, appear to be considered by shoppers in determining allegiance to supermarkets, grocers, greengrocers, clothing and furniture stores more than to any other kind of shop. Thus, whereas 69 per cent of all shoppers who mainly used one

TABLE 16.13

Customer allegiance: Percentage of shoppers naming particular stores

Shop type	number of shops named					
	I		2 or 3		Shop around	
	age <30	age >30	age <30	age >30	age <30	age >30
Supermarket	32	54	48	39	20	7
Grocer	12	39	8	31	80	30
Greengrocer	30	42	22	46	48	12
Butcher	85	93	15	7		
Fishmonger	54	64	46	36		
Baker	47	63	40	34	13	3
Clothing	26	39	67	58	7	3
Shoes	9	24	61	68	30	8
Furniture	21	46	15	33	64	21
Ironmonger	84	96	16	4		
Confectioner/newsagent/ tobacconist	63	69	37	31		
Hairdresser	81	83	18	17		
Chemist	73	88	27	12		
Café	87	90	13	10		

TABLE 16.14

Reason given for allegiance to a particular store of a given type
Percentage of shoppers

Shop type	reason for allegiance				
	convenient place	prices	better selection	quality	service
Supermarket	28	56	57	13	4
Grocer	35	47	63	54	58
Greengrocer	23	42	58	72	31
Butcher	12	17	7	85	43
Fishmonger	43	7	59	43	30
Baker	20	4	57	68	22
Clothing	5	61	74	24	32
Shoes	4	18	72	7	16
Furniture	6	69	63	33	82
Ironmonger	34	6	56	42	58
Confectioner/tobacconist/ newsagent	89	4	56	12	75
Hairdresser	32	21	—	—	94
Chemist	31	3	52	—	73

furniture store maintained that they did so because the prices were in the right range, only 3 per cent of the shoppers mainly using the same chemist felt that prices had anything to do with their choice. Indeed, it is important to note that the price factor appears to be least important in precisely that type of shop which has the highest degree of customer-allegiance.

The range of goods offered by a particular store is generally a major factor in influencing a customer's preference, except in the case of butchers' shops. Thus, over 70 per cent of all shoppers normally using the same clothing and shoe shops consider the range of goods in that particular shop to be better than elsewhere.

Considerations of quality are particularly noticeable in the choice of regular butcher, greengrocer and baker (respectively 85 per cent, 72 per cent, 68 per cent of shoppers normally using one of these types consider the quality of the respective shop to be superior to any alternatives).

The quality of service offered by the particular store appears to be especially relevant in the choice of hairdressers, confectioners, newsagents and tobacconists, furniture store and chemists: the role of service considerations in the selection of shoe stores and supermarkets, however, seems to be minimal.

The 'convenience' of a particular store appears to be a main consideration in the selection of confectioners, tobacconists and newsagents. In this particular case, 'convenience' appears to be measured in terms of store location relative to several different factors. Of the 89 per cent who said that 'convenience' was important, 38 per cent defined convenience as relative to their place of work, 34 per cent as relative to the position of a car park or bus stop, and the remainder as relative to the other shops which they were visiting on their various trips.

Rather surprisingly, perhaps, no statistical significance can be found between the evaluation of the above five factors and the under-30 and over-30 age groups. It must be concluded

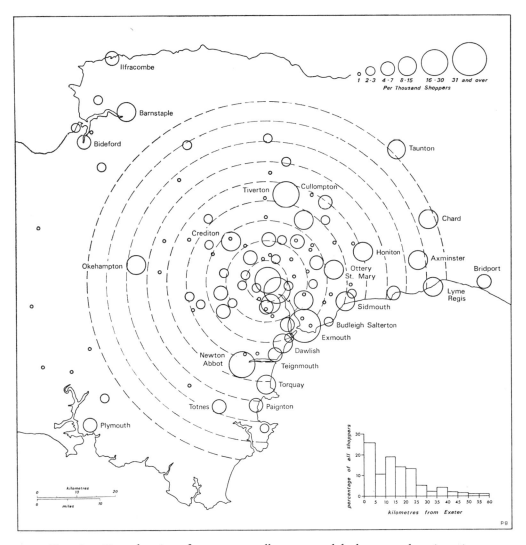

Fig. 16.2   Home location of customers on all-purpose and dual-purpose shopping trips.

therefore, that both groups of shoppers consider the five factors in the same general way. Since all of the five considerations of price, range of goods, quality, service and convenience are based on personal preferences—which in turn are based at least in part on the perception of alternative opportunities—and since, as has already been shown, such perception is less than perfect, many of the customers' allegiances are bound to be less than optimal.

As might be expected, the areas from which shoppers come vary slightly according to the type of shopping trip, though in all cases the effects of distance are apparent in causing the typical characteristics of rapid fall-off of movement near the centre together with progressively slower fall-off near the edges of the different interaction fields (Figs. 16.2 to 16.5). All-purpose and dual-purpose shopping trips involve customers from a larger geographical area than do single purpose trips. It is not, however, easy to define the absolute limits of the area involved, nor is it necessarily meaningful to do so. In the surveys conducted in Exeter, for instance, forty of the shoppers interviewed were from the USA., thirty-four were from France, and four came from New Zealand: the absolute limits of Exeter's all-purpose trade area should therefore include half of the world. A more useful definition of the trade area may be made by considering only those shoppers who regularly use the city for various shopping purposes. On this basis it can be seen that dual and all-purpose shopping trips involve customers from within a range of 60 kilometres (38 miles) from the city of Exeter, stretching from Ilfracombe to Bideford in the north-west; from the Plym valley in the west; from Bridport in the east; and from Taunton in the north-east (Fig. 16.2). Within this general area, however, there is a quite clear distance-decay function both in terms of absolute numbers of shoppers and of their frequency of visits to the central city. Thus, 50 per cent of the all-purpose shoppers come from settlements within 12 kilometres (8 miles) radius of the city, and just over half of these (26 per cent of all shoppers) live in the city itself, and whereas all-purpose trips to the centre of Exeter are mostly made about every two months by Exonians, most shoppers from distances greater than 20 kilometres (12 miles) come to Exeter only twice a year or less.

It is also clear that progressively fewer shoppers from rural villages and hamlets are attracted to Exeter as the distance away from the city increases: of the all-purpose shoppers living in the area between 5 and 20 kilometres (3 and 12 miles) away from the city centre, 53 per cent come from other urban settlements (Dawlish, Exmouth, Budleigh Salterton, Teignmouth, Newton Abbot, Cullompton, Sidmouth, Ottery St Mary, Crediton), whereas 93 per cent of those from distances of more than 20 kilometres (12 miles) live in other urban settlements (e.g. Torquay, Paignton, Okehampton). The effective rural component in all-purpose shopping is thus confined to a relatively small area.

The areas from which custom is attracted in terms of single-purpose trips vary according to whether the trips are made for fashion, food or household goods. The largest of the three trade areas is for single-purpose fashion goods (Fig. 16.3), for which shoppers are mainly drawn from settlements within 40 kilometres (24 miles) of Exeter, but again, there is clear evidence of a distance-decay function with 47 per cent of all such shoppers coming from within 10 kilometres (7 miles) of Exeter. Household-goods shoppers (Fig. 16.4) are drawn from a slightly smaller area (mainly within 30 kilometres (19 miles) of Exeter), and it is

Fig. 16.3   Home location of customers on single-purpose fashion trips.

particularly noticeable that shoppers on such trips are not attracted from north Devon (Barnstaple, Ilfracombe) or from beyond Totnes in the south-west. Well over a half of the household-goods shoppers (58 per cent) come from within 5 kilometres (3 miles) of the city centre, but it is the single-purpose food trip which involves not only the smallest interaction field but also the greatest decline rate, the majority of such shoppers coming from not further than 20 kilometres (12 miles) away, and 71 per cent of all such shoppers coming from within 5 kilometres (3 miles) of the city centre (Fig. 16.5). Statistically each of these four trading areas are significantly different from each other. By calculating the mean and standard deviation distances of each type of shoppers' home from the centre of Exeter and using Student's t test, it is found that in no case does the difference between the four distributions fall below the 95 per cent level of significance.

It can thus be seen that, although there are many different kinds of customer-movement, certain regularities and patterns within these movements may be recognised. There appear, for instance, to be marked seasonal variations in the volume of the different movements;

Fig. 16.4　Home location of customers on single-purpose household trips.

Fig. 16.5 Home location of customers on single-purpose food trips.

noticeable differences in the number of shops visited on the different kinds of trip; variations in the degree of customer-allegiance to different kinds of shop; certain basic patterns in shop-to-shop linkages and clear relationships between the types of shopping trip and the distance and frequency of movement.

It must, however, be remembered, as Harvey has pointed out, that 'we are not content to describe events in a random manner. We seek, rather, to impose some coherence upon our descriptions, to make them rational and realistic, to try to bring out what we understand of a situation by patterning our descriptive remarks in a particular way.'[5] Order is, in fact, more a construction of the imagination than a physical reality. Nevertheless, the search for such order must surely be one of the foundations of geographic analysis, for without it little progress can be made in the description and explanation of locational patterns.

REFERENCES

1 Berry, B. J. L. 'Essays on commodity flows and the spatial structure of the Indian economy' *University of Chicago, Department of Geography, Research Paper 111* (1966)
   Garrison, W. L. et al. *Studies of highway development and geographic change* (Seattle, 1959)
   Goddard, J. B. 'Functional regions within the city centre' *Trans. Inst. Brit. Geographers* 49 (1970), 161–82
   Hägerstrand, T. 'Migration and area' *Lund Studies in Geography, Series B 13* (1957), 17–158
   Ullman, E. L. *American commodity flow* (Seattle, 1957)
2 Haggett, P. *Locational analysis in Human Geography* (London 1965)
3 Berry, B. J. L. and Garrison, W. L. 'Functional bases of the central-place hierarchy' *Economic Geography* 34 (1958), 145–54
   Berry, B. J. L. and Garrison, W. L. 'A note on central-place theory and the range of a good' *Economic Geography* 35 (1958), 304–11
   Berry, B. J. L. et al. 'Commercial structure and commercial blight' *University of Chicago, Department of Geography, Research Paper 85* (1965)
   Boal, F. W. and Johnson, D. B. 'The functions of retail and service establishments' *Canadian Geographer* 9 (1965), 154–69
   Brush, J. E. and Bracey, H. E. 'Rural service centres in South-west Wisconsin and Southern England' *Geographical Review* 45 (1955), 559–69
   Carruthers, W. I. 'Major shopping centres in England and Wales' *Regional Studies* 1 (1967), 65–81
   Garner, B. J. 'The internal structure of shopping centres' *Northwestern University, Studies in Geography* 12 (1966)
   Smith, R. D. P. 'The changing urban hierarchy in Wales' *Regional Studies* 4 (1970), 85–96
   Stafford, H. A. 'The functional bases of small towns' *Economic Geography* 39 (1963), 165–75
4 Berry, B. J. L., Barnum, H. G. and Tennant, R. J. 'Retail location and consumer behaviour' *Regional Science Association, Papers and Proceedings* 9 (1962), 65–106
   Davies, R. L. 'The effects of consumer income difference on shopping movement behaviour' *Tijdschrift vor Economische en Sociale Geografie* 60 (1969), 111–21
   Huff, D. L. 'Ecological characteristics of consumer behaviour' *Regional Science Association, Papers and Proceedings* 7 (1961), 19–28
   Huff, D. L. 'A topographic model of consumer space preferences' *Regional Science Association, Papers and Proceedings* 6 (1960), 159–74
   Ray, D. M. 'Cultural differences in consumer travel behaviour in Eastern Ontario' *Canadian Geographer* 11 (1967), 143–56
5 Harvey, D. W. *Explanation in Geography* (London 1969)

NOTES

NOTES

Plate 1 Taxus trunks from the Stolford, Somerset, 'submerged forest' exposed on the foreshore. The C 14 dates for the peat deposits in this Flandrian site range from 3460 ± 90 years B.P. to 7360 ± 140 B.P. (B.P. = 1950). *C. Kidson*

Plate 2 'Interglacial' raised beach deposits resting on a shore platform cut across steeply dipping Pilton Beds at Saunton Down End near the mouth of the Taw–Torridge in North Devon. The shore platform reaches a height of +16 feet O.D where it passes beneath the deposits. While on altitudinal grounds alone it could have been developed by the present sea, it is clearly older than the deposits which themselves cannot be younger than Eemian (see text). *C. Kidson*

Plate 3 The Saunton 'pink granite' erratic resting on the shore platform and beneath the 'raised beach' sands. It is believed to be contemporaneous with the Fremington boulder clay.
C. Kidson

Plate 4 The modern shore platform and storm beach at Westward Ho, Devon, together with a raised shore platform at +27 to +28 feet O.D. bearing a raised beach of pebbles overlain by Head. Note the difference in height between the Saunton (Plate 2) and Westward Ho platforms. *C. Kidson*

Plate 5 Pebble beach overlain by Head at Westward Ho on the raised shore platform. Below is the modern shore platform on which can be seen remnants of the +5 metre platform now almost completely destroyed by contemporary erosion. These remnants are shown as 'stacks' in Figure 1.3. *C. Kidson*

Plate 6 Challacombe, looking south-west
Photo by J. K. St Joseph, Cambridge University Collection: Copyright Reserved

Plate 7 Title-page to accompany the 'county atlas' of eight sheets of the *Old Series* Ordnance Survey One-Inch Maps of Devon. By courtesy of the Trustees of the British Museum from Maps 148 e 27.

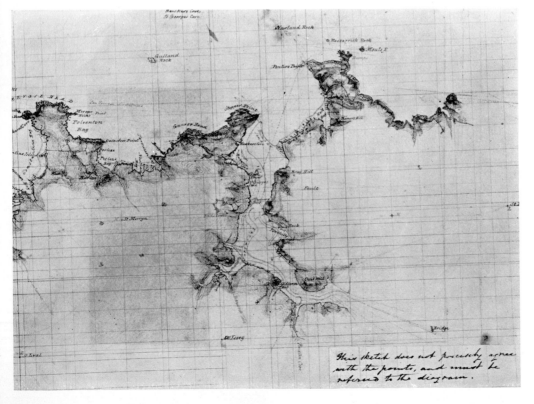

Plate 8, Revision work undertaken by Henry McLauchlan, *c* 1837, within the area of Ordnance Survey *Old Series* One-Inch map sheet 30. By courtesy of the Trustees of the British Museum, from Map Room, Ordnance Survey 2″ Hill Sketches, Serial 454.

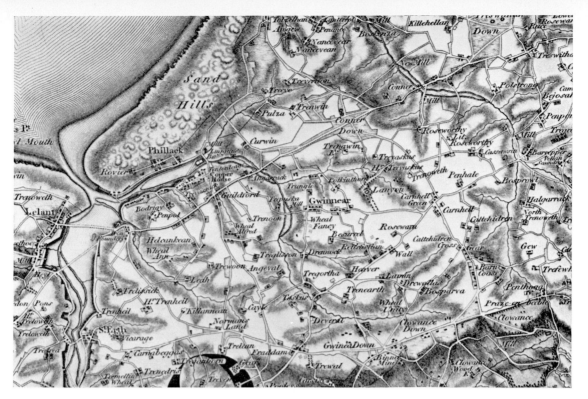

Plate 9 (a) Part of the first edition of the Ordnance Survey *Old Series* One-Inch map sheet 33 (Penzance) published 5 January 1813.

(b) The same area in the re-engraved version of the sheet published 1 January 1839. Extensive revision took place in the mid-1830s and geological symbols were added to the copper-plate at the time of its re-engraving.

By courtesy of the Trustees of the British Museum.

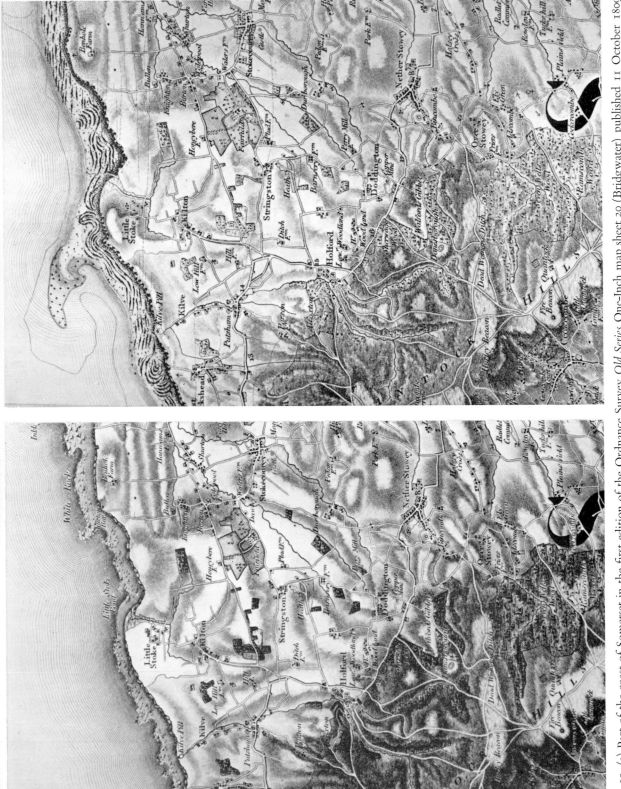

Plate 10. (a) Part of the coast of Somerset in the first edition of the Ordnance Survey *Old Series* One-Inch map sheet 20 (Bridgwater) published 11 October 1809. (b) The same area after it was partly re-engraved *c* 1838. New details were derived from a revision on land organised by Colonel Colby and from Admiralty charts. Geological symbols have been added to the copper-plate.

By courtesy of the Trustees of the British Museum.

Plate 11 Part of the 'first edition' of the Ordnance geological map of Devon (sheet 22) *c* 1836. Geological symbols were engraved on the copper-plate used for printing the regular topographical maps and colours were added by hand. By courtesy of the Trustees of the British Museum.

Plate 12 The high moor, along the West Okement Valley. *Devon County Council*

Plate 13   Car pa
at Dartmeet in la
August.
M. Blacksell

Plate 14   Clapper bridge at Postbridge. *Devon County Council*

Plate 15 Dawlish from the air. *Photo by Aerofilms Ltd*

Plate 16   The Lawn, Dawlish *c* 1864.

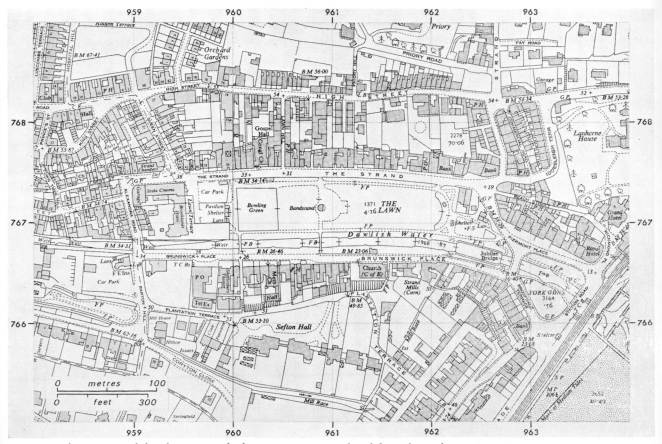

Plate 17   Dawlish, The Lawn and adjacent streets. Reproduced from the Ordnance Survey 1:25,000 map with the sanction of the Controller of HM Stationery Office, Crown Copyright reserved.

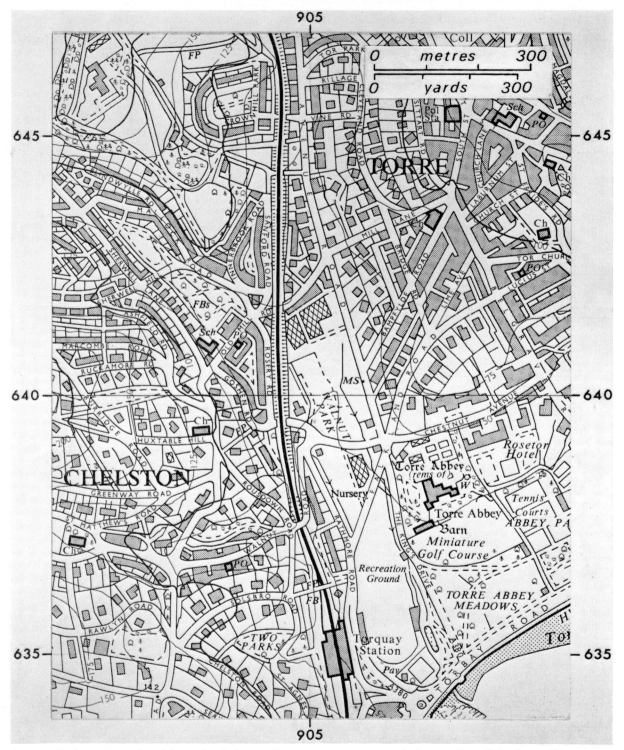

Plate 18 Chelston. Reproduced from the Ordnance Survey 1:10,560 map with the sanction of the Controller of HM Stationery Office, Crown Copyright reserved.

Plate 19 Children's play area behind Sanford Road, Chelston. *E. M. Johns*

Plate 20 Landscaped verge, Sanford Road, Chelston. *E. M. Johns*

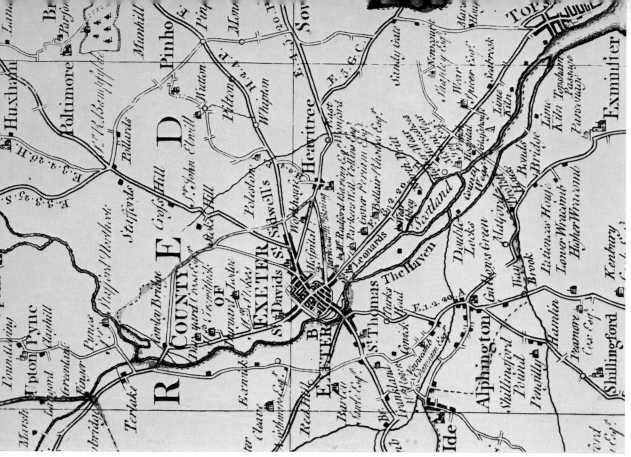

Plate 22   The Exeter area, after Benjamin Donn's map of Devon, 1765

Plate 21   Landscaped space at end of terrace, Rathmore Road, Chelston. *E. M. Johns*

List of Subscribers

John A. Agnew, Esq.

Dr R. Allison

Miss Patricia Anne Ashton

Miss Sheila M. Baggs

Miss Elizabeth M. Baker

Professor W. G. V. Balchin

Frank A. Barnes, Esq.

Miss Valerie J. Batten

Miss G. S. Beales

Professor S. H. Beaver

Dr R. P. Beckinsale

J. Bellett, Esq.

Professor J. H. Bird

J. E. Blacksell, Esq.

Dr K. W. Bolt

R. M. Borwick, Esq.

J. Bosanko, Esq.

Bernard A. F. Bowen, Esq.

Miss J. A. Brasier

Mark W. Brayshay, Esq.

Professor Eric H. Brown

L. J. Brown, Esq.

Miss Susan Buckingham

K. Bungay, Esq.

Professor Gilbert J. Butland

Professor E. M. J. Campbell

Tony Campbell, Esq.

Graham R. Cane, Esq.

Brian Cant, Esq.

Alan P. Carr, Esq.

Mrs Erlet A. Cater (née Savage)

Mrs Freda H. Cave

Professor Tony J. Chandler

Kevin A. Cheney, Esq.

R. F. John Chiplen, Esq.

B. W. Clapp, Esq.

Miss Muriel S. Clarkson

Bryan E. Coates, Esq.

J. V. Somers Cocks, Esq.

Mrs Barbara Anne Cole

Miss Alice Coleman

Miss Anne C. Cook

Sir James Cook

A. L. Cooper, Esq.

Peter Cooper, Esq.

Andrew L. Couldridge, Esq.

Miss Marilyn Coveney

Miss R. D. Cox

John T. Creasy, Esq.

D. J. Daggar, Esq.

Robert Daly, Esq.

Professor H. C. Darby

Geoffrey Davies, Esq.

Miss Glenys Davies

Professor Gordon L. Davies

Miss June M. Davies

Miss Rosemary Ann Davies

H. S. & P. J. Dennett

Miss Philippa Dolphin

Miss Tessa Dorricott

Christopher P. Drew, Esq.

Peter Drinkwater, Esq.

Mrs Mary C. Drummond (née
Cavanna)

Miss Pamela L. Eaves

Miss H. Eden

J. F. Eden, Esq.

Professor K. C. Edwards

Dr Clifford Embleton

R. A. Erskine, Esq.

Professor Estyn Evans

A. H. Forward, Esq.

Mrs Margaret I. A. Foster

Dr & Mrs F. J. Fowler

Professor G. N. Fowler

Lady (Aileen) Fox

Miss Angela M. Foyster

A. McK. Frood, Esq.

Miss Barbara J. Galois

V. Gardiner, Esq.

Professor H. B. Garland & Dr Mary Garland

R. S. Gibbs, Esq.

Professor Edmund W. Gilbert

Andrew W. Gilg, Esq.

C. James Gill, Esq.

Dr Robin E. Glasscock

Miss P. A. Grace

Miss M. R. Granger

Mrs Jean Gray (née Lambert)

Dr C. P. Green

Pete Gregory, Esq.

D. C. Hage, Esq.

Miss Ruth M. Hall

Miss Joanna M. Harper

Dr A. Harris

D. Hart, Esq.

Miss Lynda I. M. Heaney

Mrs Patricia Hemsworth

Dr A. V. Hill

Mrs Rosemary Holding (née Probert)

J. Barrie Horwell, Esq.

Miss Elizabeth F. Thurston-Hoskins

Professor John W. House

Miss Angela C. Hughes

Glanville R. J. Jones, Esq.

Miss Helen E. Jones

Miss Jenny Jones

Mrs Jill Jones

Adrian Crossley Kershaw, Esq.

Miss S. Khanna

P. B. Kirby, Esq.

Peter N. Knowles, Esq.

Peter Lacey, Esq.

Miss Vivienne E. Lake

Jonathan Lamb, Esq.

Miss Susan J. Lamb

Miss Susan M. Lambrick

Brian Langer, Esq.

Miss Mary E. Langley

O. S. Larkins, Esq.

Miss Lynn I. de Larrabeiti

Miss M. Lattimore

Professor Richard Lawton

Peter A. Lee, Esq.

Brian Le Messurier, Esq.

Miss Elizabeth J. Leppman

Dr Elvet Lewis

K. J. Lindsay, Esq.

Michael G. Livermore, Esq.

Dr F. J. Llewellyn

Miss Mary Marshall

Derek J. Martin, Esq.

Professor W. F. Maunder

Miss Jane E. May

Professor G. Duncan Mitchell

Miss Mary R. Moore

Miss Dorothy E. Morgan

Miss Rachel E. Molloy-Morley

Miss Gwladys M. Morris

S. T. Morris, Esq.

David Morrish, Esq.

Michael Morrish, Esq.

P. F. Murray, Esq.

Miss F. A. MacDowel

Miss E. Newbery

Dr M. Newson

Professor Robert Niklaus

Professor John Oliver

Miss Rosemary E. Orton

Miss Juliet T. Ory

Mr & Mrs M. Overton

Miss Alwena M. Owen

Mrs B. A. Paddon (née Barrows)

Mrs Ann M. Page (née Kirby)

Mrs M. Parkinson

Mrs Helen Parsons

Roy F. R. Payne, Esq.

Miss Margaret E. Peskett

Miss M. C. Phillips

Alec Pittam, Esq.

Richard H. Playll, Esq.

Richard Barton Pope, Esq.

Ifor B. Powell, Esq.

N. H. P. & V. A. Price

Dr R. Mansell Prothero

Professor Bruce Proudfoot

Dr C. A. Ralegh Radford

Miss S. J. Scott-Ram

B. T. Regan, Esq.

John Rendell, Esq.

Dr Thomas Revesz

Miss Christine I. Richards

Mr & Mrs A. Richardson

J. Riches, Esq.

O. B. Rigby, Esq.

Mr & Mrs Stephen N. Rigg

Miss Janet L. Roberts

Professor Ivan Roots

Roderick Ross, Esq.

K. C. H. Rowe, Esq.

P. J. Salter, Esq.

Andy Shearn, Esq.

Miss Ruth G. Scott

Miss Pamela M. Shepard

Professor Scott Simpson

Peter C. Sims, Esq.

David Singleton, Esq.

Laurence Skillman, Esq.

Geoffrey H. Smith, Esq.

Miss Jean M. Smith

Miss J. M. Drybrough-Smith

Miss A. M. Snow
D. J. W. Sowell, Esq.
Gordon & Susanne Spencer
Professor Robert W. Steel
Dr N. Stephens
Miss Jane E. Stoner
Professor Alan Stuart
Professor D. W. G. Style
Adrian R. J. Terry, Esq.
Miss Elizabeth Thorn
John Neil Thorpe, Esq.
Dr I. H. Thurston
Miss A. Tipton
R. W. Townsend, Esq.
R. P. Troake, Esq.
Phipps Turnbull, Esq.
Miss E. C. Vollans
P. G. Wake, Esq.
Dr Helen Wallis
Simon W. Ward, Esq.
Miss Lolita A. Watts
Miss Alison Weaver
B. Webb, Esq.
John P. Webb, Esq.
Miss Ann Wells
Miss Susan M. Wheeley
J. D. White, Esq.
Miss Sylvia E. Wickenden
Mrs Ursula B. M. Williams
Dr Vernon H. Williams
Professor M. J. Wise
Miss Susan E. Wood

Donald Wort, Esq.
N. A. Yool, Esq.
Dr Joyce Youings

The Library, The University College of
    Wales, Aberystwyth
The Library, The Queen's University,
    Belfast
The Library, University of Birmingham
The Library, University of Bristol
The Robert Hutchings Goddard
    Library, Clark University, U.S.A.
The Library, University of Dundee
The Cathedral Library, Exeter
The Library, University of Exeter
The Brynmor Jones Library, University
    of Hull
The Library, University of Liverpool
The Library, Bedford College, London
The Library, University College,
    London
The University of Manitoba Libraries
The School of Geography Library,
    University of Oxford
The Library, University of Reading
The Library, University of Sheffield
The Library, University of
    Southampton
The Department of Geography,
    University of Aberdeen
The Department of Geography,
    University of Cambridge
The Department of Geography,
    University of Leeds

The Department of Geography, University of Manchester

The Department of Geography, University of Sheffield

The Department of Geography, St Luke's College, Exeter

The Library, Bognor Regis College of Education

Ipswich Civic College

The Library, North Devon Technical College, Barnstaple

The Notre Dame College of Education, Liverpool

The Library, Rolle College, Exmouth

The Library, St Mary's College, Newcastle upon Tyne

The Library, South Devon Technical College, Torquay

The Library, College of St Mark & St John, Chelsea

County Secondary School, Chaddiford Lane, Barnstaple

Colston's Girls' School, Bristol

Bridgwater Public Library

Bristol Public Reference Library

Cornwall County Library

Devon County Library

Dorset County Library

Exeter City Library

Education Department Library, City of Plymouth

Plymouth Central Library

Torbay Central Public Library

Cornwall County Record Office

Unit of Coastal Sedimentation, NERC, Taunton